SCOTTISH RAILWAYS
1923-2016
A HISTORY

David Ross

'Black Five' No. 44908 passes through Hillington East Station, 1961. The factory units of the Hillington Industrial Estate are in the background. The industrial estate, Scotland's first, was established in 1934 and by 1938 there were 84 factories let. (Stenlake Collection)

Stenlake Publishing Ltd

ACKNOWLEDGEMENTS

Any student of the railways in the post-1948 period must be grateful for Dr Terry Gourvish's three volumes on British Railways. Focused very much on the attempts to achieve and maintain overall management of the system, they provide a majestic backdrop to this book's recording of a single Region's activities within – and occasionally beyond – the framework permitted by the British Transport Commission and its successor, the British Railways Board.

I am particularly grateful to Chris Green for the loan of documents and papers, and the opportunity of discussing his two periods with ScotRail, and also to Jim Summers for similar loans and valuable help in other ways. John Yellowlees of ScotRail has been, as ever, helpfully responsive. Thanks are due to Donald Cattanach, Dr John McGregor and Allan Rodger for their help, to David Spaven, on whose Waverley Route and Far North Line histories I have drawn, to Dr A.H. Urquhart for useful guidance on neo-liberalism, and to the numerous authors, academics, Ph.D. students and others whose work I have benefited from and frequently quoted, without necessarily agreeing with either their premises or conclusions. Opinions and judgements, except where attributed to others, are the author's own, as is responsibility for any factual errors.

For help in providing illustrations grateful thanks are due to John Alsop, 'big 55012', BRB (Residual), Donald Cameron of Lochiel, Alisdair Campbell (Highland Railway Society), Robert Darlaston, Freightliners Ltd, Roger Geach, the David Hills Collection, the Hutton Collection, Ed McKenna (North British Railway Study Group), Derek MacLeod, Dr John McGregor, Nigel Mundy, John G. Russell (Transport) Ltd, ScotRail, David Shirres, Richard Stenlake, Hamish Stevenson, Jim Summers, John Yellowlees, and Laura Yetton of Creative Spaces.
The maps were drawn and the book designed by Lewis Hutton.

CONTENTS

ABOUT THIS BOOK

In 1923 Scotland had a railway system that served almost every town and large village in the country, with hundreds of industrial branches to collieries, ironworks, quarries and factories. Railways were the basic means of moving people and goods from place to place. Yet they were at the brink of a long gradual decline, as newer forms of motive power brought the motor car, the lorry and the bus in ever-greater numbers on to a road system which was soon being improved to cater for the new traffic. During the Second World War the railways gave stalwart and vital service, but in the post-war world the system was old-fashioned and run down. Investment in modernisation came late and by the mid-1950s railway operations ceased to be even modestly profitable. In the 1960s the rail network and train services were drastically cut back but the expected return to profitability did not result. Eventually politicians and railway managers came to terms with a new perception of rail transport, no longer the nation's 'common carrier' but a service supported by public money for generally accepted social, economic and environmental reasons. As these values became more apparent, Scotland has seen something of a railway renaissance with new stations, new (or restored) lines, and a vigorous debate on future development.

In surveying the 93 years after 1923, this book makes a natural extension to the author's histories of the companies which formed the Scottish railway system until the end of 1922. It is not a company or business history but a general one, a survey of how the system – legacy of the final five companies – has fared and functioned under a succession of government-imposed ownerships. Between 1923 and the mid-1990s, Scottish railways were not managed as a separate concern, or concerns, but as part of UK-wide organisations: the LMS and LNER from 1923 to 1948, and British Railways from 1948 to 1997, all with London headquarters intent both on setting up a British identity, and on keeping central control. They took decisions and imposed uniform policies right across Great Britain. The distinct nature of Scotland within the United Kingdom, and the enduring sense of a national community, perhaps make it easier to detach and trace a coherent, specifically Scottish context than with other 'Areas' or 'Regions' during that era. Especially in the British Railways period, Scottish Regional management showed a growing tendency to do things in its own way – not least when English general managers were in charge. For those interested in the wider aspects of British railway history, this separating out of the Scottish dimension may help to illustrate the links and stresses between one 'region' and its metropolitan overlords.

Some of the wider background must be included because of the very large part played in railway policy by successive governments. Long before actual nationalisation, railway management was severely hemmed in by the involvement of the Ministry of Transport and of statutory tribunals dealing with wages and charges. From the start of the Second World War outright state control was imposed. And since then, the hand of the politician has never let go of the railways' vital parts. Until a partial devolution of powers in 2005, Scotland's railways were governed by the Ministry of Transport (later Department for Transport), with the gradually increasing involvement of the Scottish Office, and in 2017 control is still shared between Holyrood and London-centred agencies.

Due to the 30-year rule on making official documents accessible to the public, it has not been possible to use some national archive sources from after 1985. On the other hand, I have been fortunate in being able to speak with some of those who drove, were involved in, or witnessed events, especially in the critical period between 1980 and 1997. And apart from public and personal archives, there is also a vast amount of relevant material in books, journals, newspapers and broadcast sources. While a fully-informed assessment of 1985-2016 will not be possible until 2047, there is no shortage of information to fill an interim report. As a history should, this book presents facts, but also looks behind the facts to make connections, identify trends and the development of new ideas, and even make an occasional judgement. The different ways in which the country's railways have been governed since 1923 reflect the sequence of political and economic ideas within government and the increasing influence of management consultants – but a focus is kept on the railway's place in the community. The Notes contain many supplementary details, and the Appendices shed light on ScotRail operations and give comprehensive lists of passenger station openings and closures.

Railway histories of the United Kingdom can give only selective treatment to Scottish aspects, but in the political, social and economic context of present-day Scotland, to chart the historic continuity and the current contribution and status of this vital industry is not just desirable but very necessary. The operations of ScotRail and Network Rail are currently subsidised by the Scottish Government to the tune of over £700 million a year. Freight services attract additional support. How such a state of affairs has come about may be of more than passing concern even to those who otherwise have minimal interest in the details of railway history and management. Everyone is a stakeholder in the modern railway.

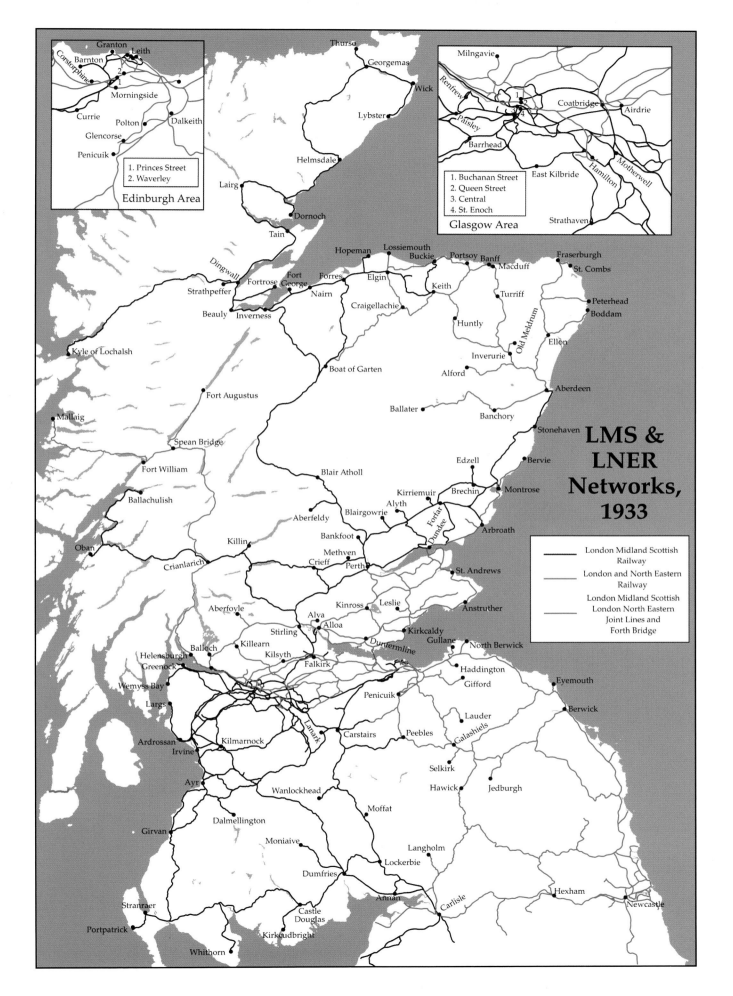

Edinburgh Area

1. Princes Street
2. Waverley

Granton
Leith
Barnton
Corstorphine
Morningside
Currie
Polton
Dalkeith
Glencorse
Penicuik

Glasgow Area

1. Buchanan Street
2. Queen Street
3. Central
4. St. Enoch

Milngavie
Renfrew
Paisley
Coatbridge
Airdrie
Barrhead
East Kilbride
Hamilton
Motherwell
Strathaven

LMS & LNER Networks, 1933

London Midland Scottish Railway

London and North Eastern Railway

London Midland Scottish London North Eastern Joint Lines and Forth Bridge

Thurso
Georgemas
Wick
Lybster
Helmsdale
Lairg
Dornoch
Tain
Hopeman
Lossiemouth
Buckie
Portsoy
Banff
Macduff
Fraserburgh
St. Combs
Dingwall
Fortrose
Fort George
Forres
Elgin
Keith
Turriff
Peterhead
Boddam
Strathpeffer
Nairn
Craigellachie
Huntly
Old Meldrum
Ellon
Beauly
Inverness
Inverurie
Kyle of Lochalsh
Boat of Garten
Alford
Aberdeen
Mallaig
Fort Augustus
Ballater
Banchory
Stonehaven
Spean Bridge
Edzell
Bervie
Fort William
Blair Atholl
Brechin
Montrose
Ballachulish
Kirriemuir
Alyth
Forfar
Aberfeldy
Blairgowrie
Dundee
Arbroath
Oban
Killin
Bankfoot
Methven
Crianlarich
Crieff
Perth
St. Andrews
Aberfoyle
Kinross
Leslie
Anstruther
Alva
Stirling
Alloa
Kirkcaldy
Helensburgh
Killearn
Dunfermline
Gullane
North Berwick
Greenock
Kilsyth
Falkirk
Haddington
Balloch
Gifford
Eyemouth
Wemyss Bay
Lanark
Penicuik
Largs
Berwick
Ardrossan
Kilmarnock
Carstairs
Peebles
Lauder
Galashiels
Irvine
Selkirk
Ayr
Wanlockhead
Hawick
Jedburgh
Moffat
Girvan
Dalmellington
Moniaive
Langholm
Lockerbie
Dumfries
Stranraer
Annan
Carlisle
Hexham
Newcastle
Castle Douglas
Portpatrick
Kirkcudbright
Whithorn

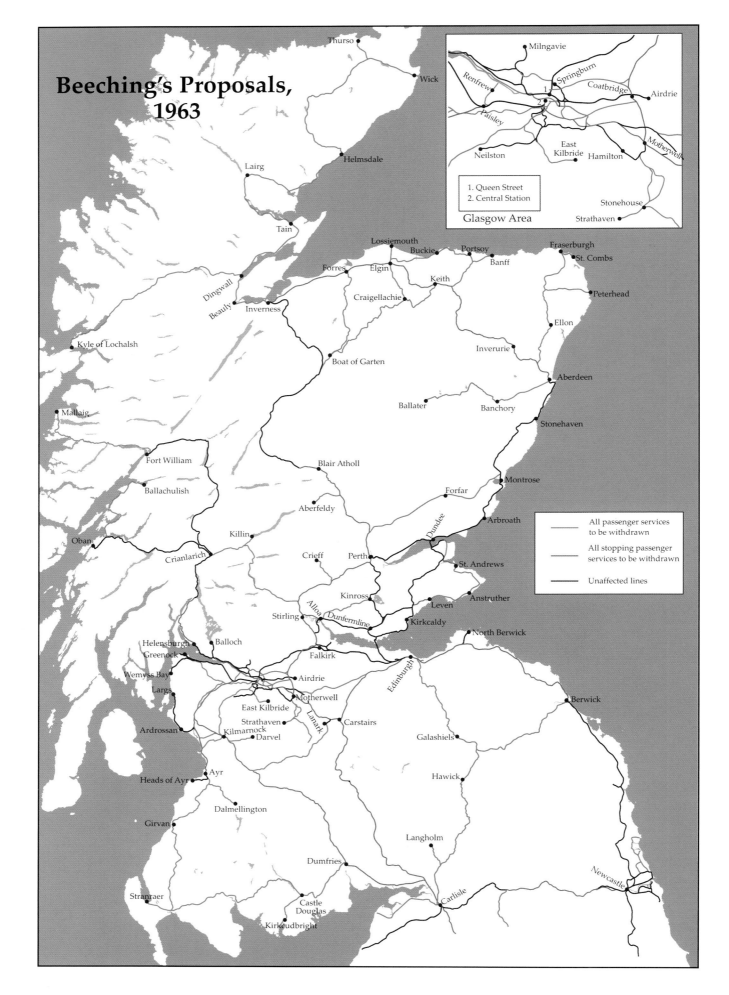

Beeching's Proposals, 1963

Glasgow Area

1. Queen Street
2. Central Station

All passenger services to be withdrawn

All stopping passenger services to be withdrawn

Unaffected lines

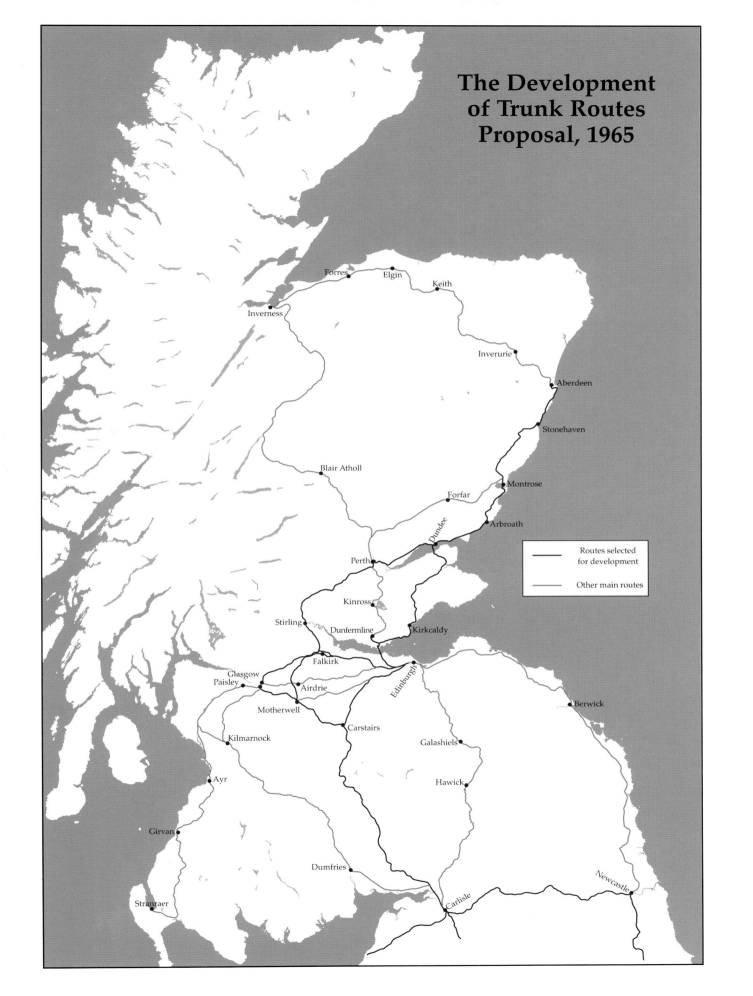

The Development of Trunk Routes Proposal, 1965

	Routes selected for development
	Other main routes

Forres, Elgin, Keith, Inverness, Inverurie, Aberdeen, Stonehaven, Blair Atholl, Forfar, Montrose, Dundee, Arbroath, Perth, Kinross, Stirling, Dunfermline, Kirkcaldy, Falkirk, Glasgow, Paisley, Airdrie, Edinburgh, Motherwell, Carstairs, Berwick, Kilmarnock, Galashiels, Ayr, Hawick, Girvan, Dumfries, Stranraer, Carlisle, Newcastle

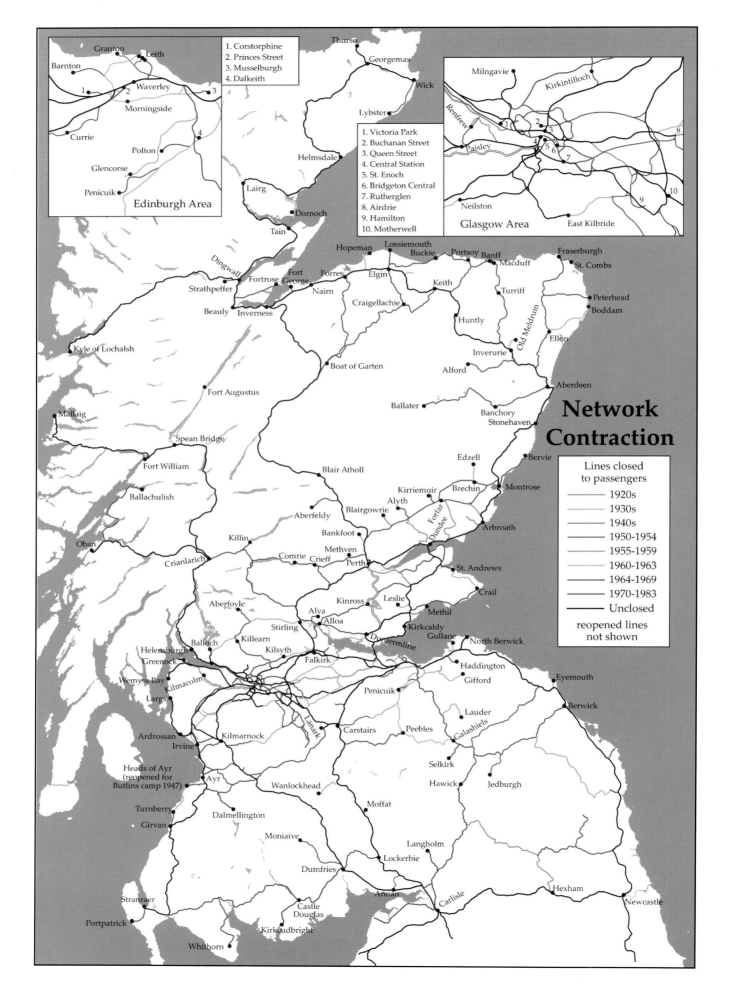

Edinburgh Area

1. Corstorphine
2. Princes Street
3. Musselburgh
4. Dalkeith

Granton
Leith
Barnton
Waverley
Morningside
Currie
Polton
Glencorse
Penicuik

Glasgow Area

1. Victoria Park
2. Buchanan Street
3. Queen Street
4. Central Station
5. St. Enoch
6. Bridgeton Central
7. Rutherglen
8. Airdrie
9. Hamilton
10. Motherwell

Milngavie
Kirkintilloch
Renfrew
Paisley
Neilston
East Kilbride

Thurso
Georgemas
Wick
Lybster
Helmsdale
Lairg
Dornoch
Tain
Hopeman
Lossiemouth
Buckie
Portsoy
Banff
Macduff
Fraserburgh
St. Combs
Dingwall
Fortrose
Fort George
Forres
Elgin
Keith
Turriff
Peterhead
Boddam
Strathpeffer
Nairn
Craigellachie
Old Meldrum
Ellon
Beauly
Inverness
Huntly
Inverurie
Kyle of Lochalsh
Boat of Garten
Alford
Aberdeen
Ballater
Banchory
Stonehaven
Mallaig
Fort Augustus
Edzell
Bervie
Spean Bridge
Kirriemuir
Brechin
Montrose
Fort William
Blair Atholl
Alyth
Ballachulish
Blairgowrie
Forfar
Dundee
Aberfeldy
Arbroath
Oban
Bankfoot
Killin
Methven
Comrie
Crieff
Crianlarich
Perth
St. Andrews
Kinross
Leslie
Crail
Aberfoyle
Alva
Methil
Stirling
Alloa
Kirkcaldy
Balloch
Killearn
Dunfermline
Gullane
Helensburgh
Kilsyth
Falkirk
North Berwick
Greenock
Haddington
Wemyss Bay
Gifford
Eyemouth
Largs
Kilmacolm
Penicuik
Berwick
Ardrossan
Lanark
Lauder
Irvine
Carstairs
Peebles
Galashiels
Heads of Ayr
(reopened for
Butlins camp 1947)
Kilmarnock
Selkirk
Ayr
Wanlockhead
Hawick
Jedburgh
Turnberry
Dalmellington
Girvan
Moffat
Moniaive
Langholm
Lockerbie
Dumfries
Hexham
Stranraer
Annan
Carlisle
Newcastle
Portpatrick
Castle
Douglas
Kirkcudbright
Whithorn

Network Contraction

Lines closed to passengers

- 1920s
- 1930s
- 1940s
- 1950-1954
- 1955-1959
- 1960-1963
- 1964-1969
- 1970-1983
- Unclosed

reopened lines
not shown

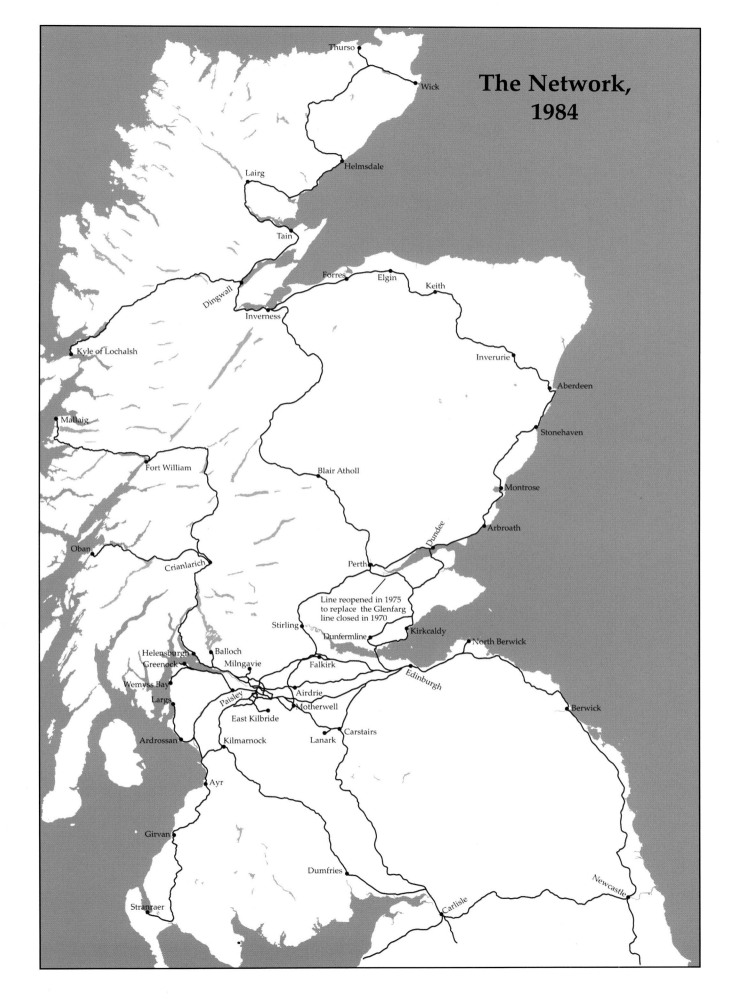

The Network, 1984

Thurso
Wick
Helmsdale
Lairg
Tain
Forres
Elgin
Keith
Dingwall
Inverness
Inverurie
Kyle of Lochalsh
Aberdeen
Stonehaven
Mallaig
Blair Atholl
Fort William
Montrose
Arbroath
Oban
Dundee
Crianlarich
Perth

Line reopened in 1975
to replace the Glenfarg
line closed in 1970

Stirling
Dunfermline
Kirkcaldy
North Berwick
Helensburgh
Balloch
Milngavie
Falkirk
Greenock
Edinburgh
Wemyss Bay
Airdrie
Berwick
Largs
Paisley
Motherwell
Ardrossan
East Kilbride
Kilmarnock
Lanark
Carstairs
Ayr
Girvan
Dumfries
Newcastle
Stranraer
Carlisle

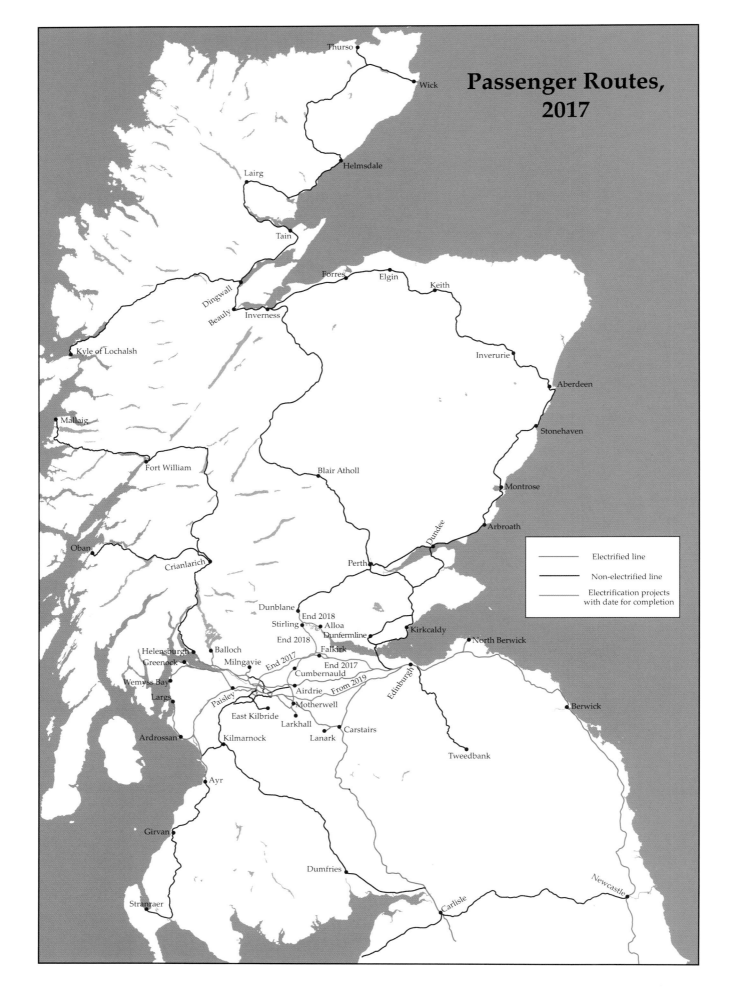

Passenger Routes, 2017

Thurso
Wick
Helmsdale
Lairg
Tain
Forres
Elgin
Keith
Dingwall
Beauly
Inverness
Inverurie
Kyle of Lochalsh
Aberdeen
Mallaig
Stonehaven
Fort William
Blair Atholl
Montrose
Arbroath
Oban
Dundee
Crianlarich
Perth
Dunblane
End 2018
Stirling
Alloa
Kirkcaldy
End 2018
Dunfermline
North Berwick
Helensburgh
Balloch
Falkirk
Greenock
Milngavie
End 2017
Cumbernauld
End 2017
Wemyss Bay
Airdrie
From 2019
Edinburgh
Berwick
Largs
Paisley
Motherwell
East Kilbride
Larkhall
Carstairs
Ardrossan
Kilmarnock
Lanark
Newcastle
Ayr
Tweedbank
Girvan
Dumfries
Stranraer
Carlisle

Electrified line
Non-electrified line
Electrification projects with date for completion

PART ONE
THE BIG TWO, 1923-47

1. The Grouping and Its Implementation

The Railways Act of 1921 and its Origins

Ex-Highland Railway No. 52 'Clan Munro', now LMS 14764, and apparently newly painted in LMS crimson, leaves Dalnaspidal with a stopping train for Perth, circa 1925. Built in 1919, it was withdrawn in 1948. (John Alsop Collection)

In the beginning, if we take the beginning as 1 January 1923, was the network. More than three thousand route miles of railway track, connecting virtually every place on the mainland with a population greater than five hundred or so to a system of main lines running north-south, and of mostly secondary lines (except for the busiest of all, Edinburgh-Glasgow) running east-west, and hundreds of branches. A ticket could be bought from any one of over a thousand stations to any other, and Bradshaw's invaluable Britain-wide timetable would show how to get from Wick to Stranraer, from Duns to Mallaig, or Fraserburgh to Helensburgh, in surprisingly few stages. Or to London and the thousands of stations in England, some of which could be reached without changing carriages: Southampton, Bristol, Harwich, even Penzance. This great nation-binding rink of steel can be seen as one of the many gifts of the 19th century to the 20th[1]. On that first day of January it was simply *there*, newly divided into the property of two giant companies whose territory stretched right down to London.

Scotland's railways had remained the exclusive preserve of Scottish companies until the end of 1922. This was largely due to happenstance: at various times one or more of the companies sought amalgamation with an English railway, but the attempts never succeeded. However, all changed at the end of 1922 when the five Scottish companies were grouped with English railways into the London Midland & Scottish Railway and the London & North Eastern Railway. Only two independent public railways survived, the Glasgow Subway, (officially known as the 'Underground' from 1936 to 2003) and the Campbeltown & Machrihanish, both of them narrow gauge and not connected to the main system.

During the war years the 100-plus railway companies of Great Britain had made an immense contribution to the national effort, and remained under unified state control until August 1921. By the end of 1918, after four years of intensive use and minimal maintenance, there was a general need for renovation, repair and replacement. Coupled with this was a widespread feeling among those concerned with the nation's economic life that a complete rationalisation of the railway system was essential. Lloyd George's wartime government accepted this and seriously considered outright state ownership, as in France, Germany and many other countries, but finally shrank from the cost implications of having to take on the unification and modernisation of such a vast industry (a later British government in 1947 had no such qualms).

In 1919 the Ministry of Transport had been established, to provide governance of all transport, rail, road, sea and air, with far more power than the Board of Trade had had. Its immediate chief task was to accomplish an overhaul of railway organisation. There was no question of leaving the

Ex-Caledonian Nos. 41 and 94, LMS 14458, built 1914 and withdrawn 1957, and 14505, built 1922 and withdrawn 1961, race through Luncarty with a Glasgow-Aberdeen express in 1925. Photo H.Gordon Tidey (John Alsop Collection)

companies to sort out their own situation: after almost a century of *laisser-faire* punctuated by occasional and often damaging interference (as far as their commercial operations were concerned), government was now taking the railways in hand and imposing a solution, in the form of amalgamation into a small number of very large companies. The very fact that such an action was possible shows how much change the war years had wrought in political and social life. The problem was located more in England and Wales, with some 95 railway companies, than in Scotland, where the five railways had largely abandoned their ancient rivalries and learned the arts of co-operation. Grouping had not been sought by the Scottish companies. They were not run-down to the point of exhaustion, but even in Scotland, a return to the quintuple set-up of boards, managements, and workshops could be seen as getting in the way of a railway fit for the 20th century, and it was generally accepted that some form of rationalisation was necessary. Once it was decided upon, the companies joined in resisting the proposal to have a separate Scottish group, or even two groups, and in this they were supported by their own employees, who feared wage reductions, and by their customers, who feared increases in passenger and freight charges. Finally they were combined into two new conglomerate companies, the Highland, Caledonian and Glasgow & South Western into the London Midland & Scottish Railway; and the Great North of Scotland and North British into the London & North Eastern Railway. The grouping arrangement was based on the lines owned by the constituent companies, and so although the LMS was predominantly 'west' and the LNER mainly 'east', both had stations in Edinburgh, Glasgow and Dundee, both ran to Aberdeen; and the LNER had the West Highland line to Fort William and Mallaig. Aberdeen and Perth remained jointly-owned stations. The Forth Bridge and its immediate approaches, though used only by the LNER, continued to be owned by a separate joint company.

The central figure in the planning and negotiations that went on from 1919 to 1921 was the first Minister of Transport, Sir Eric Geddes. Born in India of a Scots-colonial family, Geddes had been deputy general manager of the North Eastern Railway until he had been brought into the war government as a man who got things done. Forceful and confident, successful in helping to wage war, he was not a master of the arts of peace and his dictatorial style alienated many senior railwaymen and others. At one point, at the prospect of yet another civic and commercial deputation from Scotland, he refused to see them: "I've seen enough deputations from Scotland"[2]. Geddes was very much the architect of the post-war railway settlement in which the Grouping process was paralleled by another large and complex issue, centred on the termination of the wartime control system, and the railway companies' claims against the government. The 1871 Act under which the railways had been brought under state control also required the state to hand the railways back to their owners in the same condition as when they had been taken over. This was a huge obligation, estimated to cost up to £150 million. In a political master-stroke which was probably Geddes's idea, and certainly shows his style, the Government combined the two issues of amalgamation and compensation, making it obligatory for the companies, in agreeing the amalgamations, to accept and share a total amount of £60 million as full payment for all wartime wear and tear. Of this sum the Scottish companies received £6,215,000, or just over 10%[3].

Fulfilling a wartime promise, from 1 February 1919, against strong opposition from all railway companies, an eight-hour working day had been conceded to all grades of railway staff. With the government-supported wartime pay scheme due to end, the companies were determined to enforce pay cuts, and to counter this a national railway strike was called for 26 September that year.

It lasted until 5 October and for the first time all five Scottish companies were involved. Even on the Highland and Great North, the old tradition of company loyalty and 'family spirit' was gone. The era of deference was over. A settlement extended the 'war-wage' package for another year, but industrial relations were set on a stormy course, made worse by the railway unions' refusal to move imported coal, in support of the miners' increasingly bitter disputes with the coal-owners.

The Railways Act of 1921 was the first of three 20th-century Acts of Parliament which redefined the status of the railways (the others brought nationalisation in 1947, and privatisation in 1993), setting out how the system would work from 1 January 1923. This Act has been described as "the first serious attempt to grapple with the problem of scientific planning of railways", with one of its purposes being to eliminate competition as far as possible[4]. It also embodied a new perception of what a railway company was. At various times in the 19th century this matter had been half-articulated, as governments faced the existence of a growing network of company systems that simultaneously collaborated and competed in an almost total control of inland transport. Now the 1921 Act treated the railways as a public utility operated by four giant companies, which were permitted operating independence but had statutory limitations on their earnings and profits, and official controls on key business aspects: rates and charges, and wage rates (there are interesting parallels here with the franchise agreements of 90 years later, whose authors might have benefited from study of the 1921 Act and its effects). In six parts, it spelled out the final form of the amalgamations, defined the powers of regulatory bodies and of the Ministry itself, and set the framework within which the railways would operate, including their charges and the maximum amount they would be allowed to earn, and the new system for establishing wages and conditions for the half-million-plus railway workers, of whom around 56,000 were in Scotland. The railway unions had at first insisted that workers should have representation on the

Ex-G&SWR 4-6-0 No. 503, built in 1903, still retaining the old company's livery in 1924, seen here entering Ayr with an express from Glasgow. Photo C.J.L.Romanes (John Alsop Collection)

new company boards, but to Geddes's surprise and annoyance they made a u-turn on this. Instead, joint councils were to be set up to consider pay and working conditions on a broad basis, "having regard to the need for securing to the workpeople a share in the increased prosperity of the industry". Security of earnings and employment were to be guaranteed, creating an issue which would exercise the Thatcher government in 1985. The Executive Committee of the Scottish TUC was currently urging a national strike "to relieve the present untenable position of the transport workers in Scotland"[5], and at such a time of industrial turmoil it would have been extremely difficult for unions to have board representation. A Railways Rates Tribunal was set up to control rates and charges, with the aim of yielding a "standard net revenue" equivalent to that which the constituent companies had earned in 1913 (for Scottish railways this amounted to a total of £13,612,194); and a Central Wages Board to rule on pay matters, with a National Wages Board to hear appeals[6]. Not for the first or last time, the railways yielded tamely to government direction of their affairs. The vast new companies were not to be masters in their own domains. Resistance would have been difficult – at the time of the passing of the Act, which also created them, they did not exist, and the attentions of their predecessors were focused on the details of the amalgamations and the war settlement. Government control of the railways through the Railway Executive ended on 15 August 1921, and four days later the provisions of the Railways Act came into force.

The Grouping Gets Under Way

On the morning of 1 January 1923 there was an unusual sense of change in the air, an awareness that in some significant way, things were not as they had been yesterday. All appeared the same: it was of course a day of holiday. Tomorrow, shops and businesses would open again, factories return to work, children to school, trains would run normally – but here was the shift into a new and unpredictable dispensation. Until midnight, these trains had been Scottish, owned by five Scottish-based companies. Now these companies were absorbed along with English railways into two vast new conglomerate concerns, centred in London. The sense of change was most felt by the railway community, some fifty thousand families, and in the headquarters offices of the old companies. One each in Inverness, Aberdeen and Edinburgh, two in Glasgow, these proud buildings had been the centres of control for a large and vital service industry. Each had its boardroom, polished and panelled, with portraits of ex-chairmen looking down on their successors. There would be no more board meetings, no more directors to rule their empires of tracks, their hundreds of stations, their fleets of locomotives, their thousands of employees. Instead there were divisional managers, most of them the same men who had run the old companies, but now carrying out the orders of a remote set of senior officials for most of whom Scotland was a distant province counting for barely a tenth of their new company's value and activity. The Highland, Caledonian and Glasgow & South Western companies now formed the Northern Division of the LMS, which also had two English divisions; and the Great North of Scotland and North British became the Northern Division of the LNER. For some people, there was a sense of the morning of 17 January 1707, when the Scots woke up as citizens of a United Kingdom; and the Grouping of the railways was one of the biggest shocks to the Scottish system since the Union itself.

Scotland's Big Five vanished from the scene, if not from memory; though it took several years before the re-branding of stations, uniforms[7], rolling-stock and the innumerable items of equipment was complete. Their legacy was a complete railway system, indeed over-complete in some areas, and all its installations. How far the expansion of the railways led or nourished the economic development of the country has been much debated, with recent economic historians tending to play down their significance. It is certainly true that the railways, at least from the 1850s on, were as much the result of ongoing commercial and industrial expansion as generators. Yet their effect was enormous in a huge variety of ways, expanding social mobility, improving living standards, widening the horizons for local commerce though also killing off some cottage industries, and strengthening a sense of national integration. Traditionalists, and the minority of people at the time who felt that Scottish institutions should be run in Scotland, regretted the old companies' demise. Whatever the view of their efficiency and quality, they were based, managed, and largely owned in Scotland and could be held accountable at annual meetings. Their chairmen and directors were known and visible. Scotland was their territory and they had a vested interest in providing the country with a service which offered some cause for satisfaction, even pride. Each had a strong sense of identity and of its own history. Tales of rivalry, like those of Caledonian and South Western drivers racing each other on the almost-parallel lines past Ardeer, or the North British and Caledonian battling to be first at Kinnaber Junction in the 'Race to the North', or Highland porters at Elgin carefully re-labelling parcels meant to be forwarded via the Great North, are enshrined in railway folklore and reminiscence. The travelling public as a whole was largely indifferent: so long as a railway service was there, they did not mind who provided it.

Competition and Combination

The 1921 Act was intended to dispense with competition but did not entirely succeed. The four main Scottish cities were served by both new companies. While combination rather than competition had been the general policy of railway companies for thirty years, there was always an edge somewhere: a route or service over which they might vie for the traffic, if only for prestige reasons. Services within Scotland were run on a complementary basis, but when the LNER in 1923 introduced an Aberdeen-Penzance through train, as Britain's longest route, the LMS followed up with Aberdeen-Plymouth. Neither service was well-used and in February 1924 the LMS suggested they should be dropped, but the LNER refused, despite the reluctance of the Great Western Railway to treat its part of the run as an express service. The LMS train became merely a through carriage from Glasgow, and though in the late 1930s the LNER was still billing its train as Aberdeen-Penzance, in fact passengers had to change at Edinburgh[8]. The LNER's Joint Committee of Superintendents and Passenger Managers may have taken a more competitive approach, but the LMS was also ready to seize an opportunity. Already, though, the railways were facing competition far more threatening than any mutual rivalries, in the rapid spread of road transport. Between 1919 and 1921, around 48,000 army lorries were sold off to private buyers[9]. This legacy from the war years gave road haulage a huge stimulus.

The same men and women worked in the same stations, and the same engines pulled the same carriages, but everyone was braced for change. The new companies had their main operational bases at Derby, Crewe and Horwich for the LMS, and Doncaster and Darlington for the LNER. There was no immediate revolution, since daily management and service right down to station level had to be maintained. Soon it became clear that the two new companies had adopted different strategies for running their empires. On the LMS, there was a strong trend towards centralisation of control, while the LNER adopted a more devolved approach. The LNER, however, was an assemblage of companies that had long co-operated, certainly as far as the North British and North Eastern were concerned, and if the North British had had little to do in the past with the Great North, at least they had not been enemies; while the LMS was composed largely of former rivals. The Caledonian and the Highland were old allies but that could not be said of the Caledonian and the South Western. Both Groupings set up advisory committees for their Scottish areas and for some years each area was subdivided into Northern and Southern sections, the northern ones being the former Highland and GNSR systems. The LMS in Scotland was headed until 1927 by Donald Matheson, former general manager of the Caledonian, as Deputy General Manager (Scotland) – a post abolished with his retirement in October 1926. Matheson had the satisfaction of seeing his pet project, the Gleneagles Hotel, its completion delayed in the war years, opened on 2 June 1924[10]. On the LNER a more lateral arrangement was established, based on the old constituent companies. James Calder, former general manager of the North British, was appointed General Manager (Scotland) with considerable latitude on train operations, locomotive running, signalling, engineering work, property dealing, steamers and hotels. Sir Eric Geddes with typical panache suggested himself for the chair of the LNER[11], but his ex-colleagues chose to elect his doughtiest opponent in the matter of war compensation, William Whitelaw of the North British. With Whitelaw's regular presence at the Scottish Committee, there was a greater awareness of, and sensitivity to, the particular needs and requirements of the LNER Scottish lines than the LMS showed. The LNER's general manager, Sir Ralph Wedgwood, informed the general managers of operating areas that his office "decide the policy and deal with the Board. You get on with operating the railway", but the LNER historian Geoffrey Hughes noted that very often there was no unified policy and each general manager acted on his own initiative. The company had no chief civil engineer until the "craggy Scot" J.C.L. Train (ex-NBR) was appointed in 1942[12].

On the LMS, the larger of the two corporations, pulling things together was begun immediately under the chairmanship of Sir Guy Granet, of the old Midland Railway, who set up a vertical form of management structure with departmental chiefs at HQ controlling most functions. In May 1925 the chief

The branch terminus at Strathpeffer in early LMS days. The engine was originally HR No. 56 *Balnain*, built at Inverness in 1869 and withdrawn in 1926. (Highland Railway Society)

Fortrose, terminus of the Black Isle branch, in 1925. The train is vintage Highland Railway but the station has been given an LMS identity. (John Alsop Collection)

executive's title became President, a role created for Sir Josiah Stamp who came from the Nobel company in January 1926 with a reputation for brilliant analysis and effective organisation. Stamp had toured the US railways and the new structure was devised by him, with four executive vice-presidents. He also took the role of chairman from Granet's retirement in October 1927. Concentration of decision-making at Euston increased. He was a peripatetic president. Hamilton Ellis noted that he literally lived on the LMS for six days a week, "moving about in an austerely comfortable carriage with a bed and a bathroom" and also recorded an impression that Stamp "was not entirely popular in Scotland", his visits seen as "sacking tours", and even "The decadence of certain Scottish lines in his time has been noted"[13], though he offers no further detail and it is unlikely that Scottish lines decayed any more than English ones. All but the most modest decisions continued to be ratified, or taken, centrally. When the LMS arranged to take over the insolvent David MacBrayne steamer company, jointly with Coast Lines, in 1928, it was Stamp, not Matheson's successor Thomas Moffat, who did the negotiating. A well-placed observer, Michael Bonavia, considered that Moffat's post as Chief Officer for Scotland, with "something in the nature of a management committee", was the main exception to London control on the LMS, and "a concession to Scottish feeling", though he conceded it carried less direct authority than the LNER's divisional general manager role[14]. A similar comment came from a member of the Railway Clearing House secretariat, noting that in the 1920s "constituents of the four companies still continued to send representatives to Clearing House meetings… Scotland, of course, particularly liked to fly its own flag"[15]. Inherited joint concerns were dealt with by a joint LMS/LNER committee: these were the joint stations at Aberdeen and Perth, including the Perth Station Hotel, Dentonholme Goods Station in Carlisle, the Dumbarton & Balloch line, including the Loch

Lomond steamers, the Dundee & Arbroath line, the Grangemouth and Princes Dock branches; and the operation of the Caledonian/North British Agreement of 1908.

Differences first noticed by the travelling public were a set of fare reductions, bringing the level of fares down from 75% to 50% above the pre-war rate (incomes had doubled in the ten years from 1913). 'Foreign' locomotives and sometimes rolling stock began to appear on their lines, as the companies set out to rationalise their diverse inheritance of equipment. Caledonian engines began to replace Highland ones, and Midland Railway engines became familiar on the former G&SWR lines. A former Great Eastern Railway engine said to weigh 105 tons was sent from Cambridge to Craigellachie for tests of the impact of its weight on the Spey viaduct there, with a view to running heavier trains in the tourist season[16]. New liveries were devised: a young observer in the 1920s observed that "Locomotives seen previously in gamboge or royal blue startled railwaymen by appearing in apple green and crimson lake"[17]. At first LMS engines were 'Midland Red' before an austerer plain black was imposed. The LNER stuck to green for its passenger engines until 1928, when only the ex-NBR 'Atlantics' were allowed this distinction[18]. The LMS had the former companies' railway works at St. Rollox, Kilmarnock, and Inverness; the LNER had Cowlairs and Inverurie. All were kept in action, but after 1922 no more locomotives were built at any of them, except St. Rollox (to 1926). Glasgow continued to build large numbers of engines, mostly for export, at the works of the North British Locomotive Company, though 20 LNER Class A3 'Pacifics' were also built there, as were 50 of the LMS 'Royal Scot' class. It seems that the Scottish companies' works were seen as too remote and too costly by their new owners. Perhaps also the presence of former chief mechanical engineers, working out their time as hardly more than works managers, was seen as an obstacle. A Scottish MP also complained in 1923 that Scotland was losing out on orders for new carriages and wagons, "to the serious prejudice of trade and employment"[19].

Border woollen manufacturers, having worked out that road and sea transport of their products would offer considerable reduction on railway rates, wanted to send a deputation to the LNER in April 1923, but the company declined to receive it, saying it had the subject under careful consideration. A reduction was made from 50% to 33% above the pre-war rate[20]. In December 1926, representatives of the Scottish coal, steel and timber industries met Stamp to tell him that if efficiency was to be maintained, local departmental heads must have greater authority and not have to refer decisions to England. Sir Josiah did not altogether agree: he felt that Scottish managers had ample power to deal with local matters, though only as "local representatives" of senior managers based elsewhere[21]. Increasingly, the companies were realising how the rapidly developing road haulage industry was taking away business that once would have had no alternative but to use the railway. The road operators knew the level of railway charges (which the companies were legally obliged to publish) and had plenty of margin to undercut them. Not only freight but passenger transport was being lost. It became apparent that the 1921 Railways Act was not a blueprint for railway progress but a straitjacket that prevented the companies from competing on even terms with their new rivals. Sir Eric Geddes had said immodestly of his Act "… no measure of equal complexity has proved in use to be to be better balanced and a better specimen of draughtsmanship… The theory of the enactment is that the railway proprietors and railway workers should receive a reasonable and fair remuneration for the employment of their capital, or for the labour performed, and that the public should receive services for a reasonable charge"[22]. Keen to foster its reputation, he claimed from the sidelines that the railways just needed to be managed better. He had misjudged the situation. Neither the LMS nor the LNER ever came near matching the 1913 standard of earnings during their 24-year life, partly due to the slowness and inflexibility of the rate-fixing system and to economic recession, but more to the new and unforeseen competitive environment; and this failure exerted a constant drag on their ability to modernise, cope with rising costs, pay reasonable wages and a full range of dividends to their shareholders. At the time, though, the LMS and LNER, along with the Great Western and Southern Railways, still appeared huge and commercially dominant semi-monopolistic concerns, and received little political or public sympathy. Naturally enough, most users saw the railway at peak periods and seasons, when trains were often packed, with sleeping berths sold out and duplicate services needed: on 30 July 1926 the *Scotsman* noted that the 7.20 pm Highland express from Euston was run in six portions.

Troubles of the Twenties:
The General Strike

Aware of the need to weld their thousands of staff into a single body, the new companies made a real effort to inculcate a corporate spirit, encouraging social groups and promoting sports events. Football leagues, golf championships, whist drives, dances, choirs, all helped to foster the sense of belonging. Staff magazines were informative on a wide range of topics, and did not overdo exhortation. A typical *LMS Magazine* article in February 1926 described the seventeen "travelling dormitories" on the Highland line, provided with bunks and cooking facilities, enabling work gangs to spend several days at a time on remote sections of track[23]. With the co-operation of the four Scottish universities, the LNER initiated a course of lectures for management and clerical staff on railway law, geography, economics and railway operating, from January 1924. It was also the only company to operate a graduate training scheme, superintended by Robert Bell, "dry and Scots", an assistant general manager, with the aid of "a little black book"[24]. A much wider range geographical range of posts was open to those willing to move, although particularly on the LMS, many senior positions were abolished as the old incumbent retired: there was only one company-wide head of each major department (in civil engineering it was Alexander Newlands, who had started out on the Highland Railway) and there were many competitors for vacancies.

Discontent and unease among the staff increased as the post-war boom turned into industrial slump in the mid-20s. The Railway Clerks' Association deplored the reduced chances of promotion caused by amalgamation and cost-cutting[25]. In 1924 Whitelaw pointed out that while railway wages and salaries were 148% over their 1913 level, rates and charges were only between 50 and 60% above it. The ASLEF union had already mounted a strike in January of that year, in defence of enginemen's pay and conditions when the companies proposed a wage reduction in line with the (at the time) falling cost of living index, and the refusal of the National Union of Railwaymen to join them caused some hostility, though some Edinburgh NUR men came out unofficially. Charles Stemp, Superintendent of the LNER's Southern Scottish area, described the position at Eastfield Depot in Glasgow as "pretty warm", and the NUR's General Secretary, Charles Cramp, struggled to hold back unofficial strikes and what he described as "anarchist" activities by his members[26].

A portrait sketch of Norman McKillop, engine driver, ASLEF official, editor of the BR Scottish Region magazine, author of numerous books and, as 'Toram Beg', many articles on railway topics. (British Railways)

In Banffshire, rails lifted during the war were relaid in 1924-25 between Aultmore and Portessie. This reinstatement of the former HR Keith-Buckie line, which only ever had a scanty service, seems an odd decision by the LMS, but perhaps it was done at the expense of the Admiralty, which had used the old rails for its Cromarty Firth lines. Only a skeletal freight service was operated[27]. Already thoughts of expansion were forgotten. 1925 was a dire year for the railways, with revenue falling steeply. Whitelaw called it the worst year ever, not knowing what 1926 would bring[28]. On 3 May 1926, in line with a decision by the Trades Union Congress, railway and dock-workers ceased work in the General Strike which began on 4 May. This was in support of the miners' dispute with the coal-owners, who were seeking to impose both a pay reduction and a longer working day, and had imposed a national lock-out on their workforce on 1 May. A high proportion of the country's trade was effectively immobilised. In the managements' efforts to keep some trains running, the participation of volunteer workers was actively encouraged, under the protection of police and troops. The LNER enrolled 4,114 volunteers in Scotland, of whom 734 were used, 198 as porters, and 218 in locomotive depots, of whom 30 were drivers and 128 firemen[29]. Normal rules of train working were waived. Though there were no scenes comparable to the violence at Motherwell during the "Scotch Strike" of 1890-91, there were many incidents in Scotland. Some signal boxes manned by volunteers were stoned, and a railway spokesman claimed that volunteer-driven trains were "routinely stoned"[30]. On 10 May there was an angry confrontation between volunteers and pickets at Stirling, when one of the volunteers was reported to have fired a pistol. In the worst incident, a train driven by volunteers collided with wagons in the Calton Tunnel at Edinburgh on 13 May and three persons were killed. The signalman at St. Margaret's was also a volunteer, though an LNER inspector was with him in the cabin. No sabotage was involved, but the Inspecting Officer's report contrived to imply that strike pickets at St. Margaret's had refused to help after the collision. The Edinburgh Strike Committee stated that that the pickets' offer to help the injured had been refused. What they declined to do was to help in clearing the wreckage[31]. Four miners were jailed at Dunfermline Sheriff Court for loosening rails on the coal line between Kelty and Lochore[32]. At the Lanarkshire mining village of Omoa, a "flying breakdown gang" of volunteer workers came to repair the line between Holytown and Shotts, but "fled for their lives", leaving their trolley behind, after a crowd of 300-400 people, said to be mostly women and children, began throwing stones at them[33].

Far more important than the few trains run by volunteers was the action of thousands of motor drivers, many of them army-trained, in maintaining supplies by road. On 12 May the Trades Union Congress called off the strike, claiming there were good grounds for a settlement with the coal owners, though the miners disagreed and their strike went on. Returning railway workers found the companies taking a tough line, rejecting many and prompting a continuation of the dispute. For the companies it was a chance to shed staff, not only getting rid of 'troublemakers' but to reduce overall numbers, and they also compelled the unions to accept that they had committed a "wrongful act" against their employers[34] (though not an illegal one: sympathy strikes were not banned until 1927) and to commit themselves not to instruct their members to strike until there had been negotiation with the companies. James Calder told a strikers' deputation that they would be taken back "as and when there is work available for them". Three months after the general return, some 45,000 British railway workers had not been taken back. The show of industrial solidarity had been brief. Nine-year old Thomas Middlemass saw his father, an ex-NBR goods guard, return to work at Falkirk, "and understand now the conflict of emotions that must have played within him; wounding regret at the failure of the strike, inevitable sense of relief at returning to work, and, above all I like to think, a feeling of pride at having stood by his workmates in a desperate bid for social justice"[35]. With the miners' strike continuing, coal shortages forced heavy cuts in train services into 1927. The General Strike and the coal dispute were estimated to cost the LMS some £11,500,000 in lost revenue.

Constraints and Competition

The Railways Act of 1921 provided for replacement of the old system of freight charges but it was not until the beginning of 1928 that the new method, under the supervision of the Railway Rates Tribunal, was introduced. In principle it did not depart from the old one: rates were still governed by type of goods, not by the cost of carrying them. Twenty-one main merchandise classes replaced the previous eight. Section IA, 'General Merchandise', listed around 6,000 separate commodities, from bulk freight like iron ore to small high-value packages. Standard charges were imposed, subject to the possibility of some variation: with approval by the Tribunal a company might charge exceptional rates not more than 5% above, or 40% below the standard. Following the reclassification, the Tribunal permitted the companies to make changes to goods rates in February 1928. Even after this, two thirds of freight charges were 'exceptional' and the proportion rose steadily[36]. The urgency of the situation can be gauged by the example of cotton, both raw and manufactured, which had previously been carried almost entirely by rail, and was mostly now transported by road: of 676,000 tons of raw cotton 76% went by road in 1927, and only 24% by rail. Road hauliers made their charges on a basis of cost, not classification of goods: for them each contract was a one-off, and their employees' wages, not regulated like railway pay, were well below railway levels. The railways, required to act as national common carriers, depended on a charging system in which cross-subsidy between profitable and unprofitable services was implicit, spreading

The locomotive shed at Dumfries, just south of the station, showed the architectural style of the G&SWR's engineer Andrew Galloway. This 1929 view includes several ex-G&SWR engines including one of James Manson's 1901-04 'renewals' of James Stirling's 221-class 0-4-2 of 1874. All were scrapped by 1931. (John Alsop Collection)

revenue and costs across the system, to the benefit of smaller and remoter customers who would otherwise have faced impossible charges. With road haulage increasingly picking out some of their plum business, the rail goods managers were desperate to have greater freedom to compete for and claw back traffic. Freight still brought in much more revenue than passenger trains, and the companies were proactive in their relations with traders, holding goods conferences with customers to promote new services and get feedback. Long-distance freight services were improved, with some faster trains and more next-day deliveries for non-perishable items. The LMS pioneered the use of containers from 1926, with an internal report which perhaps for the first time stressed the intermodal, door-to-door aspect[37]. Telephone-based train control systems, like that introduced by the North British Railway in 1913, providing much greater efficiency in the deployment of locomotives, engine crews and wagon stocks, spread across busy districts[38]. The LNER published a timetable for the benefit of shippers, giving latest consignment times and scheduled arrival times for its best trains. Despite all the efforts, custom continued to slip towards the roads, on which a large-scale building and improvement programme was in progress, to whose costs the railways, as large payers of local rates, were hapless contributors. The railway's superior tractive power was relied on to cope with occasional out-of-gauge loads: in June 1928 two sets of turbo-alternators and a massive stator were moved from Leith Docks to the new power station at Portobello, requiring the temporary removal of ground signals – but the Continental fruit train to Glasgow was let through first[39].

In 1928 the LNER's revenue was £11,277,759, more than £3,500,000 short of the standard set by the 1921 Act, while the LMS, with revenue of £16,270,821, was £4,500,000 short. Economies were essential, and the LMS sought staff co-operation through area joint meetings with management to discuss such topics as road competition, shunting operations, speed, avoidable damage and accidents. Incidentally, among the Scottish staff in 1927 were at least 12 lady stationmasters, in their own uniforms with 'Stationmistress' on collars and caps. They were paid the same as men, with the unions' approval. England had only one stationmistress at the time[40]. Joint conferences in Perth and Glasgow were held in October 1927. In a remarkable gesture, the unions agreed in 1928 to accept a $2^1/_2\%$ cut in wages, initially for one year, to help the companies in their financial plight, and the directors reduced their own remuneration by the same amount[41]. The LMS, the world's largest joint-stock company, had paid 6% on its Ordinary stocks in 1925, but shareholders found that it was unable to pay any Ordinary dividend for 1928. In 1929 the LMS paid 4.5% and the LNER 3% (on Preferred Ordinary. Its Deferred Ordinary shares got nothing after 1925).

Sleepers and Super-Trains

Passenger rates at lower than the standard could be charged as the companies thought fit, and the 1929 Finance Act abolished the last vestiges of the old passenger duty, with the proviso that 90% of the capitalised value be used on service improvements to benefit heavy industry. To encourage first class travel, the LMS built three new Pullman cars for the ex-GSWR routes, *Meg Dods*, *Lass o' Ballochmyle*, and *Mauchline Belle*, plus an anonymous buffet car. An all-Pullman train had run between Harrogate and London since 1923, and in 1928 its route was extended north to Glasgow, with two new trains built, and a new title, 'The Queen of Scots Pullman'. Ever since the introduction of sleeping cars, there had been requests for third class accommodation, always resisted by the railway companies. In 1925 both the LMS and LNER were still claiming that there was no economic justification, but in 1928 they yielded to public demand and began an "experimental" service from Edinburgh and

Glasgow to London, which proved so successful that Inverness and Aberdeen also got third class sleepers from October that year. At first old carriages were converted but by 1931 the LNER was building new third class sleepers, of improved type with the lower bunk now of equal width to the upper one[42]. The LNER also upgraded its first class sleepers, including providing better-quality soap. Serious consideration was given to the transferring of used "soap cakes" to third class sleepers[43]. Compartments had four berths, and remained so until two-berth compartments were introduced by British Railways in 1955. The reluctance to provide cheaper sleeping cars is hard to explain, except that it was seen as an elite service: a first class sleeper in 1928 provided three tons of weight per passenger, compared with twelve cwt for a standard carriage. This gave a smoother ride but was more expensive to operate. However, while a first class sleeper carried from ten to a dozen passengers, a third class could hold 28, which should have compensated for the difference in fares.

Occasional moments of flamboyance cropped up, reminders that the movies and cinema news-reel era had arrived. Even a little glamour could go a long way. The LNER had lost some custom to the LMS's slightly speeded-up 'Royal Scot' in 1927 and responded by planning a non-stop 'Flying Scotsman', using Class A1 'Pacifics' with corridor tenders for crew change. On 27 April 1928, four days before the new LNER service began, the LMS put on the "world's longest non-stop journey", running the 'Royal Scot' in separate portions from Euston to both Glasgow and Edinburgh. An ex-Midland 4-4-0 compound engine hauled the Edinburgh train, which arrived two minutes early; a new 'Royal Scot' 4-6-0 headed the Glasgow train, which arrived on time. It was a cheeky one-day wonder – the single train, dividing at Symington, resumed next day. 'Royal Scot' facilities included a lounge car and a "boudoir compartment" with full-length mirror. More usefully, the LMS laid water-troughs in 1927, for the first time in Scotland at Strawfrank,

Ex-Highland Railway 'Clan Cameron', built in 1921, as LMS 14769, at Inverness Station, in 1929. It was withdrawn in November 1943. Boys selling fruit and sweets were a familiar sight at larger stations. (Author's Collection)

and also on the ex-Caledonian line at Floriston, Cumberland, enabling engines to replenish their tender tanks without stopping. On the East Coast, the non-stop 'Flying Scotsman's' schedule was a 19th-century one at 8 hours 30 minutes for the 392-mile journey, though improvement would come. Arriving at Kings Cross on the first run, Driver T. Henderson said he had had a wonderful run, under humane conditions, using the corridor tender, though he had not availed himself of the gents' hair salon, which managed eighteen haircuts and three shaves on the trip. Experiments were made in 1928 with radio receivers on Edinburgh-London trains, picking up broadcasts from the BBC Melbourne transmitter[44]. Behind the window-dressing, most of both companies' trains were using old rolling stock and running at modest speeds behind engines of pre-Grouping design. There was however some extension of Sunday services. From 1925 regular Sunday trains ran from Glasgow to Ayr, Girvan and Largs.

Such trains rekindled a topic long familiar to Scottish railway managements: in 1925 the General Assembly of the Church of Scotland protested against the increasing habit of travelling for pleasure on Sundays. William Whitelaw, himself an elder of the Kirk, replied on behalf of his professional colleagues: it was the Church's business to see that no public demand arose. If demand existed, the railways would supply it. In fact Sunday trains were rare, and non-existent on many lines, right through the LMS and LNER and British Railways eras, while buses and private cars were out and about in increasingly large numbers. In March 1949 Ross & Cromarty County Council refused an application by Scottish Region to run the Kyle-Kyleakin ferry on Sundays. There was no Sunday train[45].

Rescue Operations:
MacBraynes and the SMT

The Post Office made a new contract in April 1928 with the David MacBrayne shipping company for mail transport to the Western Isles (except St. Kilda, served by McCallum, Orme & Co. until all the inhabitants left in 1930). MacBraynes, with seven ships all forty or more years old, had been in financial straits since the end of the war and the LMS had been invited, and declined, to take over the contract in 1923. In February 1928 MacBraynes complained to the GPO that "we… are tired of this constant criticism of the service… The Highlands have had a better service and more Government consideration than is due to them"[46]. MacBraynes withdrew from the contract, though agreeing to work it until the end of October. A House of Commons Select Committee on the Western Highlands and Islands made a report in July, noting that a steam drifter, *Sweet Home*, owned by the Board of Agriculture, was operating from Mallaig to fourteen points on Skye and the north-west mainland – presumably a service dating from the war years. The LMS was again appealed to, and Stamp replied personally. He had holidayed on the west coast in 1927 and had been "besieged by all kinds of deputations at all kinds of stations requesting us to put up hotels, to improve ferries, to do everything to save the country, every one of which I put up to my officers and every one of which proved uneconomic as it stood". They had considered placing a cross-channel steamer at Kyle as a floating hotel in summer. Stamp also noted that letters from ministers protesting against Sunday excursions had made "an enlargement of my post-bag." Overtures to the LNER were also made by the increasingly desperate select committee, but James Calder informed it that his company would do nothing unless it was fully guaranteed against making a loss[47].

With Coast Lines Ltd, headed by Stamp's friend Sir Alfred Read, the LMS submitted two possible schemes and by the end of October a package was

A two-carriage train for Peebles leaves Symington in 1928. Ex-CR No. 66, LMS 14298, was built in 1884 and withdrawn in 1930. Photo C.J.L.Romanes (John Alsop Collection)

agreed, with a new company, David MacBrayne (1928) Ltd, capitalised at £350,000 and jointly owned by the LMS and the Coast Lines subsidiary Burns, Laird. Stamp became a director of MacBraynes and remained on its board until his death. Four new vessels were to be built, and the government would make up any deficiency each year to ensure a return on capital of 6%, with a minimum payment of £25,000 and a maximum of £75,000. Any excess profit was to be applied in fare reductions. The non-participation of the LNER caused some concern about the future of Mallaig, which was said to cater for around 60% of island passengers but had only one weekly steamer[48], but in the event there was no discrimination in favour of Oban and Kyle. The Western Highlands and Islands Transport Services Bill looked ahead to air services as well as to land-sea links[49].

Another company in difficulties at this time, more surprisingly perhaps, was the Scottish Motor Transport Co. (SMT). Bus operations had expanded greatly from 1921, even more threatening to short-distance railway passenger business than were the road hauliers to railway freight. In 1921 and 1925 attempts by the railway companies to have their functions extended to road operations had been rebuffed by the government; in 1927, however, there was a change of attitude, caused partly by the chaotic condition of the bus industry which, until 1930, had minimal regulation. In August 1928 all four main railway companies obtained Acts of Parliament allowing them to engage in road transport of both passengers and goods, though by no means with a free hand. The Ministry of Transport kept regulatory control on what they might do: if they set up a bus service they could not withdraw it without MoT permission. In order to get the Bills (as private measures) approved by Parliament, Josiah Stamp, on behalf of his fellow-managers, had to promise that the railways would not take advantage of their position by setting up intermediary businesses to run their road interests. This meant that the Railway Rates Tribunal could take the road traffic rates charged by railway companies into consideration when it was reviewing railway rates. As a result, the LMS, LNER and the others sought to buy into existing bus companies rather than set up in open competition[50]. In Scotland, the SMT offered a perfect case. Its main problem was lack of capital caused by over-rapid expansion, having swallowed up a string of local bus operators across central Scotland, and ending up with a fleet of 1,200 vehicles and hundreds more on order. In addition, a petrol tax had been introduced in 1928, and after an agreement between Anglo-American and Russian Oil Products, the price of a gallon rose to 1s 6½d in March 1929, increasing operators' costs.

Both LMS and LNER moved quickly to take advantage of the SMT's difficulties, combining to recapitalise the company, each owning 25% of it (more than 50% would have been deemed a controlling interest, making the bus company a railway ancillary and subject to regulation). The development was described as "elimination of competition" rather than a take-over; indeed the SMT managing director, W.J. Thompson, claimed success in "tying up" the railways for ten years so that they could not compete with the bus company. His shareholders, restive at first, fell into line when it was clear that they would receive at least twice the face value of their shares[51]. On 15 August 1929, the LNER and LMS arranged to relinquish their own passenger road services in favour of individual companies within the SMT group, the main transaction being the transference of the former GNSR routes in Aberdeenshire to Walter Alexander in 1930.

As the bus company's operations grew, it produced useful annual dividends through the 1930s, but the relationship remained an arm's length one and no attempt was made to align or integrate rail and bus services, though a Standing Joint Committee looked at some aspects of co-ordination, especially fares. Initiatives like the June 1930 agreement between LNER and SMT on inter-availability of tickets on routes between Edinburgh and East Lothian stations were rarities. Between 1930 and 1939 the SMT bus fleet increased from 1,750 to 3,158, and its passenger journeys (excluding tours) went from 92,021,650 a year to 295,520,000[52].

At an LMS shareholders' meeting in February 1928 to consider the company's Road Transport Bill, some unhappiness was evident. A Miss Budge demanded a freeze on capital expenditure and drastic economies until a 7% Ordinary dividend could be earned. The feeling that shareholders "do not much count" was widely expressed. Scottish-based shareholders, faced with 800 or more miles of travel to attend these meetings, asked for free passes, but neither the LMS nor the LNER obliged. In Parliament the LMS's toll on Connel Bridge traffic, 10s for a car, 2d for a foot-passenger, was held up as an example of the railways' tendency to milk a monopoly (Miss Budge would no doubt have thoroughly approved)[53].

2. The 1930s

The Slump Years

As the slump intensified, the companies had to walk a precarious line to maintain services and revenue. Pressure to reduce staff numbers grew. In Inverness a deputation from the NUR asked for the town council's support against reductions in the labour force at Lochgorm Works; by contrast the LNER had expanded Inverurie, having transferred boiler repairs there from St. Margaret's[1]. Inverurie Works enjoyed a reputation for efficiency and tranquil industrial relations. Whitelaw told his shareholders in October 1929 that "We have so much reduced fares that we have carried in the first 40 weeks of this year an increase of 10,000,000 passengers, and as a result we have received half a million pounds less as a reward for doing so." Yet any attempt to put fares up would have been refused as politically unacceptable. And in 1930 LNER passenger numbers fell by 8,500,000, with freight tonnage 10 million tons less than 1929[2]. With the LMS in the same boat, Sir Josiah Stamp issued a message to his staff "of cheer and encouragement at what is probably the most difficult time in the history of railways and, indeed, in the economic history of the modern world… above all, we need to keep up our courage." Ordinary stockholders received dividends of 2% from the LMS and Preferred Ordinary got $\frac{1}{4}$% from the LNER for 1930. But the bulk of LNER capital, £257,367,387, was in fixed interest securities on which the company was paying £23 million a year, as the unions well knew[3].

Period advertising and milk churns add to the interest of this 1930 shot of an LMS train at Annan Shawhill, heading for the Solway Viaduct. Services ended on 31 August 1931 and the viaduct was demolished in 1933. Photo D.S.Barrie (John Alsop Collection)

A Royal Commission on Transport sat in 1930-31. Its final report[4] noted that the reason for its existence was "the entirely new situation caused by the development of road transport". Little in the way of sympathy for the railways was evident: it was critical of railway speeds, noting that the 'Flying Scotsman' might be non-stop but averaged only $47\frac{1}{2}$ mph; also of the companies' attempts to cater for passengers' needs; and suggested that the capacity of the general managers might be more conspicuous if they were not restricted in their executive actions by "dilatory methods of unwieldy boards of directors". It did however express the view that a railway company should not be required to provide an unprofitable service. It had nothing specific to say about Scottish transport, except for proposing a UK-wide Transport Trust to co-ordinate all public transport (which did not happen), which might have a separate Scottish unit "to decide without delay on purely territorial matters", though it quoted Dugald MacLellan, Glasgow Divisional Engineer of the LMS: "The roads should, in fact, at least so far as passenger traffic is concerned, take the place of branch lines, which, unfortunately for the British railways, extend to 56% of the total mileage"[5]. One of the Commission's recommendations, in the interest of transport co-ordination (a buzz-word at the time) was for the licensing and regulation of public service vehicles. This resulted in the creation of Area Traffic Commissioners to grant licences for inter-town coaches and road hauliers. An early Traffic Commissioners enquiry in Aberdeen was told in April 1931 that in ten years rail passenger numbers between the city and Elgin had fallen from 114,000 to 61,000, with revenue dropping from £14,000 to £9,000; and another in Glasgow heard that railway passenger revenue had fallen by 77% between Annbank and Ayr. There was a bus every two minutes between Ayr and Prestwick[6]. Licence applications were almost invariably opposed by counsel for the railway companies. A not untypical exchange at one of these hearings went:
Railway counsel: "If you are going to run off with the cream of the business, how do you expect us to live?"
Coach operator: "That is your business, not mine"[7].

Some global figures for 1931 give an indication of how far the companies' gross receipts had fallen since 1922 (aggregate of the constituent companies), and of their efforts in cutting expenditure[8].

	LMS	LNER
Gross receipts 1922	£94,500,000	£70,500,000
Gross expenditure 1922	£76,200,000	£58,000,000
Gross receipts 1931	£70,800,000	£53,800,000
Gross expenditure 1931	£59,000,000	£45,000,000

In 1932, LMS revenues were £5 million (7.35%) down on 1931, but its expenses were down by 7.79%, by dint of 'modernisation", wage cuts, improvements in organisation, and withdrawals of unremunerative services, a programme driven by Sir Ernest Lemon, once a mechanical apprentice at Lochgorm Works in Inverness, now a vice-president. His reforms cut the types of paper used from 50 to 20, and reduced the number of forms by 40% over four years, but the company kept its reputation as a huge bureaucracy.

Having restored the voluntary $2\frac{1}{2}$% pay cut early in 1931, the companies succeeded in enforcing the same level of reductions via the National Wages Board later in the same year. All earnings were subject to a deduction of $2\frac{1}{2}$% with an additional $2\frac{1}{2}$% on any earnings in excess of £2 a week. Staff cuts had also helped: 15,931 had gone in 1931, half paid off, the others retired, resigned or died. Most losses were in the engineering shops, all of which were on short-time working until a slow return to full-time (47-hour week) began from February 1932. A Railway Wages Enquiry in 1931 found that while the LMS provided permanent status and superannuation for women, the LNER did not. The NUR was seeking a minimum adult wage of £3 a week, with a minimum twelve days of holiday, and noted that "in many cases railwaymen's wives had to go out to work or take in work"[9]: the feeling that a husband/father should be the family's sole provider was still strong. Union voices were not always united. The Railway Clerks' Association differed from the Trades Union Congress's proposal in 1931 that all those in employment should be taxed to help provide benefits for the unemployed, while noting that "The permanent character of railway employment is one of the most highly treasured traditions in the railway service, and we earnestly urge the commission to do nothing that would imperil the continuance of that exemplary tradition"[10] – an assertion that would not have gone down well with other railway workers, whose numbers continued to fall, by around 40,000 in 1930-31. Between 1931 and 1935 the percentage of insured railwaymen unemployed varied from 10% to 16.7%[11]. Finding the National and Central Wages Boards system somewhat cumbersome and not wholly dedicated to their own "stockholders first" policy, the companies proposed a new, slimmer, three-person Railway Staffs' National Tribunal, to consider claims in private and with power to enforce compulsory arbitration. The unions were concerned to retain conciliation machinery and opposed compulsory arbitration, and both sides agreed to keep a two-part system, with a Railway Staff National Council, and referral to the three-member Tribunal only in cases of non-agreement. All unions agreed that there should be no strikes until the negotiation process had been fully exhausted[12]. By mid-1937, with the railways again recruiting rather than shedding staff, pressure for pay increases became strong, with conflicting claims laid before the Tribunal. Earlier pay cuts had yet to be fully restored, but the unions were looking beyond that, with the NUR seeking a minimum adult rate of £2 10s a week. The railways' spokesman claimed that "It is not Labour but Capital that has grounds for complaint", with employees' "share of the profits" up by 107% from 1913, while shareholders' was down by 21%. NUR secretary-general John Marchbank (a Dumfries-shire Scot who had joined the Caledonian company in 1901) chose the period 1930-36 to demonstrate that employees' share of net revenue had dipped from 74% to 73% and shareholders' had risen from 25% to 27%. In 1937, against a background of falling traffic, the companies were allowed to raise passenger fares and goods rates by 5%.

Closures and Cost Savings

As early as 1924 the LMS had intentions to close the line between Strathaven and Darvel, prompting a question in Parliament: the Ministry of Transport replied that the line had been partially closed during the war, and reopened "on the understanding that full use of it would be made by farmers and others"[13]. In the event it survived until full closure in September 1939. The LMS closed around 24 Scottish passenger services in the 1930s, mostly village branches like those to Bankfoot, Edzell, Wanlockhead and Fochabers; the LNER withdrew passenger services from Kincardine-Dunfermline, Edinburgh-Glencorse, the Gifford and Macmerry branches, the Invergarry & Fort Augustus branch, and numerous others (see Appendix 7) in the early 1930s. Passenger services on the Ellon-Boddam branch were withdrawn on 1 November 1932, and the LNER's resort hotel at Cruden Bay now picked up its visitors by motor at Aberdeen, though its electric tramway to Cruden Bay Station continued to work for laundry and goods items[14]. Applying for a licence to enlarge his bus fleet, James Sutherland of Peterhead told the assessor that he was carrying from 16,000 to 20,000 passengers a month

The two tram cars of the Cruden Bay Hotel, on 9 August 1935, in LNER livery. The truck carries ash from the hotel laundry's boiler. Photo W.H.Whitworth (John Alsop Collection)

between Aberdeen and Peterhead[15]. Aberdeen's suburban trains to Dyce and Banchory were withdrawn from 5 April 1937, killed off by bus competition. While passenger services went, generally freight services were maintained, with track maintenance at a lower level than before. Coal was still a universal fuel and many stations incorporated a coal yard. Among the few total closures was the Solway Junction Railway in 1931 (the viaduct was demolished) and Leadburn-Dolphinton in 1933. Some services were defended: in March 1933 the LNER objected successfully to a bus service competing with the North Fife line (which had no Sunday service) between Newburgh and Newport. In 1932 the line had earned £355 in fares[16].

The cost-saving agreement of 1908 between the Caledonian and North British, inherited by the post-1923 companies, ended in 1932 and was immediately replaced by a new and more extensive arrangement from 1 July that year, intended to last for 50 years. Each company worked the traffic for both on certain lines, their number increasing as the years went by: the LNER between Leith North, the docks and Seafield; the Germiston branch from St. Rollox; the Camelon branch at Falkirk; and freight on the Dundee & Arbroath. The LMS handled all services to Forfar, Kirriemuir and Brechin; and all Glasgow freight to General Terminus and Stobcross. Montrose's LMS station was closed and all trains used the LNER station, and the same arrangement obtained from 1932 at Ardrossan, except for LMS boat trains to Montgomerie Pier. Dundee West Station closed on Sundays from 1 January 1935, with all trains running from Dundee Tay Bridge. Excursion services to Aberdeen were exclusively LMS from Glasgow and LNER from Edinburgh[17]. Making his inaugural speech as President of the Institute of Transport in 1933, Whitelaw insisted that there was still more room for pooling of resources: "The essential principle of conducting railway traffic ought to be the adoption of such a complete system of pooling as would put it out of the power of any railway company to earn profit by competition with another."

He wanted "a regulated monopoly" and was not averse to a single national management, though national *ownership* he saw as "ruinous"[18]. The companies combined to reduce restrictive conditions on cheap fares, accepting each other's tickets. A weekly season ticket for holiday use in specific districts, introduced by the LNER in August 1932, proved highly popular[19]. Despite economies, in 1933 the LMS spent some cash on Christmas decorations at Princes Street Station, "gay with coloured lights"[20] and evergreens: in itself this was a sign of changing habits in a country where Christmas Day was not yet a national holiday, with shops staying open and most people going to work.

Cost reduction found another battleground, between the companies and the Anglo-Scottish Railway Rating Assesment Authority, a body whose existence was needed because the local rates on commercial property were levied on different bases in Scotland and England. To charge for Scotland, as well as the value of lands and structures, the average net Scottish receipts of each company had to be established, by the Authority. For 1933 the assessor fixed these as £2,780,826 for the LMS, and £2,120,865 for the LNER, inclusive of "ancillary services", and gave them rateable values of £940,005 and £628,898 respectively, a jump of £250,000 from the previous year. The companies challenged his reading of the Railways Rating Act of 1930, and claimed that under its terms they had nothing to pay, but offered £200,000 and £100,000. The Lands Valuation Appeals Court rejected that, but altered the assessor's allowance from 40% to 55% of net receipts, bringing the LMS payment down to £704,876 and the LNER's to £445,768. Fife and West Lothian County Councils challenged the decision of the assessor to treat the Forth Bridge as part of the LNER, thereby reducing the substantial rates previously paid by the Forth Bridge Railway company, but without success[21]. County valuation officers were vigilant in noting additions and improvements to railway sites that would add value: even new signboards in stations might be counted in. After long litigation in England on railway valuation, the companies won a notable victory in July 1936, saving £1 million a year for the LMS and £700,000 for the LNER on their rates bills. Both immediately paid a full dividend to the stockholders. The National Wages Tribunal was sitting at the time, and ordered pay increases, restoring the greater part of the pay cuts made in 1931. Whitelaw noted that "This sweeps away a large part of the savings on rates, and leaves the patient stockholders with little more than the hope of expanding revenues through trade improvements"[22].

Modernisation: Aspiration and Actuality

In April 1931 a Committee on Electrification headed by the dynamic Scottish industrialist Lord Weir reported to the Minister of Transport, Tom Johnston (the Kirkintilloch-born MP who would later set up the North of Scotland Hydro-Electric Board), recommending a programme of electrification of all Britain's main line railways at an estimated cost of £261 million plus an £80 million investment by the new Central Electricity Generating Board. This was a vast sum, but the committee pointed out that some £500 million had been spent on upgrading the road network since 1921, in a totally unplanned way. With bank rate at 2%, large loans could have been raised. Although the committee was in favour of going ahead, it felt obliged to spell out that with an investment spread over 20 years, the expected rate of return after interest would be 2%: "… such a return taken by itself would not appear from a business point of view to warrant the adoption of a scheme of such exceptional magnitude." Evidently the members felt that a point of view wider than a narrow business one was needed, but the government did not pursue it, and though his general manager Sir Ralph Wedgwood had been a member of Weir's committee, Whitelaw dismissed the option of electrification unless the government would put up the money. It appears from a later LNER report, though, that the company did investigate the possibility of electrifying the line through Queen Street (Low Level) in 1935-37, with the aim of excluding steam trains altogether from the underground sections. But Whitelaw told the Railway Stockholders' Union in London on 29 January 1935 that "the company is not wasting a minute discussing the policy of electrification"[23]. Nor was Stamp in favour: noting in 1930 that electrification of Glasgow suburban railways would cost £15 million, he said that such advances "were under constant review", a statement reiterated in 1937[24].

Modernisation was selective and on a localised scale. One welcome improvement was the installation of colour-light signalling on the Queen Street (Low Level) line across central Glasgow, in 1931. On the LMS especially, only new developments that embraced efficiency and economy were acceptable, like the new electrically-operated signalbox at St. Enoch Station, which replaced five lever-operated boxes in 1933. Stamp considered research to be important, and as well as an engineering research unit, he set up a Commercial Research Section, which did much to develop container traffic: by 1938 the LMS had half of all 8,000 railway containers, in two standard sizes and of seven different types, to fit either one large or two small on a 12-ton flat wagon[25]; differential rates between 5%-20% were applied to container traffic: a 5% premium on bricks, a 20% premium on furniture removals. As a gesture to the past, the company agreed in the same year to preserve the Highland Railway 'Jones Goods' No. 103, Britain's first 4-6-0 locomotive for home railways[26]. Glasgow's Buchanan Street Station was rebuilt in 1932, with a new concourse, steel-framed but still wooden-walled, and with platform awnings transferred from the newly-closed Ardrossan North. The LNER doubled the track from Arbroath to Usan, near Montrose, in 1932. Automatic coaling plants were set up at larger locomotive depots – including Dundee (Tay Bridge) which also got a cleaning plant and new repair shop, making the operational facilities much more up to date than the

Balornock locomotive depot, Glasgow, in July 1935. Former Caledonian engines are very much in evidence, with only one LMS 'Crab' 2-6-0 on the extreme left. Photo Graham S.Lloyd (John Alsop Collection)

passenger station – and the Edinburgh-Berwick line was improved with four passing loops and colour-light signalling. A few busy freight stations like Broxburn and Bathgate were extended, and pre-heating plugs for restaurant cars were installed at Queen Street, Fort William and Mallaig[27], on-train catering now replacing the traditional pause for refreshments at Crianlarich Upper. An odd and un-modern event was mentioned by J.C. Train, then assistant maintenance engineer of the LNER southern Scottish area, in a 1934 talk to the Institute of Transport in London. A lengthman on the West Highland line had applied for a transfer because his house was haunted: "The extraordinary moving of furniture at night, and other signs, leaves no room for doubt"[28].

In 1934-35 there was much discussion about reorganising the railways of central Edinburgh, with schemes for concentration either in a new two-level Princes Street Station or a rebuilt and electrified steam-free Waverley[29], with Princes Street becoming a bus terminal, but these high-cost schemes remained only paper plans. The LNER and Town Council agreed on an extension of the Waverley Market above the station, to provide a more spacious and up-to-date exhibition hall, with an improved roof garden, and on 11 October 1936 a new Waverley West power box replaced five mechanically-worked cabins[30]. In August 1933 the LNER installed a "carrier wave circuit" telephone link between London, York and Glasgow, providing extra circuits on the existing wires to improve communication, not so much on operations as on freight quotations and business negotiations[31]. The LNER's efficient press office noted in January 1936 that in its current two-year programme it would build 207 engines, 1,154 passenger coaches, 11,046 wagons, 780 containers "of the latest type", and would renew 466½ miles of

Cars by rail in the 1930s: a scene at Kyle of Lochalsh Station. A shunting horse can also be seen. (Highland Railway Society)

track with 66,000 tons of British steel rails (the company's total route mileage was 6,590 miles). Mechanised coaling plants were installed at most of the busier locomotive depots, and carriage cleaning equipment was installed at some depots. At Galashiels a single new electrically-operated signal box replaced five others between Kilnknowe and Selkirk Junctions, a new steel bridge was built over the line at the station in 1938, at a cost of £30,000, and the station was improved, with gardens at the western end. Much of the modernisation process in both companies was out of the public eye but was nevertheless of great importance and value, in office systems using new automatic equipment, in improved telephone links, in guidance and operating advice to freight managers, and in inter-company co-operation. Both were pursuing experiments with high-pressure steam locomotives (to no avail) and making improvements on some express routes, primarily London-Edinburgh and London-Glasgow, with 20 minutes pared off the 'Royal Scot's' timing in May 1932, Euston to Glasgow in 7 hours 55 minutes, and the 'Flying Scotsman' (non-stop) now doing Kings Cross-Waverley in 7 hours 27 minutes in July of the same year, with specially-built trains running at an average 56 mph. Headphones were provided, at a charge of one shilling, for passengers to listen to BBC broadcasts or to gramophone music, with sockets fitted above each seat[32]. In March 1936 a "cinema coach" was provided by the LNER on its Edinburgh-Leeds service. On most lines little was done beyond basic maintenance except for cost-saving work, as with the LMS closure of the isolated signal cabin at Fodderty, junction for the Strathpeffer branch, and its replacement by an ingenious electric system worked from Dingwall[33].

Road Competition and Rail Freight in the 1930s

Scotland in 1930 had 82,751 motor cars, 53,798 motor cycles, 30,584 lorries and 11,257 "hackney vehicles", primarily buses. In 1935 there were 112,838 cars, 36,366 motor cycles, 35,545 lorries and 9,702 hackney vehicles[34]. An increase of over 36% in the number of private motors during the worst of the Depression years is striking: independent mobility was increasing fast among the richest and likeliest-to-travel section of the population. In 1930 the total LMS passenger train mileage in Scotland was 17,312,220 and the LNER's was 11,094,308. In 1935 the LMS figure was 18,201,402 and the LNER's 10,885,906: an increase by both companies despite service cuts. Across the UK generally and doubtless in Scotland, the proportion of reduced-price tickets had risen dramatically; by 1938 around 85% of passenger receipts came from reduced fares, compared with 34.4% in 1924[35]. The railways were working harder to earn less per passenger mile: 0.67d in 1938 against 0.86d in 1924

Modern light industries were often in out-of-town locations lacking rail connections. Goods managers adapted their services, notably by the increased use of containers: the LNER included 1,230 flat-bed container wagons in its 1936-37 building programme and by now had over 2,000 containers; and also by setting up new registered and guaranteed delivery services. One item delivered promptly in July 1934 was the 20ft-long 'Thurso Monster', caught at sea and forwarded via LMS to the Royal Scottish Museum, "a heroic gesture of monumental imperturbability which demonstrated afresh the capacity of British railways to deal, under the rules and regulations, with every eventuality". It turned out to be a basking shark, or possibly an oarfish[36]. A slight relaxation of regulations, in the Road & Rail Traffic Act of 1933, allowed railways to make "agreed charges" with individual consignors, but they still had to be approved by the Railway Rates Tribunal. The LNER's successful 'Green Arrow' service, introduced in 1933, was followed from January 1936 by a 'Blue Arrow' tracked and recorded parcel service by passenger train. It had the country's largest goods station, Glasgow High Street, extending over 3.5 acres and able to accommodate 226 wagons at its loading platforms. It handled around 1,000 wagons a day, and in 1936 it took in 122,632 tons of freight and shipped out 205,744 tons, in addition to 88,142 tons of trans-shipped freight and 487 livestock wagons[37]. Apart from meat, milk and fish, perishable items included trapped or shot rabbit, of which the LNER alone carried 238 tons in December 1933. Assuming 4lbs weight apiece, that is 133,280 rabbits.

Lemon's reorganisation of LMS systems gave more authority to district offices and goods departments in particular: local initiative was highly desirable as the men on the spot could see traffic disappearing. The Scottish Fisheries Board report for 1931-32 observed greater use of road transport: "In several cases long-distance traffic was regularly conveyed by motor lorries from the ports of landing"[38]. When the morning train on the Alford branch was discontinued in 1933, the mail went by goods train and was often late. Sir Malcolm Barclay-Harvey (later to write a history of the GNSR) inquired in Parliament what steps were being taken to improve the service. The Postmaster-General replied that it would be switched to road transport[39]. In winter snow the railways could temporarily regain traffic: March 1937 saw milk traffic from Stow to Edinburgh, fish from Granton to Glasgow, margarine from Duddingston to Sunderland and machinery from Shettleston to Liverpool all re-routed by rail because of snowbound roads[40], but the general trend was very clear. Charles Alexander, road hauliers, were refused licence to run fish lorries from Aberdeen to Manchester in 1935, when the LMS agreed to accept fish consignments for the 5.45 south express up to five minutes before departure, but in 1938 the haulier was granted licences for 20 lorries to take fish from Aberdeen. The Tribunal accepted that the railway provided sufficient facilities, but considered that the fish would be delivered "in better condition" by road and rejected the suggestion that the consignors were attracted only by lower rates. New bus routes were opening: a Fort William-Glenfinnan bus licence was granted to A.&J. Macpherson in September 1937, with an extension to Mallaig deferred for six months because of "the appalling state of the road"[41]. It was often pointed out by the "road lobby" that the railways themselves were the country's largest owners of motor vehicles: by 1939, quite apart from their bus interests British railway companies owned over 10,000 lorries and "mechanical horses", plus 11,000 horses and 24,000 carts. These vehicles, however, operated largely within towns and a narrow radius of country stations. For private motorists, long distances were still something of an endurance test. Cars had long been carried by rail, and in 1933 both companies offered car transport at $4\frac{1}{2}d$ a mile, if accompanied by one first or two third class passengers. In the mid-1930s the LNER operated a "car train" from August to October, from Kings Cross (6 pm) to Waverley (2.50 am), with up to 30 vans, to be attached to trains going onwards to Aberdeen, Inverness and Fort William[42].

Goods managers, however, had to contend with the huge inertia of a system that was only partly, and in a piecemeal way, modernised. Most freight wagons had only hand-brakes, limiting the speed of the train, and a high proportion were trader-owned, run at reduced charges and having to be returned empty. A service for all-comers had to be provided, at over a thousand depots, involving a range of consignments from single packages to trainloads of ore and coal. Frequent re-marshalling of trains and transference of items between wagons was necessary. The standard freight locomotive was the traditional Scottish 0-6-0, many dating back to the previous century, designed for slow-speed pick-up goods working. A few statistics[43] illustrate the situation:

Average freight train loads		
1930	LMS overall: 124.27 tons	LMS Scotland (North): 75.39 tons	(South): 106.73 tons
	LNER overall: 133.8 tons	LNER Scotland (North): 57.04 tons	(South): 102.31 tons
1935	LMS overall: 123.76 tons	LMS Scotland (North): 71.19 tons	(South): 104.63 tons
	LNER overall: 130.81 tons	LNER Scotland (North): 54.79 tons	(South): 101.83 tons

Average number of wagons per train	
1930	LMS overall: 33.68 of which 23.06 are loaded	LMS (Scotland): 26.73 and 19.44
	LNER overall: 34.75 of which 22.48 are loaded	LNER (Scotland): 27.46 and 18.71
1935	LMS overall: 34.44, of which 23.57 are loaded	LMS (Scotland): 27.6 and 19.69
	LNER overall: 35.02 of which 22.41 are loaded	LNER (Scotland): 28.44 and 18.8

Scottish Freight traffic in net ton-miles				
General merchandise & livestock				
	LMS (North)	**LMS (South)**	**LNER (North)**	**LNER (South)**
1930	94,444,520	341,339,811	17,964,527	262,565,599
1935	80,205,566	317,322,040	12,905,219	242,721,695
Minerals & merchandise				
1930	18,308,133	149,382,438	6,027,541	123,827,909
1935	18,051,539	129,214,802	5,042,779	103,855,125
Coal & coke				
1930	100,660,761	284,228,595	13,808,569	387,808,363
1935	90,361,560	290,430,128	11,327,068	367,901,542

Average wagon-load for general merchandise in Scotland		
1930	LMS overall: 2.86 tons	LMS Scotland (North): 2.53 tons	(South): 3.58 tons
	LNER overall: 2.94 tons	LNER Scotland (North): 2.72 tons	(South): 3.01 tons
1935	LMS overall: 2.74 tons	LMS Scotland (North): 2.33 tons	(South): 3.32 tons
	LNER overall: 2.77 tons	LNER Scotland (North): 2.48 tons	(South): 2.95 tons

Scottish freight train miles		
	LMS	**LNER**
1930	9,687,637	8,250,874
1935	9,293,126	7,484,195

These figures suggest that the LNER ran a more efficient freight operation than the LMS, with better loadings and fewer running miles. With the exception of average wagon loads, though, Scottish performance reduces the overall result for both companies.

Passenger Services in the 1930s

Peak demand on passenger services in urban areas could be very high, and somehow the companies managed to cope. During one of the 20th century's finest summers in July 1933, slump or not, the LMS ran 900 special trains in the Glasgow Fair period, and the LNER put on 250. On one day that month the LNER carried 10,000 day trippers to and from Portobello, with twelve specials on top of the normal service. An observer noted that "many of the trains resembled gigantic bathing clubs as every other person carried bathing towel and bathing costume"[44]. Taking advantage of the long daylight, both companies ran evening excursions which proved very popular, often circular tours on routes like Edinburgh-Forth Bridge-Ladybank-Kinross-Rumbling Bridge-Alloa-Edinburgh. By the end of 1933 416 evening specials had been run, carrying 194,429 passengers, and in 1934 the numbers were 682 and 247,802[45]. Like their predecessors, the companies kept substantial numbers of carriages for special use: mostly elderly stock of written-down value which could be deployed on particular occasions for events from curling matches (competitors were allowed two stones free) to Highland Games and flower shows. It was a necessity to be able to lay on trains in this way. Car ownership was still very limited and bus companies had few spare vehicles. On the normally quiet cross-country line between Crieff and Balquhidder Junction, 24 excursion trains were recorded as passing through St. Fillans Station on one day in September 1935[46]. In April 1938 26 LNER specials took 15,000 passengers to London to see Scotland beat England 1-0 at Wembley, and 45 LMS specials carried 28,000. Fare calculation had to be made with care: in 1923 when a third class fare was cut from $1^3/_4d$ per mile to $1^1/_2d$, journeys went up and revenue came down, but in March 1933 for the summer months third class return tickets were issued at $1d$ per mile, for a minimum distance of 30 miles, bringing a Glasgow-Aberdeen return fare down to 21s 3d from 31s 10d. Low fares did not please everyone: Buckie and District Traders' Association protested in December 1934 against cheap evening tickets to Elgin, drawing trade away from their shops[47], and Sunday excursions still aroused controversy. At the other end of the scale from cheap excursions, the LNER introduced the 'Northern Belle' cruise train in April 1933, a seven-day outing from Kings Cross to the Scott country and the Highlands, for 60 first class passengers at an inclusive fare of £20 each. The specially built train had a smoking room, writing room, ladies' room, hairdressing salon and shower baths. Both criticised as a wasteful luxury and admired as a feat of marketing, it was an instant sell-out, and its cost-revenue ratio appears to have been good enough for it to be re-run twice that year, and two new tourist trains were added in 1934[48]. Their operations continued until 1938. The LNER also had two special excursion sets in Scotland, each capable of taking 502 passengers and with a buffet car serving cocktails. Another immediate success was the conversion of old carriages into static "camping coaches", placed at scenic and quiet stations, introduced first by the LNER in the summer of 1933 and copied by the LMS from 1934. Yet another LNER innovation was a savings stamp scheme to pay for holiday travel, with stamps exchangeable for travel vouchers[49]. Sir Josiah Stamp took another West Highland holiday in 1935, arriving at Fort William on Sir Alfred Read's yacht (Read was chairman of MacBraynes). He inspected the locomotive depot and made a typical reply when asked for a comment on the proposed Ben Nevis electric railway: without engineering estimates and reliable data on possible users, he could not express a view[50].

In the summer schedule of 1933 the 'Flying Scotsman' had resumed non-stop running between London and Edinburgh, and Driver Robert Sheddon gave a radio broadcast on his footplate experiences. He had been a driver for 38 years, and his father had driven engines on the North British from 1848 to

Kirkcaldy in 1936. LNER Class P2 2-8-2 No. 2003 *Lord President* sweeps through with an Aberdeen-Edinburgh express. All six of the P2s were rebuilt as Class A2/2 4-6-2s in 1943-44. Photo E.R.Wethersett (John Alsop Collection)

1898. A new set of carriages for the train was introduced in July 1938, and in the same month the 50th anniversary of the 'Race to the North' was commemorated by the display of a train and engine of 1888 vintage at Waverley[51]. Smart work was required at Waverley Station where three separate portions had to be attached to the 'Flying Scotsman' before its departure at 10 am; Aberdeen carriages arrived at 9.41, Glasgow carriages at 9.45, and a Perth portion at 9.51. The incoming train from Glasgow also had carriages for Southampton and Harwich, taken forward on the 10.10 am[52]. The fastest service from Edinburgh to London was now provided by the 'Coronation' express, in six hours, hauled by streamlined Class A4 'Pacifics', introduced by chief mechanical engineer H.N. Gresley in 1935.

After a 50-year career, James Calder retired in June 1934, succeeded as general manager by George Mills, goods manager of the southern district. The LNER impressed schoolboys and many others that year by displaying Gresley's imposing new 2-8-2 'Mikado' express engine, *Cock o' the North*, at Waverley Station, the first of six Class P2 locomotives specially designed to haul heavy trains, especially sleeper trains, on the Edinburgh-Aberdeen line[53]. Another noteworthy aspect of railway promotion was the use of pictorial posters reproducing work commissioned from distinguished painters, including the Scottish artists G.S. Gillies and Duncan Carse. The LNER put on an annual exhibition of new poster work at 23 Waterloo Place in Edinburgh. Large colour posters enhanced the scene at stations. Photographs and lithographs of landscape scenes were also displayed in carriage compartments. Eighty-six Scottish resorts collaborated with the railways in posters and advertisements for visitors. Books, pamphlets, and films were also produced. The LNER had twelve films in use, and 80,500 posters on display in England, Ireland and Scotland[54]. The publicity departments strove to maintain their public image, to understand the patterns of train usage, and to maximise that usage. Aware that women often made the decisions relating to family travel, especially holidays, they aimed advertisements and information directly at a female readership, as well as at more specific groups like golfers and walkers.

A number of serious accidents happened on the LMS. Due to a signalman's error, at 3 am on 25 October 1928 the 7.20 pm ex-Euston 'Royal Highlander' for Inverness and Aberdeen ran into the rear of the stationary 1.20 am Carlisle-Dundee freight train between Dinwoodie and Wamphray, and the four crew of the express's two engines were killed. Nine people died in a collision at Port Eglinton Junction, Glasgow, on 6 September 1934, when the 5.35 pm St. Enoch-Kilmarnock collided on a diamond crossing with the 5.12 Paisley-St. Enoch train. On 10 December 1937 the worst crash of the decade happened at Castlecary, on the former Edinburgh & Glasgow line. During a blizzard the 4.03 pm Edinburgh-Glasgow express ran into the rear of the 2 pm Dundee-Glasgow, causing the deaths of 35 people and injuring 67. A signalman's mistake was blamed for allowing the express to approach under clear signals. It was the country's most intensively-used main line and the LNER rather belatedly announced in August 1938 that the Hudd system of automatic train control would be installed on 250 engines working between Waverley and Queen Street. This had not been done by the time war broke out in September 1939 and the scheme was shelved. Juvenile vandalism was blamed for the derailment on 5 August 1939 of the 12.30 pm Glasgow Central-Ardrossan Montgomerie Pier boat train on Canal Street bridge, Saltcoats, when the engine hit an obstruction placed on the line. Four people were killed[55].

The Slow Haul Out Of Recession

In the first years of the 1930s, mining and heavy industry were in deep recession, with 26.4% of insured workers aged between 16 and 64 out of work in May 1931, and only 41 out of 241 blast furnaces on the LMS system working. New industry was slow in appearance: between 1932 and 1935 Board of Trade figures showed that 104 factories in Scotland had closed, and 75 had opened[56]. By 1935 it was being felt that the British economy had turned the corner and commercial life was picking up again. Some recovery in Scotland was recorded, with the average percentage of unemployed among insured workers down to 18.7% from a peak of 27.7%; iron and steel production was growing considerably, to the benefit of the railways: 472,800 tons of pig iron and 1,642,900 tons of steel ingots represented threefold increases on 1932, and coal production, at 32,045,600 tons, was back to pre-Depression levels. But the rate of earnings was lower, and unemployment remained higher, than in England[57] and substantial pockets of high unemployment and destitution persisted until 1939. In November 1936 47% of the 18-36 age group in Scotland was unemployed. While the governments of the 1930s cannot be said to have wholly neglected the railways, what was offered were loans, not grants, requiring repayment by companies already struggling to cope with running costs, wage and dividend demands. In December 1935 a Railway Finance Corporation was set up, raising £27 million of 2.5% guaranteed debenture stock, to be repayable between February 1951 and February 1952, with £8,894,717 available to the LMS and £5,929,811 to the LNER. This was intended to be used for schemes that would not otherwise have been undertaken, and only the Southern Railway took real advantage of it, to extend its electrified network in the region least affected by the slump.

Shareholders were alarmed by the slide in railway revenues and in 1932 the Scottish Railway Stockholders Association merged with its English counterpart, also with the Railway Reform League and the LNER Stockholders Association, in the British Railway Stockholders' Union. In 1933 the two companies' revenues were less than half the standard of the 1921 Act, and neither was willing to apply to the Railway Rates Tribunal for an increase in rates and fares in case the resultant fall in traffic would make things even worse. LMS dividends were generally more regular and greater than those of the LNER, which failed on several occasions to pay anything to the holders of Ordinary shares. The Railway Stockholders' Union annual report in May 1936 objected strongly to any further restoration of railway staff pay levels. It noted that net railway revenue in 1935 was £5 million less than in the slump year of 1931[58]. Pressure from the staff side was strong, though it fell short of strike action. From 1 July 1935 it was agreed to reduce the pay deduction for railway police and shopmen to 1.25%. By mid-1936 the rail unions were insisting it was time to bring wage levels and working conditions back to the pre-1931 position. It was pointed out to the National Tribunal that the companies were paying dividends to the tune of £2.5 millions a year, but to the companies this took precedence over restoring workers' pay levels, which at £2,970,000 could not also be afforded. In 1937 the union claims were much greater than that. ASLEF were looking for restoration of the cuts, a six-hour day and 36-hour week, with double time on Sundays. Citing the demands "speeding up" made on his members, Richard Squance of the union said the claim was in some respects "excessively moderate"[59]. Though he felt that passenger traffic was developing "in a gratifying manner", William Whitelaw told the LNER ordinary general meeting in March 1937 that the company would consider no further improvement in salaries or wages "until the financial position of 1936 has been secured to the stockholders"[60]. Unfortunately in 1938, despite a brightening economy driven partly by war preparations, the railway companies' results were dire, and Ordinary shareholders received no dividend.

More sophisticated measurement of activities did not necessarily yield good news. The LMS estimated that it lost 134,460 tons of freight to road haulage in 1934, rising to 720,090 tons in 1938[61]. Railway managers were chafing more

A young spotter peers through the hedge as Ex-NBR No. 222, now LNER Class J37 9222, heads an express freight train, with containers on flat wagons. Built in 1915, it remained in action until October 1961. (North British Railway Study Group)

LMS Class 2P 647 at Ayr. The engine was built in 1931 and spent its working life in Scotland until withdrawal in 1961. Photo C.J.L.Romanes (John Alsop Collection)

and more against the obstructions still preventing them from competing on a level field with the road hauliers. They were still bound by the conditions set out in the 1921 Act, with some alleviation from 1933, when they were allowed to quote "exceptional rates" in a band between 5% and 40% below the standard maximum. But these needed approval from the Railway Rates Tribunal, and the railways were still forbidden to favour, or penalise, individual customers. Every exceptional rate had to be entered in rate books at relevant stations, and these had to be open for public inspection, making it easy for the road contractors, who could freely vary their charges, to undercut them. In 1937 permission was granted for a 5% rise in goods and passenger rates, but the real problem, as Sir Josiah Stamp pointed out, was the extensive use of "exceptional rates" which they had to apply in order to retain the traffic they still carried. An arrangement was sought with the road hauliers to have a joint charging structure, and a central consultative committee was set up in 1938, but its functions were obstructed by the Scottish Commercial Motor Users Association, which objected to the scheme[62].

The Scottish railway works, concerned with heavy and light repairs, design modifications, and dismantling of discarded engines, were back on full time work by 1938 and a degree of modernisation was under way. Inverurie switched from its own DC steam generation to the Grampian Electric Co.'s AC supply, and the iron foundry at Cowlairs was reorganised and modernised[63].

A 'Square Deal' Wanted

The national road system unquestionably needed modernisation to cope with the increasing density of traffic and the size of vehicles. Sir Cyril Hurcomb – a figure to be re-encountered in the railway story – Permanent Secretary to the Ministry of Transport, unveiled a £4 million programme for reconstruction of roads in the Highlands and Islands at the 5th annual meeting of the Institute of Transport's Scottish section in December 1935. The economic historian Gustav Sjöblom argued that the 1930s, not the 1950s, were the key period of change from rail to road, with the speed and small size of road vehicles giving "an extraordinary adaptibility to the needs of the economy", enabling new developmental and residential patterns; he concluded that "the choice of a motorised society was made in the 1930s"[64]. With ample evidence of road improvement, the railway companies launched a new campaign for a 'Square Deal'[65]. This phrase was quickly picked up on. A spokesman for the road lobby said the railways had a "square wheel"; John Marchbank said the railway workers wanted "a square meal". William Whitelaw resigned as LNER chairman in 1938, though he remained on the board of the Scottish Area. His successor, Sir Ronald Matthews, joined the other chairmen in putting their case to the Minister of Transport, and a wider campaign to attract the support of influence-groups was also mounted. Addressing the Glasgow Chamber of Commerce in February 1939, Stamp said the railways would have to take "drastic and revolutionary action" if their traffic continued to fall away, adding that "in a subsidy-ridden Europe we are the only country that has not taken a penny out of the public pocket for the railway service"[66]. Their campaign had the effect of getting the government to set up a Transport Advisory Council to consider action and in May 1939 it recommended cautiously that "the fettering regulations governing the conveyance of merchandise by rail should be relaxed for an experimental period"[67]. The government accepted the recommendation. As had happened with the Royal Commission on Railways in 1913, war began before any action was taken, and though the government had originally planned legislation for 1940, despite pleas from the companies and bodies like the Railway Stockholders' Union, no action was taken during the period of wartime and post-war control[68].

Galashiels Station with its overall roof, around 1933. Ex-NBR 'Superheated Scott' No. 363, now LNER Class D30 *Hal o' the Wynd*, at the head of an Up express. Built in 1912, it was withdrawn in 1951. (John Alsop Collection)

As far as most of Scotland's rail users were concerned, the 1930s brought relatively little change. Apart from Anglo-Scottish services from the two main cities, general speed of service did not improve, though some amenities were added, with more trains incorporating restaurant or buffet cars. It was noted in 1936 that the most popular dish in the Northern Scottish section of the LNER was bacon and eggs; in Scotland 70% of passengers drank tea in preference to coffee, while in England the proportion was 50/50. Employees had a distinctly thin time as the numbers were cut back and pay levels reduced. Many stations, repainted in company colours in the 1920s, were in a dingy state by the end of the 30s. Equally obvious to the critical eye in 1939, sixteen years after Grouping the great majority of engines were still of pre-1923 design and construction. Despite the innovations and speed records, real modernisation had not been accomplished here. Wider economic circumstances, and the unintended shackles imposed by the 1921 Act, prevented the companies from doing more. How much more they would have done is an open question: bigger dividends versus ploughed-back profits would have been a vexed issue. Counterfactual studies might indicate what could have happened if the companies had slimmed down drastically, or invested more, but they did neither. The men who ran the LMS and LNER were able and intelligent, and certainly felt that their companies had a responsibility to provide a public service and even beyond that, a service in which the nation could take some pride – Gresley's successful-by-a-whisker quest for the world steam speed record on 3 July 1938 had more than a dash of schoolboy heroics about it, but also technical interest and, not least, the issue of British prestige. One is left with the feeling that just to keep these vast concerns running was sufficiently exhausting for those in charge, without looking beyond the immediate horizon. And beyond that horizon, the omens were not encouraging. The Second World War was coming.

The LNER station at Whifflet, with the LMS goods yard beyond, in the 1930s. (North British Railway Study Group)

Docks and Steamers
in the Grouping Period

The LMS inherited the shipping fleets and routes of the Glasgow & South Western Railway, and of the Caledonian Steam Packet Company, a wholly-owned subsidiary of the Caledonian Railway, and the LNER got those of the North British. The two companies had £3 and £2.5 million respectively of capital in Scottish docks and harbours, with the LMS owning Stranraer East Pier, Ayr, Troon, Greenock, Oban, Kyle of Lochalsh, and Grangemouth, while the LNER had Bo'ness, Burntisland, Methil and Mallaig.

The LMS Stranraer-Larne services were run by the ageing turbine ships *Princess Maud* (1904) and *Princess Victoria* (1912). TS *Princess Margaret* was added in 1931 and TS *Princess Maud* in 1934, replacing its namesake, scrapped in 1932. *Princess Victoria* was scrapped in 1934 and a new ship of the same name was introduced in 1939. Competition on the Clyde, once famous, no longer existed, apart perhaps from excursion sailings, and each company served specific routes. The combined LMS fleet was much the larger. One ship, *Glen Sannox* (1892), was broken up in 1925 and replaced by a new vessel of the same name, but otherwise no new ships were built until the 1930s, by which time PS *Caledonia* (1889) was over 40 years old. Scrapping or sale, and renewal saw the disappearance of PS *Juno* (1898) in 1932, *Caledonia* and *Mercury* (1892) in 1933, of *Jupiter* (1896) and *Marchioness of Breadalbane* (1890) in 1935, and the arrival of TS *Duchess of Montrose* in 1930, TS *Duchess of Hamilton* in 1932, a new PS *Caledonia* and a new PS *Mercury* in 1934, PS *Marchioness of Lorne* in 1935, TS *Marchioness of Graham* in 1936, and new paddlers *Juno* and *Jupiter* in 1937. Between 1935 and 1938 four small motor vessels were put in service for the Cumbrae and Arran routes: *Wee Cumbrae* (1935), *Arran Mail* (1936), *Ashton* and *Leven* (1938). On inland lochs, the LMS replaced the old converted lighter *Loch Awe* (1876) in June 1936 with a small steam vessel, *Countess of Breadalbane*, while *Queen of the Lake*, built at Ailsa yard in 1907, was still operating on Loch Tay, where the Killin branch's terminal station of Loch Tay remained open for increasingly sporadic train services until 11 September 1939, when war interrupted the steamer services.

The LNER laid up PS *Dandie Dinmont* (1895) in 1926 and introduced PS *Jeanie Deans* in 1931. PS *Talisman*, TS *Atalanta*, and PS *Kenilworth* were withdrawn in 1934, 1937 and 1938; only *Talisman* was replaced, by a diesel-electric paddle steamer of the same name in 1935. The company changed its colours for Clyde steamers in 1936, retaining the red funnel with white band and black top, but black and cream on the hull was replaced by French grey with a red waterline. Deckhouses remained white[69].

The LNER was technically still owner of the Forth ferries, though the operation was leased to the boat-builders Wm Denny in 1934, who built and operated two new boats that year, another in 1949 and a fourth in 1953, running all four until the road bridge was opened in 1964. In August 1932 a daily motor saloon ferry was introduced between Mallaig and Armadale, replacing a weekly boat. Now it was possible to leave Kings Cross at 1.10 pm and be in Portree (via a MacBrayne bus) by 8.45 pm on the same day[70]. The increasing use of motor cars prompted requests for specialised car ferries rather than the improvised methods on routes like Kyle-Kyleakin. Using planks to drive on and off, around 1,000 cars were said to be carried between Gourock and Cowal in 1937; in July 1939 the LMS was reported as planning to build ramps and run a proper car ferry between Gourock and Dunoon as soon as possible[71], but the war intervened and it finally opened in 1954.

As joint owners of the former Dumbarton & Balloch line, the companies shared ownership of the Loch Lomond steamers operating from Balloch Pier Station: *Empress* (1888, laid up in 1925), *Prince George* and *Princess May*, dating from 1898, *Prince Edward*, in service from 1912, and *Princess Patricia*, bought in from London in 1914. By the later 1930s they were only in use for summer tourist traffic: *Princess Patricia* was sold in 1938 and *Prince George* was taken out of service in 1939 even before the war brought about a halt in their activity[72].

Ellon, junction for the Boddam branch, with the Sentinel steam railcar *Highland Chieftain* in 1929. In 1931 the LNER Scottish Area had fifteen such vehicles, all working on branches south of Perth. Photo D.S.Barrie (John Alsop Collection)

Motive Power and Rolling Stock, 1923-47

One provision of the 1921 Act had been for standardisation of equipment and the adoption of co-operative schemes of working among the companies. Of the former there was virtually no sign. At first it would have been impossible, with the works and stores of different companies set up to service locomotives and equipment designed to their own patterns, but the LMS and LNER went on to establish their own, rather than joint, standards. Comparative trials of various engine types were held by the LMS on the Settle-Carlisle line in 1924, including the Caledonian Class 60 4-6-0, of which 20 new examples were built at St. Rollox in 1925-26. These were the last engines built by a railway company works in Scotland, though ten Caledonian-design 0-4-4Ts were built for the LMS by Nasmyth, Wilson of Manchester in 1925. English company designs began to appear on Scottish services. Twenty-four new Great Central 4-4-0s appeared on the former North British, provided with resonant Scottish names from Sir Walter Scott's novels, in 1924, and 2-8-0 freight engines from the same source went to Thornton depot. Locomotive development moved ahead most effectively on the LNER, where H.N. Gresley expanded and improved his range of fast 3-cylinder 'Pacific' engines, and supplemented the North British 'Glen' 4-4-0s from 1925 with fourteen K2 2-6-0 engines. The LMS continued to build outmoded and under-powered pre-Grouping types until 1927 when the first of its Glasgow-built 'Royal Scot' class 4-6-0s was exhibited to the public at Edinburgh, Glasgow, Dundee and Aberdeen in November. It should not be overlooked, though, that efficiency in the locomotive works was greatly improved: the percentage of locomotive stock awaiting or undergoing repairs fell from 19.02% in 1923 to 6.13% in 1928[73]. New ways were tried for running low-density local services. The LNER ordered 31 Sentinel Cammell steam railcars for use on the Leith North and other branches where bus competition was strong[74]. Beardmores of Dalmuir were building diesel-electric units in 1929, though not for use in Scotland. The first diesel-powered service in Scotland was introduced in 1938, on the Hamilton-Brocketsbrae-Lanark route, using a four-wheeled Leyland railcar[75].

Locomotive development in the 1930s showed perhaps the most extreme example of Gresley's practice of building relatively small classes of engine to operate on particular routes, with the imposing though problematic eight-strong P2 class introduced from 1936. His six Class K4 2-6-0s of 1937 were also built specially for the West Highland, intended to eliminate double-heading on the heaviest trains. On the LMS, Stamp and the chief mechanical engineer W.A. Stanier, took the opposite view, with the 'general utility' engine, exemplified by Stanier's 'Black 5' 4-6-0 introduced in 1934, which worked passenger and goods trains everywhere between Wick and Bournemouth. Even before Gresley's death, the LNER would also adopt this policy, with the versatile Class V2 2-6-2 in 1938, and continue it with Edward Thompson's B1 4-6-0 class of 1942.

Gresley was also innovative in carriage design, having saved train weight by building articulated carriages, two bodies on three bogies, from 1907. His attention to detail was remarkable; in his reconditioned sleeping cars of 1934, even the coat-hangers were redesigned: "… the rod for the trousers is conveniently above the coat hanger instead of below it, as a practical recognition of the order in which the garments are removed and put on again"[76]. In the 1930s, wood was still a prime component in carrriage bodies, though with steel frames, but all-steel carriages were being built by the end of the decade. Both companies still ran gas- and even oil-lit carriages in 1930 though by 1939 oil was phased out and gas was rare. On the LMS, Sir Ernest Lemon pushed forward unit-assembly and production-line techniques that

A LNER road-rail lorry on the West Highland line at Arisaig in 1936. Compare the 2016 picture on page 201. (J.L. Stevenson, courtesy of Hamish Stevenson)

The one-coach branch train at Alyth, in 1936. LMS 15229 is an ex-Caledonian 439-class 0-4-4T built in 1915 and withdrawn in 1961. (John Alsop Collection) Photo Miall

had begun on the Midland Railway in 1919. Construction of a carriage from laying down of the frame to putting on the roof had once taken six weeks: in 1931 it was six hours[77].

The most antique engines, and those belonging to very small classes, were being scrapped, and by 1935 the LMS was operating with 24% fewer locomotives than in 1923. At the amalgamation it had 393 locomotive types, by 1938 the number was down to 220. Over 360 G&SWR engines were scrapped between 1923 and 1939, with only eleven surviving into the 1940s, compared with 54 ex-Highland and 60 GNSR. One reason for the survival of GNSR engines was their low axle-weights, designed for the numerous iron bridges of relatively light construction on the former Great North lines. Most trains in 1939 were still being worked by the 753 ex-Caledonian and 687 ex-North British engines still in action.

Railway Air Services

With their shipping and road transport interests, the Big Four did not see themselves as exclusively rail businesses, and they took due note of the new field of air transport. The LMS obtained Parliamentary authority to run air services in 1929, but did not take any action until small pioneer air companies began operations in the early 1930s. Railway Air Services was formed by the Big Four in 1934 with an LMS vice-president, Sir Harold Hartley, as chairman, to work in association with Imperial Airways (whose chairman was Sir Eric Geddes, until his death in 1937). Its initial service was from Croydon, departing at 9.30 am, to Renfrew, arriving at 1.40 pm, at a fare of £9 10s. Midland & Scottish Air Ferries had been running flights from Renfrew to Campbeltown and the Inner Hebrides since early 1933, and Renfrew was also the base of Northern & Scottish Airways from November 1934. Northern & Scottish amalgamated with the Inverness-based Highland Airways to form Scottish Airways on 12 August 1937, and the LMS took a 40% interest in the company, which operated flights to Orkney, Shetland and the Western Isles. Also formed in 1937 was Western Isles Airways, in which MacBraynes had a 50% interest. The aircraft of the time had limited accommodation and passenger numbers were small, but nevertheless represented a loss of mostly first class fares on trains and steamers. In 1937, the 'General Instructions for the Railways Air Service' required the pilot, in the event of an emergency landing, to telephone the nearest railway station, whose stationmaster would arrange cars, etc[78].

3. Wartime and After

Preparation for War

In the late 1930s it was becoming increasingly clear that war was likely, and a five-year rearmament programme was initiated in 1937. Although after the Munich Agreement of 29 September 1939 Prime Minister Neville Chamberlain announced "peace for our time", active preparation for war intensified. Expenditure on new munitions factories went from £0 in 1934 to £12.7 million in 1939. A new factory at Bishopton, Renfrewshire, partly on the site of the First World War Georgetown factory, was begun in April 1937 and within two years two further factories were being built alongside it. Ultimately almost 20 miles of standard-gauge railway were laid inside the perimeter, worked by small diesel locomotives and linked to both the LMS lines between Paisley and Greenock[1]. A new ordnance factory was built at Dalbeattie in 1939 and in the early years of the war others were set up at Cargenbridge (Dumfries), Carsegowan (Wigtown), Powfoot (Annan), Grangeston (Girvan) and Charlesfield (St. Boswells), with railway access one of the key considerations in location. Wartime stations for workers at the Ardeer chemicals and explosives works were set up by the LMS as Garnock East and West, from 8 January 1940[2].

An interdepartmental Railway Communication Committee was established in November 1938 to plan concerted action, with representation from the Department of Health for Scotland. By July 1939 intensive planning for civilian evacuation was going on, with Glasgow, Edinburgh, Clydebank and Dundee listed for evacuation of children, also the communities adjoining the Forth Bridge. When the order "Evacuate forthwith" was given on 31 August, the plan snapped into action. In three days, 123,639 evacuees were moved from Glasgow and Clydebank, and in all around 176,000 Scottish children were moved to a wide range of places like Buchlyvie, Comrie, Turriff and Wigtown, which had railway stations, with buses, cars or carts to take them to nearby places. It was another tribute to communal organising capacity and to railway efficiency, though it turned out to have been a premature precaution. In the first "phoney war" phase the anticipated aerial attacks did not happen, and by Christmas three quarters of the evacuees had been brought back to their homes. Further plans made in anticipation of massive air attack included provision for casualty evacuation trains, as well as preparation of vehicles for military ambulance trains[3].

Children evacuated from Glasgow arrive at Forgandenny Station, September 1939. (Photo A.C. Cowper, Perth)

In 1937 the railway companies were asked to outline proposals for the financial arrangements of a control scheme in the event of war, but no progress was made on this until the government presented its own proposals in June 1939. As in August 1914, the Regulation of the Forces Act of 1871 was invoked on 1 September, enabling the government to put all railways under state control for the duration of a national emergency, and a Railway Executive was set up to manage operations across the entire system, though now with only four rather than 100-plus companies to control. It was headed by Sir Ralph Wedgwood, who had just retired as general manager of the LNER. The financial arrangements, established after negotiation, were not the same as in the First World War[4]. All railway receipts were to be paid to the government, which would pass a regular standard amount back to the companies, who suggested hopefully that the "standard revenue" of 1921 should taken as the basis for this, but they had never earned as much as that, and instead, payments were to be based on their averaged actual revenues for the years 1935-37. These amounted to £40 million. If the total revenue in a war year should exceed that, the extra up to £3,500,000 would be shared, with 34% going to the LMS and 23% to the LNER. Any surplus beyond that, up to £56 million, would go half to the government and half to the companies. Anything above £56 million would be taken wholly by the government. The companies did not regard this arrangement as particularly equitable, but hostile voices were saying their share was too big, and as it was not a time to seem greedy and unpatriotic, they accepted what was on offer, having to take on trust the functions of the Railway Executive, which had not yet been defined. This time, however, they were not obliged to carry government traffic free of charge as they had done in 1914-18, though the rate was at anything down to a third less than the standard. In August 1941 the rates were adjusted, ranging from £3 4s 6d a ton for Stationery Office material to £1 6s 5d a ton for Ministry of Food traffic. A special rate of £1 16s 9d was made for shipments by the Scottish Agricultural Department, within Scotland only[5].

Damage from enemy attack was provided for, up to a point: £10 million from the 'control account' could be paid in any one year, with any extra paid by the companies, subject to "any general compensation which the government may ultimately pay" after the end of hostilities. In August 1941 the control scheme terms were revised, backdated to 1 January 1941: the four companies were now to share £43 million a year – the LMS receiving £14,736,000 and the LNER £10,148,000 – and everything over that went to the government. With the inevitable rise in traffic created by war production, the government earned more from the railways than the companies themselves did – £45,700,000 in 1942 and £62,000,000 in 1943, the peak year of the war for railway earnings. While this may seem unfair to the railway companies – which protested – Christopher Savage pointed out that the revised arrangement was not merely to stop the railways from earning too much, but partly because the original assertion by the companies that they could cope with virtually any increase in traffic was no longer valid, and the Ministry of War Transport realised that traffic must now be diverted from the railways rather than towards them[6].

The Scotland Street tunnel originally dug for the Edinburgh Leith & Granton Railway was adapted as location for the LNER Scottish central and Edinburgh district control rooms, and as an air-raid shelter for 3,000 people[7]. The LNER moved its locomotive running office there from Glasgow on 1 July 1939. Protected accommodation was set up at Kilmarnock, Motherwell, Polmadie and St. Rollox, while initially at least, Aberdeen, Perth and Inverness had to make do with a supply of sandbags. Sand dumps were placed at key points, and emergency engineering depots, with stores and equipment, were set up at Carstairs and Perth. Steel shelters of a d.i.y. sort for inside use were provided for some signal cabins[8]. Certain sites were inevitably highly exposed: on the Forth Bridge, the painters were commended for continuing work even when Rosyth was subjected to an air raid early in the war[9].

Wartime Operations

Railway operations in Scotland continued under the two separate managements, with close co-operation in maintaining services and ensuring the flow of supplies. Operations were organised on a divisional and district basis, with the LMS Northern Division forming control districts centred on Carlisle, Edinburgh, Aberdeen, Inverness, Kilmarnock, Motherwell, Perth, Glasgow (Polmadie and St. Rollox) and Stranraer; and the LNER at Aberdeen, Burntisland, Edinburgh and Glasgow. Selected stations in each district reported on the traffic position at set times. From the autumn of 1940 emergency wireless equipment was installed at some places, and by 1943 fixed sets were at Ayr, Carlisle, Dumfries, Glasgow (Thornton Hall), and Perth (Forgandenny); road mobile sets at Glasgow and Stirling; and railway vehicle sets at Aberdeen, Dalwhinnie, Forfar and Inverness, all on the LMS; and the LNER had fixed sets at Aberdeen, Montrose, Burntisland, Glasgow, and Galashiels, with a mobile unit based at Edinburgh[10].

Resumption of total war, after a twenty year gap, meant that many railway workers at all levels had already experienced war conditions. They knew what to do and got on with it. Some jerky decisions were made: restaurant cars were taken off all services on 11 September 1939, then partially restored in October, offering "standard meals" for 2s 6d[11]. By the summer of 1942 they had mostly gone again, due to lack of staff and the need to provide the maximum number of passenger carriages in the overcrowded trains; only 61 trains had restaurant cars, "a few essential business trains and trains in the North of Scotland"[12]. To allow for freight requirements, the full pre-war passenger service could not be maintained. In 1943, although 50% more passengers were being carried than in 1939, passenger train miles in 1943 were 30% less[13]. After the war Sir Ronald Matthews remarked that LNER passenger numbers were 20% above pre-war levels but passenger train mileage was 22.5% below[14]. Of course, before 1939 many trains had been only lightly occupied, and it was on the main trunk lines that overcowding was the wartime norm. In April 1940 some platforms at Glasgow Central were extended to allow for extra-long trains. Platform 11 at 1,107 ft could hold seventeen carriages and two engines. Working timetables for wartime conditions had been prepared before war was declared, and the companies, and the nation, settled gradually into wartime mode.

Service cuts within Scotland were relatively few, because of the high level of demand (despite posters asking "Is Your Journey Really Necessary?") though express speeds were reduced by 10-15% to save coal, with times lengthened accordingly. The journey time from London to Glasgow, 6 hours 30 minutes in October 1938, was 9 hours 35 minutes in October 1939, with London-Inverness up from 13 hours to 16 hours 14 minutes. January 1940 saw a modest re-speeding-up, though not to pre-war standards, with the 7.52 night train from Euston reaching Inverness at 9.52 am rather than 11.15[15], and summer timetables that year showed Britain's fastest point-to-point timings to be in Scotland, with the 7.50 am and 11.38 am from Perth both averaging 58.9 mph between Coupar Angus and Forfar; and 50-plus mph on Gleneagles-Perth and Paisley-Kilwinning trains. Special regulations applied on some routes: for most of the war, passengers had to place all hand luggage in the guard's van of trains crossing the Forth and Tay Bridges, unless the item was too small to hold a bomb. Pre-planned arrangements covered virtually all traffic, even fish – from 9 September 1939 under the control of the Director of Fish Supplies. Fish traffic was routed from the seventeen main receiving ports to railhead receiving stations: Carlisle, Stranraer (also a despatching port), Glasgow (Sighthill), North Leith, Perth, Dundee (East), Aberdeen, and Inverness, which sent on the wagons as directed[16], and the Ministry of Food took over two floors at High Street Goods Station in Glasgow. Coal shortages affected train services at times, with drastic cuts in the sleeper services in the early Spring of 1940. All sleeper berths were taken over from 12 January 1942 by the Ministry of Transport (renamed Ministry of War Transport from 1 May 1941) for official use, and handed back for civilian use only if not needed on the day. Some first class sleeping cars were modified in 1942 to have two-berth compartments at each end, to increase accommodation. In 1943 the LMS put on a "secret" unadvertised sleeper train leaving Glasgow (St. Enoch) at 9.27 pm and arriving at Euston at 6.50 am; the northbound times were 8.40 pm and 6.05 am. With five first and two third cars, it was intended primarily for US servicemen and its bookings were controlled by the Air Ministry. Mail trains still ran, including the Euston-Aberdeen 'Postal', but on-train sorting of letters was dropped in late 1940 for the duration of the war. The Railway Executive governed the level of passenger train services with a firm hand, to ensure the passage of freight trains. No more passenger services were allowed in 1943 than in 1942. One non-essential service that it allowed to remain was pigeon trains in the racing season; cancelling them in 1943 but rescinding the decision[17]. The LMS hotels at Gleneagles, Turnberry, and Strathpeffer were closed to visitors during September, and by the end of 1939 all the resort hotels, including Cruden Bay (LNER) were requisitioned for government or military use.

Fear of aerial photography and the potential landing of paratroops led to the removal of many station nameboards and covering up of the numerous station names spelled out with painted stones at the lineside. Many signal box nameboards were also taken down. Eventually the policy was deemed to have gone too far, bewildering passengers, and in the case of signal boxes, confusing engine crews. By autumn 1940 many names were back in place[18]. Finally the Railway Executive Operating Committee ruled that signal box names could be restored so long as the lettering was no more than six inches high. Injunctions to railway staff to maintain silence about military and special trains were regularly repeated. An apocryphal tale tells of a passenger who leaned out at a nameless station to ask where he was. The porter replied, "I'm nae allowed to tell strangers". Similar invasion concern led to drivers being instructed on how to immobilise their engines. The Censorship Department of the Ministry of Information helpfully offered its services to railway chairmen, to vet their speeches at annual meetings, lest some nugget of useful information should inadvertently reach the enemy[19].

Wartime Working Conditions

Unlike the position in 1914, the railways did not suffer an immediate shortage of staff due to volunteers joining the armed forces. Conscription was in force from 1 September 1939 and people waited to be called up. Railways were among the reserved occupations: enginemen and signalmen were not subject to call-up, and most other railway workers were exempted if over 25 or 30 years of age, depending on their function[20]. Late in 1939 the rail unions put in a claim for increased pay due to war conditions, and the Railway Executive awarded a flat £10 a year to all salaried staff, 4s a week to conciliation grades and 5s to shopmen: the first of numerous increases to cope with the increasing cost of living[21]. By March 1944 war advances had reached £53 6s for salaried staff and £1 0s 6d for the weekly-paid. Increases were awarded by the Railway Wages Tribunal but paid by the companies, which

The armoured train at North Berwick, 1941. It is manned by Polish troops on this occasion. (Wikimedia Commons)

usually argued against them. In February 1942 a companies' spokesman informed the Railway Staff National Tribunal that equal pay for equal work by women was "unsound on social grounds"[22], and the Tribunal rejected the union claim that women clerks were performing duties similar in character and value to those of men. Women's increases were always less than those of men; in August 1942 adult males received an additional 4s a week while the women got 3s[23]. From 1943 staff shortage was added to the dificulties of operation. More women workers were recruited – from 1941 single women aged between 21 and 30 were liable to conscription for civilian service in reserved occupations. At Perth, the women porters got the porters' mess-room and space was found for their male colleagues in an annex to the gents' toilets[24]. By 1944 15% of the LNER's male staff were in the armed forces, and one in six of its employees was female. Reflecting the intense activity and heavy traffic, shareholders did better in the war years than in the 1930s, with both LMS and LNER paying full dividends on Preference shares, though LNER Deferred Ordinary shareholders remained unrewarded.

Volunteer railwaymen manned an armoured train that patrolled the East Coast Main Line, commanded by Captain W.J. McLeod, a top-link Haymarket driver, with a crew of 20. The locomotive was in the middle and the train carried a 6-pounder gun, Vickers machine gun, a twin-barreled AA gun and Bren guns[25]. Many others joined the Home Guard or became Air Raid Precaution (ARP) wardens. The entire lengths of the LMS and LNER between London and Glasgow and London and Edinburgh were single Home Guard zones, with battalions centred on major stations. The 1,000 members of the 8th City of Glasgow Home Guard were all LNER men. Railway works were adapted to produce war supplies as well as their normal business, with Cowlairs among the first, its paint shop converted to make aircraft wings. Tank turrets, high-angle gun mounts and Inglis bridge units (precursor of Bailey bridges) were also made by a workforce that was two-thirds female[26].

The nature of warfare had changed and the need for a 'blackout' against air attack made many operations, especially shunting, more difficult and dangerous. Permissible lighting had three grades: (A) only shunters' handlamps; (B) low-power lighting that might be continued even under air raid warning, until "purple" or "red" warning was received; (C) screened lighting for larger depots and stations, to be extinguished on air raid warning. Signal boxes were permitted lighting slightly above basic Category B[27]. Locomotive cabs had window shutters or tarpaulins fitted. Numerous experiments were made with signal boxes: at Waverley their windows were coated with translucent blue paint and yellow lighting was fitted which did not show outwards. More frequently inner sides were lined with cellophane.

Inevitably the number of accidents increased, most of them minor. But blackout conditions and intensity of train movements played a part along with human error in the disaster at Cowlairs East Junction on 30 January 1942, when the 4 pm Edinburgh-Glasgow express collided head-on with a light engine, and fourteen people were killed or died in hospital. Polish soldiers on the express helped in the rescue operation[28]. After the Castlecary smash of 1937, LNER operating rules on the Edinburgh-Glasgow line required the brake van, or a vehicle with a brake compartment, to be next to the engine; by "a sad coincidence of operational circumstances" this vehicle was at the wrong end. Most serious accidents during the war years had nothing to do with the blackout. On 5 March 1940 a mineral train had just entered the crossing loop at Slochd Summit on the Highland Main Line when 21 loaded wagons broke away. The guard jumped to safety, while the wagons rolled back down the steep grade for 9¼ miles and collided at high speed with the following train, a freight pulled by two engines, killing the driver and fireman of the leading engine. At Gretna Green, on 5 November 1940, the 6.09 pm Euston-Perth express ran into the 8.55 pm Glasgow (Shawfield)-Carlisle freight which was crossing its path off the Dumfries line, and the express's driver and two passengers were killed. Other fatal accidents during the war years included the deaths of three permanent-way men hit by a train in the Falkirk Tunnel, on 18 June 1942; and of three passengers on the 8.40 pm Euston-St. Enoch express, derailed at 55 mph at Mossband on 15 May 1944. There had been work on the track there, but no speed limit had been imposed. The 1 pm Glasgow Central-Euston express inexplicably passed two red signals at Ecclefechan on 21 July 1945 and hit a freight train which was backing into a refuge siding to clear the path, and its driver and fireman were fatally injured. An unusual incident occurred when a 44-wagon vacuum-fitted freight train halted in the Haymarket Tunnel on 7 November 1939 and both enginemen got down to look for a brake fault. They restored a parted coupling in the vacuum system, but the driver had left the regulator open and the engine moved off. The driver hastened to find a telephone. His train ran through Waverley Station, and was diverted on to the Granton line, where it finally collided with a shunting engine. Both locomotives and twelve wagons were derailed, and the guard was slightly injured. Fortunately it all took place around 3 am, with no other traffic[29]. Most of Edinburgh's Lothian Road Goods Station was destroyed in a fire on 18 November 1939. Aberdeen's Palace Hotel, owned by the LNER, burned down on 30 October 1941, with the deaths of six women workers. The cause was not confirmed. Any usable surviving items were removed from the building[30].

Coping with Problems

At the start of the war the railways had expressed confidence in their ability to handle the increased and more varied traffics that would arise, but demands, conditions and pressures became increasingly intense. The official history of wartime transport on the home front sees the autumn and winter of 1940-41 as a dangerously critical time: "By October, it was apparent that the railways were not doing their job; they were carrying badly and not enough" was the judgment of Sir Ralph Wedgwood himself[31]. As so often, it is difficult to establish the situation in Scotland. There were certainly problems. A huge tonnage of imports was coming to the Clyde ports, much it being American steel, and there was a critical lack of bolster wagons to carry it. Unloading of ships was delayed, while others waited for a berth. The limited capacity of the Highland Main Line and the 'Port Road' to Stranraer were also serious difficulties. Another key factor was the bottleneck at Carlisle, on which three Scottish and three English main lines converged. Firm and fast action was taken, with an overhaul of methods, planning and requirements, and a programme of new installations. Wedgwood retired and on 7 August 1941 Sir Alan Anderson, of the Orient Line shipping company, was appointed Railway Controller and head of the Railway Executive Committee.

From March 1941 an Inter-Railway Freight Rolling Stock Control system was operated, to ensure that wagons, especially coal wagons, and vans were distributed in accordance with traffic needs, something vitally important for seasonal traffic like seed potatoes. In the 1944 harvest, trains carried 326,000 tons of seed potatoes from Scottish stations, reckoned to produce a 1945 crop of 2,600,000 tons[32]. But the total crop that year amounted to 470,000 tons – more than the railways could cope with, and road transport had to be deployed to assist[33]. Special provision was made for the control of specialised wagons for perishable foodstuffs, steel, explosives and timber (a priority here was for the LMS Highland Section). In Scotland the main new works were: Carlisle-Stranraer: lengthening of thirteen crossing loops, July-October 1941

Carlisle-Stranraer and Dumfries: new loops at Holywood, Ruthwell, Eastriggs (Annan) and Gretna Green, September-December 1942

Highland Main Line: Improved telephone circuits, September 1942

Highland Main Line: Five loops installed, and three block posts, September-December 1942

St. Margaret's: improvements to depot, May 1943

Aberdeen: control telephone system, November 1943[34].

Large-scale work was also undertaken at Carlisle to reduce the delays there, which had been causing Scottish controllers to divert freight trains over the already hard-pressed East Coast Main Line. Some use was also made of the former Border Counties Railway between Riccarton Junction and Hexham, but its gradients and traffic capacity did not allow for more than a couple of special trains a day.

Freight flows were rationalised as far as possible, with operations dominated by the need to stretch inadequate resources to meet imperative demands. But Britain after all remained a nation of shopkeepers with a capitalist commercial system. For the railway operators, the fact that Scottish brewers owned tied houses in London and wanted to send their beer there[35], had to be accepted, even though there was plenty of beer brewed in London. Many other products required the same kind of cross-haulage, and the Railway Executive's efforts to minimise this could only be partially successful. Manufacturers needed national distribution for their products whether these were food, clothing or domestic utensils. Scrap metal, always a good freight item, assumed great importance, the railways

Stanley was where the Inverness & Perth Junction Railway diverged from the Scottish North Eastern (later Highland and Caledonian). Since the complete closure of the line to Forfar in 1982 it is no longer a junction. Photo H.R.Norman (John Alsop Collection)

themselves being a large contributor, with districts competing for which could supply the most, though managements had to be careful about lifting unused and unwanted rails, since that could impair their ownership rights on the track bed itself[36].

The blackout, together with rationing of food and many other commodities, including cigarettes, encouraged pilfering. More than a million towels were stolen from carriage lavatories in 1941-42: they were not replaced. Huge numbers of light bulbs were also removed, despite being the wrong voltage for domestic use. The railways ran short of cups and glasses, and appealed to passengers to equip themselves with tin mugs[37]. This spate of theft was linked to the black market in consumer goods, which sprang up as soon as rationing of food, clothes etc. was introduced. In the whole year of 1939 the LMS paid out claims of £73,897 against stolen or lost items: in the first nine months of 1944 the figure was £887,500. The LNER's figures were £42,058 and £526,000[38]. Vandalism also increased, and chairmen's speeches at company meetings deplored the lower moral standards which appeared to prevail[39].

Railway Traffic Officers (RTOs) were stationed at major stations and junctions to liaise between the military and railway. Troop movements were constant, including the return of the 24-hour plus 'Misery' between Euston and Thurso, from summer 1940[40]. By January 1940, volunteer canteens were providing refeshments for servicemen and women on the move at all transfer stations between Dingwall and Dumfries. At Aberdeen the first class ladies' waiting room, the gentlemen's waiting room, the milk bar and ambulance hall were all handed over to the YMCA to be run as canteen and rest-rooms. Civilian travel into the Highlands and Islands was restricted from 27 February 1940, with passes required for entry to the region. With the exception of 1940-41 and 1941-42, the wartime winters were comparatively mild. In 1941 heavy snowfalls persisted into April, when over 100 passengers were snowbound for three nights between Kinbrace and Forsinard, and the rescue plough tunnelled under 20ft drifts. Ten months later the RAF station at Wick proved helpful when a northbound train with 200 passengers became snowbound at Kinbrace, and a southbound one was stuck near Forsinard. Emergency food supplies were dropped from a low-flying Whitley bomber and a trainer aircraft[41].

Scottish railways suffered much less material damage due to enemy action than those in south-east and eastern England. An RAF training aircraft crashed on Luncarty Station on 11 September 1940, killing its two occupants[42]. Kittybrewster engine shed at Aberdeen was hit by a bomb on 31 October 1940 and the carriage sheds were bombed on 21 April 1943, but damage was relatively slight. Clydeside suffered heavy German bombing raids on 13-14 March 1941, around Clydebank, and on 6-7 May, on Greenock, with devastation of property, hundreds of civilian deaths and many more injured. On the north bank both railway lines between Dalmuir and Dumbarton were blocked for several days. Among much other damage goods sheds and the Ladyburn locomotive shed at Greenock were hit and a locomotive destroyed. In the wake of these attacks, an evacuation scheme was reintroduced in Greenock, Dumbarton and Port Glasgow, but though sporadic air raids continued at various locations, primarily east coast towns and Edinburgh, and an attempt on the Lochaber aluminium plant was made in 1941, there was no further intensive bombing, and most children soon returned home. Altogether 188 bombing incidents were recorded in LMS Scottish districts, 158 in the greater Glasgow area, one in Perth, seven in Edinburgh, five at Irvine (close to the large Ardeer chemical and dynamite works), and one at Inverness[43]. Passengers on a train crossing the Forth Bridge saw the first Spitfire engagement of the war when a wave of German bombers attacked naval ships in the Firth of Forth on 16 October 1939, but the two great East Coast bridges, defended by anti-aircraft batteries, survived the attentions of the Luftwaffe. The South Esk Viaduct at Montrose was hit by a bomb on 8 August 1941, and a freight train was derailed. For two weeks traffic was rerouted by way of Guthrie and Dubton Junctions[44]. Glasgow's subway was out of action for four months after bomb damage in September 1940. Josiah Stamp (a baron since 1938) was killed when his house in Kent was hit by a bomb on the night of 16 April 1941. His place as LMS chairman was taken by Sir Thomas (later Lord) Royden, more remote as a public figure but who maintained Stamp's general line of management, until 1946.

Little-used lines like the Carstairs-Dolphinton-Leadburn cross-country link, long closed to passengers east of Dolphinton, saw new traffic as trains were re-routed to avoid main line congestion[45]. Sidings were laid on the Kyle line at Fodderty Junction and Duirinish to accommodate munitions traffic[46]. All camping coaches, by May 1942, were requisitioned for Home Guard or other war-related purposes[47]. Perhaps the most intensively-used lines were the former Caledonian and South Western lines to Greenock. On 6 October 1939 a special goods train brought £6 million worth of gold bullion, to be shipped over to Canada for safe keeping, but there were very many other more workaday shipments both outwards and inwards. From America's entry into the war in 1941, traffic increased enormously. Between May 1942 and December 1944, 339 troopships docked at Greenock, disembarking 1,319,089 servicemen, the vast majority of whom were carried onwards by train, helping to lift Glasgow Central's passenger numbers to 35 million in 1943[48]. Unsurprisingly, at a time when efforts were being made to maximise the use of railway resources, few lines were closed during the war years, compared to the periods on either side, though one victim of total closure was the branch from Wick to Lybster, in 1944. Balerno, Catrine, Dalkeith, Fort George and Moniaive lost their branch passenger trains but not the freight service (see Appendix 7).

Harbours found their functions changing. Methil had shipped 2,771,034 tons of coal in 1938, but only 687,890 tons in 1944, by which time Fife coal was going mostly by rail. Railway tracks were laid along the outer jetties at Methil and Burntisland, with an assemblage of trucks loaded with "any kind of scrap which came in handy" ready to be pushed into the harbour mouth if an invasion force appeared[49]. Atlantic-facing ports were exceptionally busy in the winter of 1940-41. Craigendoran became an emergency freight port from 11 October 1940, with barges landing cargo from ships anchored offshore. Seventy London dockers transferred there reportedly "found it difficult to understand the Scottish dialect"[50] – but perhaps the boot should have been put on the other foot. New harbours were constructed to supplement and if necessary replace the older Clyde ports. In the south west, a branch line of 5½ miles and a large railway installation were laid to serve the military port of Cairnryan, north of Stranraer, begun on 20 January 1941 and operational by 20 July 1942. The Cairnryan Military Railway remained in use until 1959 and was closed in 1962. Another branch of 2½ miles was laid from the West Highland line, branching off high above Shandon Pier to a deep-water port at Faslane on the Firth of Clyde in 1941, from which much of the *matériel* for the North African landings was shipped. Heavy naval traffic of stores, ammunition and personnel also used the Rosyth branch from Inverkeithing and the Charlestown branch extension to the ammunition depot at Crombie.

For the Americans, beginning to plan the joint assault on the European mainland, the over-pressured British railway system was a problem to be tackled. Operation BOLERO was the build-up of troops and equipment, started on 29 April 1942, which brought 1,340,000 US troops into Britain, with all their equipment. To make this possible, 400 new 2-8-0 locomotives were imported from the USA. Though US Army property (returnable in good condition on 14 days' notice), they were worked by British crews. With them came 700 flat cars for large loads, 500 tank transporters and 42 refrigerator cars[51]. Much of this personnel and equipment came in via the Clyde and had to be despatched on to southern England in BOLERO trains under conditions of strict secrecy.

Planning for Post War Service

With the entry of the USA into the war, the feeling grew that ultimate victory was inevitable, and railway managers began to plan for the post-war period. On 1 January 1942 the chairmen of the Big Four met, and set up the Railway Companies Association Commission, headed by Sir Ernest Lemon, "to advise on how the efficiency of the railways can be improved in the broadest sense"[52]. A Post-War Development Committee was set up by the LNER in September 1943, its members including two from the Scottish Area, A.E.H. Brown, Assistant General Manager, and H.G. Sayer, Assistant Superintendent. Another member was James Ness, a future general manager of British Railways' Scottish Region, at that time with the North Eastern area. They came up with what was basically a manager's wish-list, showing little sign of thought about how different the post-war situation might be. For Scotland, this included reconstruction of Waverley, with escalators to replace the Steps, and Dundee (TB), where the inconvenient access was to be replaced by a new superstructure at the Union Street end: "Tay Bridge Station has been the object of strong representation for many years… deficient in almost all aspects judged by modern standards"[53]. Complete reconstruction of Queen Street Station to nine platforms, with a second tunnel to Cowlairs, was recommended, with reconstruction of St. Margaret's depot (north side), a new Edinburgh marshalling yard, joint locomotive depots with the LMS at Perth and Stirling, and completion of automatic train control on the Edinburgh-Glasgow main line (£12,000 worth of materials had been acquired

LNER class O6 locomotive No. 7655 with a breakdown train near Kelso, 10 January 1946. The LMS Stanier class was chosen by the War Department as its standard heavy freight locomotive. The Railway Executive Committee ordered 60 of them from the LNER, 25 of which were subcontracted to the Southern Railway's Brighton Works, No.7655 was one of those. It had a brief history in the LNER after the war, during which time it was renumbered twice, before it was handed over to the LMS in October 1947. (Stenlake Collection)

for this but not installed). All were pre-war schemes, in some cases, like the Edinburgh marshalling yard, from as early as 1923, which lack of funds, or doubt about the financial return, or the advent of war had prevented from being pushed forward[54]. A scheme for a gravitation yard of 3,100-wagon capacity on the south side of the suburban line between Duddingston and Niddrie had been put forward in 1923 but the city took the site for a housing scheme. In 1929, Up and Down hump yards and a 30-engine locomotive shed were proposed for the north side of the suburban line, but not pursued because of cost considerations[55]. There was no further action until the Millerhill yard was proposed by British Railways in 1952-53. At the LNER's twenty-first ordinary general meeting Sir Ronald Matthews pointed out that the railways' policy of running uneconomic lines as part of their total service was now of great national benefit, citing particularly northern Scotland, where before the war, "owing to the lavish expenditure of public money on providing roads, and the laws regulating railway charges, the continuance of many miles of railway had no economic justification"[56].

The transatlantic influx of war materials and soldiers placed demands on the railway service far beyond what was anticipated when the war payment terms were agreed. In March 1945 both the LMS and LNER annual shareholders' meetings passed unanimous resolutions, backed by the directors, condemning the government's refusal to alter the terms of the 1941 agreement on railway finances, despite "the new circumstances of a major character which arose in December 1941" (i.e. the American involvement), but the government was unmoved. Movement of freight and passengers by road and canal actually fell in the war years, whereas railway passenger traffic rose from 18,993 million in 1938 to 35,248 million in 1945, and freight went up from 16,266 million ton-miles to 22,023 ton-miles, with the biggest

rise being in general merchandise, up by 77%[57]. Unquestionably the railways had borne the brunt of sustaining the war transport effort. Wartime conditions and controls thus temporarily stemmed the growth in road transport which had so much, and so rightly, concerned the railway managers.

PS *Waverley* under construction at A. & J. Inglis's yard on the Clyde, 21 September 1946. (Hutton Collection)

Air and Sea Services in the War

Most railway steamers were commandeered for war service as minesweepers, warship tenders or troop carriers. On the LNER only *Lucy Ashton* remained, running a Craigendoran-Dunoon service. Of the others, Waverley was sunk at Dunkirk on 29 May 1940, and *Duchess of Fife* and *Marmion* were also among the railway steamers there. *Marmion*, refitted as an AA gunship, was sunk by bombs off Harwich on 8 April 1941. *Jeanie Deans* and *Talisman* returned to be refitted for service in 1945. LMS routes to Arran and Bute were maintained by *Marchioness of Lorne*, *Duchess of Montrose*, *Marchioness of Graham* and *Glen Sannox*, using Fairlie Pier rather than Ardrossan from November 1939. The turbine-powered Duchesses also ran supplementary services on the busy Stranraer-Larne route. The LMS's new *Princess Victoria*, converted to a minelayer, was sunk by a mine off the Humber in May 1940. Other victims of the war were *Mercury*, mined on 25 December 1940, and *Juno*, hit by bombs in the Thames on 19 March 1941. In February 1941 the Loch Lomond steamers were requisitioned to accommodate ratings of the Royal Indian Navy, and in May PS *Prince George* housed some of the evacuees from the Clydeside blitz. *Prince George* was scrapped in 1942, leaving *Prince Edward* and *Princess May* to resume service after the war.

The companies did not delay in making renewals, though their fleets remained depleted compared with pre-war. On 27 August 1946 the new 2,500-ton *Princess Victoria*, with room for 1,500 passengers and 40 cars, was launched at Denny's, Dumbarton, for the Northern Ireland route, and a new PS *Waverley*, to carry 1,350 passengers, was launched at A.&J. Inglis's yard on 2 October 1946. Only sixteen seagoing railway steamers and motor vessels were transferred to the British Transport Commission in January 1948.

Internal air services had become a somewhat riskier affair in wartime, but were not discontinued. Civil aviation was placed under government control and "cross-water" services in particular resumed after a brief pause in September 1939. From March 1940 Scottish Airways were allowed to fly the Glasgow (Renfrew)-Campbeltown-Islay route, also Inverness-Wick-Kirkwall and Inverness-Sumburgh; and Kirkwall-Sanday-Stronsay-North Ronaldsay[58], and by 1942 also Glasgow-Tiree-Benbecula-North Uist-Stornoway. Service and administrative personnel were the prime users.

In 1944 the railway companies combined to produce a plan for the future of their air service, describing themselves as "transportation companies affording the public co-ordinated transport by rail, sea, road and air", and emphasising the aim to make the air routes a primary, not an auxiliary, service, to be run by a new company, perhaps incorporating shipping lines in its ownership, and certainly not requiring any kind of public subsidy[59]. RAS schedules in April 1945 included Prestwick-Croydon, and Scottish Airways operated direct Glasgow-Stornoway flights on Tuesdays, Thursdays and Saturdays, and Glasgow-Inverness three times a week, in addition to the existing Hebridean services.

Political Change

The generation born in the early 1920s, coming of age in 1945, had witnessed the aftermath of the First World War, industrial strife, the Great Depression, and the Second World War. For most of them there were few reasons to feel that the old order of things had been satisfactory. As the prospect of eventual victory became more assured, a general resolve that the future should be different became more clearly defined, and a political programme was widely debated, which included state ownership of the basic industries: coal mining, iron and steel, electricity and gas, long-distance road transport, air transport, and the railways. For the railways, nationalisation was a far older issue than for the others, going right back to Gladstone's ideas a hundred years earlier, and periodically revived when railway charges and facilities became an issue – most recently in 1918-20 when the future of the companies was under review. Railway directors were fully aware of this and joined the debate about their companies' future. From 1942 onwards, the LMS and LNER, with the Southern and Great Western, ran publicity campaigns to emphasise their service to the nation and to highlight the problems that state ownership would bring: not an easy task since they were currently functioning effectively as a single state-controlled organisation. Within the companies there was a real feeling, enhanced by the war, that the railways were a public service and not merely commercial concerns. Citing their own record in the 1930s, of maintaining services, making technical improvements, and showing social responsibility in holding rates and fares steady, they were keen to emphasise their readiness and ability to meet the post-war challenges. They were not trying to turn the clock back to the pre-war era, but rather campaigning for something like the "new deal" that had been accepted as necessary in 1939. For many of their employees, probably a majority, resolutions passed at union branch and general meetings showed a desire for more radical change in how the railway system was run.

Wartime travel had generally been a dismal experience, especially on long-distance trains, their corridors and vestibules packed with people who could not find seats, toilets inaccessible, and delays the norm; and travellers were more conscious of their own discomfort than of the extraordinary efforts being made by railway workers to keep the whole pattern of transport flowing. With the return of peace, more people wanted to travel, and did not relish the condition of their trains, while the old standard reply to all complaints, "Don't you know there's a war on?" would no longer do. By the end of the war, Scottish railways, relatively unscathed by enemy action, were in a run-down rather than damaged state. Maintenance had been on a priority basis, and there had been virtually nothing in the way of routine renewal. Rolling stock, much of it dating back to pre-1923, was dilapidated and ingrained with dirt and soot. Sir Ronald Matthews, in a newspaper article in February 1946, spelled out the overall task: arrears of maintenance amounted to 18 months' worth of work; passenger stock was 12% down on pre-war and 15% of it was awaiting repair, with vandalism playing a large part in its condition; 150,000 wagons also awaited repair, making a queue almost 600 miles long; the workshops themselves were in need of renewal. And staff was short, with 94,000 railway workers yet to be demobilised[60]. In an almost-bankrupt Great Britain, faced with huge reconstruction costs and international debt, the railway companies found it hard to impress the travelling public, though they tried hard to restore service levels and to demonstrate plans for an effective future. That as ever might include cutting costs wherever possible, and West Perthshire saw protests in October 1945 against the LMS's intention to close the line between Crieff and Balquhidder. A Strathearn Railway Committee was set up, managing to stave off execution to 1951. Some other unremunerative lines were not spared: the Boddam branch was totally closed in November 1945 and Strathaven North and Strathpeffer lost their passenger services in September 1945 and February 1946. Many more would follow after Nationalisation (See Appendices 6 and 7).

The Grouping was doomed. Planned as a compromise between private enterprise and state control, its model did not fit actual conditions: the companies could neither satisfy their shareholders nor modernise to the degree that was technically possible and socially desirable; they "were both over-capitalised financially and under-capitalised physically"[61], paying dividends on no-longer productive capital investment but unable to fund large-scale network improvement. Jonathan Roberts remarks that "Whether or not there had been harmful disinvestment between the wars is still an area of debate, but it seems likely that some assets were not replaced when they might have been, thus storing up trouble not evident at the time. The war manifestly created disinvestment (Derek Aldcroft estimates £200 million at least)"[62]. That does not mean, as some writers have stated, that the companies were either bankrupt or demoralised[63], on the contrary, they were ready and willing to work out a new arrangement, and if the political will had been different, their privately-owned but state-regulated status, with a "square deal", could have been maintained. But the Labour Party claimed that only through nationalisation of key industries could post-war reconstruction be achieved. The companies had not run out of money, or of steam, but they had run out of time. Following the 1945 general election result, a new dispensation was going to be imposed.

PART TWO
STATE OWNERSHIP, 1948-1996

4. Scottish Region: the First Years

Prelude to Nationalisation

"Co-ordination of transport services by rail, road, air and canal cannot be achieved without unification. And unification without public ownership means a steady struggle with sectional interests or the enthronement of a private monopoly, which would be a menace to the rest of industry." So stated the Labour Party's manifesto for the July 1945 general election, in which 37 of Scotland's 71 seats were won by Labour, three by Independent Labour, and one by the Communist Party. With an overwhelming Parliamentary majority (including 32 MPs sponsored by railway unions), the new Labour Government embarked on its nationalisation programme. For two years, the Big Four continued on borrowed time, though they went on doing the things that would have been expected of companies with a future. New locomotive types were introduced, including Britain's first main line express diesel-electric engines: the first, LMS 10000, introduced on the eve of the company's demise. Through 1947 the LMS Scottish Committee was still busy: a new link was opened between the former G&SWR and Caledonian lines at Stevenston on 16 June, enabling closure of the CR Stevenston-

A grubby No. 64636 of St Margaret's depot heads an Edinburgh-Leven train with extremely varied carriages past Inverkeithing in 1949. Although it carries a BR number, the ex-North British 104, built in 1921, still has LNER lettered on the tender. It ran until October 1964. Photo E.R.Wethersett (John Alsop Collection)

Kilwinning section; its traffic sub-committee reporting that £3,595 was to be spent on improving the smoke uptakes of Polmadie engine depot, to stop smoke blowing into the offices and canteen. The claims committee had to deal with extensive pilfering of whisky and cigarettes; also the disappearance of 161 packs of bananas – a rare fruit – between Glasgow and Stornoway. The land & rating sub-committee was authorised to buy land at the Turnberry golf courses because the company had a right to use the ground only if golf was played on it: the hotel had just been relinquished by the Air Ministry and restoration of building and grounds would take some time[1]. The LNER was building 60 new express 'Pacifics', and sent a mechanical engineering team to the USA to study locomotive development on American railroads, where diesel-electric traction was already widely used. Though impressed by diesel performance, they commented on the high capital cost of diesels, and also found maintenance costs to be higher than for steam which, they found "is vigorously answering the challenge of the Diesel"[2]. When the Forth Road Bridge was proposed, it decided not to oppose the project after agreement was reached to exempt railway companies from any element of rates levied for bridge construction, plus annual compensation of £15,000 for ten years after the bridge opened[3].

The companies continued to campaign against nationalisation, claiming it would be a "calamity", that they were engaged in "vast development", that they were already "under public control" and that the present units were as large as could be effectively manageable[4], but they were willing to compromise. In January 1946 they combined with the Road Haulage Association to present the Ministry of Transport with a national scheme for co-ordination of road and rail transport[5]. Even William Whitelaw, always the most vocal defender of shareholders' interests, suggested that the government might take ownership of the rail network and let the companies operate the trains – this intriguing presaging of what would happen in 2002 was published by the LNER in October 1946, after his death in January that year. But the buffers were coming into view. An ambitious new Transport Act was passed in August 1947, providing for state ownership not just of the

Former NER 0-6-2T No. 2098 heads north under Aberdeen's Union Street Viaduct, 1947. Built in 1901, it was withdrawn in 1955. (Stenlake Collection)

railway system but of most transport services except for those operating on a local basis (25 miles radius or less), under the control of a new body, the British Transport Commission.

What were the railways worth, if the state was going to acquire them? The Chancellor of the Exchequer, Hugh Dalton, offended many railway people in describing the system as "a very poor bag of physical assets" and a "disgrace to the nation", so shortly after the railways had made a vital and sustained contribution to the nation's war effort. The railways were still under government control, and would remain so until nationalisation took effect. Based on the Stock Exchange valuation of the four companies' shares, stockholders were issued with £907.8 million of British Transport Commission stocks, redeemable in 40 years, with annual 3% interest guaranteed by the government. LMS Ordinary shareholders got £29 10s of BTC 3% shares for every £100; LNER Preferred Ordinary shareholders got £7 6s 2d, and Deferred Ordinary got £3 12s. Sir Ronald Matthews of the LNER condemned the terms of nationalisation as such as "would bring a blush of shame to the leathery cheeks of a Barbary pirate", but most economic historians agree that they were not unreasonable. Interest payments, at £27.2 million a year, were to prove a heavy burden on the new British Transport Commission. Left-wing critics felt the new set-up was too like the old: *Socialist Standard* called it "state capitalism"[6]. At the last ordinary general meeting of LNER shareholders, in March 1948, a proposal to reward the directors with the sum of £63,000 was lost on a show of hands; instead the last dividend on 5% Preference Ordinary shares was raised from 18s 2d to 19s 2d.

External circumstances made operating conditions very difficult in the companies' last years, 1945-48, with coal shortages caused by a shortage of miners and industrial disputes in the coal industry. With the rapid run-down of war traffic, net earnings of the railways fell from £62.5 million in 1945 to £32.5 million in 1946[7]. Problems were exacerbated by harsh winters, particularly in early 1947, when there was prolonged snow into March. Among many tales of hardship and of heroic endurance by train crews and permanent way workers, there was probably the maximum delay ever encountered by a Scottish train. The 8.15 pm train to St. Enoch left Stranraer with eighteen passengers on Wednesday 12 March, rerouted via Dumfries because of fresh snow. It reached Dumfries at 12.20 am on Thursday and was held there because of snow blocks until the following Monday. It reached the Glasgow terminus at 6.45 pm on Tuesday 18th, five days, eighteen hours and 50 minutes late[8].

A government paper on industry and employment observed that, "The economic position of Scotland is fundamentally different to pre-war. The difficulty is finding the manpower and materials required both for current production and for the capital investment necessary to secure proper future development"[9]. This was as much a problem for the railways as for manufacturing industry.

The BTC, the Railway Executive, and Scottish Region

The British Transport Commission was set up from 1 January 1948, and Sir Cyril Hurcomb, formerly Permanent Secretary to the Ministry of Transport, was appointed to chair it, with a set of executive bodies to manage specific sections of the industry: a Railway Executive, a Docks and Waterways Executive, a Road Transport Executive and a London Transport Executive. A Hotels Executive was also added to take over railway-owned hotels, of which sixteen were in Scotland. It was a vast organisation, a testimony to the faith of the time that giant enterprises were inherently more efficient than smaller ones. Herbert Morrison, the minister supervising the nationalisation plans, wrote, "The country will have a splendid opportunity to wield an efficient instrument to meet its transport needs. The new concern will be absolutely free to go for sheer efficiency right from the beginning and use assets in a way that is best. They will be able to write off these miserable rolling stocks in which the middle and lower classes have to travel"[10]. One effect of nationalisation was to finally confirm the position of the railways as a general national utility, ending their ambivalent relationship with the state as privately-owned corporations working under government-imposed conditions and limits. This happened just as the switch in transport usage from railway to road was about to become definitive. The railways' diminishing role in ground transport had been obvious for two decades, while they still bore the load of being 'common carrier' to the nation. The Minister of Transport, Alfred Barnes, described the main object of socialising transport as "to consolidate the various elements of transport… into a single whole which would operate as a non-profit making utility service at the least real cost to trade, industry and the general public"[11]. With the British Transport Commision also responsible for road freight over 25 miles, some kind of rationalisation might have been anticipated, but within five years road haulage was back in private hands and no co-ordination was attempted in the meantime.

The government purchased Railway Air Services from the companies for £550,000, for incorporation into British European Airways on 28 February, though the railways retained their legal entitlement to operate aircraft. Otherwise, the BTC had acquired not only "the whole of the undertakings" of the railway companies but also all their historic rights and liabilities, including those relating to rates and charges. Restrictions which had been admitted to be obsolete and excessively confining in 1939 remained in place, and a new Transport Tribunal was set up to replace the Railway Rates Tribunal. The Transport Act empowered the Commission to withdraw transport services between specific places, but did not make clear whether the state-owned British Railways was intended to maintain and provide a nationwide service, or was meant to operate profitably on behalf of the nation. The assumption that the railways would operate profitably obscured this issue.

From the Scottish point of view, the most important aspect of the 1947 Act was that British Railways was to be divided into six regions, five in England and Wales, and a Scottish Region. The separate Scottish region owed its existence to political pressure rather than operating considerations. It had been strongly argued for both by Scottish MPs and by Scottish peers, particularly the Earls of Selkirk and Airlie, in the House of Lords[12]; indeed there was pressure for a completely separate Scottish Transport Board, which the government rejected. As a result, while the English regions were based very much on the territories of the former companies, the Scottish region had to combine the properties, staffs and working methods of both the LMS and LNER into a single working entity[13]. Enthusiasm for the arrangement was muted by the limited powers allowed. The *Scotsman*, commenting on the Region's lack of executive powers and decentralised authority, felt that it was "difficult to resist suspicion that devolution in railway management will prove as unsatisfactory from Scotland's point of view as that conceded for civil aviation or mining" and noted that the proposed Scottish Transport Users' Consultative Council would need "activity and aggressiveness"[14]. However, for the first time, albeit as one division of a vast organisation whose central HQ was in London, the Scottish railways were to be administered as a single entity. The new Region had 3,730 route miles (Scotland's road

BR Class A1 *Bonnie Dundee*, built in 1949 to an LNER design, heads the southbound 'Queen of Scots Pullman' past Prestonpans. The British Railways lion-and-wheel emblem was created in 1949. Photo E.R.Wethersett (John Alsop Collection)

mileage was 26,392 in total, with 1,949 miles of trunk road) and 3,957 miles of sidings, and employed 31,640 men and 3,650 women. It had 1,020 stations handling both passengers and freight, and 302 that were freight only; 56 marshalling yards, three hump yards and 170 other freight yards; its freight traffic in 1948 was 8,039,000 tons of minerals and 7,885,000 tons of general merchandise, and it provided 66,226,000 passenger journeys. It owned sixteen prestigious hotels[15]. The headquarters were to be in Glasgow, with 2,000 staff, and a further 600 in Edinburgh.

To Sir Steven (later Lord) Bilsland, a businessman who had been a member of the LMS Scottish board, Scottish Region was "an administrative fiction", headed by a chief regional officer without the powers of a general manager, and its technical officers primarily responsible to departmental heads in London[16]. Hurcomb was determined to operate British Railways as one huge integrated enterprise, with the Railway Executive setting up standard practices across the system and using regional managements as agents to implement national policy – yet avoiding "excessive centralisation". He was anxious lest the Commission should find itself running six semi-independent railways; in his view "individual regions were not intended to be viable economic bodies" but administrative areas set up for operational convenience[17]. Instruction No. 1 on the first day of 1948 from Miles Beevor, chief secretary of the BTC to regional chiefs informed them that "The CRO will assume responsibility for general administration, within the policy and general instruction of the Railway Executive… It is desirable that the various steps should be taken as quickly as possible, and the co-operation of all involved is sought to this end… Matters local to regions and coming within the sphere delegated by the Railway Executive are… to be disposed of quickly at regional level"[18]. Incidentally, members of the Commission and Railway Executive, including Hurcomb and Beevor, though public servants, assumed the privilege of having locomotives named after themselves. Later BR practice was not to name engines after living people, though one or two exceptions were made. As the policy and general instructions of the Executive were not defined, it amounted to an instruction for the CRO to do the Executive's bidding. When regional chiefs began holding regular meetings to discuss common problems, they were instructed to stop[19]. Chief Regional Officer for Scotland was T.F. Cameron, LNER Scottish general manager since 1946, at an annual salary of £3,750 (his London Midland Region colleague earned £7,500), and Scottish interests were represented on the BTC by a part-time board member, Sir Ian Bolton, a Glasgow accountant, who had previously been a director of the LMS and who saw his role more in terms of representing the BTC to Scotland. The Minister of Transport, Alfred Barnes, insisted on naming the members of the Railway Executive himself, not allowing the British Transport Commission to appoint the people who would effectively run the railway system for it. The Railway Executive had a part-time Scottish member in Sir Wilfred Ayre, of the Burntisland Shipbuilding Company (he served until 1950). A pale shade of blue, faintly reminiscent of the Caledonian's blue, was assigned as the Region's colour, as a background to nameboards and other station signs.

Tension soon arose between Commission and Executive over which was to formulate policy, and how instructions should be passed to the regions. Regional chiefs in turn disliked the ability of functional heads in the Executive staff to give orders to their department heads, and as early as June 1948 Cameron joined his fellow CRO's in pointing out that divided loyalties made for serious complications in management. The response was uncompromising: the Executive was in charge[20].

The Region Gets Down to Work

Regional autonomy might not be on the agenda, but there was plenty for Scottish Region to do, quite apart from combining its two parts into one. The network had to be maintained, or brought up to standard after the war years.

Queen Street Station, its sign painted in the blue colour scheme assigned to Scottish Region. (Stenlake collection)

Services had to be devised and operated, locomotives and rolling stock kept available, stations managed, freight customers sought and cultivated – all the basic routines of railway management. Significant changes had happened to the main customer base – coal, iron and steel. Managers of coal companies or collieries were transformed into area or regional officials of the National Coal Board; a single Scottish Gas Board (of enviable independence) replaced the multiplicity of local and municipal gas companies; and the iron and steel works were also nationalised. While this produced a rather different relationship, there was no statutory requirement for co-operation, and customer-supplier stances were maintained.

The Regional management had an early test when torrential rain in the eastern Borders caused disastrous floods in late August 1948, with massive damage to railway lines and much else. Reaction was prompt and effective. The Edinburgh-Berwick main line was closed for eleven weeks while temporary bridges were built, and trains were diverted onto the Waverley Route as far as St. Boswells, then along the former North British and North Eastern lines via Kelso to Tweedmouth. 'Flying Scotsman' drivers took some pride in maintaining the non-stop practice over the detour whenever they could, with A4 'Pacific' *Walter K. Whigham* first to make the 408.65 mile run non-stop – a world record for steam – northbound, on 24 August, repeating the feat on the Down service next day[21]. There had been no direct trains between Edinburgh and London via Symington and Carlisle since the LMS-LNER cost-saving days, and "Regular Traveller" asked on behalf of himself and others why in this emergency they were not reinstated. Probably congestion on the West Coast Main Line would have lost as much time as the 90 minutes involved in the detour via St. Boswells. Three freight trains were trapped between wash-outs and had to be unloaded *in situ*. Bus links were laid on to isolated stations. The almost-parallel line between St. Boswells and Reston Junction was breached west of Earlston, and though the track was restored, the passenger service between St. Boswells and Duns was not. The Jedburgh and Lauder branches, also flooded, were reinstated in 1950 for goods traffic only (Lauder had lost its passenger trains in September 1932).

Elsewhere, new services and accelerations were beginning, with timings claimed as "nearly into line" with pre-war performance. The 7.30 pm Euston-Perth sleeper was extended to Forfar and a new 10.30 pm Euston-Perth sleeper was provided. The 4.30 pm Inverness-Euston sleeper via Forres now left at 5.35 pm and ran via Carr Bridge. Third class sleepers underwent some improvement from May 1949, with "full bedding and washing facilities" in each compartment". A new 11.15 pm train from Edinburgh Princes Street to Carstairs made a connection with the 11.25 pm Glasgow Central to Liverpool and Manchester[22]. In reply to "Regular Traveller" and others, Sir Eustace Missenden, chairman of the Railway Executive, pointed out during a visit to Edinburgh in November 1948, that the Scottish Region was "a bold and wide experiment", as the only one to combine large sections of two previously separate systems. He blamed a shortage of carriages for some service limitations, and said that the old practice of attaching/detaching Edinburgh portions at Symington had been dropped because the trains to and from Glasgow already formed full engine loads[23]. By May 1950, full repairs were complete on the main line, in time for the summer timetable.

Industrial Relations: No 'New Dawn'

Two union men had been appointed to top management, John Benstead of the NUR to the BTC and W.P. Allen of ASLEF to the Railway Executive. The unions were disappointed that no greater degree of worker participation was allowed. Any supposition that nationalisation would herald a new dawn of industrial relations did not last long. In May-June 1949 a series of unofficial strikes by enginemen in the Scottish and North-Eastern Regions, objecting to new arrangements in their "lodging turns" (staying away overnight) which were being imposed in the interest of improved efficiency, set what was to be a continuing, if sporadic theme. Restiveness among railway workers was reported, when the Conciliation Board rejected demands for a £5 10s weekly minimum wage[24]. From the beginning, Regional management took its cue from the Commission, with its membership of senior railwaymen, captains of industry, eminent trade unionists of the more tractable sort, and former civil servants, making it clear that railway management would remain a command system, albeit one with employee representation committees, conciliation procedures, and a staff magazine to make everyone feel that their involvement counted. Amalgamation of former districts was instituted from 1 January 1949, with eight LMS and four LNER districts merged into seven, centred on Aberdeen, Ayr, Burntisland, Edinburgh, Glasgow (two) and Inverness, each responsible for operational and commercial activity. Behind this was a mass of detailed preparation involving new rule books, new ways of keeping records, and of course new operating schedules to maximise the efficiency of the altered set-up. Even though the LMS and LNER had set out to eliminate competing services, there were still transfer yards, notably at Greenhill, where freight trains from each company were separated or combined. Single control made the point-to-point flow of through loads possible throughout the Scottish network, particularly of commodities like coal and minerals that formed full trainloads. Integration was a step-by-step process, and the measure of progress can seem modest: freight train miles per train hour rose from 9.59 in 1948 to 10.93 in 1950[25], but a 14% increase is a significant achievement

While many operating methods had been modernised, and greater changes were already in the air, industrial relations appeared to remain set at a primitive level. There were real difficulties in trying to break this mould. Ever since the old companies were finally compelled to recognise trade unions in 1909, confrontation, not collaboration, had dominated the relationship between management and the mass of employees. Union men still remembered their gesture of accepting pay cuts in 1928, and the years it had taken for these to be restored. Departmental heads and managers, imbued with the more authoritarian culture of the 1930s, found the more democratic and challenging post-war spirit hard to cope with, especially as they had responsibility for a vast system that required strict disciplines to maintain a service schedule and safety requirements. The basic problem, which remains in the 21st century, is that the unions, financed by their own members' contributions, exist to maintain and advance the interests of their members. This is a perfectly proper function and most people would agree it is still necessary. Railway managements are there in order to provide an efficient and sufficient service to meet the requirements of the national community. The responsibilities of each side are liable to conflict when systems are changed, as the following chapters will amply show. An industry owned by the nation was supposed to show a good example in industrial relations, and a system of district committees was set up to deal with changes in operating practice, which were particularly marked in Scottish Region. The prevailing tone was not that of a partnership, however: "If every member of the Operating staff takes a proper pride in his particular job, and if that spirit of co-operation which has pervaded all ranks during the last two and a half years continue to prevail, then notwithstanding the difficult times ahead, there is no reason to be apprehensive about the eventual result"[26]. Scottish Region at that time employed over 35,000 staff.

Investment and Renewal

A trust fund worth £150 million[27], created during the war years against possible compensation for railway damage, was held over from the companies and applied to the nationalised railways, but despite this money and Herbert Morrison's rhetoric, signs of early progress on the nation's railway were hard to find. Hard winters, coal strikes and shortages, devaluation of sterling and a return to increased defence spending all combined to keep development slow. At the end of 1948 40% of engines, 24% of wagons and 28% of passenger coaches were over 35 years old, pre-dating the LMS and LNER era[28]. The Railway Executive's first (and only) 5-year plan, for 1948-52, stated that it was neither practicable nor necessary to replace all rolling stock over 35 years old, and noted that there were many locomotives of 35-plus engaged on shunting and other work where replacement could not be justified "even under normal conditions"[29]. At one of the country's largest locomotive depots, Polmadie in south Glasgow, hardly altered since 1924 though modernisation had been decided on in 1941, a full renewal programme was finally begun in 1951, providing an "efficient layout" at a cost of £181,681, and other depots were modernised, including Dunfermline, with modern steam locomotive handling plant including a 200-ton skip-hoist coaling plant, an electric ash elevator, and a vacuum-operated 75-ft turntable[30].

The scale of the Region's engineering operations was revealed when the third Annual Conference of BR Mechanical, Electrical and Carriage & Wagon Engineers was held in Glasgow in May 1950. Iron foundries at Cowlairs and St. Rollox produced 18,000 tons a year, plus non-ferrous metals. Inverurie and Barassie Works produced 2,200 tons of castings annually. Locomotive repairs were made at Cowlairs, St. Rollox, Inverurie, Kilmarnock and Inverness; carriage and wagon building was done at Cowlairs and Inverurie, carriages at St. Rollox, and wagons at Barassie and Germiston, where the 260,000 sq ft former government factory was allocated on 31 December 1947 to the Railway Executive (it closed in the early 1950s). In the immediate post-war years railway wagons were also built at the Dalmuir Royal Ordnance Factory. Another site of 211,000 sq ft at Newmains was sold in 1948 to the Costain

Ex GNSR 4-4-0 *Benachie* as BR 62274 (withdrawn in 1955) shunting at Fraserburgh. Most of the wagons are fish vans. (Stenlake Collection)

construction group for a concrete sleeper works. The Region also kept on inherited civil engineering depots at Hawick and Irvine, where concrete units were prefabricated, and the plant for creosoting sleepers and telegraph poles at Greenhill. Total engineering staff was 11,972.

Accidents and Service Problems

Two successive train fires happened in the summers of 1949 and 1950. On 25 June 1949 a carriage (built in 1947) on the 7.30 am Waverley-Kings Cross train caught fire as it entered Penmanshiel Tunnel. Its wooden inner lining had been sprayed with a type of cellulose lacquer that was highly flammable and it was assumed that a cigar end or pipe ash had caused the fire. Prompt action by railwaymen prevented disaster, though one person was seriously injured in jumping from the train before it stopped. A more disastrous fire affected the 11 am Birmingham-Glasgow train on the approach to Beattock Summit on 8 June 1950. Probably caused by a cigarette end thrown under a seat, a smouldering fire generated carbon monoxide which killed five people before a sudden flash of flame broke out. A lineside ganger, Adam Moffat, was awarded the Railway Executive's Certificate for Courage and Resource, and the British Empire Medal, for his efforts in rescuing passengers from the burning carriage. The fires caused both public and official concern and resulted in changes to carriage building and painting procedures. More typical were the incidents caused by wintry weather. Two passengers died at Alloa Junction on 10 January 1951 when signals were out of action due to snow, and despite a flagman's warning the 7.00 am Perth-Glasgow express hit a light engine. On 17 February 1951 the 3.46 Glasgow-Fort William train was stopped near Corrour when the engine was derailed in snow. A relief train stuck a mile and a half to the south. Eventually an engine and snowplough pushed through from Fort William, after a delay of 30 hours. Fortunately the train had a restaurant car[31].

Public criticism over service standards was strong in 1950, with poor connections a prime source of complaint. The 2.25 pm train from Carlisle

A 1950s platform scene at Aberfeldy. (Highland Railway Society)

arrived in Galashiels at 4.13, three minutes after the last train from there to Peebles had gone. The last train over the Waverley Route reached Waverley Station at 10.20, five minutes after the last train to Glasgow had gone. Sometimes such lapses were ascribed to poor planning, sometimes, especially in the case of lines known to be vulnerable to closure, a purposeful approach was suspected, in order to further deplete the traffic. Letters accused the Scottish Region officials of "living in a world of their own". A hidebound administrative stiffness was most obvious in the public relations department, whose letters to newspapers in response to public comments and complaints were stilted and filled with railway jargon. The unfortunate public relations officer, Mr Hunter, was accused of writing replies "too difficult for anyone but a railwayman to understand"[32]. New competition came with the opening of Edinburgh Airport on 19 May 1947, with flights to Aberdeen and Shetland. Anglo-Scottish services were challenged in 1950 when British European Airways offered to deduct the return part of an Edinburgh-London railway ticket if the holder wished to return by air, leaving only £2 16s 3d to pay[33]. At least a lot of the stations looked nice. The nationalised system kept up the old companies' practice of making awards for best kept station gardens, with 211 stations receiving prizes or commendations in 1950, the list topped by Gleneagles and Kinross, followed by Aberdour and Kilmacolm[34].

Cuts and Closures

Under Nationalisation, in one respect even experienced railway managers were working in uncharted territory. A limited company had external disciplines, of share price, shareholders' interests, and borrowing potential, which helped its directors to decide what was possible or not. The British Transport Commission and the Railway Executive had no such framework, merely a very wide and rather loosely-worded brief from the 1947 Act. Their resources came from the government and were subject to arbitrary cuts, and the government also controlled their ability to raise money by fare increases. They had no-one to compare themselves, their problems and their performance against. It is not surprising that they found housekeeping difficult. As costs began to rise faster than income, regional heads came under increasing pressure from the centre to find savings. At both regional and headquarters levels it was well-known that some services or sections of line were losing money, but from 1949 it became also apparent that costs were mounting in such a way that it could no longer be safely assumed that profitable services would cancel out losses on others and still leave a sufficient surplus after other costs, like interest payments on loans, had been met. The Railway Executive set up a Branch Lines Committee in 1949 to consider potential closures and regions were instructed to set up their own committees to examine "every branch line whose earning capacity may be in question" and pass on proposals. The approach was tentative and also made reference to the possibility of developing the traffic of a dubious line, perhaps by using "light units"[35]. Transport Users' Consultative Committees, already mentioned above, largely modelled on LMS/LNER practice of joint area committees representing industrial or commercial user groups rather than the travelling public, grew in importance from their formation in 1950 as passenger railway closure proposals increased. They were in no sense "watchdogs" but saw themselves as part of a necessary apparatus to maintain an efficient system. English findings had to be endorsed by the Central Consultative Committee; Scottish findings went straight to the Minister of Transport. Goods line closures required no formalities, and in November 1949 Stirling County Council protested to Scottish Region about the removal of freight services on the Longriggend-Slamannan line, causing problems for farmers and prejudicing future development in a run-down mining district[36].

The terminus of the short Moffat branch, with a mixed train ready to leave for Beattock, on 14 August 1950. When not working branch trains, the engine, formerly CR No. 431, built in 1922, banked heavy trains to Beattock Summit. It was withdrawn in 1961. Photo A.C.Roberts (John Alsop Collection)

The Scottish TUCC was set up in July 1949, with eighteen members, drawn from agriculture, commerce, industry, shipping, labour and local authorities, as well as nominees of the Ministry of Transport and the BTC. Its terms of reference were fairly narrow, centred on how much "hardship" a closure would entail, and it could do no more in opposing than pass a suggestion for delay or modification to the Minister of Transport. Even such opposition was rare, not least because the railway witnesses could present 'facts' whereas much of the opposers' evidence boiled down to feeling. At this time, when a general head of steam against railway closures had not yet built up, lay members might well defer to the certainties of the professionals. Still, by 1950 the closure of under-used branches was becoming an issue. Lord Bilsland deplored the BTC's "defeatism" in shutting down branch passenger services without prior attempts to improve traffic, and with no provision of alternative arrangements. From Alford to Whithorn, 35 passenger services were withdrawn in Scotland between 1948 and 1953, seventeen of them in 1951. As with closures of lines or stations made by the former companies, in most cases goods services were maintained into the early 1960s, presumably for the same reason, that domestic coal was still an important freight item. The railways' role as 'common carrier' also played a part. Freight services could be shut down without the public procedures required for passenger services, and many workings became sporadic or seasonal in the later 1950s.

Scottish Region was by no means reluctant to put forward closure proposals. Along with the Alford branch (closed to passengers on 2 January 1950), it proposed the North Fife line, between Newburgh and St. Fort, for closure. At the time the line carried two passenger trains each way daily, between Perth and Dundee. Basing their case on an agreement made in 1897 by the North British Railway to operate the line "in perpetuity", Fife County Council, Cupar District Council, Newburgh Town Council and eight local residents obtained an interdict on 5 June 1950 in the Court of Session against closure of passenger services. Following an appeal by Scottish Region, the interdict was removed on 25 January 1951 and closure went ahead on 12 February[37]. Such strong local resistance was not typical of the time, even though Scottish Region was distinctly casual about the existence of alternative transport. At a public meeting in the County Buildings, Peebles, in March 1950, T.F. Cameron had "no definite plans to put forward" about services to replace Peebles-Biggar-Symington trains, but agreed to have a meeting with SMT managers "in the near future"[38]. Among other passenger closures approved and effected in 1950 were Portpatrick-Stranraer, the Bothwell branch, and Newton Stewart-Whithorn. Sir Ian Bolton, addressing a press conference after a meeting of the Scottish Transport Users' Consultative Council on 1 December 1950, warned of "drastic" curtailment to come of local and branch services, all of which were under review. Noting the report of a Committee on Transport in the Highlands, headed by John Cameron KC, which had proposed more favourable goods rates for remote stations, with mileage rates "tapering" after a certain distance, Sir Ian discouraged any prospect of special treatment, observing, correctly, that "the BTC are, generally speaking, obliged to treat all their customers alike". John Elliot, chairman of the Railway Executive from 1951, exhorted regional chiefs to be vigorous in achieving line closures[39], and Scottish Region continued to respond vigorously. In 1951 the Carstairs-Dolphinton and Strathpeffer branches were closed completely and the Kilsyth branch lost its passenger service, as did the lines to Macduff, Penicuik, Polton, Wilsontown, Selkirk, Duns, Bothwell, Aberfoyle, Inverbervie, Fortrose and Ayr-Muirkirk. On 22 June that year Forfar lost its through sleeping car from Euston[40]. At Morningside (Lanarkshire), like Dolphinton the site of LMS and LNER stations, the goods service was withdrawn from the former LMS station, leaving the ex-LNER to exploit the diminishing traffic of this once-busy iron industry location. The process was reinforced by the Railway Executive's institution of a census of passenger train traffic in 1952, which revealed that over the system as a whole, only 33% of the seating capacity was being occupied. In 1953 Geoffrey Wilson of the BTC helpfully picked out certain services as candidates for closure: the Cathcart Circle, and trains to Kirkhill, East Kilbride (already being developed into a new town), and Uplawmoor[41]. BTC figures showed the Region producing a small net surplus of £0.1 million in 1951, which by 1953 became a shortfall on revenue of £2.6 million[42].

On a visit to Glasgow in June 1951, John Elliott pursued his theme, asserting that they had come out of the railway age into the transport age: "Where better alternative services were offered, it was not their intention to compete with bus services. What the railway can offer must be considered part of the general transport facilities of a country." He claimed that Scottish Region had saved £200,000 since 1948 in the co-ordination of goods services[43]. At this time coal was still the prime freight traffic; new lines were built around Kelty and Oakley in Fife to serve new collieries and a new control centre was established at Burntisland, covering all lines in Fife and Clackmannan, and north to Kinnaber Junction, under a deputy chief controller, assistant and five section controllers. It also controlled the seasonal sugar beet traffic, carrying from 80-90,000 tons each autumn to the processing factory at Cupar[44].

Post-war reconstruction and planning were active in many other fields, and Cameron and his team were closely involved with the Glasgow and District Transport Committee, chaired by Sir Robert Inglis, another former general manager of the LNER Scottish Division, which sat between 1949 and 1951 and produced a report which recommended the phasing out of the city's trams and electrification of the suburban railway network. It was an ambitious though not new proposal, first mooted in the 1920s[45], which though it did not attract the backing of the BTC, remained an obvious and desirable solution to the run-down and obsolescent condition of Glasgow's railways. However, town planners at the time showed minimal regard for railways: the 1951 City of Glasgow Development Plan ignored the Inglis recommendations, and the planning of the new towns of East Kilbride and Cumbernauld treated railways as peripheral in every sense[46].

5. Reorganisation and the Modernisation Plan

The 1953 Transport Act

Tensions between the BTC directors and the Railway Executive remained and by 1951 Hurcomb was discreetly campaigning for the Executive's abolition. In this he had the support of the regional chiefs, who hoped that greater independence would result[1]. With the second general election of 1951, in October, and the return of a Conservative government pledged to restore road haulage to private enterprise, the policy of creating a unified pan-British transport system came to an end. A new Transport Act in 1953 provided for this, though its effect was only partial and the state-owned British Road Services continued operations until 1982. Hurcomb's desire to abolish the Railway Executive was fulfilled and it ceased to exist from 1 October 1953, leaving the BTC to run the railways with a larger executive staff and no intermediate tier of management between it and the regions. At this time bus services remained under state ownership, but little was done by way of co-ordination, except for possible replacement buses when a rail passenger service was closed.

The 1953 Act also increased the BTC's board from eight to fourteen, with two to be appointed on the advice of the Secretary of State for Scotland, and the Commission was given a year to submit a new scheme for railway management. It was made clear that the Government expected to see considerable devolution of management to Area Authorities, "each with its own pride of identity", intended to be "policy-forming at area level, and supervisory. They are not intended to be executive organs of day-to-day management, nor will they be suitably composed for that purpose. In this they will resemble the boards of the former railway companies". A Scottish Authority was specifically provided for, with the possibility of further subdivision, and the Minister of Transport was required to consult with the Secretary of State on all Scottish matters[2]. The BTC was, however, to to continue to have general financial control and "general control of the charges to be made for the services and facilities provided". Some latitude on rates and charges was given to the industry, with the restrictions on "undue preference" and equality of charges removed. Only maximum rates now had to be published by the BTC, and in certain circumstances it could exceed these. The Transport Tribunal remained in being, with powers to rule on maximum charges and deal with customers' complaints and queries on charging matters[3]. The 1953 Act's references to the Secretary of State indicate the growing role of the Scottish Office, though at this time it had no direct involvement with railway operations.

On Hurcomb's retirement in September 1953, a new BTC chairman, Sir Brian Robertson, a former Army general, was appointed, and some changes were made. From 1 October 1953 Cameron's title was altered to Chief Regional Manager, in common with other regional chiefs, with authority over departmental officers, though these still also had "dotted lines" to functional heads in London. Robertson turned out to be as reluctant as his predecessor to cede real powers, and set up a somewhat military-style 'general staff' at the London headquarters, with the dotted lines to the regional functional heads tending to assume continuity. Area boards remained advisory. Donald (later Sir Donald) Cameron of Lochiel joined the BTC as a part-time member

Sir Donald Cameron, chairman of the Scottish Region board from 1959 to 1964. (Courtesy of Donald Cameron of Lochiel)

on 1 September 1954. Terence Gourvish is dismissive about Lochiel's usefulness to the board other than being Scottish. Much later, an obituary of Cameron noted that he had "an almost boyish passion for railways"[4], but he was also a prominent businessman, a practising accountant, like Bolton, and gave more than a decade's active service to the railways, including chairmanship of the area board.

Scottish Issues

Donald Cameron's home base was Lochaber, and farmers and other rail customers in the Highlands were concerned about charges for long-distance transit of their necessities and their produce (the flat-rate postal system was often noted as an instructive example) and in March 1954 there were high hopes for British Railways' proposed new freight charges, which would have a tapering element, reducing the rate per mile as distance increased. Sir Brian Robertson met the Advisory Panel on the Highlands & Islands in March 1954, with T.F. Cameron and Bolton, and explained that the new charges would set out new maximum rates, but that local officials would have greater latitude to quote special rates. He also pointed out that BR already operated at a loss on the Highland and West Highland lines, and left his hearers with little hope of the special treatment they felt their remoteness deserved. Robertson pronounced himself against the notion of subsidies for specific lines: he felt that overall the BTC should be able to balance its accounts[5]. From the Highlands' point of view, of course, that left the Commission with the option of improving its balance by taking away their railway services. In May 1954 the completion of a two-mile diversion of the Dingwall-Kyle line around Loch Luichart, to allow the level of the loch to rise as part of a hydro-electric scheme, might have given some confidence as to its future, but the cost was borne by the hydro-electric project.

As required by the 1953 Act, from 1 January 1955 the Scottish Region set up an advisory area board, intended to extend its links with business and commerce. Sir Ian Bolton was chairman and its members were Lochiel, Lord Bilsland, Sir Hugh Rose, a director of the Bank of Scotland, Sir John Denholm, of the eponymous shipping agency, W.G.N. Walker, of Jute Industries Ltd, and Councillor P.J. Meldrum, a former trade union official. From 1958 it included Frank Donachy, a former member of the NUR national executive, who also succeeded Bolton as one of the designated Scots on the BTC board from October 1959. From Scotland, departmental heads could call on Central Services, including research, advertising, film, archives, police, stores (renamed Supplies in 1956), paper and printing. A central staff, formed of functional heads including accounting, motive power, passenger and freight, was in overall charge of railway operations, while the general staff and a railways sub-commission of BTC board members was responsible for policy and for the ever-closer liaison with government[6]. A new multi-level headquarters structure was also introduced on 1 January 1955. The chief regional manager's executive authority was still limited. In 1956 he was allowed to agree expenditure of up to £50,000 (£100,000 from 1959) and make appointments up to the level of departmental head without reference to London. At both headquarters and regional levels, these structures were put to extreme test by the need – apparently suddenly perceived in 1954 – for a wide-ranging Modernisation Plan.

Camping coach at Eddleston Station. (Stenlake Collection).

T.F. Cameron retired in 1955[7] and was briefly succeeded by A.E.H. Brown, who died soon after taking office, and then by James Ness, whose career had begun with the North British in 1919 and who had held senior positions in the BTC headquarters staff. Cameron had done well in welding his two divisions of the former companies (still harbouring many memories of their predecessor companies) into a single body, helped perhaps by the Scottish sense of identity, but to run a mix of local and suburban services in the densely-populated Central Belt and long-distance services across wide tracts of thinly-populated territory in the south west, Southern Uplands and the Highlands was a challenge, when passengers and freight customers were increasingly using the private car, the bus or coach, and the heavy lorry.

Around £7 million was spent on new works in the Region between 1948 and 1953, the main project being the modernisation of Cadder marshalling yard at Bishopbriggs. Traffic innovations centred, as in the past, on Anglo-Scottish services, though with popular rather than prestige trains. Overnight 'Starlight Specials' introduced in 1953 ran from Easter to September on Fridays, returning on Saturday, between Glasgow (St. Enoch) and London (St. Pancras) and Edinburgh (Waverley) and London (Marylebone). Classed as excursion trains, with an all-night cafeteria car, and priced at £3 10s return from Glasgow, little more than half the normal £5 17s 4d, they proved very popular and required duplicate services at holiday times. At local holiday times 'Starlight Specials' also ran from other places, including Gourock, Dundee and Clydebank[8]. A new non-stop Edinburgh-London day express, the 'Elizabethan', was introduced in the Coronation year of 1953, taking six hours 45 minutes, with no supplementary fare. Internal services were run to much the same pattern, and with the same motive power and rolling stock, as pre-1948. Pride in punctuality is evident in the Region's monthly section in the British Railways staff magazine: it consistently led all others in punctuality of steam services, with an average of 84.85% of trains arriving on time or within five minutes in the September-March periods between 1949 and 1956[9]. Freight was still the backbone of the Region: in a talk to the

Railway Studies Association in Aberdeen in September 1957, the transport expert Professor Andrew O'Dell noted that the revenue proportions of the Aberdeen District in 1956 were: passenger 22.5%, parcels and fish 33.4%, and general merchandise 44.1%[10]. This was at a time when the Buchan and Deeside lines were still running. One of the last of the war and post-war rationing systems to be abolished was that of meat. With decontrol of the livestock and slaughtering trade, and its transport, from July 1954, road hauliers were quick to make local contracts and though the railways were well-equipped with meat vans, their share of this traffic went into decline. The spread of myxomatosis disease put an end to rabbit traffic, though other game remained a significant item. Scotland's last railway horses were retired in May 1955, bringing a long tradition to an end, including the annual horse parades in Edinburgh and Glasgow (Glasgow had two, at Eglinton Street and Buchanan Street). The 1,522 still at work were replaced by 693 motor vehicles, bringing the Region's total motor fleet up to 1,456, with 3,000 trailers. A new road motor maintenance depot was set up at Kilbirnie Street in Glasgow, dealing with heavy repairs to all Regional vehicles and running maintenance of the 800 motor units and 1,500 trailers of the Glasgow area[11].

A minor though cash-productive aspect of operations was the camping coaches inherited from the old companies and reinstated after the war: in September 1952 there were ten in Scotland, but holiday rentals could also be taken of railway cottages at Aberfeldy, Banchory, Cairneyhill, Culross, Gullane, Old Meldrum, Torryburn and Whitehouse[12] – most of them by this time accessible only by road.

Closures continued under Ness. Dundee's two lines to Strathmore (1955), and the old Border Counties Railway from Hexham to Riccarton Junction (1956) were left with only a limited goods service. Scottish Region closed 488 miles of passenger railway between 1948 and 1955, more than any other region of British Railways[13].

Granton Harbour, Edinburgh in 1952. Ex-NBR No. 47, built in 1916, and withdrawn as BR 69172 in 1958, passes the tram terminus. Route 9 ran via the city centre to Juniper Green. (Stenlake Collection)

Working methods in the Regional offices were brought up to date with what was then known as "mechanical accountancy", particularly useful for wages calculations and for recording train movements. Records of engine and wagon mileage were centralised at Edinburgh, using the Hollerith punched card system; 7,000 daily reports came in from drivers and guards. The operating superintendent's office at 302 Buchanan Street, Glasgow, prepared

new diagrams for train services. Drawn on waxed sheets with Indian ink, they showed where each train ought to be on each section of line. The sheets were sent to Derby where the requisite number of copies were run off and returned to Glasgow. In the 19th century, the railways had been pioneers of telegraphy and the telephone, and made much use of electricity, but in the 1950s and 60s, many Scottish stations and signal cabins were still lit by acetylene, gas or oil lamps. An innovation of the 1950s was to provide motorbikes for stationmasters supervising more than one station in rural areas, to enable them to get from point to point without waiting what might be several hours for a train[14].

The Motive Power Question

Apart from its Southern Region, British Railways was very much a steam-powered system. In July 1947, with nationalisation already certain and imminent, the LNER board approved a plan to obtain tenders "from all possible builders" for 25 diesel-electric locomotives to work on the East Coast Main Line. It is hard to see this as anything other than a pre-emptive move by traction "modernists", to be followed up by the new regime[15], but in the event no more was heard of it. No main line diesel locomotive, even for testing purposes, was ordered between 1948 and 1953. Steam was to remain the means of traction, and following the example of the grouped companies in the early 1920s, BR's chief mechanical engineer, R.A. Riddles, arranged for some inter-regional tests of locomotive types in July-August 1948, an exercise of

BR Southern Region 'Pacific' 34004 *Yeovil* on an Inverness-Perth train at Blair Atholl, on 14 July 1948, during the inter-region locomotive exchanges. (Highland Railway Society)

doubtful value except perhaps for fostering contacts among the many regional engineers in his empire, but much appreciated by locomotive enthusiasts who had never expected to see a Southern Railway 'West Country' 'Pacific' haul trains over Druimuachdar Summit. New engines of old company designs continued to be built in the post-war years, to a total of 1,487, sometimes with experimental modifications; and in 1948 533 wartime 2-8-0s were added to 200 already purchased from the government by the LNER, plus 150 2-10-0 types all of which were employed in Scottish Region. Riddles was also developing a set of BR standard steam locomotives which might be expected to have an operational life of 25 years or more. Almost 40% of British Railways' engines were more than 35 years old in 1947, and in April 1948 the BTC asked the Railway Executive to investigate, from an economic angle, the future balance of advantage between the various types of motive power available to the modern railway[16]. In response, the Executive set up a committee the following December, which did not report until October 1951, when it recommended a large-scale pilot scheme of diesel traction. Riddles was not a member of the committee. A parallel Railway Executive report on electrification, made by a group including the British Railways' chief electrical engineer, but no mechanical engineers, looked forward to a "considerable switch" to electric traction over the next 25 years. It recommended overhead power lines at 1,500 volts (just as an earlier Ministry of Transport-appointed committee had done in 1927) but said nothing about which lines might be electrified, or at what cost[17]. By this time Riddles was already building the new range of standard steam types, and his response was that motive power policy should be founded on coal rather than on imported oil, and that steam traction "is in every way adequate and economical for working the traffic of British Railways"[18]. There had been a brief period in 1948 when during a coal shortage, BR had begun, then cancelled, a conversion programme of coal burning to oil burning: a panic measure like that in 1921 when the pre-grouping companies had done the same thing. Riddles's view was that electrification should be the next phase and that steam should serve until that was achieved. 'Standard' types in relatively small numbers were allocated to Scottish depots – 36 in September 1950[19]. Many pre-1923 locomotives were still in use. Around 130 Caledonian, almost 230 North British, and two Great North veterans were still active in 1960. In January 1950 the first of BR's 'Clan' class light 'Pacifics', *Clan Buchanan*, was displayed at Glasgow Central. The ten 'Clans', based at Polmadie and Carlisle (Kingmoor) depots, never operated on the former Highland line, as had apparently been intended; though *Clan Cameron* made a trip on the West Highland line to Fort William in 1956 on a special train arranged by BRB board member Donald Cameron of Lochiel in connection with a clan celebration.

Ships and Ferries, 1948-57

Railway air interests were transferred to the state-owned British European Airways in 1948, but Scottish Region was responsible for the operation of the steamer services inherited from the former companies, the Caledonian Steam Packet Co., the Clyde & Campbeltown Shipping Co., the Stranraer-Larne route, and the Loch Lomond steamers; also the Skye ferry from Kyle to Kyleakin. The railways had entered the shipping business when direct transfer between train and ship, whether of passengers or goods, was the norm. In the post-war era, there was increasing demand for the ships to carry cars and lorries. Coastal connections were becoming more part of the road rather than the railway network, and provision of capacity for road vehicles was still very limited and primitive.

One of the first demands on the Railway Executive was to provide new Clyde steamers. Investment was essential as the fleet, *Waverley* apart, was mostly elderly and severely depleted. In 1938 there had been 20, and in 1948 only nine remained in service. Requests were being made for restoration of services from Princes Pier, Greenock, but R.D. Kerr, the marine superintendent, could not hold out hopes for this with his reduced fleet[20]. Delays on the Clyde services were frequent in the winter of 1949-50, with "not a ship capable of keeping the schedule", and the *Talisman* (built 1935) especially criticised[21]. Such things may have played a part in a unique event, a 4-hour "lightning strike" by all the steamer captains, to highlight their grievances. Scottish Region denied that there had been any deterioration in relations between management and officers since nationalisation[22].

A new Forth ferry, *Mary Queen of Scots*, was launched by Denny's on 5 March 1949 to replace the 74-year old *Dundee*. Things improved on the Clyde in 1953 when four general-purpose motor vessels were put in service on Clyde routes, *Maid of Ashton*, *Maid of Argyll*, *Maid of Skelmorlie*, and *Maid of Cumbrae*. In November 1953 the 650-ton *Arran* was launched. The new ships brought a large increase in passenger numbers, with an additional 207,000 in 1954. On Glasgow Fair Monday, 19 July, 48,000 were carried, double the number in 1963. A new *Glen Sannox*, built at Troon, entered service in the summer of 1957, able to carry 1,000 passengers and 60 cars, or 40 cars plus 40 tons of containers[23]. A new *Maid of the Loch* for Loch Lomond was kit-built and assembled at Balloch. Improvements to the Gourock-Dunoon ferry raised the number of cars carried from 58 in 1953 to 3,926 in 1954. In July 1950 a new four-car Kyle-Kyleakin ferry was ordered from Wm Denny & Co. at Dumbarton. A six-car vessel, *Lochalsh*, joined it in service from 12 April 1957, and in July 1960 *Kyleakin* followed, making a fleet of four boats[24].

Tragedy struck the Stranraer-Larne route when on 31 January 1953 the relatively new MV *Princess Victoria*, one of the first drive-on car ferries, foundered in the North Channel during a violent storm, with the loss of 133 lives. The legal and compensation officers had to deal with claims that ran far in excess of £200,000. In 1961 *Caledonian Princess* was launched for the route, holding 1,400 passengers and 103 motor vehicles, and equipped with a bow thruster[25].

The Modernisation Plan

Following the Conservative election victory in 1951, Sir Reginald Wilson, BTC's Comptroller or financial chief, prompted the Railway Executive to prepare a report on its long-term financial needs, which appeared as 'A Development Programme for British Railways' in April 1953. With the Transport Bill going through Parliament, it was the Executive's last fling. The BTC followed up with 'Reorganisation of the Railways' a year later, as required by the Transport Act of 1953; and finding the government, even the Treasury, to be in receptive mode, it submitted its plan for 'Modernisation and Re-Equipment of British Railways' to the Minister of Transport in December 1954, and he allowed it to be published in January 1955. Outlining a strategy to be implemented within five years and completed within fifteen, it was intended to be a vision of the new railway and its place in national life as a major element in freight and passenger transport, and, of course, a financially self-supporting one. It anticipated an investment of £1,240 million. Its main elements were the improvement of track and signalling, the gradual elimination of steam power and its replacement by electric and diesel traction, the replacement of conventional rolling stock by self-powered multiple units, and a drastic remodelling of freight services incorporating continuous-braked trains, larger wagons, and reduction of marshalling yards from 150 to 55; also improvement of the railway ports. Further items were the improvement of staff welfare and a research and development fund of £10 million. Electrification was seen as the ultimate goal, with diesel power chosen as an interim measure. A 1956 report under the 'Modernisation of BR' rubric, 'The System of Electrification for British Railways', dumped the 1951 recommendation of 1,500 volts in favour of 25kV AC current to be the standard, and listed some electrification schemes including that of the Glasgow suburban network both north and south of the Clyde[26]. With freight in Scotland a bigger earner than passenger trains, the Plan included proposals for more efficient handling, with large new marshalling yards at Thornton (a project dating back to 1948. Ground had been cleared for it in 1953, but no funds were provided for further action), Millerhill, to the east of Edinburgh, and Perth. A smaller, non-hump yard at Alloa, primarily for coal, was already being laid out. Existing marshalling yards at Cadder, on the Edinburgh-Glagow line near Bishopbriggs, and at Mossend were also designated for modernisation. The Plan was widely welcomed, quickly approved by Sir Anthony Eden's Conservative government, and implementation went ahead.

Freight Innovations in the 1950s

Regional management had to quickly form its plans for modernisation, including selection of motive power, adaptation of steam depots, a timetable for route conversion, and a staff training programme. Change soon became visible as diesel traction spread, and long lines of redundant steam locomotives stood dead on sidings. New engines and wagons fitted with automatic brakes[27] made new express goods services possible and Scottish Region, with a dynamic chief operating superintendent, F.C. Margetts (later to be Dr Richard Beeching's right-hand man and a British Rail director) took advantage of this. The number of Class C "fast-fitted" freight trains rose from 215 services running 26,231 miles in 1954, to 331 services, running 42,237 miles in 1956. Margetts told the staff magazine in December 1956 that the 'Hielan' Piper' (introduced 1955) running nightly between Paisley, Glasgow,

Ex-LMS No. 44255 of Perth depot running downhill over Glen Ogle Viaduct with a goods on 2 September 1959. (Robert Darlaston)

Aberdeen and Inverness, provided next-morning arrival for traffic loaded at 44 points on Clydeside to 105 points in the north-east and north; with second-morning arrival at a further 66 locations[28]. It was followed in 1956 by the 'Killie' between Aberdeen, Perth, Stirling, Glasgow, Irvine and Kilmarnock and similar services between Edinburgh, Johnstone and Stranraer (the 'Galloway Piper') and Dumfries and Aberdeen. By 1958 the Paisley train ran as far as Wick (435 miles, via Aberdeen). Another overnight express freight was introduced between Greenock and York, picking up wagons despatched from Grangemouth, Falkirk, North Clydeside, Renfrew and Govan[29], and the Region was running 80 Class C fitted freight trains daily, more than any other region, carrying such assorted items as grass seed, china, gas meters, hams, nylon hose, carpets, boots and shoes, jute, wool, grain, animal feed, biscuits, newsprint reels, plants, whisky and beer – in fact every commodity now transported in articulated lorries. These initiatives were followed up by a next-day Assured Arrival service for smaller items from Glasgow and Edinburgh to Dundee, Aberdeen, Elgin and Inverness, from April 1958. By January 1959 140,000 consignments had been made, all delivered on time. January 1958 saw the inception of the 'Blue Spot' fish specials, using 275 fish vans fitted with roller bearings for high-speed running between Aberdeen and Kings Cross[30], and in July an 'Export Express' service was introduced for delivery to the quays at Glasgow, Grangemouth and Liverpool. Its 36,047 tons delivered between July and December that year is modest, but also evidence of an effort to capture new custom. In 1959 the 'Condor' (container door-to-door) express began running from Gushetfaulds freight depot to Hendon in London, claimed as the fastest long-distance goods train in Europe. These innovative freight services were helped by the railways' new ability, from 1 January 1957, to exercise what James Ness described as "relative charging freedom" to negotiate one-off deals with customers at rates below the pre-set maxima. Proposed by BR to the Transport Tribunal in 1955, it brought in "loadability" as a criterion in classifying charges, a significant move towards basing charges on costs, and gave Regions more authority and flexibility in managing freight traffic[31]. Even as these innovations were being

Two buffed and burnished J37s from Dunfermline Upper depot pull the Royal Train along the branch to Rosyth, on 22 June 1955. In the background the main line rises towards the Forth Bridge. (North British Railway Study Group)

The departures indicator and bookstall at Aberdeen Station, 1956. The John Menzies company opened its first station bookstall in 1833 and ran all station bookstalls between 1923 and 1998, when it was acquired by W.H. Smith. (Stenlake Collection)

introduced, roads overtook railways in 1956 as the biggest carriers of freight in Great Britain.

A BTC-commissioned report on freight operations in 1958 noted that the universal availability of road transport had effectively made the railways' continuing obligation as common carriers redundant and that "it should be made known that the Commission are no longer prepared to perform, except at a profit, any service which is physically capable of being performed by someone else"[32]. Nevertheless, the report accepted that the BTC had to maintain a comprehensive service for small, especially rural, customers because no-one else would, even though it would make a loss on this. This did not deter Scottish Region from withdrawing freight services from Aberfoyle and stations on the Stirling-Balloch line on 9 October 1959[33].

A record of items handled in 1959 at Nairn, a typical country town station, is of interest: in the course of a year 30,000 parcels, 50,000 gallons of milk, 300 tons of salmon, 700 tons of whisky, 4,000 tons of granite chips, 1,000 tons of timber and 6,000 tons of grain passed through its modest-sized goods depot[34]. Almost all of this would have come and gone in wagons without continuous brakes, shunted by steam locomotives already marked down for scrapping. Scottish goods trains in general were far from punctual: in September-October 1956 57% arrived at their final destinations on time, with 23.7% up to 30 minutes late, and 19.3% more than 30 minutes late[35], and transit times were unpredictable. Here of course was one of the problems which modernisation was also intended to address, through the provision of large and efficient marshalling yards. The new marshalling yard at Thornton opened in January 1956, as the first of British Railways' new mechanised yards. Replacing six older yards or groups of sidings, its 35 sorting roads were intended to serve an increase in coal production estimated at 15,000 tons a day. A sophisticated automated system of track retarders was installed to speed up shunting and train formation, but suffered from what Margetts described as "interesting problems" – these were new developments "which can and should provide a testing ground"[36] and needed to be got right for the yards still under construction.

Modernised Passenger Services

Diesel-powered trains between Waverley and Queen Street began running on 7 January 1957. Scotland's first diesel suburban services began in Edinburgh on 3 February 1958, with a Corstorphine-Waverley-North Berwick service, followed on the 17th by Waverley-Peebles-Galashiels. "Land cruises" on diesel units were said to be well patronised[37], and in 1958 the popular 'Freedom of Scotland' ticket was introduced, giving seven days' unlimited travel for £9 (first class) or £6 (second class). Diesel operations spread steadily, with rail-buses on the Dalmellington and Beith branches and the Devon Valley line by May 1959 and two-car units on the Buchan, Dundee-St. Andrews and Perth-Blair Atholl services by September. In passenger services, another successful novelty was the drive-on car-sleeper introduced between London and Perth in 1955; three years later five Anglo-Scottish car-sleepers ran between Perth and Kings Cross, Inverness-York, Glasgow-Marylebone, Glasgow-Eastbourne, and Stirling-Sutton Coldfield, with (as the LMS had done before) onward car conveyance possible to Aberdeen, Wick, Thurso, Fort William and Mallaig[38]. Diesel railcars were tried out in 1956 on the Crieff and Galashiels lines, and a battery-powered railcar on the Deeside line in 1958 (Neil Sinclair notes that in the Highlands the railbuses were dubbed 'sputniks' after Russia's pioneering satellite[39]). From 9 July 1956 an observation car was run on the Fort William-Mallaig line, and another innovation in August 1957 was the TV Train, a set of carriages with an on-board TV studio broadcasting on closed circuit to the passengers. It was used on excursion services from Glasgow, as far afield as Blackpool, for the illuminations, but the gimmick failed to catch on and by the end of the year it was converted into a charterable exhibition train[40]. With the introduction of new multiple-unit rolling stock, the designation of third class was abolished in June 1956 in favour of second class (in turn to be replaced by standard class in May 1987).

Sir Ian Bolton, Tom Johnston, chairman of the North of Scotland Hydro-Electric Board, and James Ness, at Ballater for the inauguration of the Deeside line's battery railcar service, in June 1962. (BR Scottish Region Magazine)

Modernisation work in 1956-57 extended to a new electro-pneumatic signalling system at Cowlairs, colour light signalling at Glasgow Central – the largest contract yet placed by BR for power signalling – new signalling at Thornton Junction, commencement of work on a new marshalling yard at Millerhill, to the east of Edinburgh, and the new marshalling yard at Perth. A single new freight depot at Dundee concentrated the city's goods traffic at one place[41]. Some 'blue sky' thinking was being applied to Glasgow terminals at this time, with current opinion in the Scottish HQ in favour of closing Queen Street Station and transferring its services to an enlarged Buchanan Street[42], though simultaneously work was in progress on a new signalling system and power box at Cowlairs, replacing eight mechanically-worked signal boxes on the route from Queen Street out as far as Cadder Yard.

Scottish Region's proposal in 1957 on future motive power visualised a five-year plan, revised in 1959 to set the end of 1963 as the time when income and expenditure on passenger services would balance each other. By then the Region expected to have

AC diesel railcar Sc79979 at Comrie, with the 18.05 from Gleneagles, on 3 September 1959, a year after the service began. (Robert Darlaston)

reduced its locomotive fleet by 43%, with 55% of the remaining engines to be diesel-powered. One diesel could replace two steam locomotives on main line work, not in terms of power but in greater availability through reduced maintenance time and turn-round time at termini. The 23 Type 2 1250hp engines introduced in December 1961 were intended to replace 45 steam locomotives. Achieving the reduction in locomotive numbers was described as "a stiff task"[43]. Loaded diesel passenger mileage in 1959 was 3,986,520, compared to 1,863,660 in 1958. It was noted that while some diesel schemes were intended to increase traffic, like Perth-Dundee-Arbroath (38% increase in the first years of diesel) and Glasgow-Ayr-Girvan, others were seen only as reducing operating costs, like the Buchan lines (7.2% increase), Edinburgh-Peebles-Galashiels, and the Edinburgh suburban lines. Initial growth rates were never likely to be maintained, but increases showed a tendency to level off, as shown by the Edinburgh-Glasgow route, which earned £334,018 with steam traction in 1956, and £429,759 with the introduction of diesel units in 1957 (up 28.7%), £451,496 in 1958 (5.1%) and £487,156 in 1959 (7.9%). The impending demise of steam, leading to both poor maintenance and demotivation of engine crews, knocked punctuality badly. In December 1957, when 'on time' still meant just that, only 35.6% of Scottish steam trains achieved the standard, rising to 44.7% arriving within five minutes of time. Even so, the dismal steam figures were the best in the UK. The diesel figures were 70.9% and 87.6%[44].

While introduction of railcars showed concern for services on rural lines, railway management was aware, or soon realised, that modern vehicles might reduce but not stem the losses in many cases. By mid-1955 the BTC's

Dunblane Station on 31 August 1959. Class 5 4-6-0 No. 45465 of Perth depot heads the 15.30 Aberdeen-Glasgow Buchanan Street, and the 17.15 Glasgow-Oban is entering. (Robert Darlaston)

Joint Traffics Committee, with regional members, resolved that area boards should be more closely involved in dealing with unremunerative passenger services. That same year, however, Scottish Region, in its contribution to passenger traffic policy under the Modernisation Plan, noted that "it would be unrealistic to contemplate wholesale closure of branch lines… railways have a social obligation to communities served"[45]. In view of its own closure record, this was surprising, unless it was felt that the Region's dead wood had already been trimmed off. In any case, practice did not march sentiments. When in March 1956 the need for an accelerated closure procedure was put to the TUCCs, almost simultaneously Scottish Region's chief commercial manager, T.H. Hollingsworth, announced the closure of 30 stations on the Glasgow and Edinburgh routes to Perth, Dundee and Aberdeen, already approved by the TUCC. By that time 233 rural stations had been closed to passengers since nationalisation.

In May 1958 the BTC asked area boards to submit proposals for closures. Scheduled passenger trains on the former G&SWR line between Kilmacolm and Greenock (Princes Pier) were withdrawn from 2 February 1959, though occasional boat trains still ran in connection with liner sailings (the era of the jumbo jet had not quite arrived). The Lauder and Fort George branches were closed down in 1958, the Dornoch and Black Isle branches in 1960. Already wider closures were mooted. On 12 May 1959 Scottish Region announced the intention to close thirteen stations and reduce freight operations north of Inverness. Meeting a deputation from Highland bodies in January 1960, Donald Cameron defended branch and station closures in the north as the price of keeping the Further North and Kyle lines open and insisted that the Scottish area board was anxious to retain the lines and improve long-distance services[46]. In February that year an agreement on "combined operations" was made with Highland Omnibuses, with the railway providing long-distance and the buses intermediate and short-distance services, to a co-ordinated timetable[47], in anticipation of closure of the majority of intermediate stations on the Inverness-

Wick line. This was effected on 6 June. More positively, a sleeper service between Edinburgh and Inverness was introduced on the Highland Main Line, running via Dunfermline, from 15 June 1959. Leaving northbound at 10.55 pm and arriving at 5.30 am, it allowed passengers to remain in their berths until 8 am. The supplementary fare was 30s in first and 12s in second class[48].

At this time there was some interest in the Ministry of Transport (under a Conservative government) in giving financial aid to certain lines for social reasons, though no concrete proposal was made, perhaps because the BTC was wholly opposed to the idea of government subsidies for specific services. Why this should have been is not entirely clear, but would seem to be connected to the BTC's belief that the Modernisation Plan would restore its overall profitability, enabling it to balance losses against profits, and maintain its increasingly tenuous independence. Despite this, as part of a 1959 reappraisal of the Plan, the Ministry of Transport selected three areas for appraisal as potential subsidy candidates, including the Highland lines[49].

Reappraisals of the Modernisation Plan

By 1957 the cost of the Plan had mounted to £1,660 millions and the Treasury was becoming alarmed. Harold Watkinson, Minister of Transport since 1955, asked for a full and detailed reappraisal, receiving a defensive reply from Robertson in 1958 which insisted that the basic plan was sound: "Subsequent events have made desirable some modifications, but these are not many, and are principally in the direction of accelerating its execution. Where the financial forecasts of 1956 have not been realised, the causes lie predominantly in forces which were expressly excluded as being outside the scope of the Commission"[50]. Later commentators have been severe on Robertson and his colleagues: "too late… not properly thought out… did not result in an all-out attack on the many fronts of the problem"; and "… all too often the BTC's organisation and planning mechanisms were unequal to the task"[51], and with good reason. The railways' share of passenger traffic, 21.4% in 1951-53, was down to 14.3% in 1960-62 and their freight share fell from 45.3% to 29.2%. It was of course, a time of booming motor car sales. In 1951 there had been 176,166 licensed private cars in Scotland, and at 30 September 1961 there were 446,270, with the number rising year by year to 668,600 in 1965[52].

A reappraisal of the Modernisation Plan published by the BTC in 1959 was largely a matter of detail, though it noted that "the essential requirement of the next five years is a more compact system and a more economical scale of operation". It proposed to reduce station numbers by concentrating traffic at selected railheads, citing the reduction of stations on the Glasgow-Dundee-Aberdeen route from 51 to 21 (effected on 11 June 1956) as a source of "considerable savings". Continuing provision of diesel traction and maintenance for the Scottish Region would require £30 million, with only the Eastern and Western Regions needing more (£40 million). A note of self-justification is evident in the comment that the BTC was expected to act as a "normal commercial undertaking" while also "the Commission's activities are often expected to be guided primarily by the public interest" and the document assumes that this will continue although "economic benefits to the community… are often substantial, these benefits are not reflected in the revenue account of the Commission". Sadly for the BTC, cost-benefit accounting had not yet appeared on the scene. A plea was made for increased fares, with the claim that fares in 1959 were cheaper in real terms than in the 1930s. The price of a monthly third class return ticket was 2d a mile compared to 1.63d a mile in 1948: a 23% increase, but the Commission would need an increase of double that just to keep abreast of the falling purchasing power of money[53].

Connel Viaduct, built in 1903, carried the Ballachulish branch over the narrows at the mouth of Loch Awe. The 08.14 Ballachulish-Oban train is crossing, on 31 August 1959. (Robert Darlaston)

The reappraisal document barely hinted at actual trading conditions. With new traffic initiatives in both freight and passenger workings, new locomotives and new trains, so much appeared positive, yet during the second half of the decade railway usage in general was slumping. Even as the modernisation plan was taking shape, British Railways was plunging into the red. The 1956 results showed gross revenue of £481 million and operating costs of £497.5 million; by 1962 gross revenue would be down to £465.1 million and operating costs up to £569.1 million. The welcome given to the Modernisation Plan in 1955 turned into harsh criticism. While the Plan had achieved a great deal, its operational strategy lay in ruins. This was not wholly the fault of its authors, who would have been shocked in 1953 to know that their fifteen-year timetable coincided with the inexorable decline of heavy industry. Coal, iron and steel, shipbuilding – in every industrial district the smokestacks were falling and the cranes being dismantled. The railway planners were not alone in grossly underestimating the increase in private car ownership and usage. They were however responsible for over-haste in what became a dash for complete dieselisation. The Clean Air Act of 1956, creating smoke-free areas in urban centres, may have contributed to the sense of hurry – the railways were long-standing contributors to the coat of soot which then masked buildings in the cities. British Railways were under pressure to buy new motive power from British makers, many of whom were relatively small, and mostly with minimal experience in building main line diesels. New types were often ordered without proper prototype trials and were found to have problems only after being put into line service. Worst example was Scottish Region's Type 21, of which 58 were built between 1958 and 1960 by the North British Locomotive Company in Glasgow. Hopelessly prone to breakdown, spurned by other regions, they lived out brief and ineffectual lives based at Eastfield Depot. The North British Locomotive Company went into liquidation in 1962. From 1959 the workers at the 22 railway works knew that ten were expected to close by the end of 1963, some of them by the end of 1959. In that year two Scottish Region engineering works were closed down, at Inverness and Kilmarnock, with staff from the latter being transferred to the wagon works at Barassie.

In 1958 BTC chairman Robertson was still insisting that merchandise traffic in less than wagon-load consigments could be retained by "proper charging and good service". On a visit to Scotland in October 1959, he announced that "The Commission are adopting a very bold forward policy in Scotland. Undeterred by the fact that the setbacks in the heavy industries… are gravely affecting our traffic receipts, we are intensifying our efforts to modernise this part of our system, and we are showing faith in Scotland's economic future." About the Glasgow electrification, he remarked, "there will be no better rolling stock on any suburban service in the Kingdom. It has, as you know, been built in Scotland"[54]. The unit bodies were being built by Pressed Steel at Linwood, Renfrewshire.

Government concerns were heightened by the report of another committee, set up at Watkinson's instigation, between BR and the National Union of Manufacturers, in March 1959 to consider how the decline in rail freight – 36 million tons in 1958 compared with 55 million tons in 1948 – might be stemmed. Its exposure of railway shortcomings was unsparing, including

Kirkcaldy's harbour branch was notoriously steep and on 13 November 1954 Class J88 0-6-0T 68341, of Thornton depot, ran away and plunged into the harbour with thirteen wagons. The enginemen survived. The locomotive was lifted out in January 1955 and went for scrapping. A similar incident had occurred in 1905. (North British Railway Study Group)

slowness, delays, lack of progress-tracking systems, poor salesmanship and public relations, and an inability to respond to the needs of modern industry. Robertson insisted that it should not be published[55]. Even as the Modernisation Plan was being driven on, railway management, with an apparent belief that the Plan would resolve everything, was failing in a key area of modern management, particularly in a competitive environment: the study and fulfilment of customer needs. Awareness of this prompted Scottish Region to create the new post of planning officer in late 1959[56].

The complete failure of the Modernisation Plan to realise its financial objectives created a lasting feeling in government that the railways could not be relied on to carry out a large-scale investment programme competently and with reliable financial results. In October 1959 a Conservative government was re-elected and a new Transport Minister, Ernest Marples, was appointed. He speedily requested a further reappraisal, which produced essentially the same response as before. A Ministry of Transport note observed that "The present management seems unlikely to be able to re-orient their ideas to produce a realistic programme"[57]. An intention to make economies by station or line closures was included in the reappraisal, though these were not detailed or quantified. However, the regions were once again instructed to put forward proposals for possible closures.

Industrial Relations: Pay and Productivity

For the railway unions, the issue of pay was a permanent concern. While so much was being invested in modern equipment, railway wages were slipping down the industrial scale. A judicial inquiry into railway pay in 1954 established the principle that parity with private industry should be maintained, and at the end of 1958, in an unusual departure, the BTC and the three railway unions commissioned the economist C.W. Guillebaud to

Train cleaners at Craigentinny Depot, Edinburgh, circa 1958. A Class 105 diesel unit stands behind, with the original 'speed whiskers'.

inquire into the respective pay rates of the railways and comparable industries. Since the railways had 40 wage rates for 153 conciliation grades of staff, this was a complex task and the final report did not emerge until 2 March 1960, by which time it had been necessary to implement a pay rise, though this was understood to be within whatever discrepancy Guillebaud would reveal. In fact he found the monetary gap to be 10%, though various benefits of railway employment reduced it to 8%. On 10 March Prime Minister Harold Macmillan accepted that "fair and reasonable" wages had to be paid, though he explicitly linked this to corresponding obligations: "the industry must be of a size and pattern suited to modern conditions and prospects", including a remodelling of the railway network, some higher fares and rates, and a radical reorganisation of the BTC's structure, with its regions "as far as possible to be fully self-accounting and responsible for management of their own affairs"[58]. Successive governments would press British Railways to link pay rises to productivity, making the increases self-funding in a more efficient industry. To the unions productivity had wider implications, including job losses, fewer members, and less influence, which made it difficult for both sides to keep up a constructive dialogue. The Modernisation Plan's failure to generate surpluses left the management squeezed between the demands of the unions and government pressure to hold down costs, and railway pay levels continued to slip back by comparison with other industries.

Scottish Region at the End of the 1950s

Something quite unrelated to regular railway operations was a manifestation of Cold War precautions against a nuclear strike. Action in the case of such an eventuality was discussed between the Home and Scottish Offices and the BTC, including the possible dispersal of Glasgow control to Cumbernauld or Burntisland, and of Edinburgh control to Ratho. An emergency control centre

Achnasheen in 1958: the engine of the morning Kyle-Inverness train is about to couple onto the restaurant car at the rear of the Inverness-Kyle train and attach it at the front of its own train. The restaurant car was discontinued in 1963. (Highland Railway Society)

was constructed at Burntisland, one of five in Great Britain, in 1956. Ten years later, Scottish Region also had two mobile train control centres, of four cars: control & apparatus; office; stores and mess-room; generator & battery. They were stabled at Perth and Carstairs[59].

Throughout the 1950s the managers of Scottish Region could not but be aware that theirs was in many ways the least productive BR region. Of course it had never been formed as a distinct commercial unit: its genesis was political and the Select Committee on the nationalised industries referred to it in 1959 as "a geographical entity"[60]. Population distribution, climate and topography provided operating difficulties on a scale greater than other regions had to face. Scottish performance was below the British Railways average in many, though not all, respects, as these 1959 figures[61] reveal:

	All Regions	Scottish Region
Passenger train miles per total engine hours in traffic	12.72	10.64 (lowest)
Freight train miles per total engine hours in traffic	4.14	4.41 (2nd highest)
Net freight ton miles per engine hour	1127	908
Net freight ton miles per total engine hour in traffic	606	454
Train load per engine mile in tons	146.19	102.84

Their place at the bottom of most statistical tables doubtless kept board and management focused on economy, with a degree of success in containing their deficit:

	Gross Receipts (£millions)		Working Expenses		Net Deficit	
	BR total	Sc Reg	BR total	Sc Reg	BR total	Sc Reg
1957	501.4	50.6 (10.09%)	528.5	57.6 (10.9%)	27.1	7.0 (25.83%)
1958	471.6	46.3 (9.82%)	519.7	56.1 (10.82%)	48.1	9.8 (20.37%)
1959	457.4	44.3 (9.69%)	499.4	52.6 (10.5%)	42	8.3 (19.9%)

A broad statistical summary[62] of Scottish Region's extent and activity in 1959, eleven years after nationalisation and four years into the Modernisation Plan, shows:

Route miles: 3,392, of which 2,444 in use for passenger traffic
Stations: Passenger & freight 572, passenger only 161, freight only 515
Marshalling yards: hump 5, flat 140
Locomotives: steam 1,796 (2,021 in 1958), diesel 239 (175 in 1958)
Multiple units: diesel 396 (169 in 1958), electric 47 (2 in 1958)
Passenger journeys: 66,038,000 (up 1.1% on 1958)
Passenger receipts: £11,731,000 (up 2.4% on 1958)
Passenger train miles: 21,065,000
Freight tonnage (coal): 17,240,000; receipts £10,022,000
Freight tonnage (other minerals): 5,759,000; receipts £3,538,000
Freight tonnage (merchandise): 4,519,000; receipts £11,043,000
Livestock 129,000 (12.3% down on 1958); receipts £268,000
Total freight receipts: £24,871,000 (9.4% down on 1958)
Parcels & Mail receipts: £5,346,000 (7.3% down on 1958)
Freight train miles: 12,765,000
Train working costs per train mile: 7s 5.3d (highest among BR regions except for London Midland, 7s 5.4d)

6. The 1960s – 1. From Modernisation to Reshaping

The 1960s were a decade of profound and far-reaching changes for Scottish railways, not only brought about by policies adopted and decisions taken in London. Programmes of drastic service cuts and line closures were pursued simultaneously with a complete overhaul of regional management to a form different to that of other regions, and the introduction of new services intended to secure a profitable future, all against a background of increasingly rapid social, industrial and commercial change. By the end of the decade, a new perception of the "social railway" had begun to be formulated. To trace all the different events as they happened would make for confusing reading, so this and the next chapter follow separate though interlinked themes. This chapter covers the final phase of the Modernisation Plan, the introduction of a new regime with a radically different approach, and the impact on Scottish Region. Chapter 7 looks at Scottish Region's service adaptations, its change of management structure, and the important implications of the 1986 Transport Act.

The Need for Action

A leaked Scottish Region document from October 1960 appeared in *Modern Railways*, giving examples of revenue against movement costs on certain passenger trains. The 5.48 am Kilmarnock-Dumfries was earning £7 against a cost of £176; for the 12.00 noon Carstairs-Muirkirk the figures were £14 and £106; for the 9.30 am Oban-Buchanan Street, £84 and £336; and for the 7.56 am Berwick-Waverley, ten shillings and £164[1]. For the general public, cuts to rail

A wet day at Ballachulish in 1961. The slate quarries rise behind the station, which was closed in 1966. No. 55263 was one of ten Caledonian-design 0-4-4T engines built by the LMS in 1925. It was withdrawn in 1961. (Stenlake Collection)

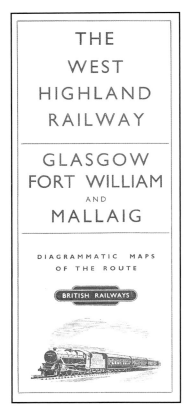

Far left: Cover of a passenger brochure for the West Highland line, from the 1950s. (British Railways, Chris Green Collection)

Left: Observation cars information 1960s Information for prospective passengers on Scottish Region observation cars in 1966. (British Railways, Chris Green Collection)

services and threats to others had been familiar since the 1950s. In December 1961 Scottish Region withdrew 125 trains on 20 main and branch line services, causing the NUR to threaten strike action, but a further 160 services were cut from 8 January 1962[2]. A saving of £200,000 was expected, but the Region's annual deficit was said be £12 million, and these were mere tinkerings compared with what was to come. Railway managers at all levels could not fail to realise that things had gone badly wrong and the situation had to be addressed. They were running a system which was losing revenue year after year both in its core traffic and its still numerous peripheral services. How could this be happening?

The answer lay around them in many forms. Although their trains were rapidly being modernised, they were maintaining a service pattern which had taken scant account of changing conditions. Between 1955 and 1962 the number of cars on British roads doubled, to almost 5 million, and the first section of motorway opened in 1958. Road haulage was booming. Patterns of work, shopping, leisure, holidays all were changing rapidly. New concepts of efficiency in commerce, industry and shipping required short lead times for delivery and a flexibility of supply that road transport could provide and railways could not.

Politicians and civil servants could not ignore the worsening finances of the railways. A House of Commons Select Committee on British Railways noted in July 1960 that the British Transport Commission was caught in a conflict between social and economic viability in its provision of services. The Committee decided that "the best test of what the public needed was what it was prepared to pay for", and that British Railways should leave social considerations to the government[3]. Marples appointed a special advisory group, headed by the industrialist Sir Ivan Stedeford, to look at the structure, finance and working of the BTC. Stedeford's report was not published, but Ministry of Transport files reveal it was highly critical of the Commission, as non-commercial in outlook, obscure in organisation, and unclear in its objectives. It noted that "Large parts of its organisation, including the railway regions, have no separate accounts and no systematic financial yardsticks by which to judge the results and prospects of managerial actions". In its diagnosis the committee was united, but not in its prescription. Stedeford believed the solution should be a small holding company with management devolved to the regions, while one member who in particular had impressed Marples, Dr Richard Beeching, seconded from Imperial Chemical Industries, recommended a strong central command structure, with only functional responsibilities executed at regional level[4]. The government preferred Beeching's approach to Stedeford's, and it was certainly a more likely one to achieve the extent of cost-cutting now viewed by the Treasury as essential. No more was heard of Macmillan's desire to have semi-autonomous regions.

Robertson, who was not given a copy of the Stedeford Report, sent his proposals for a continued modernisation programme over the next four years to Marples on 19 December 1960[5]. His board proposed to spend its already allocated investment for 1961, £140 million, entirely on the West Coast Main Line electrification. For the ensuing three years its investment requirement was £175 million a year. Typically short on detail of how specific aims were to be managed and achieved, the proposal reiterated the 1959 reappraisal's intention that a more compact system and more economic scale of operations should be achieved more quickly, and included a list of closure proposals submitted by Regions. Scottish Region listed only 31 miles of line, encompassing four closures. This has prompted some commentators to suggest that the Region was dragging its heels on the closure issue – Western Region was proposing 80 cases and 1,138 route miles. But as we have seen, Scottish Region had been the most assiduous in the past. It kept its place at the top of the closure table, having closed a further 149¾ miles since 1955; in all it closed 65 branch lines between January 1950 and August 1962[6]. By now it had little to offer other than much deeper cutting than had yet been suggested;

Former 'Devon Belle' observation car, now SC280M, and a Post Office van at Kyle of Lochalsh, in July 1961. (Stenlake Collection)

Killin Station in 1961. The branch
engine is a Caledonian-design 0-4-4T
built under LMS auspices in 1925. It
was withdrawn on December 1962.
(Stenlake Collection)

indeed Robertson's proposals went on to state that closure of stations had now
"passed its peak" and that an average of 100-150 stations a year was as much
as could be foreseen in the next few years. Scottish projects listed for the
period were a new steel trough floor for the Tay Bridge, installation of
Automatic Warning System (AWS) on both routes between Carlisle and
Glasgow, stage two of the Glasgow suburban electrification, "complementary
to Stage 1 and essential if the system is to become viable", the Millerhill and
Perth marshalling yards, a "Glasgow South" marshalling yard, reorganisation
of terminal working at Sighthill, and new Glasgow office accommodation[7].

Marples sent a copy of Robertson's document and its supporting papers to
Beeching (by now chairman-designate) on 21 April 1961[8]. Meanwhile his
Ministry had responded with a battery of questions, most of them designed
to prise out details that the proposals had glossed over. Robertson retired on
1 June, two years before the normal date. By that time British Railways'
earnings were some £60 millions a year below running costs, apart from the
requirement to make interest payments of another £75 millions. He was
awarded a peerage and a lump sum of £12,500 above his pension: a notable
instance of the UK establishment's way of easing the exit from high-level
failure. Beeching became BTC chairman, with a brief to review the entire
range of railway operations and frame a strategy for a profitable system. His
contract was for five years at a salary of £24,000, far more than any previous
nationalised industry chairman, and, as often pointed out, equal to the
combined salaries of 38 railway clerks. Rapid action was to follow, by
Beeching and his staff, and by the Ministry of Transport, which was drafting
a new Transport Bill. At the same time Marples headed a Ministerial Group
on Modernisation, which commissioned a report from Sir Robert Hall, the
MoT's Economic Adviser, on 'The Transport Needs of Great Britain in the
Next Twenty Years'. It was not published until February 1963, but Hall's

views probably influenced the provisions of the Transport Act. His estimates gave a gloomy but accurate prognosis for the railways of zero growth in passenger services over the next twenty years. His forecast for the increased number of cars in Great Britain was greatly understated, like all others: he anticipated 18 million by 1980 but there were already 19 million by 1971. He expected minimal growth in rail freight unless gross domestic production should rise by at least 4% a year, and his only positive comment on railways related to urban lines, which he felt should be retained (increasing urban road congestion was a prime issue at the time)[9].

Inevitably, with major changes expected following Beeching's appointment, and despite the availability of post, telephone and telex, there was much coming and going between Scotland and London: James Ness observed to a London colleague that 90 first class sleeper berths each week were taken up by Scottish staff attending meetings in London[10]. Nevertheless, while the Government, the Transport Ministry, and their various advisers and consultants considered the reshaping of the railway system in the early 1960s, railway managers were also getting on with the day-to-day job. At this point, it is apposite to note that the management itself – never a static body – was undergoing change as a new generation came in. For the first time, these were people who had grown up in the post-war era, who shared the attitudes and the ideas of their peers and were less deferential, more questioning and more open-minded than most of their seniors. As graduate entrants or school leavers, men like Chris Green, Jim Cornell, Chris Leah, Jim Summers and others who would play significant roles in Scotland and across the wider system, joined the industry at a time of uncertainty and corporate gloom because they wanted to work for the railway: things were pretty bad, and would get worse, but they could envisage a better future. It would take time for this generation to achieve seniority and power – and of course there were executives in senior positions who adopted and encouraged the spirit of challenge – but the seeds of future development were planted. Commercial management as a subject in its own right was assuming a stronger role, with a mix of textbooks and popular works like *Parkinson's Law* (1958) or *The Peter Principle* (1959) that all showed the value of standing back from the business, analysing what it was doing, discovering what it wasn't doing, and putting into practice what it should be doing. Corporate planning was a new discipline, on which consultancy firms would grow rich.

The Transport Act 1962 and Scottish Region

Some statistics show the continuing scale of Scottish Region operations between 1959 and 1962[11]:

	1959	1960	1961	1962
Total receipts £million	41.9	43.85	43.68	43.60
Passenger receipts £million	11.7	18.14	18.81	19.5
Freight receipts £million	30.2	25.72	24.88	24.1
Passenger journeys million	66	64.9	63.4	n/r
Freight tonnage	n/r	29.8	28.1	n/r

The figures show the increasing convergence of passenger and freight receipts as the one rose (though numbers fluctuated) and the other steadily fell. During this period bus journeys also fell; in 1959 773 million journeys were recorded on BTC-owned buses and 954 million on municipally-owned buses. In 1961 the figures were 751 million and 897 million.

In March 1962 it was recorded that Scottish Region was "vigorously closing branches and cutting services"[12]. Passenger receipts were holding up, but running costs were not recorded by the Scottish Office, and in August 1962 a traffic survey conducted in Scotland revealed that 2,000 of the 2,750 daily services ran at a loss[13]. Dr Beeching made a four-day tour of the Scottish Region at the end of the month, encountering a protest demonstration by apprehensive railway workers; he had informed the unions in July that closure proposals for Berwick-St. Boswells, Lugton-Beith, Hamilton-Motherwell-Coatbridge-Glasgow, and some Edinburgh suburban services, were already "with the Minister" pending his national report. The Beith branch closed in November that year, and the Buchanan Street-Coatbridge-Motherwell-Hamilton and Coatbridge-Holytown passenger services were closed.

The unions were said to be surprised by lack of protest from railway managers[14], but Scottish Region's previous history showed it had no desire to provide services that even with modern traction were little used by their communities. It lacked interest in promoting them, and also lacked the necessary marketing techniques to do so effectively[15]. With the threat of closure moving from rural branches to main lines, and the TUCC increasingly seen as having neither influence nor power, national and local pressure groups began to be formed in defence of railway services and promoting a positive view of their role. The Scottish Railway Development Association, later Scottish Association for Public Transport, was established in 1962. Such groups could raise issues that the TUCC, confined to its narrow remit, could not bring to public attention, such as the correctness of the railways' figures in bringing a case for closure and the alleged practice of deliberately running down a train service in order to enhance the case for closing it. Steadily improving their game, they played a substantial part in the gradual changing of public attitudes towards the railways. British Railways did not always help. Bradshaw's guide to all train services ceased publication in June 1961. While all regions issued their own timetables, BR did not issue a comprehensive Britain-wide timetable until 1974, though a general timetable of "principal passenger services" was issued in June 1961.

When the latest Transport Act came into force in August 1962, a shadow board, the 'British Railways Committee' had already been practising its steps since April, with Cameron of Lochiel and Frank Donachy among its members. The Act provided for the dissolution of the British Transport Commission into five separate public bodies, one of them to be the British Railways Board, with a set of regional boards, including Scotland, to come into operation on 1 January 1963. The continued existence of a Scottish board had been recommended by the Stedeford committee, because "financial assistance will always be required" and "it would please the Scots"[16]. Regions were permitted, though not enjoined, to delegate responsibilities to regional boards as allowed by the BRB, on lines settled from time to time with the approval of the minister[17], but there was little sign of this happening; general managers were possessive of their powers. Lochiel, chairman of the Scottish Board since 1959, retired from the chair in 1964 though he remained a member until 1972. Until 1971, when Thomas Taylor, President of the Scottish Co-operative Wholesale Society (later Lord Taylor of Gryfe) took over, the general manager was also chairman of his own advisory board. Ships and hotels remained within the remit of the regions, though the only actual railway-run harbour in Scotland was now Stranraer (East Pier). The Act also relieved the BRB of interest payments on the British Transport Commission stock of 1947, transferring all rights and liabilities to the Treasury[18]. A significant provision allowed Parliament to make grants to the BRB to make up any deficit on its revenue account, up to an aggregate of £450 million, in its first five years, but not thereafter; and the board was required to "so

A pair of Class 21 diesels with an Oban train in the Pass of Brander, in 1961. The lattice post mounts three signals. The two in the clear position are connected to rock-fall wires on the hillside above. The other is the distant signal for Falls of Cruachan Halt which the train has just left. (Stenlake Collection)

conduct their business as to place themselves at the earliest possible date in such a position that their revenue will be, and continue to be, not less than sufficient for making provision for the meeting of charges properly chargeable to revenue, taking one year with another"[19]. Beeching was chairman of the new BRB, and unlike previous arrangements there was no specific provision for Scottish representation on the Board, though members were expected to be chosen for their knowledge of the various parts of Great Britain. With this Act the railways' obligation as common carriers was finally removed, along with restrictions on charges and rates. The Transport Tribunal still existed with a role in passenger fares, but its relevance to railways was much reduced. At last there was something like an even playing field between rail and road, but by 1963 fully two thirds of inland freight was being moved by road.

The 'Reshaping' Report

Teams of analysts were hard at work examining the traffic patterns and revenues of the railway system, and drawing conclusions. Under the title 'The Reshaping of British Railways', the findings were passed to the Ministry of Transport, published in March 1963 and endorsed by Parliament in April. Mostly written by Beeching, the report began with a brief critique of previous management, noting that the railways had "paid their way" until 1952, with a surplus on the operating account vanishing by 1955 into annual losses culminating in £86.9 million by 1961. The 1955 Modernisation Plan did not embrace basic changes in the scope or general mode of railway operations, and the effects of modernisation had been neither so rapid nor pronounced as the forecasts had claimed, failing to overcome the downward trends. Through the company era and into nationalisation, the degree of cross-subsidisation involved in carrying "bad" traffic on the back of financially "good" traffic had been very largely ignored, but this could not continue:

"Now… it is no longer socially necessary for the railways to cover such a preponderant part of the total variety of internal transport services… This situation requires a much more analytical examination of the Railways' business with a view to reshaping their system, their mode of operation, and their pattern of services and traffics"[20].

Scottish Region was still running December meat specials from Aberdeen to London, and an Aberdeen-Crewe express fish train, in 1962[21], but the great bulk of its merchandise traffic was in wagonload trains: a system condemned for its inefficiency and lack of tracking detail: "… we are compelled to think of the system of freight movement as one which produces statistically measurable and predictable results, but which does not produce a known or foreseeable result with any one consignment". The future of rail freight was defined as "Liner Trains" on high-density routes, which could carry 16 million tons a year of containerised road-rail units[22]. A few specific comments on Scottish routes include a note that air transport "makes quite serious inroads into the loading of day trains" and some will have to be withdrawn. Sleepers however "attract a satisfactory level of traffic". A pre-emptive comment also notes that in the north of Scotland the ownership of private cars is 11.7 per 100 of the population, equal to the British national average, and that demand for rural public transport is falling[23].

Beeching's actual figures have been heavily criticised for a "snapshot" approach, with observations taken during a single week, 16-23 April 1963, though his conclusions also incorporate historical statistics. His track and signalling costs were based on national averages with no consideration of the actual position on targeted routes. As two of his sternest later critics point out, "the railway has always been run as a network, and any attempt to produce a separate balance sheet for an individual line means allocating costs which may or may not arise"[24]. Appendices to the report include figures relating to three Scottish routes, Gleneagles-Crieff-Comrie, Banff-Tillynaught,

Ten years after its closure to passengers, a rail-tour visits Brechin in 1962. Since 1993 the station has been preserved as part of the heritage Caledonian Railway. (Photo Nigel Mundy)

and Aberdeen-Ballater. The 15-mile Comrie line, with eight stations, had ten railbus services daily each way. Passenger miles accruing to this service were 340,000; train miles were 65,000 a year: simple division yielded an average of five passengers per train. The line earned £1,900 a year; train movements cost £7,500 and terminal costs were £3,480; track and signalling costs were put at £8,200, making a total of around ten times the revenue. The line's contribution to onwards rail services was estimated at £12,000, of which £9,000 would be lost by the closure. Overall, closure would mean a financial improvement of £8,400[25].

Banff-Tillynaught, six miles, with 37,400 train miles a year, earned £800 a year plus £6,130 on onwards journeys. Movement expenses were £14,150 and the closure gain was put at £10,900. Aberdeen-Ballater was not be spared for its royal connections. Over its 43-mile length, 161,000 train miles were clocked up each year. Its earnings were £14,370, its gross contributory revenue was £21,980. Against these were movement expenses of £19,850, terminal expenses of £9,250, and direct track and signalling expenses of £20,980, giving a closure gain of £28,710[26].

'Reshaping': Implementation

The sledgehammer blows came with the actual closure proposals. In the country at large they caused a great deal of dismay, with people feeling the country was about to be filleted. Full implementation would leave vast areas of Scotland without railway transport. Fifty-one passenger train services were up for withdrawal, including main and important secondary lines. Edinburgh-Hawick-Carlisle and the other Border lines, Ayr-Stranraer, Dumfries-Stranraer, everything north and west of Inverness, the Deeside, Moray and Buchan lines, the Fife coast line, the Dunblane-Crianlarich line, the line through Strathmore past Forfar, the Glasgow Central underground line, and all railways to and beyond Crieff. To the nineteen stations currently slated for closure, the report added a further 423 (incidentally, an internal regional document in August 1964 listed the Scottish stations to remain open following the reshaping procedure. These were naturally the busier stations. Sixty-seven were still lit by oil or gas[27]). Forty-one per cent of Scotland's railway mileage would be removed. In the midst of the wave of protest, James Ness announced that the *Maid of the Loch* was "doomed" after the summer season: there would be no railway to Balloch Pier[28].

Beeching and his team understood the shock-value of global statistics, and the messages were reiterated through the media: a quarter of BR receipts came from a mere 34 of the 7,000-odd stations; a third of the railway mileage was carrying only 1% of traffic, as expressed in ton- and passenger-miles (the same was true of the road network); the average revenue-earning travel of a goods wagon was only 45 miles per week. The 1962 Act had speeded up the closure process, enabling the BRB to give six weeks' notice of closure, and had also tightened up the procedures and reduced the powers of the TUCC, which could not challenge the figures on which closure was based or make contra-recommendations, including suggestions for more economical operation, but only give details of possible hardship on an individual basis: economic impact on a community and its future were excluded. Indeed, one review of the 'Reshaping' paper pointed out that "... there is no way of preventing the Board from pricing itself out of any service which it may consider to hinder the discharge of its main statutory duty, to pay its way"[29]. Local authorities, other organisations, and thousands of individuals combined in local and national groups to fight the proposed cuts, with J.S. Campbell, of Larkhall, Secretary of the District Councils' Association for Scotland, acting as a co-ordinator of protest. In Edinburgh a joint Citizens,

Rail Users and Rail Workers Committee was formed[30]. Supportive voices for the closure policy were few, though they did include the Council of Scottish Chambers of Commerce[31]. The campaign cut across the political divide, with local Tory MPs joining in, and not merely because a general election was impending in 1964. In a by-election in Dumfries-shire in December 1963 the Conservative majority slumped from 7,000-plus to 971, with railway closures a prominent issue in the campaign.

Though Beeching is remembered as drawer-up of the indictments, and axe-wielder, and certainly believed firmly in his proposals, the real driver behind the 'reshaping' was Marples, with strong encouragement from the Treasury as well as from the civil servants of his own department. One railway historian has written "... with motorway-loving Ernest Marples as Conservative Minister of Transport the destruction of Britain's railways moved into top gear following the publication of the 'Report'"[32]. But it would be both crude and insufficient to say that Marples was a pro-roads man and leave it at that. Deep political and commercial schemings by anti-railway theorists and capitalists have been seen by some commentators as the background to the "re-shaping"[33]. They were a disparate range of groups and individuals, whose cumulative efforts were more effective in influencing public opinion against the railways than in nudging a government which by 1960 was convinced that action was necessary and a policy must be formulated. Those who favour the idea of an anti-railways conspiracy ignore not only the part played by the BTC in its own demise, but also that the real enemy was the immense popular appeal of the motor car itself. Railways had first made it possible for individuals to travel far and wide, in a collective transportation mode; the car improved on that by enabling individuals and families to travel independently and randomly from their own front doors. It was only to be expected that bodies with a financial interest in roads: haulage

Ex-North British Class C15 4-4-2T No. 135, built 1912, now BR 67460 working the Arrochar push-pull service, takes on water at Craigendoran Pier, around 1961. The West Highland station is above on the right. (Stenlake Collection)

companies, car makers, fuel companies, civil engineering groups, would campaign for road investment to replace railways: "We should build more roads, and we should have fewer railways. This would merely be following the lesson of history…"[34], and that a Conservative government with a belief in the economic and social virtues of private enterprise should be sympathetic to their case (though informed support for railways could be found in both main political parties). Even if BR had been able to apply marketing and adaptive management skills of a high order, it is most unlikely that the surge in car ownership and use and consequent loss to the railway would have been stemmed.

That the railways by 1960 presented a huge problem which had to be addressed is incontrovertible. The British Transport Commission had dug a hole for itself. Adaptation of the network to serve current circumstances had only been attempted in a limited and piecemeal way. Since the Commission under Robertson appeared content to let the situation continue, the government would have failed in its duty if it had taken no action. From the number of committees and the extent of internal discussion that went on between 1959 and 1962, it is evident that the Cabinet was concerned to be sure of the policy and its implementation. Marples, previously Postmaster-General, was given the job of investigating solutions and implementing the chosen one by a Prime Minister, Harold Macmillan, who had once been a director of the Great Western Railway and was known to be a proud wielder of his gold pass. The Conservative government of 1953 had spiked its Labour predecessor's movement towards a national road/rail transport policy, and the railway system was expected to survive on its own. With continuing general acceptance of the belief that a reformed system would be self-financing, some version of the Marples-Beeching solution was the only one available.

Like nationalisation before and privatisation later, reshaping was done in a hurry. Given five years to bring the railways to break-even point on costs and revenue, and with a lack of historic statistics to work from, Beeching devised blunt economic criteria to identify stations and lines which were failing to pay their way – even his fiercest critics accepted that for many of these closure was inevitable – but he proved no better than anyone else in predicting future trends. In the case of many of his cuts, most people are scarcely aware that once a railway existed; but in others, the axing of a railway left serious problems in its wake, with one of the most obvious being that of the Dumfries-Stranraer line, where container traffic for Northern Ireland, eminently suitable for rail, congests the A75 'Euroroute'.

News presentation and damage limitation

Braced for protest, Beeching and the government were anxious to minimise the opportunities for public campaigns against closures. Anyone who supposes that news management is a recent invention would be surprised to find how much time Macmillan's Cabinet devoted to presentation of the 'Reshaping' report and of the closure proposals that swiftly followed[35]. Grouping of closure notices by region alarmed the politicians. In the week beginning 22 June 1963, Scottish Region issued closure notices for passenger services between Aberdeen-Fraserburgh and Peterhead, Ayr and Dalmellington, Ayr-Kilmarnock (reprieved), Elgin-Lossiemouth, Berwick and St. Boswells, Berwick and Edinburgh (local), Craigendoran-Arrochar (local), Fraserburgh-St. Combs, Gleneagles-Crieff-Comrie, Kilmarnock-Darvel, Kilmarnock-Ardrossan, and Langholm-Riddings Junction-Carlisle. In November 1963 the BRB notified intention to withdraw passenger trains from Dumfries-Kirkcudbright, Dumfries-Stranraer, Ayr-Stranraer, Inverness-Wick

Class 26 and Class 24 diesels with an independent snowplough, embedded in snow and possibly derailed, at Dava Moor in the winter of 1962-63. (David Hills Collection)

and Thurso, and Inverness-Kyle of Lochalsh, but the Scottish TUCC deferred its hearings until late February or early March, prompting the Ministry of Transport to ask British Railways to defer some further closure announcements, "which may be particularly embarrassing in the light of our policy for regional development", in order to minimise the period between proposal and TUCC hearing. These included Edinburgh-Hawick-Carlisle[36]. Marples and Beeching agreed that TUCC hearings should be given only three figures: earnings of the line or service (excluding contribution to onwards travel), working costs, and capital expenditure needed if it were kept going for a further five years. 'The Reshaping of British Railways' had given more detailed figures of some examples, as noted above[37].

Scottish Region management's job was to get on with implementing the decisions made in London, and fights against individual closures were not conducted across the area board table but in public meetings, newspaper columns, radio interviews, petitions and even sermons. The Region's response to Beeching is a matter for speculation: Beeching resolved that the industry must be reduced to an extent far beyond anything that professional railwaymen had contemplated. Was there internal resistance? Dr Charles Loft wrote: "the chairman [Beeching] was able to compel Scottish Regional Board to put forward major closures (like the Far North and Borders lines) which it would not have done on its own initiative (and which it privately invited the Scottish Secretary to direct it to retain in 1963)"[38]. This is most improbable. The Secretary of State, at that time Michael Noble MP, had no power in railway matters and could not have given any instruction to the area board (and gave none), though he could, and did, impress on his Cabinet colleagues the political dangers of closures, obtaining a deferral of the decision to close the Aviemore-Forres line from September 1964 until after the general election of October that year. The line was shut under the new Labour government in

October 1965. The Scottish Development Department, with a brief to grow industry, reported railway closures year by year without comment, and devoted far more attention to roads, for which the Scottish Office had reponsibility. Among Noble's civil servants in the Scottish Office, pro and anti-closure supporters could be found, with a senior planning officer, Frank Spaven[39], active behind the scenes in bolstering the case for keeping the Highland lines to and beyond Inverness, both at the Scottish Office and later with the Highlands and Islands Development Board. These lines were the most notable survivors of the closure era. The evident inadequacy of the roads spared the Kyle of Lochalsh line. Estimated annual receipts of the Wick and Thurso line had been stated as £88,340 and direct costs as £209,030. Total loss of passenger revenue from closure, including the line's contribution to other lines from through tickets, was put at £202,500. Gourvish records a conversation between Marples and Beeching, in which the Minister pointed out the modest difference, and Beeching stated that a further £235,500 would be saved on track and signalling costs as the board intended to close the line completely if the passenger closure was allowed[40] – something not known to the general public. Discussion reached the topmost level: on 30 September 1962 Macmillan wrote to Marples: "If the government decides that on social grounds a railway from Inverness to Wick is necessary then… Dr Beeching will quote a price… for keeping the line open… the government will pay this, if it decides to do so, as a social service". His letter[41] notes that "social grounds" were not part of Beeching's remit, but implies that closure of this line, at least, would not go ahead, though Macmillan's government did not legislate for subsidies to specific railway services. At this time the concept of the social railway was too new and unformulated to form a basis of policy, and Sir Brian Robertson's insistence that the Modernisation Plan would balance the railways' books did nothing to advance it.

There was a bad-tempered episode when Beeching refused to release

The departures board at Elgin 's East Station in May 1968. Notices about impending withdrawal of its trains are posted. (Stenlake Collection)

anything more than the basic figures for the Waverley and Wick/Thurso lines to Michael Noble, a cabinet minister. John Brewis, MP for Galloway, had obtained the detailed Dumfries-Stranraer figures from general manager Willie Thorpe (who was entitled to do so, at his discretion, until Beeching removed the discretion and the entitlement). The furious Noble threatened to complain to the Prime Minister, but Beeching was unmoved. His view was that no-one should have more information than the TUCC had. His reluctance is understandable when the savings on the Dumfries-Stranraer line as shown to the TUCC were £122,260 whereas those shown on the detailed statement were a less than a quarter of that, at £29,940. Beeching had called in Sir William Carrington, a former president of the Institute of Chartered Accountants, to confirm the validity of his figures, which were based to a considerable degreee on estimates of cost.

The two sets of figures for the Wick/Thurso line were[42]:

1. As supplied to the TUCC.
Estimated direct earnings: £88,340
Movement costs: £86,030
Terminals (i.e. stations): £15,180 (most wayside stations already closed)
Track & signalling: £107,820
Total costs: £209,030
Saving: £120,690

2. As supplied to the MoT:
Estimated direct earnings: £88,340
Contributory gross revenue: £196,800
Expected loss in total revenue from closure: £202,440
Estimated direct expenses: £209,030
Estimated net financial effect: £6,590
Balance of track/signalling cost saving on complete closure: £235,250

By 1960 Class 26 diesel locomotives had taken over the Inverness-Kyle service. Tokens are exchanged as the Kyle-Inverness train enters Achnasheen. (Highland Railway Society)

Marples ultimately refused the closure of the northern lines in April 1964, and of the Ayr-Stranraer line in July. Beeching, deprived of his cost-saving, wanted losses made on reprieved uneconomic lines to be shown separately in the British Rail accounts[43]. Other areas were less fortunate. Against vehement protests, the Dumfries-Challoch Junction line was shut down on 14 June 1965, and Stranraer trains were re-routed via Kilmarnock and Ayr, adding 35 minutes to the timing of the 'Northern Irishman' from Euston. Closure of the Waverley Route was held off for four years, while the Labour government hesitated. It was sponsoring a Central Borders Plan for Expansion, but the plan, when delivered in April 1968 to William Ross, the Secretary of State, did not insist on the need for the railway, and though Ross made a final appeal to Prime Minister Harold Wilson: "I would beg you to look at the cumulative consequences of our course of action on our standing in Scotland"[44], consent for closure was given in July, and effected on 6 January 1969, except for an Edinburgh-Hawick coal service which lasted until 28 April. The Borders were described as the largest area in Europe to have no railway service. An attempt was made to form a private Border Union Railway to purchase and work the line, and lifting of the rails was delayed until 1971. The Ministry of Transport seemed to foster the proposal[45], but it foundered on failure to secure adequate financial backing. Scottish Region, not keen on seeing a private venture take over a line it had declared as unable to make a profit, asked for £745-960,000 for the freehold, with a deposit of £250,000 and an annual access charge for running powers into Carlisle and Edinburgh of £125,000[46]. Hopes for reinstatement did not disappear and strengthened in the 1990s, with ultimate success in the opening of the new Borders Railway as far as Tweedbank in 2015.

Beeching's Second Report

Two months after the election of a Labour government in October 1964, it was announced that Beeching would return to ICI in June 1965, a year earlier than his agreed secondment[47]. One railway magazine noted that he had transformed management attitudes, introducing new research, costing, production and marketing[48]. Though Labour had made heavy and cogent criticisms of some of the closure decisions, most notably by Bruce Millan, a future Scottish Secretary[49], there was no immediate change in policy towards the railways. The new Minister of Transport, Tom Fraser, MP for Hamilton, made little impact compared with his predecessor or successors; he had no policy for railways and inherited a ministry which still had a full head of steam on closure plans. Completion of closure procedures went on through the rest of the decade, so that Labour ended up cutting more of the system than the Tories.

Beeching's second report, 'The Development of the Major Trunk Routes'[50], was published on 16 February 1965 and indicated the lines for development. In Scotland, these consisted only of Carlisle-Carstairs-Glasgow and Edinburgh, and its northward continuation via Perth and Dundee to Aberdeen; along with Edinburgh-Glasgow and Edinburgh-Dundee. The corollary, not spelled out in the report, was that routes not marked down for closure in the reshaping programme, and not listed among the trunk routes, would not undergo any development. Scaling down began immediately, losing double track in many cases, along with sidings, goods yards and loops, and providing no more than essential levels of maintenance. The Highland Main Line's double track sections between Blair Atholl and Inchlea, and Daviot and Millburn Junction, were singled in 1966, with tokenless block signalling installed, and the Inverness-Aberdeen line was singled from Millburn Junction to Dalcross and from Keith to Dyce (later right into Aberdeen)[51].

Between 1963 and 1968 the number of freight yards fell from 39 to 23, signal boxes from 995 to 606, motive power depots from 77 to 23, passenger stations from 671 to 359, freight depots from 960 to 215, and route mileage from 3,138 to 2,344. The Region's locomotive stock fell from 1,000 to 400, and the number of passenger coaches from 2,400 to 700. In the same period Scottish passenger train mileage fell from 23,830,000 to 20,787,000, with a much sharper fall in freight mileage, from 12,937,000 to 7,528,000[52].

Officials of the Ministry of Transport still took a keen interest in certain Scottish lines – arrangements were made for a party of seven to inspect the West Highland in the spring of 1969. To the surprise and relief of many it had escaped Beeching's list, but was still considered a potential closure by Scottish Region. While the senior civil servants looked forward to the pleasure of riding in the official saloon, it was asked if some younger members of their group might be allowed to ride in the locomotive cab. The trip was arranged while the going was still possible: as the Ministry man wrote, "we envisage only a short-term future" for the line. As a helpful hint to his railway colleagues, he suggested that if it were kept open for a time because of its winter reliability, special high winter fares could be imposed[53].

The total saving made by British Rail from closures in 1961-73 was estimated at a maximum of £16,872,104, with £7 million of this in the peak years of 1964-65. This is certainly much less than Beeching envisaged, though he never specified a total, and while some of the difference is due to refused or postponed closures, a substantial amount must be due to overstatement of the actual savings achievable by the cuts. Analysing various conflicting estimates, Dr Gourvish concluded that the true value of savings achieved "is anybody's guess"[54]. In the same period, British Railways' annual losses on operations and unpaid interest were covered by Exchequer grants totalling £822 million. In the view of one management insider, these grants, enabling the BR accounts to show "an apparent break-even" each year, created a "dangerous unreality in the financial discipline of BR management" into the 1970s[55].

The Beeching Cuts: A Footnote

Numerous analyses of the post-1994 problems experienced by railway privatisation in Britain have been produced by exponents of neo-liberal economic and commercial theory (See Appendix 1), and a recurrent *motif* is that of surprise that the general public should continue to have a "sentimental attachment" towards railways. This was expressed as early as 1973, "railway romanticism" and 1975: "railways today seem still to be seen as a national necessity, and not just as one player in the market for movement". A generation later a Labour transport minister was quoted as saying "train-spotters" had an undue influence on railway policy, by a writer who went on to say "Just what gives rise to to the British obsession with railways, rarely to be found elsewhere… is not very easy to define, but the sentiment is very real and shows no sign of going away"[56]. Accustomed to considering individual consumers as marginal units and concerned only to find the most efficient way of transporting them from point to point, they do not seem to understand that railway users might find a train the best option in their own personal terms, which might include space, comfort, speed, safety, and the totality of a pleasant travel experience, and consequently resist attempts to diminish the inherent values of rail travel or to replace it with something more cost-effective and less pleasant. To dismiss this as "sentiment" is worse than a mistake, it is a condescension. They might do well to look at the reactions to Dr Beeching's proposed cuts in the 1960s.

The furore aroused then, still evoking strong feelings 50 years later, showed

Ex-LMS Class 4F 44255 at Fort William engine shed, where it was based from 1958 to 1962. It is fitted with a snowplough and a tender cover. Ben Nevis rises above. (Stenlake Collection)

how much the presence of railways had etched itself into the national consciousness as a system whose solidity, durability, regularity, dependability and – whether well used or not – availability made an important contribution to the general sense of a linked-up and providing society. British railways faced a critical juncture in the late 1960s, which might have led to further cutting and reduction; instead, the concept of the 'social' railway began to be accepted, and with that, other positive aspects, including its low environmental impact and its increasing speed between places, became more apparent. Had the concept of a market-driven society been taken up a decade earlier, the subsidised railway would not have happened. Even so, a vocal group of economists and politicians deplored subsidisation of railways as an expensive waste of resources. The idea of converting them to roads was canvassed in some circles, but no subsequent government tried to replicate the Marples-Beeching solution. Apart from political prudence, there was also the fact that Beeching's large-scale reduction of railway mileage and services reduced the level of losses only briefly. Only once, in 1969, did the British Railways Board achieve the requirement to earn sufficient revenue to meet its running costs. The modern railway had to be seen as a necessity which required the support of public money – for successive governments and managements, the great concern would now be how that money was most efficiently spent.

7. The 1960s – 2. Adaptation and Reorganisation

Partial Decentralisation, Blue Trains

In January 1960 Scottish Region's original vertical management structure was partially decentralised, with the creation of three traffic divisions, centred on Glasgow, Edinburgh and Inverness, incorporating the commercial, operating and motive power functions. Managers took up their posts from 2 May. The divisions were headed by a traffic manager, with a team formed of commercial officer, operating officer, district goods and passenger managers, district operating superintendents, and district running and mechanical engineering officers. Although this was designed to produce a focus on maximising revenue, the commercial officer quoting rates was not responsible for investigating traffic costs, and "all important decisions on rates and fares, staff levels, and quality were taken at regional or national headquarters". Three head office positions were dispensed with: chief commercial manager (this was Stanley Raymond, later BR chairman, now promoted to assistant general manager (Traffic)), chief operating superintendent, and motive power superintendent[1]. The reorganisation, made by James Ness, was possibly made with enhancement of the general manager's role in mind, at the expense of the functional heads, but it set a precedent for Scottish Region to adapt its management methods in its own way.

From November 1960, the Caledonian Steam Packet (Irish Services) Company was formed to take over the Stranraer-Larne service from the dual control of Scottish Region and BR's Irish Shipping Service, "in accordance with the BTC's policy of decentralisation"[2], though its manager was listed among senior Scottish Region staff. Co-ordination of services continued. When from 16 December 1962 TS *Caledonian Princess* was introduced on the Stranraer-Larne route, allowing daytime crossings with a 2.30 pm sailing, the 11.30 am Glasgow-Girvan was extended to Stranraer Harbour and speeded up to make a connection[3].

Late in 1960 the Region had a major urban line problem to deal with. Phase 1 of the Glasgow area electrification was completed in November, the line running from Balloch and Helensburgh to Airdrie, crossing Glasgow on the old City & District line through Queen Street (Low Level) Station, with a loop by Drumry and Anniesland, and branches to Milngavie, Bridgeton Central, and Springburn. A special staff had been set up by Regional management in 1957 to control the project, all housed in one building. Apart from adaption of the lines for installation of the electric catenary, a new connection had to be laid between the former North British and Caledonian lines at Dunglass, to include Dumbarton East Station on the electrified line. The original electricity supply was predominantly 25kV, with sections at 6.26kV, the lower voltage allowing for reduced insulation and installation requirements in the central area (Later the whole system ran on 25kV). Glasgow's 'Blue Trains' were launched with considerable fanfare on 7 November, the new

Timetable for the new Glasgow Electric Train Services. (Hutton Collection)

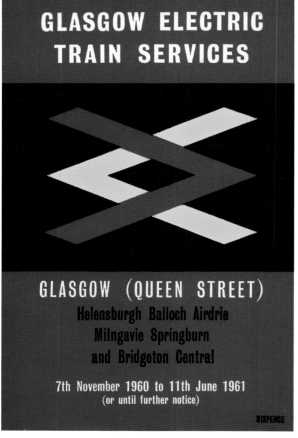

Following the withdrawal of Glasgow's new electric trains in December 1960, steam engines returned. Four ex-LNER V1/V3 2-6-2Ts, two from Glasgow Eastfield and two borrowed from Heaton (Newcastle), line up for duty. (Stenlake Collection)

line described as "the virtual demolition of an obsolescent system and the creation of a new one over its ruins"[4]. Helensburgh Central to Queen Street now took 51 minutes rather than 64. Soon, however, it became clear that there was something wrong with the Class 303 electric units. A series of explosions and fires indicated serious problems with the voltage transformers. On 30 December the Region withdrew the new trains until matters could be investigated and rectified. An emergency steam-powered service was hastily put together – no easy task as much of the necessary infrastructure for steam power had already been cleared away. Staff rallied valiantly to achieve it, but the travelling public was understandably unimpressed. Nine months elapsed before the electric units were restored, from 1 October 1961, with 400,000 journeys made in the first week: 6% less than the initial opening week, but weekly takings were noted as £17-18,000 compared with £7,000 on the previous steam workings, with five passengers for every two carried before[5].

Electrification south of the Clyde was under way and Blue Trains started running from Central Station to Kirkhill and Motherwell eastwards, to Neilston westwards, and on the Cathcart Circle, from 27 May 1962. In the first week they carried 150,000 people, three times the previous level, and taking "175% more revenue". The Corporation's transport manager was reported as saying that his department was losing £50,000 a year to the electric trains[6]. A Glasgow area timetable for September 1962 (price 6d), as well as giving Blue Train times, listed diesel-unit "Green Trains" on the Lanarkshire lines, but the label failed to stick. Electrification of Glasgow's commuter lines was clearly proving a success, and a go-ahead for the electrification of the Gourock and Wemyss Bay lines was given by the Ministry of Transport on 7 October 1964 – one of Ernest Marples's last actions before the Tory election defeat nine days later. The £6.5 million Inverclyde scheme required the lowering of the floor of Scotland's longest tunnel, Newton Street in Greenock, to provide electrical clearance from the Princes Pier line tunnel which crosses diagonally just above it[7]. Completion of the Erskine Bridge over the lower Clyde in 1967 improved road access into Renfrewshire but June of that year also saw completion of the Inverclyde electrification. Apart from providing faster and more pleasant journeys, the Blue Trains made a strongly positive contribution to the modernisation of Glasgow's public image as the city struggled to cope with the demise of its former heavy industries.

Blue Train branding also played a part in a wider exercise. A well-planned, thorough, positively intended and well-executed reform, underlining that modernisation was still on the menu as well as cuts, was the updating of British Railways' public face in 1965-66 by the introduction of the famous double-arrow logo, along with a standardised approach, using prescribed colour schemes and typography, for everything from locomotives and rolling stock to signage and documents[8]. A massive four-volume corporate identity manual was put together. The two-way arrow, created by Design Research Unit, was inspired by the double-vee intersecting blue and yellow arrowhead shape designed for the Glasgow electrification in 1960 by F.H.K. Henrion, pioneer of European corporate design. Perhaps the least successful aspect of the programme was the design of a new uniform for staff, featuring "German-style" caps and trendy 60s-style jackets that soon began to look outdated. The re-uniformed staff were working in largely-unmodernised stations, though a post-steam clean-up was

The new and the old: cover of a BR brochure explaining the reasons for closing Buchanan Street and St Enoch stations, 1966. (British Railways, Jim Summers Collection)

gradually going ahead. Clearance of old items and disposal of property was briskly under way. A queue 200 yards long formed at St. Enoch on 9 August 1968 for an event quaintly styled "Ye Old Curiosity Shoppe", selling off items from the now closed terminus and all over the Scottish region, including 10,000 prints and photographs formerly mounted in carriage compartments[9].

New Services in the 1960s

From 4 April 1960 a three-hour service was reintroduced between Edinburgh and Aberdeen, the first since 1939, for two trains with restaurant cars, making four stops, and hauled by pairs of BR-Sulzer 1160hp diesels[10]. From 1 July the fastest-ever Aberdeen-Inverness trains were put on, as a test of public demand, using diesel multiple units to make the 108-mile run in two hours 30 minutes, compared with the previous east-west 3 hours 18 minutes, and west-east three hours 32 minutes. Unsurprisingly, the public liked it, and the summer service was extended for a winter test: by April 1961 the service level was doubled, with the trains making a stop at Huntly as well as Inverurie, Keith, Elgin, Forres and Nairn[11]. Another try-out was the 'Griddle Car' on Edinburgh-Inverness trains, offering snack-type eats rather than the formal meal of the restaurant cars: a Regional press release observed that "the catering taste of the public is beginning to undergo a change"[12], and the clear subtext was "Scottish Region is keeping up with the times". The summer of 1961 saw the last non-stop trains between Waverley and Kings Cross, hauled by A4 'Pacifics' with corridor tenders. When the new 3300hp 'Deltic' locomotives took over, a stop was made at Newcastle to change crews (the journey took six hours, matching the pre-war 'Coronation' but with three trains each way daily). Competition spurred these improvements – from April 1961, with British European Airways providing 10,500 seats a week on the Glasgow-London route, "for the first time in Great Britain air travel became a real competitor in the domestic market not only for first class travel"[13].

Steam and diesel trains at St Enoch, 1961. BR Standard Class 4MT 2-6-4T 80051 of Corkerhill depot, and a Class 103 dmu (introduced 1957) on an East Kilbride service. (Stenlake Collection)

Displacement of Gresley's A4 'Pacifics' was just another detail in this most disruptive and reformative decade in railway history, but Scottish Region, troubled by the frequent failures of Type 2 diesels on the three-hour Aberdeen trains from Glasgow, took an imaginative step by replacing the diesels with redundant A4s, which maintained the route's three-hour timings until September 1966[14] To the pleasure of steam enthusiasts, this reversed the modernisers' mantra of "one diesel replaces two steam engines" with one 30-year old steam locomotive replacing and outperforming two new diesels. Other lines too were speeded up, though with diesel traction. Reviving an LMS name, the Inverness-Wick and Thurso 'Orcadian' ran the Far North line in four hours, and in June 1965 the 'Hebridean' had the fastest-ever timing between Inverness and Kyle of Lochalsh, at 2.5 hours. On the West Highland, 54 minutes were lopped from the Glasgow-Fort William timing[15]. By April 1968 the reduction in intermediate stops brought Edinburgh-Aberdeen services down to 2 hours 40 minutes and Inverness-Edinburgh and Glasgow to four hours. Observation cars were withdrawn from the Kyle and West Highland lines in January 1968; the vehicles condemned as obsolete, and the earnings insufficient to justify replacing them. The Inverness-Kyle car had been built in the First World War for the 'Devon Belle', rebuilt in 1947 and acquired by Scottish Region in 1958, running first between Glasgow and Oban, then transferred to Inverness in 1961. The two West Highland cars came from the 'Coronation' trains of 1937, rebuilt in 1958[16].

Elimination of minor stations on surviving lines enabled faster timings in the later 1960s, though the speeding-up hailed with each new timetable was of no value to the users of closed stations. Automatic Warning System installation was complete on all the electrified lines and between Glasgow and Edinburgh and Edinburgh-Berwick. Following the long freeze-up of the winter of 1962-63, as part of a BR-wide policy, 129 sets of points heaters were installed at key junctions[17]. In early 1962 Glasgow Central's acreage of soot-

Class 40 diesel No. D265 on the 'Queen of Scots Pullman' at Queen Street Station. (Stenlake Collection)

smeared glass roof panes was replaced by translucent polyester-resin sheets. "Face lift" improvements were made to nineteen stations in 1963, with seventeen more due in 1964[18].

A victim of the times was excursion traffic, due both to changing travel habits and new costing techniques which showed the practice of retaining large numbers of passenger coaches for use only at peak summer periods to be uneconomic. The 'Starlight Specials' came to an end with the 1962 season. Coaching stock, siding space and maintenance costs were substantially reduced. Once upon a time providing for the needs of the travelling public would have been the prime consideration, but private cars and luxury road coaches had eaten too far into rail usage for these cuts to generate public feeling.

Elimination of steam traction in Scotland was completed in June 1967 when the former North British (LNER Class J36) 0-6-0 engines Nos. 65288 (built 1897), and 65345 (built 1900) were withdrawn from Thornton and Dunfermline depots. The last scheduled steam-hauled passenger train had already run on 28 April that year, the 17.03 Gourock-Glasgow Central[19]. With steam power swept away, six snowploughs were mounted on converted tenders at Cowlairs Works, to be propelled by diesel engines, whose construction did not allow for the fixing of large snowploughs to the frames[20].

Freight and the
Fate of the Marshalling Yards

"Reshaping" effectively killed off what was left of the Modernisation Plan as such, though the established programmes continued, with new diesel locomotives and multiple units being deployed, and the withdrawal of steam

In 1957 two pannier tank engines (built 1951) were transferred from BR's Western Region to work the Dornoch branch, until it closed on 11 June 1960. The pair remained in the north until 1962 and No. 1649 is seen here shunting at Dingwall in 1961. (Stenlake Collection)

continuing. The Plan left in its wake three great monuments which emerged in the 1960s as a testimony to the intentions and aspirations of ten years earlier. The original plan had been for five main marshalling yards, two of which, Cadder and Mossend, already existed and would be modernised. The other three would be new. Work was already in hand on the first, at Thornton Junction in Fife, which opened in 1956, fitted with sophisticated automatic equipment imported from the USA. Coal was by far its principal traffic and the adjacent new Rothes "super-pit", opened in 1958, was expected to bring up 5,000 tons a day. In fact its output was far less and flooding brought about premature closure in 1962. Coal output from Fife was steadily falling, and the yard was progressively reduced in capacity and lost its hump shunting facility. It survived as a secondary yard into the 1980s. On 12 March 1962 the Perth yard opened. Intended to replace four old shunting yards, with six reception roads, 30 sorting sidings, and a fully automated hump-shunting system to sort wagons for 55 different destinations, it was even more than Thornton a state-of-the-art installation, with sophisticated retarders to protect whisky traffic from undesirable shocks. Providing far more capacity than the about-to-be truncated system required, and designed to handle the wagonload consignments that Beeching wanted to get rid of, the Perth yard was redundant almost from its opening. The 1962 timetable shows 58 scheduled arrivals and 54 departures, but with the closure of the Strathmore line and of most freight depots on the Highland lines, its traffic shrank far below the viability level and it was effectively closed from the late 1980s. In 2016 it was owned by DB Cargo, who were granted permission by Network Rail and the Office of Rail and Road in 2016 to sell it for non-railway purposes[21]. Millerhill yard, even bigger, was in full operation from August 1963, replacing six former yards in the Edinburgh area, with 80 sorting sidings, able to deal with 10,000 wagons a week. In 1962 coal traffic flow was improved by the Craiglockhart spur linking the line from Carstairs to the

South Suburban in Edinburgh and giving access to Millerhill. The yard straddled the Waverley line to Carlisle, but the intimated closure of that route, combined with previous closures in the area, and the demise of wagonload freight, brought about the abandonment of its Up hump yard by 1970. Residual coal, limestone and cement traffic kept the Down yard in action through the 1970s, but in 1983 it was drastically reduced, to handle a few Speedlink trains a day. Cadder yard, on the Edinburgh-Glasgow line near Bishopbriggs, received little in the way of modernisation and was run down in the 1970s. The one yard which survived and flourished was Mossend, strategically placed in the middle of the Central Belt. Its little-changed 1930s layout as a 'flat' yard was a positive advantage by 1966, when with the focus on trainload freight, hump shunting, for all its modern techniques, was becoming irrelevant to the traffic pattern. Mossend became the country's prime freight yard and a key point in the Britain-wide Speedlink network[22].

Meanwhile a vision of the trainload freight future was realised at Dunbar, where the new Blue Circle Cement works opened in September 1963, producing 400,000 tons a year to be distributed in special tanker trains, with automatic loading and unloading[23]. Britain's first regular merry-go-round coal trains, using high-capacity 33-ton hopper wagons, began between Monktonhall Colliery and the new Cockenzie Power Station in 1966. The service caused a dispute between BR and the National Coal Board, which wanted to impose a levy on tonnage carried to finance its construction of rapid-loading bunkers. After both chairmen became involved, a payment by BR of 7d a ton was agreed. Full implementation of the merry-go-round service was delayed until March 1967[24].

Rationalisation of freight was a far less public affair than for passenger services, with no need for statutory processes. Beeching's emphasis was firmly on traffic between main centres, which he expected to double between

The locomotive yard at Oban in July 1961, with the automatic coaling plant and assorted snowploughs. 0-6-0 No. 57667, ex-CR No. 311, was built in 1918 and broken up in 1962. (Stenlake Collection)

1964 and 1984, primarily in block and liner trains. Unavailing protests came from the west coast when the carriage rate of shellfish was raised by 50% and a minimum consignment of one cwt was implemented. Cancellation of a crofting co-operative's special rate meant an 87% increase on the charge between Oban and London. Scottish Region replied that it had been charging an uneconomic rate for a long time[25]. A continuous programme of freight station closures went on through the 1960s, including many branches and stations that had lost their passenger trains 30 or more years before. Aberlady and Gullane, Bonnybridge, Edzell, Fortrose, Fyvie, Kelty, Wilsontown and many others now lost their final rail links (see Appendix 7). A closures programme for 1969 listed 33 locations, nine in the Highland area, eleven and sixteen in the Glasgow and Edinburgh areas respectively[26]. In some cases, like Lesmahagow, Neilston (Low Level) and New Cumnock, freight closure preceded that of the passenger service. The "feeder" contribution of these lines and stations was discounted: in single wagonload quantities at best, it was too expensive to collect and deliver. The veteran steam goods engines built to deal with such traffic had gone to the breakers.

In line with the aim of a slimmer and profitable service, local closures were paralleled by new developments in liner freight, using permanently-coupled wagon sets operating from point to point. One of the first Freightliner container terminals was opened at Gushetfaulds, Glasgow, on 15 November 1965. Vigorously marketed[27], the service got off to a successful start, almost too much so in the case of Gushetfaulds, where lack of containers and difficulties with handling equipment made it struggle to cope with the demand from customers. It was controversial both with the road haulage industry and the rail unions; the former seeing serious competition over long-distance carriage and the latter refusing to countenance non-BR vehicles using the terminals. An indication of the road hauliers' reaction was seen in the 87 objections made to British Rail's application for licences for sixteen articulated lorries to take containers to and from the Glasgow and Aberdeen terminals: the licence was granted but the hauliers appealed (in vain) because the railways started running the lorries before the appeal was held[28]. Freightliner terminals opened in Aberdeen and Edinburgh (Portobello) in January 1968, the new facilities expected to almost double the 1967 turnover of £800,000. The Edinburgh service was reported as running at 96% capacity[29]. The "dry port" terminal at Coatbridge, also opened in 1968, was set up primarily to handle deep-sea containers to and from harbours.

There was more controversy in 1967 when the state-owned Transport Holding Company, concerned with road haulage, bought first a 50% stake, then full control of Tartan Arrow, a private haulage company which had made a 20-year contract with BR in mid-1965 for a chartered railfreight service between mechanised terminals at Bridgeton (Glasgow) and Kentish Town (London), with Tartan Arrow doing the deliveries at each end. The NUR interpreted this as an aggressive move that could threaten the whole Freightliner venture, and the British Railways Board also objected. The dispute was resolved when the BRB took a 50% share with the Transport Holding Company, and a final settlement with the union, enabling open use of the terminals, was made on 7 June[30]. An £8 million 10-year contract was signed with Colvilles in May 1965, for coal haulage of two million tons a year from twenty collieries in the Central Belt to the Ravenscraig and Clyde steelworks. Imported ore traffic from the General Terminus quay in Glasgow was booming, with an increase from 915,146 tons in 1962 to 1,894,569 tons in the first eleven months of 1964. Fifty wagons were rebuilt to carry timber on the West Highland line from a concentration point at Crianlarich to a new pulp mill at Corpach[31]. There was a follow-up to the Second Stage, providing an evaluation of the contribution made by remaining supply or feeder lines to the designated trunk routes, but its findings were never made public[32].

In 1966 the Region ceded management of its Sundries (parcels) traffic to a new Freight Sundries Division which included the British Road Services parcels operation, and the 1968 Transport Act created a new body, the National Freight Corporation, which absorbed the substantial surviving remnant of British Road Services and was also given a controlling 51% share of Freightliners, leaving BR with a minority stake and no control over what was now a 'standalone' company. It also took over the Freight Sundries division, renamed National

Supporters of Hibernian FC at Princes Street Station, Edinburgh, in the early 1960s. (Author's Collection)

Carriers Ltd, acting as BR's cartage agents under a contract-hire arrangement. The reorganised rail freight services were required to earn revenues at least matching their costs. Despite a succession of action plans – "Freight Action Programme IV" was launched in November 1969 – and a drive on punctuality and performance, with a new post of General Manager (Movements), plus two assistants, created to monitor freight movements[33], and valiant efforts to achieve cost-effective ways of maintaining single wagonload consignments, including an early computer-based system, FRATE (formulation of routes and technical equipment), usage and earnings continued to fall[34].

The Setting Up of 'Two-Tier' Management

James Ness departed to BRB headquarters in London in 1963, appointed board member for planning. He was succeeded by W.G. Thorpe, from the London Midland Region, who also took over from Lochiel as chairman of the area board from 1964. Terence Gourvish remarks that there is no evidence that Ness had been involved in any radical initiatives in the Robertson regime, which is a little unfair as there were numerous positive actions, and labels him "obviously a Beeching man" and one of Beeching's "leading disciples". Ness appears to have had difficulties with colleague relationships: James Stevenson (later Scottish Region Planning and Investment Manager), who worked for him, regarded him as "the outstanding General Manager in Scotland in the early years… a complete autocrat but a man of constant drive and immense ability". When Stanley Raymond succeeded Beeching as BRB chairman, he "got rid of Ness"; their antipathy going back to Raymond's time in Glasgow. Ness "was asked to retire early" in January 1966, eighteen months before his contract date[35].

The new post of regional planning officer had been approved by the BRB in 1959. It took eight weeks of correspondence, for a middle-range position with a salary in the £2,400-£3,025 range. Things seem to have slipped back from 1959, when the Region was authorised to fill all posts up to the level of deputy head of department[36]. Forward planning became a formalised procedure for the first time with the creation of a planning group from December 1964. Chaired by the deputy general manager, it was intended to spread the planning function across all activities, not just new works, and had authority to accord priority to projects and to allocate technical time, but it did not achieve a strong presence. Under Thorpe, planning began for a big change in the Region's management structure. The three traffic divisions had been operating since 1960; now it was proposed to remove the divisional management level altogether and enhance the role of local area managers, who would report direct to Regional HQ. The supporting argument was that ongoing cuts and closures would diminish workload and administration, with a estimated fall in staff numbers from 35,000 in 1965 to 25,000 in 1970; efficiency and coping with change would be improved; and the clincher – 300 managerial jobs would be eliminated, with a saving of £350,000. It was also felt safe to assume that Scottish Region had a future (Beeching was known to favour a reduced number of regions). An outline paper was drawn up in July 1966 and sent to the chairman of the BRB Management Staff Committee. Stating that effective production needed management close to the ground, and "a lot of it", it proposed a total of 88 second-tier posts, 50 as area managers, the others as managers of freight and motive power depots, and the three major stations. Maintenance engineers would be reorganised on a similar but not necessarily co-terminous basis. At the same time, organisation of head office staff would be changed to ensure effective reporting and response. There would be five service planning managers for suburban passenger, InterCity, trainload freight, wagonload freight, sundries and parcels, but no passenger sales manager: "decisions to travel by rail result mainly from service planning factors rather than because people respond to a direct sales effort. The pattern of train services, i.e. the timetable, the fares structure and general publicity campaigns which are integral parts of the responsibility of a service planning manager… will generate the great bulk of passenger travel"[37]. The quotation shows that Regional thinking had some way yet to go before the concept of adjusting the service to passenger needs, rather than vice versa, could take hold. But the same was true at BRB headquarters, where the paper was circulated to directors and departmental heads, drawing a cautiously favourable response in most cases. However, a more detailed proposal was asked for, and a steering group and a set of working parties were formed to produce a blueprint. Rumours of a new Scottish Region set-up were circulating in the railway press from early 1965[38], suggesting that *districts* were abolished, leaving the three divisions as "the one internal tier of command except in sales promotion": the reverse of actuality. At this time, however, a unique arrangement was made for the Inverness Division, which became responsible for every aspect of railway management: traffic, locomotive running, civil engineering, signal and telegraph engineering, and estate, from Kyle to Inveramsay and from Thurso to Stanley Junction, under the rubric of 'Highland Lines', headed by Bernard Allison. This was the first phase of a deliberate experiment, with the future regional management pattern very much in mind.

The departures indicator at Inverness, circa 1961. The lack of Sunday trains is notable. (Stenlake Collection)

In 1967 Thorpe was moved to London, where he would be deputy chairman and ultimately chief executive of the BRB: his presence at the top no doubt helped acceptance of the Two-Tier scheme, now taken up by his successor, Gordon Stewart. While the final proposal was still being compiled, an investigation into the possible disbandment of the Highland Lines organisation was begun in January 1967[39]. Having been for a short time a test-area for devolved management on a divisional level, the Highlands were now to be used for a try-out of complete elimination of the divisional tier. In August the go-ahead was given for this to happen, and its replacement by a set of eleven area managers reporting directly to head office in Glasgow. Stewart wrote in August to A.R. Dunbar, another Scot in the upmost echelon of BR, who had joined the North British in 1922, and could claim, like a diminishing number of others, to have experienced three forms of railway management: "… the reasons for the setting-up of the Highland Division are well-known to you and it can be said that the task of rationalisation it was set up to perform is well-nigh complete[40]. This was implemented by 1 January 1968 and the staff at Inverness was reduced from 72 to 55. A three-man management unit team remained: commercial officer, outdoor superintendent, and depot engineer[41]. Three management structures had been tried out at Inverness within a few years: divisional (essentially traffic management), autonomous, and two-tier. The altered system worked satisfactorily, especially to the satisfaction of the chief civil engineer, who once again had direct functional control of the area engineers[42]. Erosion of divisional responsibility was already happening: a Regional train planning unit set up in 1967 took this out of divisional managers' hands, leaving them responsible for achieving divisional budgets but without control of the trains[43]. With a comment from Stewart that "Our experience with two-tier management in the Highland territory and the results of the wider examination point quite definitely to two-tier as the logical development of Scottish Region organisational pattern" ('Territory' was a buzz-word at the time: McKinsey was proposing to scrap regions in favour of eight territories), the detailed proposal was submitted to the Scottish Area Board on 5 June 1968, which gave its approval, and the BRB approved it on 8 August. Implementation of 'Two-Tier' went ahead through 1969, with everything in place by 3 November[44]. At a time when the British Railways Board, as required by Section 45 of the 1968 Transport Act, was contemplating a wide-ranging shake-up of regional management, the acceptance of this bold initiative (no outside consultancy involved) from a single region was surprising, but it was seen by at least some as an experiment which, if successful, could be a model for application elsewhere.

The head office structure was now: chairman & general manager, with five assistant general managers covering staff, technical, commercial, movements, and finance. In addition were the legal adviser and the manager of the Caledonian Steam Packet Co. The assistant general managers' teams amounted to 32 functional managers, who were in constant touch with the 64 area/depot managers (see Appendix 2).

In January 1968 the civil engineering department, with 4,213 employees, was reorganised on its own divisional basis, with four divisional heads reporting to the chief civil engineer, and signals & telecommunications (955 employees) were reorganised on similar lines but for some unexplained reason, not in the same geographical areas. The chief mechanical & electrical engineer's department was reported in May 1968 as "run presently from HQ to Divisions, with area managers, depot engineers, etc." Some 500 staff would move to the head office. It was stressed that reallocation of reponsibilities was directed *upwards*, in the now reduced operating system[45].

During the years it took to set up Two-Tier, there were changes which affected Regional activity. Efficiency-related pay agreement had been reached with clerical staff, other staff had been transferred to National Carriers and Freightliner, and a new Parcels operation, as required by the BRB, had been set up. The net result of the restructuring, in terms of savings, was a good deal less than the forecast: 126 jobs were lost, at a saving of £165,890, or 190 posts and £193,890 if the merging of the accounts and audit offices were added in. But the new arrangement undoubtedly was beneficial, tightening up lines of communication and making the Regional business faster on its feet. As part of the McKinsey 'Field' project, a survey of the area managers was conducted in 1970, with broadly positive findings. Respondents complained mostly about their salary levels, while finding their jobs to be usually "interesting, exciting, varied, giving a sense of achievement and making use of their skills and abilities". Also noted was the "here we go again" reaction to organisational change, though most felt this particular change had been necessary and beneficial[46].

Scotland's biggest commercial office building, Buchanan House, with 210,000 square feet of offices, was completed on 3 November 1969 on the site once occupied by Buchanan Street Station's carriage sidings, to house Regional HQ's 2000 staff. (It was renamed ScotRail House on 3 January 1985). Publicity and public relations employed 49 people, legal affairs 35, finance 752, stores control 30.

In September 1967 Scottish Region employed 28,963 staff, down from from 34,994 in 1965. Apart from managerial grades, they included 2,597 drivers and 1,781 firemen (though no steam locomotives), 390 cleaners, 1,642 guards, 2,112 signalmen, 830 shunters, 1,674 porters, 228 ticket collectors, and 703 other traffic grades. Goods handling accounted for 1,538, cartage for 1,045, locomotive sheds for 431, carriage & wagon staff for 1,260, police for 231, and 'others' for four. There were 3,618 employed in maintenance & construction and 2956 in engineering workshops. In addition there were 740 shipping staff and 186 in docks and wharves.

Industrial Relations in the 1960s

Discussions on different aspects of the business were going on in other ways. Among them was a seven-year dialogue from 1960 to 1968 with the unions, increasingly centred on productivity bargaining rather than on comparison with other industries. New technology and new ways of doing things all ended up in reduction of staff numbers, with the most obvious examples being the lack of need for a fireman in a locomotive with no fire and designed to be driven by one man; and the lack of need for a guard and his brake van on a freight train fitted with continuous automatic brakes. Weapons of industrial dispute, working to rule, strikes, go-slows, were deployed as the rail unions fought first for jobs to be retained, then for pay levels to rise in line with the responsibility of one-man train operation, or of signalmen who had to master electronic systems covering dozens of miles. Productivity – more revenue from fewer staff, was what the management sought. Much of the productivity savings were absorbed by higher costs of equipment, as mechanised methods in track-laying and maintenance were introduced, and British Railways was also an early user of computers[47], while the unions argued for a share of the productivity savings to be paid to the depleted workforce. In 1965 the government-established Board for Prices and Incomes rejected cross-industry wages comparison. Eventually, in 1968 a productivity deal was negotiated with the NUR and ASLEF as Stage One of an ongoing pay and efficiency review. The old railway job descriptions gave way to a new set of job titles: railman, senior railman, leading railman, chargeman, with pay differentials based partly on length of service and partly on responsibility.

The 1968 Transport Act

A change of political outlook from the Marples-Beeching period was expected with the election of a Labour government in 1964. A new perspective finally came in 1965, when Barbara Castle took over from Tom Fraser after his brief term as Minister of Transport. While the presence of numerous rail union-sponsored MPs might be expected to make a Labour administration look more favourably on railways than a Conservative one, this was not axiomatic: antipathy to the railways was entrenched as strongly in the mighty Transport & General Workers Union, and other road industry unions, as it was in the boardrooms of the road transport companies, and backroom pressure against concesssions to rail transport could be strong. However, the Transport Act of 1968 marked an important new step in the political management of railways in Britain by accepting the necessity, for social reasons, of subsidising selected railway services. These would receive grants, for specific periods of time, to keep them running. Twenty years before, the LMS and LNER had proudly claimed that Britain's railways had never required a subsidy. The maximum period of grants initially was three years, and among the Scottish lines to be supported were Glasgow-Perth-Inverness (£294,000), Glasgow-Dundee (£249,000), and Aberdeen-Inverness (£290,000), sums eclipsed by grants to the Glasgow North and Glasgow South electric systems, of £1,445,000 and £1,051,000 respectively in 1969. In 1969-70, £9,463,000 of subsidy went to maintain 30 Scottish routes[48]. The Act also wrote off much of BR's very large capital debt. In order to focus on the transport needs of large conurbations, Passenger Transport Authorities were to be set up (none in Scotland at this time). The railway freight business was also addressed, with British Railways' loss-making sundries-carrying business

Will such a scene be repeated? A Class 101 diesel unit at Leven Station, pre-1969. (North British Railway Study Group)

hived off as a subsidiary of a new entity, the National Freight Corporation, becoming National Carriers Ltd. In 1968 NCL had fifteen depots in Scotland, deploying 841 small articulated vehicles, 100 rigid lorries and 2,388 semi-trailers[49]. As already noted, the NFC also took control of the Beeching-inspired Freightliner container service, though British Rail would retrieve control in August 1978).

Regions had lost responsibility for engineering workshops in another Beeching-instigated change, in 1962, which hived them off into a separate management unit. Now a further provision of the 1968 Act was to give the workshops, facing a lower workload from the slimmed-down system, freedom to seek contracts from outside customers. They were incorporated in a separate company, British Rail Engineering Ltd (BREL), which promptly embarked on "rationalisation" of its facilities. Cowlairs Works was shut down in 1968, and Inverurie, where the works and 580-strong workforce were the mainstay of the local economy, followed in 1969: despite low costs, an excellent industrial relations record, and the installation of new equipment in 1964[50]. Barassie Works were closed in 1972, and Townhill in 1982, leaving only St. Rollox (renamed Glasgow Works) as a railway engineering facility in Scotland. Ships, hotels and property management remained responsibilities of BR, for the time being.

The 1968 Act also established the state-owned Scottish Transport Group, including the Caledonian Steam Packet and MacBrayne companies with the former Scottish Bus Group (originally formed in 1961 and part of the Transport Holding Company since 1962. In 1968 it operated 4,700 buses). Scottish Region now ceased to have any control over the CSP and the Kyle-Kyleakin ferry. Section 38 (4) of the Act removed the requirement on the BRB to maintain regional boards, though it did not formally abolish them, and the

Largs Station on 18 July 1968. The holiday period is reflected by the number of trains, with three class 107 and one Class 105/6 diesel units visible, and a BR Class 20 locomotive on an excursion train. (Photo John Alsop)

Scottish area board continued in being. For Scotland an important aspect of the Act was its citing the Secretary of State and not the Minister of Transport as the authority on certain Scottish matters, necessary because of the integrated rail/road aspect of the National Freight Corporation, and the possible formation of Scottish Passenger Transport Authorities. Section 20 (4) of the Act enabled PTAs to make payments to the British Railways Board in respect of passenger services. Section 24 (3) required the Railways Board and the new Scottish Transport Group to co-operate in co-ordinating passenger services. However, the MoT continued to have responsibility for railways in Scotland while the Scottish Office had charge of roads. This separation of roles was a distinct hindrance to any sort of co-ordinated approach on transport, and certainly did not encourage the Scottish Office to take any initiative where railways were concerned.

The Last Hotel

Scotland's last railway hotel opened at St. Andrews in June 1968, built on the site of the one-time goods station. The town's railway link to Leuchars Junction was already earmarked for closure in January 1969: not a Beeching cut but a Scottish Region one – a further indication that regional management fully embraced closure mode. The resultant loss in receipts was put at £32,380 and the estimated saving in direct costs as £47,110. Here was a prime example of a branch which could have been made profitable if it was not already so[51]. Scottish railways had once built stations for their hotels, as at Turnberry and Cruden Bay – now a hotel was built where a railway was being shut down. The hotel was, however, the responsibility not of Scottish Region, but the British Transport Hotels Division, of which W.G. Thorpe, Regional general manager from 1963 to to 1967, was a director. Its construction budget of £700,000 was overrun by 20%. In 1970 it made a loss of £60,000 instead of the £123,000 profit forecast[52].

8. The 1970s

In the 1970s a sense of comparative stability was restored to the railway system, but with stagnant passenger numbers, falling goods traffic and rising costs the issue of finance remained dominant. The future did not look promising. For Scottish Region the decade held new relationships and new opportunities to grow freight traffic.

Will the Railways Ever Break Even?

In 1969, Lord (as he by then was) Beeching had the satisfaction of hearing that the Railways Board had met its target, achieving a surplus of revenue (including grants) over working costs. Unfortunately, this was the only time such a thing happened. By 1971 its annual deficit was again large and growing, despite the subsidies to selected lines, and it became clear that an annual, and accumulating, deficit was unavoidable. Back in 1960, only one answer to this had been available, and a powerful element in the Ministry of Transport, including its Permanent Secretary, Peter Baldwin, clung to the notion that further slimming down of the network would produce a profitable "core railway". Richard Marsh, who had succeeded Barbara Castle as Minister of Transport in 1968-69, left a political career for big business as chairman of the BRB in 1971, holding the post until 1976, commissioned studies on the effect that further cuts would have on costs. The conclusion was that the impact would be minimal, due to the fixed costs that would remain, against diminished revenues because of the loss of income from 'feeder' services to the trunk routes. There really was no such thing as a profitable core railway, and any attempt to create one would require huge capital spending. Further cuts would also have a social and economic (not to mention political) impact, which the 1968 Act had already acknowledged. Social factors had to be included in future railway costing. Cost benefit analysis, using a financial formula to balance the benefits of a scheme against its costs, had been introduced into official planning procedures in the 1960s. Though not applied in the Beeching reviews, it was now increasingly used as a tool. These findings strengthened the BRB's resolve, though scepticism in the Ministry of Transport remained strong[1]. The Scottish Office by now had more involvement in railway matters, including powers to award grants for railway and railway-related projects, but its view of the value of railways is not clear. An inside observer noted that when the Ministry of Transport and BR joint committee on grant applications came to Edinburgh in 1968 to consider Scottish lines, the Scottish Office representatives "were not the most unbiased reviewers of grant applications : after all, it was Whitehall money, from another department's vote, which was being spent"[2]. Scottish civil

Waverley Station's booking hall before modernisation. It could almost be the interior of a church. (Stenlake Collection)

Passengers head for an Edinburgh train at Glasgow Queen Street in the early 1970s, with a 'Derby Sulzer' at each end. D7579 was renumbered 25229 on 31 December 1973. Built in 1963, it was withdrawn in 1985.

servants would have been well aware of the still-raw wounds left by the Beeching cuts, and of the potential public anger if more were enforced.

Though the 1968 Transport Act is remembered for its acknowledgement of the "social railway", it failed like the 1962 Act and the Beeching reforms in its principal intention, which was to make the railway balance its books. Apart from the brief flicker of 1969, British Rail appeared incapable of making ends meet. The extremely large sums of public money involved attracted the attention of neo-liberal economists to this failure and whether there was any remedy. For any advocate of a free market economy, Britain's railways, state-owned, subsidised, loss-making, were a glaring example of what should not be allowed. As neo-liberal ideas spread from think-tanks into the public and political domain, the status of the railways would remain an irritant. This should not be confused with an inherently anti-railway outlook. For Pryke and Dodgson, for example, subsidisation of railway passenger services was a "costly and inefficient way of dealing with the social and environmental costs to which roads give rise", and also a bad case for public subsidy because they were used primarily by the better-off[3]. They considered it was preferable to increase road pricing. Noting that in 1974 the output per man-year on BR had increased by only 2% since 1969, they also identified both the need for and the possibility of a vast increase in efficiency. Their figures[4] for the contribution of the total population's five income groups to railway earnings showed:

First quintile (poorest 20%): 5% of total
Second quintile: 8.8% of total
Third quintile: 13.5% of total
Fourth quintile: 21.7% of total
Fifth quintile (richest 20%): 51% of total

Of course, first class fares help to swell the wealthiest quintile's contribution. These figures, no doubt based on estimates and limited surveys, were widely influential. Their accuracy with respect to Scotland, where such a large proportion of rail travel is within the former Strathclyde Region, is uncertain. The general inference that railway travel is beyond the means of the poorest members of society can be answered in different ways: it is equally true of all other forms of consumption. But just as the notion of the social railway was taking hold, so the damaging one of "the rich man's railway" was emerging. Gradually, a new ideology was shaping up and by the end of the decade its influence on railway management would be strong.

Regional Affairs

Back in the realm of the actual, in November 1969 a landslip on the Dingwall-Kyle line at Attadale had offered a closure opportunity, but remedial work was prompt and it reopened after two weeks. In 1970 the BRB listed the line for closure when its grant of £175,000 a year was to expire in 1971 and the (Labour) Minister of Transport was said to have made the "tentative conclusion" that it should be closed as not representing value for money[5]. Neither William Ross, the Secretary of State, who had fought his Cabinet colleagues over the Waverley Route closure, nor his Tory successor in June 1970, Gordon Campbell, was prepared to accept this conclusion. Campbell said in December 1972 that "he was not currently engaged in any discussion of reorganisation of the railway system in Scotland" and that there was no threat to the main Highland lines[6]. Still, uncertainty over the line's future continued until June 1974 when the Transport Minister, Fred Mulley, asked BR not to proceed with a re-proposed closure. Oil industry developments helped to ensure its survival. Despite Labour's more positive view of the "social" railway, it instituted some closures. A significant one was the line between Kinross and Bridge of Earn in Spring 1970, which had not been on the Beeching list. This appeared to have been at government instigation in order to use part of the trackbed for the new M90 motorway, and services from Edinburgh to Perth and the Highlands had to be redirected by Larbert and Stirling. In 1975 the Ladybank-Bridge of Earn railway, which had lost its passenger traffic in 1955, had it restored to provide

Carstairs Station in 1970, four years before the West Coast Main Line electrification was completed. (Photo Nigel Mundy)

a slightly more direct route. However, apart from that, new closures virtually ceased, for political rather than operational reasons. Charles Loft makes the shrewd point that "politically, cutting investment was much easier"[7], and service cuts were made, with the Scottish TUCC approving withdrawal of passenger trains between Glasgow and Kirkcaldy, and Dalry and Kilmarnock in 1972, also the closure of Fairlie Pier[8]. Perhaps as a headquarters rather than a regionally-inspired action, the BRB identified the Far North, West Highland and Oban lines to the Ministry of Transport as suitable candidates for closure in 1974 and the same lines were listed among 44 services reported by the Board in 1975 to the Minister of Transport as having a "limited future, but neither Tory (1970-74) nor Labour governments (1974-79) made any move to shut them down.

To an extent, the Region took stock of itself in a 1970 report[9] which though primarily on the Central Belt gave some all-Scotland figures.

	January 1963	**October 1970**
Route miles	3100	1954
Track miles	4781	3157
Passenger stations	671	283
Freight stations	891	124
Signal boxes	995	485
Staff numbers	47,063 (including workshops)	22,462 (excluding workshops)

Scottish Region's freight tonnage in 1969 was 21.1 million tons, compared with 21.4 million tons in 1966, and receipts were £20 million against £22.6 million (of the 1969 figure over 30% came from coal, and 20% from iron and steel). Passenger journeys in 1966 numbered 65.8 million, rising to 68.5 million in 1969, with receipts rising from £14.47 million to £16.7 million. The railways' estimated share of all passenger journeys (including private motoring) rose from from 4.57% in 1966 to 5.41%. For British Railways, 1970 was the "break year" when passenger revenue surpassed that of freight[10] but in Scotland freight was still ahead, though the gap was closing.

The report did not venture into the field of costs against revenue, but though it congratulated its own begetters on their "energetic and creative approach", the results, positive though they were, were modest enough after a substantial shedding of costs and the assumptions of growth put forward in the Modernisation Plan. The two-tier refocusing of management no doubt helped to keep traffic figures up, and a sense of optimism in the Region's management is detectable. Freight traffic was set to gain from new car factories at Bathgate and Linwood, and new steel works at Motherwell and Glengarnock. The coal industry was contracting, but 26 collieries were still at work in the Central Belt, while proving of the North Sea oil deposits began in the late 1960s, showing Scotland to have large off-shore reserves. Planned capital investment was a little over £7 million in 1970, rising to £12-14 million in 1972-73 before falling back again. This took into account the Region's share of the West Coast Main Line electrification (approved between Weaver Junction and Glasgow in 1970), improvements between Edinburgh and Glasgow, alterations at the Mossend yard, and the rebuilding of the Eastfield motive power depot. Beyond that, the report envisaged electrification of the Hamilton Circle in 1974-75 and noted that the Greater Glasgow Transportation Study of 1968 had recommended the reopening and electrification of the Glasgow Central low level line (The study also recommended the forming of a north-south 'crossrail' link in Glasgow with

Carstairs Station in 1970. These buildings have since been demolished, apart from the footbridge, and replaced by a modern structure. (Stenlake Collection)

200 yards of new track curving between High Street and Bell Street, not mentioned in the Scottish Region report). The Region was receiving £9.4 million in grant aid for unremunerative services, of which £7.7 million was for services within or originating in the Central Belt. Critical observers noted that in the mid-70s Scotland still had very few pay trains and 88% of the Region's stations were still staffed. In 1972 automatic ticket barriers had been introduced on the Inverclyde lines, resulting in receipts rising by an estimated 11%[11], but the initiative was not being followed up.

Planning of the electrification of the West Coast Main Line caused the re-airing of an old controversy from the early 1840s, over whether the Carlisle-Glasgow railway should go by Lockerbie and Carstairs or by Dumfries and Kilmarnock. Particularly as electrification of the Carstairs-Edinburgh line was not part of the original plan, a strong body of opinion felt that the electric catenary should follow the old G&SWR route, tapping larger centres of population and industry. As before, though, the Caledonian route was preferred[12]. Completion of electrification into Glasgow Central was celebrated on 6 May 1974. New Class 87 electric locomotives with a continuous rating of 5,000 hp could pull 500-ton trains at speeds of up to 100 mph, and regular block sections of 1,340 yards enabled a 2.5 minute headway. A single signal box at Motherwell controlled the entire distance from Carlisle to Glasgow[13]. On this route, for the first time, standard class carriages had air-conditioning.

Scottish Region and Strathclyde

In 1973 a very important new partnership was formed, when the Greater Glasgow Passenger Transport Authority was established. This body, which also took responsibility for transport throughout the newly-formed Strathclyde region in 1975, owned and operated Glasgow city buses and the Subway, and was responsible for co-ordination of Scottish Bus Group, British

Loading timber at Crianlarich (Lower) in the 1980s. Class 37408 *Loch Rannoch* of Eastfield Depot heads the train. (Photo: Roger Geach)

Railway and Cal-Mac steamer services, all state-owned. It had an interest in more than half of the Scottish Region's business, and held the purse-strings of public subsidy. Also in 1973, important long-term implications for the railways were to be found in the Local Government (Scotland) Act, a Conservative measure which gave regional and island councils responsibility for roads, traffic management, and "promotion and provision of a co-ordinated and efficient system of public transport". This last point brought about a new approach to regional transport planning, known as Transport Policies and Programmes, with each region developing a structure plan, on five-year time-spans. Involvement and liaison in these was seen by Scottish Region management as vital, and the rail side quickly discovered that regional planners often had little notion of what the railways could do, especially in freight traffic. Information and education were necessary and it was at this time that a Director for Public Affairs was first appointed, in the person of Bert Gemmell, formerly an area manager. He quickly attracted the notice of Sir Peter Parker, BR chairman from 1976 to whom he wrote on 4 December 1978: "If we are honest the world thinks we are: Victorian and fuddy-duddy, bureaucratic, inflexible, non-commercial, unsympathetic and witless, expensive and poor value for money, an overpaid, unreliable army of tea-drinkers." Parker, most approachable of chairmen, cordially agreed[14]. It was not enough to be in contact with actual and potential customers – transport was now within the remit of other bodies, not only the local authorities but the Scottish Development Department, the Highlands & Islands Development Board, and the Scottish Development Agency. Positive relationships with all these were essential if the railway, whether commercial or social, was to keep a profile. Restoration of double track on the Highland Main Line from Blair Atholl to Dalwhinnie was helped by £3.7 million worth of support from the Scottish Development Department[15].

The 1974 Transport Act

The years between 1972 and 1979 were a difficult time, with economic recession including the "three-day week" of January-March 1974 and the "Winter of Discontent" in 1978-79, and accompanied by currency inflation which compelled substantial increases in rail charges and pay rates. British Railways were hit in three ways. The price of oil doubled between 1973 and 1976. The economic slow-down reduced traffic, which was also affected by coal strikes in January-February 1972 and February-March 1974. Inflation of the currency (the pound sterling lost almost 27% of its purchasing value in 1974-75 and inflation reached 26.9%) caused urgent wage demands from staff. Meanwhile the government was struggling to hold down inflation through a policy of wage restraint, by which public service employees, including railway workers, were most directly affected. In Scottish Region, general managers came and went: four within the decade, and other senior staff were often transferred from region to HQ or another region, under a long-established policy perhaps designed to avoid personal fiefdoms, but which at least gave its executives experience of the whole system. Usefully, too, it enabled contacts, friendships, and exchanges of favours which helped to bypass potentially lengthy procedures, or the opposition or inertia of the occasional functionary who did things only by the book. Having done its own restructuring in the 1960s, the Region largely escaped the BRB's attempt to reorganise its regional operations through the 'Field' system devised at enormous expense by the McKinsey management consultancy, and abandoned in January 1975 because of "implementation problems"[16].

In January 1973 the BRB drew up an "Interim Rail Strategy" for the next nine years, estimating that subsidies apart, there would be an annual loss of £70 million a year. Offering 73 cuts to provincial services and staff reductions of 40,000, it sought investment of £1,787 million over the period. The new Labour government in 1974 duly produced a new Transport Act, the first that had to make its provisions comply with European Economic Community regulations.

Adopting the terminology of a British Railways policy review submitted to the preceding Tory government in December 1972, the Act distinguished between the "viable" (i.e. profitable) railway, basically InterCity trains and the freight business, and the "necessary" (but not profitable) railway. It also accepted that overall viability was not possible and that the necessary railway should be more effectively provided for than in the 1968 Act. While nothing specifically relating to Scotland is included in the Act, its provisions undoubtedly helped to secure the preservation of lines and services which made a loss. Firstly, it accepted that viability of the whole system could not be achieved even by further large-scale closures; secondly it scrapped the time-related subsidies for specific lines in favour of a global block grant to fund the "Public Service Obligation" of the railway, up to £1,500 million a year, as provided for in EEC regulation 1191/69[17]. None other than Margaret Thatcher pointed out in the debate on the Second Reading of the Bill that the EEC regulation also allowed grants for individual lines: the reason for switching to the blanket grant was that virtually all lines appeared to have a claim for support. Thirdly, the Act stated that the BRB should provide a public service comparable with its current one. This did not deter Scottish Region from continuing to put up closure prospects. In 1975-77 the only passenger closures implemented were Ayr-Ardrossan and Ayr-Mauchline. A leaked BRB document of September 1979 proposing a range of lines across England and Scotland for closure listed Ardrossan-Largs, Stranraer-Ayr, Markinch-Cowdenbeath, Fort William-Mallaig, Dingwall-Kyle, Crianlarich-Oban and Drem-North Berwick[18]. None was implemented by government, though the proposals may have originated within its own Ministry of Transport. Stewart Joy, formerly chief economist at the BRB and a keen proponent of a reduced railway system, wrote: "Hardly any member of the general public knows that British Rail only makes it (sic) closure proposals at the invitation of the Minister, and after he has decided a prima facie case for closure exists"[19]. The effect of this batting to-and-fro of closure suggestions between Marylebone and Whitehall was to increase public uncertainty about the lines' future, while at regional level no attempt was made to improve marketing or services on lines which might be summarily axed.

Traffic Plans and Innovations

New investment was largely confined to InterCity, London commuter services and trainload freight[20], but Scotland had two areas of modernisation. Passenger numbers on Glasgow-Edinburgh trains, formed of 1957-vintage diesel m-u sets, were falling from 1970 onwards. With much of the M8 motorway open even before final completion in 1980, and 70 mph road coaches anticipated, arrangements for a speed-up began in 1971, re-signalling the route for 90 mph operation (at this time 75 mph was the maximum on any Scottish line) by Class 27 locomotive-hauled trains, one at each end, reducing journey time from 55 to 45 minutes. This was a unique traction arrangement for British Rail. Colin Boocock, then regional rolling stock engineer, recalled that it was a difficult service to maintain, especially in winter, but 5% traffic growth was maintained. In 1977 authority was obtained for new trains, using 34 up-to-date Mk 3A coaches from London Midland Region, twelve class 47 engines, modified as 47/7, and ten Mk2F brake vans fitted with driving cabs to enable push-pull working[21]. The engines were uprated to run at a maximum of 100 mph, as much a publicity point as an operational one[22]. Introduced from 22 October 1979, they provided a more comfortable and reliable service until replaced by new multiple unit stock in 1990. Even where no investment was made, it was possible for an active area manager to make service improvements by analysis and reshaping of existing traffic patterns: this was done in Fife in the early 1970s, where the local Kirkcaldy and Cowdenbeath services acquired the suggestive identity of 'Fiferail'.

In 1974 a joint Scottish Region and GGPTE 'Clyderail' proposal was drawn up and submitted to the Scottish Office for an infrastructure grant. Phase 1 of the programme included electrification of the cross-city line through Glasgow Central (Low Level), closed since October 1964, and the construction of an underground-overground interchange station at Partick. A £12 million government grant was authorised. Phase 2 included improvements of the Queen Street electrified line and provision of the often-discussed north-south link in Glasgow, but no funding was granted and these projects went into abeyance[23]. As one of the first results of the Scottish Region-SPTA partnership, the Central line was reinstated with electric traction in November 1979, and renamed the Argyle Line, with trains initially between Dumbarton and Motherwell. A study of its impact on city traffic five months later showed a lower increase in rail patronage than had been expected, and the proportion of 19% of new passengers being former motor car users was considered disappointing[24].

Across the region, however, the diesel locomotives and multiple units introduced in the late 1950s were showing signs of age, and replacements were not in sight. Standards of performance and the state of operational morale were both low. BR's new chairman Sir Peter Parker, thought the railways' fortunes at "an achingly low ebb"[25] in 1986. Parker got off to an uncertain start, succumbing for a time to the enthusiasm of the BRB's political overlord, Antony Crosland MP, Secretary of State for the Environment (with Transport a sub-department) for replacing trains with buses[26], before pursuing a positive vision of railway development. An ebullient and enthusiastic figure, he paid a visit to Scottish Region in April 1978, travelling in best chairmanly style in a special train with the inspection saloon over the newly-reinstated Highland doubled section, and going on to Inverness and

A charmless Cumbernauld Station with two two-car Cravens Class 105 diesel multiple units. These were introduced on Scottish Region in 1959. (Stenlake Collection)

Aberdeen. Confidential talks going on at the time between the National Standing Joint Committee of BR and the Scottish bus operators (at that time National Bus Co. and the Scottish Transport Group) centred on the possibility of closing the line between Crianlarich and Oban, and replacing it with additional bus services. Annual rail passenger revenue between Glasgow and Oban was £84,000, while the cost of working the line was put at £846,000 of which passenger working accounted for £521,000. Allowing for an additional dmu service to operate between Glasgow and Crianlarich, an annual saving of £665,000 could be effected. Closure between Crianlarich (Lower) and Oban was recommended[27], but not immediately pursued. Studies made in Scotland suggested that feeder bus services to selected stations would provide "a better and more cost-effective service" than diesel multiple-units on rail, and an agreement on marketing co-operation was made with the bus groups in February 1979. These initiatives, however, lapsed in a changing political scene. Thoughts of fix-ups with the state-owned bus operators came to an end with the election of a Conservative government under Margaret Thatcher in May 1979, and the looming threat of deregulation of bus services. From the winter travellers' point of view the dropping of 'bustitution' was highly desirable, as the late 1970s had successive severe and snowy winters. On 17 February 1979 police moved northbound motorists onto the Edinburgh-Inverness train at Dalwhinnie when the A9 trunk road was blocked. In the previous year, though, the train too had fallen foul of snow, when the 17.15 Inverness-Wick ran into a drift-packed cutting on the Far North line at Altnabreac. Five coaches were derailed and the track torn up. Seventy passengers were eventually taken to safety by helicopters[28].

At Shields Junction on 30 August 1973 the 21.35 electric train from Wemyss Bay to Glasgow Central passed a signal at danger and ran into the back of the 21.10 diesel train from Ayr to Glasgow Central. Its driver and four passengers were killed. Two serious accidents happened in 1979. On 16 April the 19.40 Glasgow Central-Wemyss Bay emu was struck head-on at Wallneuk Junction, just east of Paisley Gilmour Street Station, by a diesel mu forming the 18.58 special from Ayr to Glasgow, which had passed a danger signal. Both drivers and seven passengers were killed. On 22 October 1979 the late-running 08.44 Glasgow-Dundee train came to a stop through engine failure 540 yards east of Invergowrie Station. The following train, the 09.35 Glasgow-Aberdeen, passed a semaphore signal set to danger but not fully in position, and ran into the back of the halted train. Its driver, his assistant, and three passengers died. Two carriages were thrown right over the sea-wall into the Firth of Tay, and the Tay Bridge rescue craft was summoned to help[29].

Freight in the 1970s

Thirteen years after closure of the Dumfries-Stranraer railway, the ports of Stranraer and Cairnryan were handling almost 220,000 freight units a year, all by road. Seven ferries were at work, and Sealink was building the 7,000-tonne *Galloway Princess*. In the north, expansion of the North Sea oil industry brought some regeneration to declining freight traffic on lines still extant, with haulage of pipe sections and other construction materials: a proposal for singling of the Aberdeen line between Montrose and Stonehaven was dropped, and the axe hanging over the line to Kyle of Lochalsh receded in 1973 when a platform erection site was established at Loch Kishorn. By the end of 1976 around 60,000 tonnes of material had been moved by rail to Stromeferry[30]. But the rails between Maud Junction and Peterhead were lifted in 1970 before the oil industry got under way, and oil traffic was not enough to prevent the complete closure of the Fraserburgh line in 1979. Efforts to claw back freight traffic continued: a fast wagonload freight service between Glasgow and Bristol was introduced in 1972, using air-braked rolling stock: a precursor of the Speedlink goods service which began in 1977, by which time more air-braked stock was available, providing fixed-timetable trains between some 200 locations across the UK, with Inverness the northernmost pont. At the end of the 70s a new bulk freight route was established with the opening of the Hunterston deep water terminal, where huge loading hoppers could fill three 100-ton ore wagons simultaneously and a set of 21 wagons in in 30 minutes. From here the heaviest freight trains seen in Scotland, 2,100 tonnes, served the great new steel works and strip mill at Ravenscraig. British Rail had established a new Freight Business Plan, and it was noted that the

Stranraer Harbour, around 1975. The railway steamers are by now car ferries. MV *Ulidia*, introduced to the route in December 1974, is on the left. (Stenlake Collection)

Grain traffic for the distilleries is still in evidence at Cameron Bridge, in this 1970s view. The passenger station was closed in 1969. (Stenlake Collection)

Region would have to fully exploit performance improvements and economies to offset its heavy dependence on coal and steel and gain more general merchandise traffic. Greenock's Clydeport container terminal, on the site of the former G&SWR Princes Pier station, opened in 1969, was being extended in 1970, and had a new rail link installed in 1971 at the cost of the Clyde Port Authority (this line is no longer in use although Greenock is now an important cruise ship calling point with over 50 ships a year).

Most of the new freight services were trainload as specified by Beeching, rather than wagonload. By 1971 it was accepted that wagonload absorbed a disproportionate amount of resources and British Railways gave up pursuing this type of business at surviving goods stations, except at Speedlink depots where it was hoped adequate trains of individual wagon loads could be assembled. Freightliner, in which BR had a minority interest until 1976, was growing as container traffic increased. As part of the enhancement of the East Coast Main Line to allow the use of containers 8ft 6in high, work was going on to lower the floor of Penmanshiel Tunnel, between Dunbar and Drem, when its roof collapsed on 17 March 1979, killing and entombing two men. The track was realigned in a cutting to replace the tunnel.

The management of freight services was transformed with the introduction of the computerised TOPS (total operations processing system) for identifying, tracking and deploying all wagons. Purchase of the system, pioneered by the American Southern Pacific Railroad, was approved in 1971 and gradually introduced in the various regions. TOPS operated in Scotland from the Spring of 1975, introduced first in the Inverness traffic area, the only area freight centre to be combined with a district control office, and was completed with Mossend in June. This ambitious scheme was a great success, achieved by railwaymen without the involvement of external consultants. Locomotives and carriages were also included in TOPS by 1977 and 1983 respectively, firstly by Western Region, but Scottish Region received credit for being second to resolve the difficulties with union members who clung to the former ways of doing things, with an agreement in July 1977. For most people, TOPS was very much to be preferred to BOTTOMS (back on to the old manual system)[31]. TOPS or not, Leslie Soane, Scottish Region general manager, was quoted in 1977 as saying that Dutch lorries could take fish from Mallaig to the Netherlands within 48 hours, and the railways could not. His difficulty was that the traffic was volatile both in volume and arrival time, and British Rail could not keep resources "lying round for use at the drop of a hat"[32].

Government financial support for non-passenger railway business stopped at the end of 1977. The 1978 Transport Act transferred full ownership of Freightliners Ltd to the BRB, at the same time supplying an £18 million-plus bailout to cover the company's unsecured interest payments[33]. BR was now able to offer a wider range of services. The 1974 Transport Act had aleady made it possible for businesses to claim up to 50% of the capital costs of laying new sidings and facilities for freight, where there are environmental benefits, and the 1978 Act extended this to include the cost of new rolling stock.

Industrial Relations and
Organisational Reform in the Later 1970s

The background of union/management dialogue was changing in the late 1970s. Since nationalisation its tenor had been one that assumed collaboration and co-operation in running the business – an assumption that partly masked the degree to which a command structure was maintained. Since 1905 both sides at the negotiating table had got used to the idea that when railway management and workers were at loggerheads, the government, rather than have to deal with the consequences of a strike, would step in and provide a solution which, if less than the workers had wanted, was more than the employers had been willing to concede. By now, however, a rail strike, though damaging, could no longer paralyse commercial and industrial life. Even before the election of the Thatcher government, determined to confront and curb what it considered to be the excessive power of trade unions, and intending that the state-owned industries should lead the way, a new robustness in railway management attitudes was apparent. In February 1976 there was deadlock with union representatives over a review of HQ staff, and general manager David Cobbett took the step of writing to inform individual staff members that economies had to be made, and unnecessary work cut out, and that the new arrangement would be imposed on 6 June[34].

Determined to bring innovation to an industry that had seemed almost bankrupt of vision as well as money, Parker found an ally in Robert 'Bob' Reid, the BRB member in charge of marketing, who had cut his managerial teeth in a succession of roles in Scottish Region from 1960 to 1968, finally as planning manager. New views on the historical, actual and potential future contribution of railways to the economy, increasingly aired in courses, articles and books on economic history and economic theory through the 1970s, were finding their way into the intellectual background of politicians and their advisers, and of railway managers. Now, with the expensive disaster of 'Field' as a reminder that consultancy had its perils as well as virtues, the BRB began its own version of organisational reform. Existence of the PTEs, five in England and one in Scotland, with their need to know what they were paying for, was one of the factors that would impel the British Railways Board to divide its passenger business into four cost and revenue centres from 1977: InterCity, London & South East, PTE Services, and Other Provincial Services. All Scottish Region trains fell into the last category, with its far from uplifting name. For Parker and Bob Reid, this was a deliberate step towards a much more substantial change.

9. The Advent of ScotRail, 1980-1985

The 1980s formed the decade in which the system's future development took shape. Four issues dominated these years: the working relationship with Strathclyde PTA; deregulation of coach and bus services and the resultant competition; a crisis in industrial relations; and a radical change in management's approach to running the system. Closely interlinked, they form the subject matter of this and the following chapter. This chapter sets the scene and describes a problematic period in the Strathclyde-Scottish Region partnership.

The Serpell Report and the Beginnings of 'Sectorisation'

Margaret Thatcher's hostility to the principle of nationalised industry was well-known, as was that of her advisers, of whom one or two were also ardent rail-to-road enthusiasts. Her Parliamentary party however held many members with a positive view of railways (including, perhaps, William Whitelaw, grandson of the LNER chairman). Thatcher had taken the trouble to study railway finances, but she made a mistake in assuming that the managers of state-owned industries must be second-rate types compared to their counterparts in private industry. Most of the top and up-and-coming BRB executives were career railwaymen, committed to their industry, but as capable and effective as their counterparts in any very large organisation; and after two decades of bruising change and enforced adjustment, they were

SPT liveried train at Dalmuir in 1984. The creative use of old motor tyres may be noted. (Stenlake Collection)

working in a corporate culture different to that of the 1950s and 1960s. At the end of the 70s the railways' financial problems were just as bad as earlier in the decade, but they were about to be tackled in a new way.

Though the concept of railway privatisation simmered, there was a difficulty – how to sell off an industry whose survival depended on large amounts of public money being regularly pumped into it might challenge the most determined free marketeer. None of the Thatcher governments attempted to de-nationalise the railways, though a start was made by identifying parts which could be detached and profitably sold off. In the past, sale of redundant sites and disused equipment had brought income to British Railways. In the new process, the beneficiary was Her Majesty's Treasury, starting with the disposal of British Transport Hotels. Even before the 1981 Transport Act, which made provision "with respect to the disposal by the British Railways Board of part of their undertaking, property, rights and liabilities", and set up British Rail Investments Ltd for the purpose, the BRB Hotels Division had begun to sell part-ownership of the remaining Scottish properties, with Gleneagles, Edinburgh's Caledonian and North British hotels in June 1981, followed by the Old Course Hotel at St. Andrews in March 1982, Turnberry, Lochalsh, the Central (Glasgow) and the hotels at Inverness, Perth and Aberdeen in March 1983; and finally the North British (Glasgow) in January 1984. Of the other hotels, Cruden Bay was not reopened after 1945, Ayr was sold in 1951, Strathpeffer in 1958, Dornoch was sold in 1965, and St. Enoch was demolished in 1974.

The Transport Act of 1980 abolished quantity control of express road coach services and reduced controls on other services, including that of price. New companies emerged, including Stagecoach (1980) which grew to call itself "Scotland's Own Transport Revolution" by 1983, the same year in which Scottish Bus Group launched Citylink. Coaches were competing with one another as well as with the railways, and by 1984 long-distance coach travel had increased by 50%. In the Dundee area an attempt was made to co-ordinate passenger transport, with the Tayway Bus Service, run by Tayside Regional Council, Northern Scottish Bus Group, and BR (Scottish Region), with standardised fares and interchangeable tickets between Carnoustie and Dundee. The scheme ran until 1986 but was not extended or replicated elsewhere.

Bob Reid was appointed as BR chief executive from 1980, and on 11 June 1981, he and Sir Peter Parker arranged a dinner for George Younger, Secretary of State for Scotland, and top civil servants, to meet Leslie Soane and discuss "the Scottish dimension". This followed a meeting on 7 May between Scottish Office, senior Regional staff, and four members of the Scottish Area Board. Soane's concern was for rural lines, which had had little more than basic maintenance since the 1960s and if current budget constraints were maintained, would require speed restrictions adding seventeen minutes to journey time between Ayr and Stranraer, 40 minutes between Crianlarich and Oban, 44 minutes on the West Highland, 37 minutes on the Far North, and 24 minutes on the Kyle line. Scottish Region passenger revenue was down 5% between May 1980 and May 1981, still a better showing than the BR average fall of 10%, but an extra £5 million was needed to maintain the present level of speed on these routes[1].

One government initiative of 1982-83 was an inquiry into British Railways' financial position and prospects, set up in May 1982 with a small team headed by Sir David Serpell, a former civil servant who had worked with Beeching in the 1960s, and had been a BRB director since 1974. Its terms of reference were virtually hijacked by one member, Alfred Goldstein, of the

This scene at the south end of Aberdeen Station could be any time in the late 1970s or 1980s. A Class 08 diesel shunter is moving a single carriage while a train hauled by two Class 47s pulls in. The British Railways Universal Trolley Equipment (BRUTE), used between 1964-1999, holds mailbags and parcels. (Stenlake Collection)

engineering consultancy Travers Morgan. This group had provided Serpell with a consultancy document recommending, among other things, that BR engineers should abandon the practice of replacing signalling equipment on grounds of age, because they could not forecast the cost involved: "Replacement is therefore justified only when the old equipment becomes so unreliable as to be a potential hazard or unable to cater for the timetabled service", and adding "At present, equipment failures delay trains by only 3,500 hours a year, with only 600 failures a year causing delays over 10 minutes. *No consideration seems to have been given to the cost savings available from a less good performance*"[2] (my italics). No consideration was apparently given to the possibility of a "less good performance" actually killing people. Goldstein insisted on the committee setting out options for the future scale of railway operations in Britain. Their report in January 1983 gave a detailed and critical analysis of the BRB's accounts and financial projections before setting out four main options. While making no specific recommendations, it gave prominence as 'Option A' to the proposition that Great Britain could get by almost without railways at all, and that all Scotland needed was the West Coast Main Line to Glasgow and Edinburgh: nothing else. As an attempt to provide the basis for more large-scale cuts and closures, it was a failure. Feebly and briefly defended by the Minister of Transport, the report was very quickly shelved. Railway managers, however, found it contained much useful information for a programme of internal reform which was already under way.

Reid introduced a restructuring of the basic organisation in January 1982, which was to have a vital effect on the future. From nationalisation and before, the industry had a vertically-arranged command structure, with central officers in charge of major functions passing orders to regions which themselves were similarly organised (only Scottish Region had modified this with the two-tier system). Now the commercial structure was reformed into five market sectors, each with its own Director and separately accountable, with its profit or loss shown. These were InterCity, Rail Express Systems (parcels, mail, newspapers), Provincial Services: regional and inter-regional passenger services), London & South East (later renamed Network Southeast), and Freight, split into Trainload Freight and Railfreight Distribution. Parker and Reid chose to superimpose the sectors on the regional structure, and a complex 'matrix' format ensued, with regional general managers, sector directors and functional chiefs all at the same level, and reporting to the chief executive. Reid's matrix model, with its potentially conflicting lines of command (said to be known internally as "Rubik's cube"[3]), has been seen as a device to make a radical reorganisation without prompting interference by the Ministry of Transport. It was a deliberate programme to promote change, not a solid rearrangement of senior posts. For the first time, the rigid divisions of function-based management, with only the regional managing director having any cross-functional authority, were taken down. Sector directors, charged with responsibility for the bottom line of their 'businesses', began to set up their own market-oriented management teams.

Reid became chairman on Parker's departure in 1983. Speaking to the House of Commons Transport Committee in 1986, he described sector management and changes in regional and HQ organisation as "the single most important change in BR since nationalisation"[4]. Quickly, however, it became clear that the sector directors were the ones who called the shots and neither the BRB's 'barons', the regional managers, nor its 'bishops', the HQ functional heads, were allowed to stand in their way or obstruct the new emphasis on commercial goals.

Scotland's northernmost junction, at Georgemas, in the British Railways era before the introduction of radio control in 1984. One side of the snow-blower situated just south of the station can be seen. (Stenlake Collection)

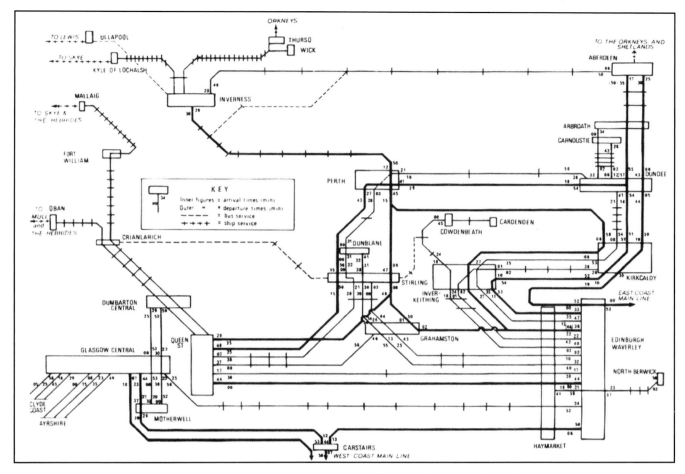

The base diagram for the Scottish Region's new even-interval timetable of 1982-83. (Jim Summers Collection)

The Politics of Profit

Sector directors discovered that the existing accounting methods provided information on their business sector revenues, but not on the associated costs, and new methods of identifying and calculating business sector costs and profits had to be devised. This developing management accounting system supported a new managerial outlook, which might be characterised as "the politics of profit". Using the new accounting information, sector directors were able to change the terms of reference in operational discussions. Short-term profit considerations began to displace traditional operating norms as the rationale for decision making. Rolling stock was reallocated between routes on the basis of where it could earn the most profit. Timetable alterations were introduced to create customer traffic, rather than suit the operating convenience of the timetable. Extensive track maintenance, which would normally have been done in conjunction with the associated signalling maintenance, was postponed to reduce short-term expenditure. In 1983 the sector directors were nominated as principal officers on the BR Board, confirming the displacement of the regional managers as the controlling force within the corporation[5]. When the Scottish Region management committee considered singling the ex-G&SWR line between Annan and Bank Junction (at Old Cumnock), and also between Mauchline and Kilmarnock, it could only develop the project to submission stage and then inform the Director, Provincial Services, who by now 'owned' the line[6].

It was a profound and skilfully executed change in corporate culture. Now the function of Scottish Region's general manager was reduced to maintaining the physical elements of the railway: stations, depots, tracks, rolling stock – everything necessary to facilitate the traffic of InterCity from London to Edinburgh, Glasgow, Aberdeen and Inverness; and for the freight sectors, while final responsibility for the Region's own passenger services, including the vital relationship with the Strathclyde PTA, resided with the director of Provincial Railways, as the new sector was called: not a name likely to win friends in Scotland. Naturally the general managers were not pleased, and Leslie Soane, general manager of the Scottish Region, took a lead in calling for an alternative approach, making the regions themselves for the first time "fully accountable profit centres"[7]. This was ignored, though some Scottish services were transferred from InterCity to Provincial. Sectorisation was imposed and became the main basis of British Railways' management structure in the course of the 1980s. General managers were not abolished but in effect became "contractors" to sector managers who were "commanders"[8]. With multiple users of the railway track, "prime user costing" was introduced, with the main user bearing the infrastucture charges, and enabling others to use them at a marginal cost. This was replaced from 1984 by "sole user" costing, when sectors were charged with the cost of facilities required if they were the sole users[9]. These changes were not intended as a quick fix, though with rail patronage falling from 61.5 million passenger journeys in 1980-81 to 49.5 million (an all-time low) in 1982-83[10], the urgency of the need to turn things round was obvious.

Scotland (with the Western Region), was used to try the BRB's "open stations" initiative from October 1981. No more queues at platform gates: instead tickets were inspected on the trains by a conductor-guard. Though it was stressed that it was not a staff reduction exercise, this was not accomplished without long and difficult talks with the National Union of Railwaymen. Training was essential: 235 sets of ticket punches were on order, of four different types. The Far North, Aberdeen, and Perth lines (to Blair Atholl) were the test routes. One of the intentions behind the change was to

Class 26 No. 26040 with an Inverness-Kyle train, around 1975. Built in 1959, the engine was withdrawn in December 1992, but is preserved. The road alongside was made in the late 1960s to avoid the Strome Ferry crossing. (Stenlake Collection)

A Red Star parcel delivery van stands outside the cleaned-up façade of Stirling Station in 1997. (Stenlake Collection)

reduce the possibility of fraudulent travel, estimated to cost the railways many millions each year; another was to ease the movement of passengers through stations. A 1982 spot-check on the test lines showed that 99.5% of passengers had a valid ticket, and another in 1983, after the policy was extended to all stations outside the SPTA area, found more passengers without tickets passing through stations with barriers than through the open ones[11]. The relatively self-contained nature of the Scottish system, with most journeys and consignments made within the country, perhaps led to Scottish Region's choice as a test area for a new parcel service, Red Star Plus, offering same-day delivery, from October 1984.

Scottish Region Takes an Independent Line

Its self-contained aspect helped Scottish Region to stand out as something of an exception even as sectorisation was spreading its wings. Although in theory the Director of Provincial Services had control of all Scottish Region train services, Regional management had already taken the future into its own hands. The decision of Provincial's first director, John Welsby, a former civil servant in the Department for Transport, to at first "leave service provision largely alone… it would have involved major rows with general managers who would have gone out of their way to make sure I screwed up"[12] made things easier. Evidence of a new and somewhat independent spirit had been growing within the Regional management from around 1980, beginning under general manager Leslie Soane, from 1977. Perhaps sparked in part by the devolution debate and referendum of 1979, the Regional team embarked on a programme which in effect treated the Scottish system as an integral and independent unit. Central to this was the chief operating manager from 1980 and deputy general manager from 1983, Chris Green, a graduate entrant from 1965 who had had a succession of roles in English regions and a stint at headquarters before coming to Scotland as the relatively youthful holder of a senior management role.

Importantly, he had the confidence and tacit support of Bob Reid. He had gained the understanding that if progress was to be made, passengers' total experience of their railway journey had to be catered for, from entry to a smart station to a punctual arrival in a clean, comfortable and up-to-date train. Green had plenty of ideas, and the will to implement them through a coherent approach. Scottish Region did not lack achievements in the 70s but many stations remained drab and cheerless, speeds in general were slow, with many restrictions because lines had not been fettled up to a modern standard; the rolling stock introduced in the late 50s and early 60s was showing its age, and the operational focus was still on running trains for the public to use, rather than on how to get the public to use the trains. On his arrival, Green felt that he had come to a region which provided a reliable service but was not at the cutting edge of progress[13].

Green identified three immediate vital issues: the imminent deregulation of inter-city coach services, the relationship with Strathclyde PTE, and the BRB's plans to make further cuts in Scotland, including the Kyle, Oban, Ardrossan/Largs and North Berwick lines. The Regional team now embarked on a programme whose mission was to enable the system to fight for its life against new and ruthless road competition. His messages to operating staff were clear, specific, and often took them into his confidence. Detailed annual plans were introduced from 1981, setting out a range of objectives and targets and how they would be achieved, from train-cleaning to freight train punctuality and better station services. As a preliminary to further changes, an administrative streamlining was effected in 1981, retaining the two-tier system, described as "a robust, if arduous structure which offers remarkable opportunities for fast communication and action"[14], but with 27 areas reduced to twelve "business groups" by 1982: Aberdeen, Ayr, Edinburgh, Fife, Fort William, Glasgow Central, Glasgow Queen Street, Inverness, Motherwell, North Transclyde, Paisley, and Tayside. Green was quoted as "cutting loose" the area managers to go out and find business[15], and a reduction of 52 posts in headquarters operation was made.

Train-cleaning, a mundane and often neglected task, was hauled out and exposed to headline treatment in staff reports, making the Region a pioneer in this field, with a manager to supervise it and help achieve targets: "Scotland has become the only Region to assess the quality of Cleaning in a

Two Sprinter units heading towards Mallaig on the West Highland Line, with the islands of Eigg (left) and Rum in the background.

numerate manner"[16]. Mechanical aids, mobile cleaning units and controlled emission toilet equipment for Mark III sleepers were provided, and a mobile heavy cleaning gang was set up. A war on the "Paper Railway" was declared, and in 1984 the working timetables for passenger and freight trains were combined and the system of traffic notices and staff circulars rationalised. In each area past progress and new developments and targets were recorded year by year.

For 1982-83 a new basic interval timetable for internal services was introduced, based on Dutch and German practice, and especially the Swiss Railways' *Taktfahrplan*. Taking the hourly arrivals and departures of East Coast expresses from Waverley as a basis, it eased passengers' journey planning by setting out regular-interval connections across the country. Unique on British Railways, it was drawn up by Jim Summers, who saw it as "a product we can operate and sell aggressively". It was also devised to reduce journey times, taking full advantage of increased maximum speeds in many places, and new traction, like the Glasgow-Aberdeen push-pull trains[17]. It had some subtle touches, including certain public departure times earlier than those given on the staff's Working Timetable: "where the punctuality of the passengers themselves at the station is crucial to the punctual departure of their train. An instance is Falkirk High". Establishment of this was helped by the fact that most Scottish services and passenger journeys began and terminated within Scotland. Operational managers became adept at 'borrowing' High Speed Trains sets with time to make an extra run between InterCity duties. Scottish Region was the first to introduce differential speed restrictions for the 125 mph HSTs, enabling full use of their superior acceleration and braking powers, and so to run more revenue-earning miles. The BRB was reported as "not happy" about this, but it soon became standard practice across the system[18].

ScotRail management resisted acquiring the bus-type 'Pacer' diesel units initially ordered by the Provincial Sector, preferring to use more expensive, and older, locomotive-hauled trains on most non-electrified routes rather than these lightweight vehicles which would not shine on Scottish gradients, nor against Scottish wind and weather; and the travelling public also preferred "proper trains". It turned out to be a prudent move in other ways: the 'Pacers' were unreliable and unpopular with passengers. In 1985 the Region was operating 287 main line diesel locomotives and 428 carriages, some of the latter being rather elderly but given "BR's cheapest face-lifting programme". Even Provincial's improved 'Sprinter' units, Class 150, introduced in January 1986, were restricted to six sets on Edinburgh local services[19]. A hopeful indicator of better things to come had been British Rail's high-speed tilting Advanced Passenger Train prototype, which made occasional runs into Scotland; in October 1981 it was recorded going south from Beattock Summit at 125 mph, a speed which has not been equalled there since, and on 12 December 1984 it ran from Euston to Glasgow Central in three hours, 52 minutes and 40 seconds, at an average speed of 103 mph. BR's abandonment of the project in 1985 due to soaring costs, design problems and delays was a serious setback to Scottish Region, which had great faith in the project and had put in for 55 sets[20]. That would certainly have transformed the timetable. Countering this failure was the great success of the 125 mph 'High Speed Train' with a Class 43 diesel power car at each end. Introduced in 1976 and originally envisaged as an interim provision until the APT was in full production, it was still very much in service in 2016 and refurbished units were due to be deployed by Abellio between Edinburgh, Glasgow, Inverness and Aberdeen from 2017, 41 years after their first appearance. In 1985, though, Scottish Region had no HSTs on order.

Behind all the detailed planning and action was a holistic view of the regional railway, intended to transform it in the eyes of the travelling public and of its own staff. What was happening was just what Hurcomb and Robertson had sought to prevent, but things were different in the 1980s. The culmination was the re-branding of BR (Scottish Region) as Scotrail (changed soon to ScotRail), in September 1983. The chosen name was a brilliant one, national, modern, clear and memorable, and public response was highly favourable. Colin Boocock noted that public criticism of the Region's "second-hand" or "clapped-out" rolling stock had quietened in the mid-1980s even though "the fleet is older now than it was then". But now it was spruced-up ScotRail rolling stock[21]. In 1984 Green was made general manager on George Mackie's retirement, evidence that top management did not look unfavourably on the Scottish initiatives. It seemed that in Scotland at least, regional tradition and identity could be successfully fused with the dynamic, market-oriented, sectorised approach. The authors of *Diverging Mobilities* suggest that Green took the decision to adopt as autonomous a policy direction from London as was possible: "In a precursor to the rebranding that was to become commonplace across the rail network later in the decade, Green capitalised on the re-emerging pro-devolution political mood by launching the new ScotRail identity in a blaze of publicity"[22]. It could be said, though, that the appearance of a "national" railway was one of the factors that helped to create the new sense of Scottish identity. The Provincial sector was decentralised into four subsectors in June 1984: Eastern, Midland, Western, and Scotland. Though still with a sector management based in Birmingham, for the first time ever, passenger railway services within Scotland were managed as an individual commercial unit, with the ScotRail/SPTA partnership a vital element. Green also pays tribute to the Scottish TUCC, headed by Col. Bill Dalziel, for its positive attitude and suggestions for improvements.

Works are in progress at Glasgow Central in 1984. The line-up from left to right shows West Coast Main Line Class 85 and 86 locomotives, a class 303 emu, and a class 101 diesel unit. (Stenlake Collection)

The Strathclyde Strategy

The SPTA was concerned about the increasing gulf between revenues and operating costs in the train services it supported, caused in part by the declining numbers of passengers. Asbestos removal from its Class 303 'Blue Trains' was a major expense. In 1983 it had to provide £28.9 million, more than three times the 1976 figure (though inflation played a part). It had withdrawn support in 1981 from the Glasgow-Paisley (Canal)-Kilmacolm line, an action seen as a signal to the railway unions that it was not going to keep railways open at any cost. The line was closed by Scottish Region in January 1983. Impending deregulation of all bus services and their removal from PTA control helped to focus the Authority's attention on the railways, and a ScotRail initiative produced a joint planning group in 1983. The group eventually agreed on a strategy which ensured retention of all the existing network, with new or life-extended rolling stock provided until 2000, and with the Strathclyde subsidy to be reduced by one third in real terms by 1989. Four conditions were considered necessary: (i) 75% government and 30% European Regional Development Fund grants for rolling stock and infrastructure; (ii) no government reduction of Strathclyde Region's permitted capital expenditure; (iii) efficiency measures to be put in place, particularly in relation to improved staff working practices; (iv) the level of bus services not to be significantly in excess of the 1983 level. Item (iv) was taken out of Strathclyde's control by deregulation. It was a positive programme, combining cost-reduction, modernisation and operating efficiency. It recommended electrification to Ayr, Ardrossan and Largs, East Kilbride, and Cumbernauld; improvement of the Barrhead and Kilmarnock services; new stations at Auchinleck, Kilmaurs and Cumbernauld South; and driver-only operation, "the key cost-saving element for the network", to be effected on all electric and Class 150 DMU services between 1985 and 1990.

A Class 314 at Balloch Pier Station, 1981. Sixteen Class 314 three-car electric multiple units were delivered from November 1979, initially to work the Argyle Line. The TransClyde name and logo were applied to all Strathclyde PTA vehicles: trains, buses and the Subway. (Stenlake Collection)

New signalling centres at Paisley and Yoker would replace 57 existing boxes. The final comment in a document introducing the agreement to staff was, "Support payments are not unlimited. Any service ceases to be good value for money if it fails to cover at least 40% of its costs from passenger fares. Almost all the diesel services were in this category at the beginning of the Review. Positive action will bring all these routes above performance level"[23].

The SPTA and ScotRail were setting themselves a stiff task. A record of financial performance by route showed that Glasgow southern electrics covered 35% of their costs by fares in 1983 (target for 1988 55%); north side electrics 39% (46%); and Glasgow-Shotts-Edinburgh 41% (43%), but also on lines exceeding the 40% mark, new targets were set, as with Glasgow-Ayr/Largs, raising the bar from 57% to 93% and Glasgow-Barrhead/Kilmarnock from 46% to 76%. The Ayrshire electrification gained government approval in 1983. Financial support for its £80 million cost came from several sources: fixed electrification equipment at £25 million was met by Strathclyde Regional Council, with a 30% grant from the European Regional Development Fund (Green also took full advantage of Scotland's eligibility for EC development grants, appointing a liaison officer specifically to research and apply for these, 21 new Class 318 and twelve refurbished Class 311 electric units, at £20 million, by the Regional Council with a 55% government grant from the Scottish Office; and British Rail funding the £35 million of track improvement and resignalling, again with a 30% ERDF grant[24].

Two years on, things looked dicey. In 1985 Strathclyde set up a review of the 1983 plan's progress. One result was a ScotRail message for staff in December 1985, with some straight talk from Green: "Either we can continue to achieve investment in a new railway hand in hand with constructive cost reduction, or be forced back into drastically cutting services through our failure to

Twenty-six Class 107 diesel units were built in 1960 for use in the Scottish Region, and ran until 1991, though displaced from the Ayrshire lines by electrification in 1986-87. This spruced-up centenary train has the G&SWR crest in the windscreen. (Stenlake Collection)

deliver on the economies we agreed with Strathclyde at the time of the Rail Review in 1983. None of us want cuts. But we must deliver on the economies agreed, including operation of trains by Drivers and Commercial Guards, to obtain the investment in new trains, new signalling, better stations that was promised when we delivered". Strikes in 1984 and 1985, and strong competition from road coaches had pushed ScotRail's earnings in the SPTA area well off target, threatening a million-pound gap in 1986. Strathclyde had already agreed in 1985 for electrification to Largs to go ahead for a further £4 million, but further decisions, including electrification to East Kilbride and provision of Class 150 DMUs to Kilmarnock, would depend on the Regional Council feeling confident that ScotRail was progressing with the agreed economies. It was crunch time[25].

Industrial Relations in the 1980s

Looking back, Chris Green regards the trade unions as essentially supportive of the ScotRail project, and the often-difficult negotiations as an inevitable part of the renewal project. The unions, naturally operations-oriented, were confronted with a new customer-service ethos, and a cost-reduction strategy focused on changed working methods and reduced staff numbers. Like many railway managers before and after him, he ascribes considerable influence in unofficial action to a small number of highly politicised and persuasive union members whose aims go beyond the welfare of members within the existing system, and who use industrial disruption for political ends.

Wages and working conditions were a stormy theme within the railway industry during the 1980s. Through the 1970s, inflation and the rising cost of living had made regular increases necessary, but railway wages had risen less than other industries'. The numbers employed had shrunk but were still substantial (almost 16,000 in Scottish Region in 1985) and the industry was in need of new capital investment and also had a workforce whose union representatives were naturally dedicated to maintaining jobs for their members and to ensuring that savings from new equipment and work practices were shared with the workers. Though a 20% increase was made in 1980, the retail price index had risen by 21.6% since the previous pay rise in April 1979[26]. A reduction in the working week from 40 to 39 hours was implemented from January 1982, but industrial relations across all BR regions and sectors remained troubled, with Scotland no exception (ScotRail's 1981 Operating Plan had noted that "Scottish Region Establishments are inflated by the heavy sickness and absenteeism that all industries face in Western Scotland").

Jimmy Knapp, General Secretary of the National Union of Railwaymen from 1983 to 1990 and of the RMT 1990 to 2001.

The tough attitudes that had emerged in the 1970s were heightened on both sides. Negotiation on pay and conditions was virtually constant, with a new settlement expected each year. ASLEF mounted strikes in January-February and July 1982, and the government kept in close touch with the British Railways Board. A Cabinet minute noted in June that the Board was anxious to avoid a situation in which the NUR went on strike and ASLEF men turned up for work, and would have to be paid, though "present indications were, however, that ASLEF would be on strike within a week or so". At the time, the BRB's handling of the dispute was constrained by "the 1919 Guaranteed Work Agreement" and it was suggested that "the strike might provide the opportunity for removing this constraint in the future"[27]. On 14 July the BRB stated that if no settlement was achieved it would close down the system on the 21st and sack the strikers. With the help of the Trades Union Congress a settlement was made on the 18th. As a measure of the change in the industrial climate, British Rail lost more working days through disputes in 1982 than in the entire period between 1948 and 1981[28].

In 1983 the NUR elected a new General Secretary in Jimmy Knapp, a Scot from the ranks of the signalmen, born in Kilmarnock's railway suburb of Hurlford. Described by one reporter as "six foot two of Scottish socialist"[29], Knapp fostered a tough style of negotiation while also proving successful at keeping public opinion on the railway workers' side even when successive one-day strikes were disrupting everyone's travel plans. In his union's tradition, however, he was willing to compromise. A key issue here was the abolition of guards on commuter trains, where their prime duty was to open and close the doors, and their partial replacement by conductors whose main function would be ticket inspection, while the doors were operated by the driver. Some trains might have only a driver on board. This was hotly resisted by the NUR, citing passenger safety as a main concern. An intriguing aspect of the dispute was the involvement of a third party, the SPTA, whose council-appointed members were largely from the then-dominant Labour Party.

Green told the ScotRail staff at the start of 1984 that the past year had cost the Region £1,200,000 in lost income due to strikes and the threat of strikes elsewhere on British Rail: "We really have to stop involving our customers in our disagreements if we are to be serious about survival." Through 1984 the NUR refused to move coal traffic while the miners were on strike. A "closed shop" agreement going back to 1975, by which all waged workers were

In the mid-1980s some Class 104 diesel units (first introduced in 1957) were allocated to Scottish Region. Here one calls at Lochwinnoch (formerly Lochside) in June 1985 shortly after it was renamed, en route for Ardrossan or Ayr. (Stenlake Collection)

required to join the appropriate union, was ended by the British Railways Board in May 1985. Union membership remained strong, however, and they continued to negotiate on behalf of the workforce.

The late summer of 1985 brought eight weeks of crisis. One of the main points in the Strathclyde/ScotRail agreement had been the institution of driver-only operation of trains. On 2 August that year the guard of the first DOO train, on the Gourock line, refused duty and was sent home. After that, 186 of his Glasgow colleagues walked out on unofficial strike, halting most services. ScotRail management refused any concession. Strathclyde councillors had to consider their constituents, who wanted to keep their railways, with their (relatively) low fares, and on the 10th, the SPTA announced that if there was no agreement on a return to work, the plan for future rail development in the region, including the Ayr and Ardrossan electrification, would be in jeopardy. On 13 August ScotRail stated that the guards would be dismissed if they did not return to work by the 16th. The guards did not return: dismissal notices were issued and 121 vacant positions were advertised. This brought a one-day walkout on the 19th by other guards in the Strathclyde area. These actions were still unofficial, and the NUR arranged a Britain-wide ballot among guards, which resulted in a majority, 4,815 against 4,360, opposing a campaign of industrial action. ScotRail refused to reinstate the strikers unless the NUR now accepted DOO working, and at a special union delegates' conference on 12 September this was accepted, with reservations. The guards returned to work on 23 September, and a new target date for DOO operation was set for January 1986, as an "experiment" on the Gourock and Wemyss Bay lines[30]. Between the unions, ScotRail and the SPTE, a 'Strathclyde Manning Agreement' was worked out. Really a joint understanding, it permitted driver-only operated (DOO) trains on the SPTE lines, on the acceptance that a ticket inspector would normally be on the train, but did not have to be. Even so, implementation was gradual, and other issues remained, or would arise.

Establishment of 'Social Benefit'

With working agreement in place, electrification to Ardrossan and Largs went ahead swiftly. At Paisley a single signalling centre replaced 36 mechanical boxes, controlling signals allowing the Class 318 electric units to run at 90 mph with trains only 90 seconds apart (in theory rather than practice). Glasgow-Ayr and Glasgow-Largs journey times were reduced to 51 and 53 minutes respectively, cutting thirteen and seventeen minutes from the diesel timings. The Ayr service began on 29 September 1986, six months ahead of the original schedule, with Ardrossan (South Beach) and Largs following on 19 January 1987.

Another review of railway services was made by a Strathclyde working party which reported in October 1987, looking at the supported lines and applying the same type of social cost-benefit analysis as was used for road schemes: a significant move which went beyond the guidelines for grant funding set out in the 1968 Transport Act. The exercise showed that while some rail closures would produce a financial gain to the council, this would be more than offset by the resulting increase in social costs[31] – road congestion, more accidents, air pollution, etc. The social benefits of the railway had become an established factor. However, the same review rejected the Glasgow Crossrail link as of insufficient value from a social cost-benefit analysis, a view which was endorsed by the council in 1989[32].

ScotRail sought collaboration with other regional and local authorities, resulting in station improvements across the country, and the restoration of trains between Edinburgh and Bathgate in March 1986 – a line funded by Edinburgh and four other authorities. Carrying double the anticipated number of passengers, its success confirmed a new, positive sense of the railway being seen and used as a community asset. Finding money was always a problem, but here the BR policy of moving managers around the system helped: Green had useful contacts, not least at BRB headquarters. Government money came to the railway on an annual basis and any unspent funds had to be returned at the end of the year, ultimately going back to the Treasury, with no benefit to the railways. Scottish Region, quick off the mark, found that here was a regular source of useful top-up cash to balance any calculated overspending, but also made savings whenever possible on its own approved schemes, releasing money to be spent elsewhere: some £10 million was saved on the Ayrshire electrification scheme by dint of finding cheaper but equally good ways of doing things.

Doing Battle with the Buses

Complete deregulation of bus and coach services came in 1984, unleashing a price war until the operators with deepest pockets or greatest determination won through. It was a reverse re-enactment of the 1920s bus wars which had prompted regulation of the industry in the first place. Seeing it coming, Scottish Region established a 'Nightrider' service in 1982 from Glasgow and Edinburgh to London, recalling the 'Starlight Specials' that had run from 1953 to 1962, but on a daily basis and at a much higher quality level, using first class (non-sleeper) carriages that had been displaced by new High Speed Trains on main line services in England, and including video and refreshment cars, all at the attractive fare of £17. With the success of 'Starlight Express' on the London stage in 1984, ScotRail's publicity-conscious management got the composer Andrew Lloyd Webber to relaunch the service, which ran until 1988[33]. Road/rail competition was intense, and a *Modern Railways* article in February 1985 talked of a "bloody battle" on the A9 between rail and road, with ScotRail taking the offensive, as passenger manager Euan Cameron introduced the limited-stop 'Jacobite' train with a video carriage, and the Highland line's first 100 mph section between Aviemore and Kingussie[34]. In April 1984 InterCity had introduced the first HST service on the Highland line, the eight-hour Kings Cross-Inverness 'Highland Chieftain', described in 1985 as "a major success"[35], demoting the 'Clansman' which had been running via Birmingham since the early 1980s as the prime daily service between Inverness and London, though the 'Clansman' did have "tartan-clad hostesses who distribute tourist literature and provide copious advice"[36]. Adroit usage of other regions' HST rolling stock saw Britain's longest railway run, Elgin-Penzance, 797 miles, an initiative by the Elgin area business group and also providing an early-morning (05.52) service to Aberdeen. Fort William's business group, under area manager Colin Shearer, introduced successful Sunday excursion trains between Fort William and Mallaig, worked by steam from 1984[37].

Despite ScotRail's preparations and efforts, the bus war, offering all-but free fares on many routes, dealt a heavy blow, drawing off a great deal of passenger traffic, estimated at 20-23%[38]: the only consolation for ScotRail being that it could have been a lot worse if they had been less active in improving their own 'offer'. The eventual domination of key bus routes by single companies, with consequent diminution of services and rises in fares, restored a degree of balance to passenger transport. Entrepreneurial spirit in these bus companies was strong – in a few years they would be expanding into railway operation[39]. Bus competition notwithstanding, Dyce Station was reopened on 15 September 1984 as an experiment which, with usage double the forecast, soon became permanent[40].

Operation Phoenix, and Other Ingenuities

Though control of costs, and improvement of efficiency (in the accounting sense) and consequent reduction of the Public Service Obligation bill were prime considerations, Mrs Thatcher's government was not seeking major closures. But Gordon Pettitt records that "while no closures were on the table, fear of them remained intense"[41]. A real change of thinking had happened, from the days of 'closures are necessary to achieve efficiency' to 'we have failed if closure is the only option left'. Even before Dr Beeching's day, the Far North and Kyle lines had been prime candidates for closure, and since then, improvement of roads in the northern counties lessened their claim to be essential for economic development of the region. In January 1978 the collapse of 40 miles of the Wick line's telegraph wire in a snowstorm put the block signalling system out of action and jeopardised services, but BR's Research & Development and Signalling & Telegraph divisions devised a solution by installing radio contact between the signal boxes, operative by August 1980[42]. By 1983 the levels of subsidy required to maintain these services were felt by the Regional management to have reached proportions that "do not appear to make economic or political sense and which are becoming politically unacceptable". Earnings of the Kyle line were £256,000 and of the Wick line £685,000, against train running costs of £677,000 and £1,478,000 respectively. Complete closure was regarded as a highly undesirable last resort. Green was aware of British Rail's Derby-based R&D

A message to staff from Chris Green about Radio Train despatch. Scotrail has not yet acquired the capital R. (British Railways, Jim Summers Collection)

division's ongoing work on radio train control, and agreement between Scottish Region, the signals & telecommunication department, and R&D led to the selection of the Kyle line for a full-scale try-out of radio electronic token block (RETB) operation. Using solid-state interlocking and radio contact between train driver and a central controller, it was possible to dispense with traditional signalling methods (and signalmen), by the issue of an electronic 'token' giving the train secure occupancy of a section. In July 1983 'Operation Phoenix' was proposed and agreed, and installation of RETB was implemented from 28 October 1984. Conversion of the Wick/Thurso line followed in December 1985. The control station was moved from Dingwall to Inverness in August 1988. RETB, with an investment cost of £415,419 (supported by a 30% EEC grant), though central to the exercise, was not the only aspect of change. 'Operation Phoenix' set out a full set of options and proposals for line operation and accounting, noting potential staff savings at £194,000 a year and that if actual local costs were used rather than centrally allocated charges, reductions of £1,655,000 on track costs and around £500,000 on administration costs could be effected[43]. Installation of RETB followed on the Fort William-Mallaig line on 7 December 1987, on the line from Helensburgh (Upper) to Oban on 27 March 1988, and from Crianlarich to Fort William Junction on 28 May 1988. Installation and successful operation of RETB ensured the survival of these long rural lines for a

relatively modest cost and substantial savings. Remedial and enhancement work on the RETB system was done in 2003 and 2006-10, and further improvements with the aim of increasing flexibility and line capacity (and an enforced change of radio sub-band) were under way in 2015-18 with the aim of extending the system life to 2035[44].

The Kings Cross-Fort William sleeper crosses Rannoch Viaduct, hauled by a class 37 with ETHEL train-heating vehicle, in the late 1980s. (North British Railway Study Group)

In other ways ingenuity made up for limitations on investment. Jim Cornell, deputy general manager, with an engineering background, was among the first to appreciate that new trains with lower axle-weights exerted much less grinding pressure on the rails, which could therefore be safely used, at higher speeds, for years or even decades longer[45]. Scottish Region engineers devised the 'two-wire' system, using the train's electric lighting circuit, between driving cab at one end and locomotive at the other, to work the push-pull expresses operated at speeds of up to 100 mph by Class 47/7 engines. The Fort William-London sleeper service, threatened with closure in 1983 because the West Highland line's Class 37 engines were not fitted for electric heating as needed by the new Mark III sleeping cars, was rescued by the conversion of old Class 25 engines into ETHELs (electric train heating ex-locomotives), their traction equipment removed and their generators used to provide the necessary power. By the late 1980s, Class 37 engines fitted for electric train heating took over, and the ETHELs were retired[46].

The First Years of ScotRail: a Summing-Up

One of the striking things about the Scottish Region's self re-invention was that it was achieved by its own management. Like other very large organisations, the BRB had a tendency to hire grand consultancy firms to advise it on on how to organise its own activities (though they were sometimes wished upon it by the government, or employed in the hope of justifying rail policy to the government). ScotRail picked outside help only for specific tasks, like the industrial psychologist Valerie Stewart, whose ideas on customer-oriented business strongly influenced Green before he came to Scotland, and whom he recruited to lead staff training. She in turn was so impressed by what was being achieved that she co-authored a book with Vivian Chadwick, ScotRail's deputy general manager, drawing on their experience to show how a production-oriented concern could be turned into a market-oriented one[47]. Green himself became a familiar public figure, giving a previously faceless organisation a top-level spokesman whose utterances were crisp and frank and whose commitment to the service was obvious.

"ScotRail: image or substance?" inquired a railway journal in September 1985, in an article typical of the attention ScotRail was beginning to receive beyond Scotland (including a cover feature in France's *La Vie du Rail* in October that year) which cited some of the problems which the Scottish railway continued to face – slumping coal traffic, strikes, increasing road competition. If it did not altogether answer its own question, that was symptomatic of the fact that new ways of doing things might be as hard to grasp by the railway press as in some other sections of the railway industry[48]. ScotRail put its own case with verve in a paid-for supplement modelled on a with-it company's annual report. Glossy, in colour, it was intended to display the considerable substance of a business with an annual turnover approaching £150 million, explaining a four-point strategy: Station Upgrading, Customer and Staff Care, Business Expansion, and On-Train Improvements, as if to shareholders. Informative rather than bland, it set out an interesting and carefully selected range of figures:

Gross income of Region: £147.6 million
Passenger revenue: £113.1 million, of which Strathclyde PTE accounted for £29.3 million
Parcels revenue: £5.21 million
Freight revenue: £29.4 million
Regional expenditure: £287.5 million, of which track and signalling took £98 million, general costs £23.1 million, and train services £166.4 million

Passenger trains run daily: 1,544, with 227 staffed stations and 60 unstaffed. Punctuality was best of all BR Regions, with 92% of arrivals on time or within five minutes.
Freight train run daily: 218, with 50 terminals. Freight forwarded amounted to 6.8 million tonnes and freight received to 8.1 million tonnes.
Route miles: 1,707, of which 241 were electrified.

Locomotive stock: 287 main line diesel and 58 diesel shunters; ten InterCity power cars; nineteen main line electric.
Diesel multiple units: 260; electric 306.
Coaching stock: 395 Mark I and II, 52 Mark III.

Total staff: 15,798, of whom drivers and assistant drivers numbered 2,530, gaurds and other train crew 1,190, signalmen 755, traffic staff 2,162, engineering 3,272, others 2,167; and salaried staff 3,782. Numbers had fallen by 4.2% in the year.

Property sales and leases brought in £13.78 million in 1984-85. Station and on-train catering earned £10.78 million.

Investment in the period was £37 million, including £15.9 million in signalling, £2 million in telecommunications, and £9.7 million in passenger stations.

Some statistics from the early 1980s show both the volatility of rail usage and the divergent trends of passenger and freight revenues. The passenger figures for 1982 and the freight figures for 1984 partly reflect strikes on the railway and in the coal industry.

	1980	1981	1982	1983	1984
Passenger receipts £millions	81.4	87.9	76.6	91.4	91.7
Passenger journeys (millions)	61.5	58.4	49.3	54.6	52.0
Freight receipts £millions	34.3	40.4	34.8	33.1	23.7
Freight tonnage (millions)	24.4	25.3	21.5	19.4	11.9
Coal tonnage (millions)	6.0	6.0	5.1	4.0	1.0

Total staff numbers were 18,627 in 1980, declining year by year to 15,798 in 1985. At the start of 1985 ScotRail had 277 main line diesel locomotives and 64 diesel shunters, five HST sets, 19 electric locomotives, 106 three-car electric multiple-units and 86 DMU sets. It had 458 carriages, of which 20 were sleepers[49]. Under British Railways, three generations of carriages were built, each one going through successive modifications, beginning with the introduction of Mark I in 1951, vacuum-braked, steam-heated at first, and for running speeds up to 75 mph. Use of asbestos insulation in construction caused Scottish Region to scrap most of its Mark I's around 1980. From 1964 until 1975 Mark II were built, at first fitted with vacuum brakes and dual heating, later air-braked and electrically heated, then air-conditioned, and with a 100 mph running speed. The Mark III carriage was first designed for the HST and so for a speed of 125 mph, with a new design of bogies and suspension. Ten feet longer than the Mark II, it was of integral construction with great strength and crash-resistance and is used in most multiple-unit trains. A further advantage of Mk III was noted in the ScotRail Operating Plan for 1982, after a particularly hard winter: "The main lesson learned is that BR is just not generally equipped to operate successfully in temperatures below 100 with the notable exception of Mark III vehicles[50]. Carriages in use on the East Coast Main Line are designated Mark IV, and the new Caledonian Sleeper cars from 2017 as Mark V.

The departures board and ticket office at Glasgow Central, designed by James Miller and Donald Matheson, seen in 1984 before modernisation of the station in 1985. (Stenlake Collection)

10. The Later 1980s:
ScotRail, Provincial and InterCity

Chris Green in 1994, Director of ScotRail. (ScotRail News)

Chris Green was whisked south in January 1986 to tackle a greater challenge in the newly-formed 'Network Southeast'. In his own words, he had found the Scottish Region to be the equivalent of a chemistry set, with "freedom to experiment"[1]. He left it with a complete and tested formula that could be successfully employed elsewhere. ScotRail was well-launched and confident. Apart from the Region's relatively early adoption of a marketing approach which focused on customer needs and wishes – some people disliked the idea of a passenger being a 'customer' but it reminded railway staff that people paid for the service, and very often could choose an alternative – other factors may have played a part. The preservation of lines to the northern and western extremities helped to give the system a national character, rather than merely that of a transit operation for high-density traffic. The restoration of several lines and numerous stations closed only a decade or two before was another positive aspect. Stations were being smartened up and modernised and even those which were unstaffed and provided only with bus-shelter type refuges from the weather might have information screens and train arrival announcements. An old railway practice was brought up to date by using flowers to give colour and character to stations, with annual prizes for the best displays. Also, as the public became more educated in, and more aware of, the real threats to the 'natural' environment, railways were seen as environmentally friendlier than road traffic (even if the response on carrying bicycles was somewhat grudging). Imaginative happenings were planned, with the Tay Bridge's centenary celebrated by a series of events including the first fireworks display to be set off from a moving train as it crossed the bridge.

ScotRail was not, however, an autonomous outfit, and in the later 1980s as Provincial management matured, it began to exert greater control over its widespread and variegated empire. Its brief from the government was to reduce the public service obligation from £736 to £555 millions over three years from 1987 to 1989[2], and with ScotRail one of the largest consumers of public funds, a focus on its activities was inevitable and no doubt seen as overdue by some. Sector chiefs and their senior managers were expected to be robust as well as competent in pursuing their objectives and though the brand was such a success it could only be admired, there were certainly those who felt it was time to pull the Region into line. From 1 April 1986 Scotland had both a regional general manager, Jim Cornell, and a 'Provincial Manager ScotRail', Chris Leah (formerly ScotRail passenger business manager); while the former was concerned with "production" and the latter with "business", cohabitation between the regional and sectorised set-ups was not wholly comfortable. 'Old railway' and 'new railway' attittudes were often at variance in a cultural clash which was very different to the combinings made in 1923 and 1948, where working methods had been different but the fundamental approach had been the same. Now 'old railway' felt its values of technical know-how, public-service spirit, and operational experience was ignored or even scorned by 'new railway's' pursuit of efficient (in the economic sense) working, which might include improvements which simply transferred cost to another budget or reduced service effectiveness. In the mid-1980s, studies were revived of bus substitution for some services seen as underused and expensive to maintain. The lines from Stranraer to Ayr,

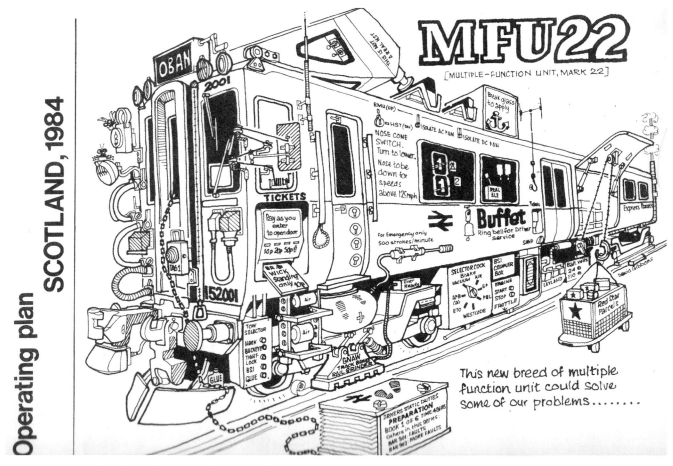

Operating plan   SCOTLAND, 1984

The cartoon-style cover of the ScotRail Operating Plan for 1984 displays the new directness and informality of management information. (British Railways)

Kirkcaldy-Ladybank-Perth, and those north and west of Inverness were investigated in December 1985 and April 1987; Fort William-Mallaig also in 1987 and Ladybank-Perth again in March 1988[3], though the matter was not pursued. Locomotive haulage decreased rapidly as new Provincial dmu types became available in the form of the Class 156 "Super Sprinters" first used on scheduled service with the 11.35 am Inverness-Wick on 26 January 1989. Unfortunately, as had happened all too often with new traction in the past, the new units, particularly the 90 mph Class 158 'Express Sprinters' from late 1990, suffered from initial problems ranging from couplings coming apart at speed to breaking crankshafts and defective lavatories. In 1991 Sir Bob Reid described them as "still running in"[4] (See also page 169).

Under John Ellis, general manager from 1987 to 1990, a further overhaul of the Regional management structure was effected from 22 May 1988, seen as "absolutely necessary to… reflect modern railway practices; to devolve greater authority to 'the manager on the spot'; and to make real cost savings". A somewhat reduced HQ staff now supervised the activities of five management areas, whose managers had a greater degree of authority and "a contractual relationship with the railway businesses based on specified quality and financial requirements", and were expected to contribute to forward planning and to make more decisions at area level. The new areas were South West, based in central Glasgow, with sub-offices at Ayr, Dumfries, Motherwell and Paisley; North West, based at Yoker Operations Depot, with sub-offices at Queen Street and Fort William; North, at Perth, with sub-offices at Aberdeen, Dundee and Inverness; East, at Edinburgh (Waverley), with sub-offices at Stirling and Kirkcaldy; and Freight, based at Motherwell, and providing specialist support to the geographic area managers.

In the Provincial scheme of things, new profit centres, partly route-based, partly territorial were established: ScotRail Express; West Highlands & North; South West; East Coast Locals; Strathclyde PTE lines. In the first year, 1986-87, the cumulative earnings were £52 million, 2% over budget and 9% better than 1985-86, with only the Glasgow-Aberdeen service, hit by cutbacks in the oil industry, failing to meet or exceed its budget[5].

1988 figures	Route Miles	Staff	Annual Budget	Passenger Revenue	Stations
South West	440	2,092	£24.3 million	£24.6 million	101
North West	290	984	£10 million	£8.7 million*	80
North	600	1,250	£13 million	£17 million	57
East	281	1,720	£21 million	£40 million	50
Freight		830	£9 million	£40 million	14 locations
Total	1611	6,876	£77.3 million	£130.3 million	298 stations
* Total passenger, freight and parcels revenue					

These figures do not include total operating costs or subsidies, nor non-ScotRail stations[6].

Members of the Elgin Business Group see off the unofficially-named 'Penzance Pirate' from Elgin at 05.52 on 14 May 1984. Aberdeen was the train's official departure station. (Jim Summers Collection)

Rail passenger journeys originating in Scotland fluctuated through the 1980s, influenced by rail strikes and the bus war, from the low point of 1982-83 to a maximum of 57.5 millions in 1985-86. Another low point came in 1989-90, with 51.3 million journeys. A decade of intense activity and service transformation had done little more than hold the line as far as passenger travel was concerned, though revenues improved and costs were controlled.

Of virtually identical design to the earlier Class 303, 19 Class 311 electric units were acquired for the Inverclyde lines services in 1967. They were withdrawn in 1990. One is preserved at the Summerlee Museum of Scottish Industrial Life, Coatbridge. (Stenlake Collection)

Strathclyde PTE was also looking ahead, publishing a document in 1989 with the title 'Public Transport for the 21st Century' which listed possible projects including a 'light rail' link from Gilmour Street Station in Paisley to Glasgow Airport. Its Yoker operations centre, later known as an Integrated Electronic Control Centre, using solid state electronics, was fully effective from December 1989, replacing 17 signal boxes on the North Clydeside lines and the West Highland to Helensburgh Upper, where RETB took over[7].

Protests were made in the House of Commons when the Carlisle-Dumfries-Kilmarnock-Glasgow line was "demoted" by the InterCity sector, with the removal of through services from English cities and of the sleeper service. InterCity was due to receive no public service operation payments from the end of the 1987-88 financial year, and as one of British Rail's commercial businesses was required by the government to contribute towards a combined 2.7% return on net assets, before interest, by 1988-89. ScotRail services on the line were still supported by subsidy, but the InterCity action showed the effects of removal of support[8]. In March 1988 the director of InterCity, Dr John Prideaux, announced that there was "no case" for electrification of any line between Edinburgh and Glasgow, as the requisite investment criteria could not be met[9]. Sharp disputes arose between InterCity and ScotRail over usage of InterCity's tracks into Waverley and through Haymarket. From 1984, sectors were charged for infrastructure on a "sole user" rather than the previous "prime user" basis, i.e. they bore the cost of only those facilities necessary for their use of the line. InterCity reduced the four tracks though the Calton tunnels into Waverley to two, against the protests of ScotRail, who also ran on the tracks as secondary users. BR's top management perhaps saw such local spats, even sector heads' bullying tactics, as part of the price to be paid in the pursuit of profitability and cost reduction, but they did not ease the task of regional planners and operators, and made inter-sector relations difficult, and on occasion, downright hostile.

Highland Lines:
A bridge that wasn't, and a bridge that was

In 1984 a long-requested road bridge across the Dornoch Firth was officially approved as a major improvement to the A9 trunk road, and a campaign was launched by the Railway Development Society and ScotRail's Inverness Business Group to incorporate a railway line on the bridge, providing a cut-off between Tain and Golspie which would reduce the length of the Far North railway by 23 miles and help it to compete with the new, more direct road. Chris Green made an approach to the Scottish Office, then with Malcolm Rifkind as Secretary of State, in November 1984, but while the response was favourable, it was made clear that no government funding would be available. As the June 1986 deadline for incorporating a railway approached, the only official funding commitment was £1 million from the Highland Regional Council. While ScotRail, under the general management of Jim Cornell (1986-87), continued to back the scheme, it was in no position to even partially fund a project which did not meet the BRB's government-imposed standards for return on capital invested. The project went ahead as a road bridge only. In response to an outburst of media criticism, the Scottish Office blamed ScotRail for not producing a detailed follow-up proposal, but without British Railways Board backing this would have been impossible for ScotRail to do. Even with a likely EEC contribution, refusal of government support left an impossibly large funding gap[10]. The leaking of confidential Scottish Office papers from ScotRail HQ to the *Glasgow Herald* in February 1987 enabled the newspaper to expose the Scottish Office as "villain of the piece", and produced a memorable but unsuccessful hunt in Buchanan House for the 'mole', instigated by deputy general manager Vivian Chadwick and involving close inspection of office staplers. In 1999 a Tain-Golspie direct line, costed at £20 million, was included in a published list of £1 billion-worth of rail projects planned for the next ten years[11].

The first Ness Bridge, in 1965, with a Class 24 engine on a Far North line train. (Robert Darlaston)

When the Ness Viaduct collapsed on 7 February 1989, by chance John Ellis, general manager of ScotRail, was in Inverness on the same day. Almost immediately he was able to announce that the bridge would be restored, endorsed by Sir Bob Reid on the following day. Provincial management might feel that its hand had been forced, but the promise was public. Engines and rolling stock on the north side provided an interim service from Dingwall and the commitment to introduce Class 156 Super Sprinters was honoured with the transfer by road of six units from Inverness to Invergordon, in April, as well as fifteen coaches for charter and heritage trains. Thirteen goods vehicles and 2 Class 37 locomotives were moved south. Later moves in October included two snowploughs, the return of the tourist coaches and an exchange of Class 37s. Persuasion was necessary to get Provincial sector's agreement that a full-strength viaduct should be built rather than one suitable only for lightweight diesel units. Scheduled freight services had been withdrawn in 1984, and while arrangements still existed for trainload freight, they were not Provincial's baby[12]. The survival of the Far North and Kyle lines is a remarkable story: much of the argument for retention in 1964 related to the inadequacy of a road system that by 1990 was much improved. It is almost as if reiterating commitment to their preservation is a necessary token of ScotRail's claim to be "Scotland's Railway"; it also says something about how the Northern Highlands are perceived within Scotland. They exert a claim with a different resonance to other rural regions, as the vestigial remains of railways in Buchan and in Galloway show.

Freight Traffic in the 1980s

Scottish Region's Operating Plan in 1982 noted that freight traffic was changing radically both in volume and composition. It was proposed to completely phase out vacuum-braked wagonload business by 1985, later advanced to 1984, and to concentrate on building up "a far more selective air-braked Speedlink network of about 120 trains and to develop all possible Company/Freightliner trains". The emphasis on "tailored" freight services brought about a programme of yard closures and the establishment of a single Network Yard at Mossend as the centre of the Speedlink network. Of the 100 general merchandise freight terminals in 1980, the top 20 generated around two thirds of the total tonnage. By 1982 the number had been reduced to eight major terminals, with handling facilities, and 83 unmanned terminals without handling facilities. An active policy to improve freight efficiency brought about reductions in capacity as a result of changing or declining traffics, including a reduction in domestic coal terminals from 89 to fourteen hopper-discharge points by 1984. Millerhill Down marshalling yard was closed in 1983 (the Up yard had closed in 1969).

Speedlink point-to-point services with wagonload freight saw growth in the early 1980s, with 177 trains originating each week in Scotland in 1982, rising to 257 by the end of 1983. Between these years the positions of Speedlink and the old-style "vacuum network" was completely reversed: Speedlink train miles rose from 670,000 to 2,097,000 and the other fell from 3,970,000 to 507,000. From May 1984 all Scottish freight trains were air-braked except for a few block trains operated for individual companies. The Region was running 200 Freightliners (See Appendix 3) and around 250 company trains, though this sector was very irregular with companies often not meeting the agreed schedules. Unfortunately, though, the Speedlink operation ran at a substantial loss, with accumulated losses of £211 million between 1982 and 1991[13], and was shut down in July 1991.

In November 1984, Green told his staff that in 1983, coal and iron had accounted for 46% of the Region's freight revenue. "This year no coal has

Two Class 116 3-car Derby dmu just south of Brownhill Junction, Glengarnock, June 1985. The huge white buildings to the left of the signal post are part of the Glengarnock Steelworks, which had ceased production in 1978 and closed completely in October 1985. (Stenlake Collection)

moved since 23 June and no iron ore since 28 June", and £250,000 a week was being lost in revenue[14]. The year-long miners' strike in 1984-85 drastically reduced coal transport and railfreight revenue. An innovation in May 1984 was the provision of a container service between Aberdeen and Wick, with containers added to the 1.55 pm Aberdeen-Inverness and the 5.40 pm Inverness-Wick passenger trains[15]. The locomotives had dual braking systems, as the container wagon had vacuum brakes and the carriages air brakes. The replacement of locomotive-hauled trains by diesel units ended the possibility of such "mixed train" services.

Freightliners Ltd closed their Edinburgh, Dundee and Aberdeen depots on 6 April 1987, as part of a "restructuring" to "more closely match its resources to customer requirements and improve profitability to acceptable levels"; the traffic was now mostly to and from container ports. Their Scottish operations were now concentrated at Coatbridge[16], though Railfreight opened an intermodal terminal at Guild Street, Aberdeen in 1987, primarily for coal, in a partnership with the John G. Russell transport company[17].

As a function of ScotRail, freight achieved its £40 million earnings budget in 1987-88. Coal traffic had made a good recovery from the crisis year of 1984, and metals earned a record £19 million. In October 1987 sectorisation of the UK-wide freight business was effected, with the creation of Trainload Freight, incorporating specialist sub-sectors for coal, construction, metals and petroleum; and in October 1988 Railfreight Distribution, Rail Express Parcels, and Railfreight General (briefly until 1989) were formed. Railfreight Distribution consisted of Freightliners, Speedlink, and Railfreight International. Scottish Region provided "production" facilities for these business groups, and the specialist ScotRail freight office at Motherwell, in addition to managing freight business in the central area, supplied specialist services as needed to the four area managers, South West, North West, North and East. With trainload working as a major element, the Scottish contribution to freight was probably a positive one (Trainload Freight made a profit in 1988-89), but the general rail freight market was in a state of increasing deterioration and Railfreight Distribution made large losses every year from 1988 to 1996, on a turnover falling steeply from £176.7 million in 1989-90 to £70.4 million in 1995-96[18]. Even in a time of recession this was a disastrous decline.

In 1982 confident predictions had been made for future profitable carriage of premium parcels (under the Red Star brand), newspapers, and parcels and letters for Royal Mail, and a drive was made in 1984 to build up parcel services, with Night Star and Red Star Plus (same day delivery) supplementing the Red Star service, though there were complaints in Scottish Region, always the leader in punctuality, about delays from the south, particularly on the West Coast Main Line[19]. A new five-year contract for letter mail had been signed in 1984 but the Post Office was already expressing concern about UK-wide delays, which incurred abatement payments to the PO of £414,000. Carriage of Royal Mail parcels by rail, which had been making a loss, ended in 1986. Newspaper traffic, once lucrative, ended with the termination or cancellation of contracts in 1987-88. In that year, the Red Star service in Scotland, at 76 stations, earned around £5 million, with traffic volume 12% higher than in the previous year. Aspects of the service which had not been profitable were cut. Parcels collection and delivery was ended on 1 July 1981. General collection and delivery of goods ceased in March 1982 with the closure of the High Street Goods station in Glasgow, replaced by a multi-role parcels, freight and international terminal at Salkeld Street.

Negative Actions:
Vandalism, Trespassing: From the 1970s

Concentration of goods in one place, like a warehouse or goods shed, or a standing freight train, has always been an enticement to the criminal-minded and was a problem for the railways from the beginning. The railways had always needed constables to protect their own and consignors' property. Petty

Kilwinning Junction, 1985: a Class 101 dmu takes the Ardrossan line. A ballast-tamping vehicle is in the siding. (Stenlake Collection)

pilfering and organised theft were rife during the wartime blackout, and it was estimated that in the first quarter of 1948, theft by employees cost British Railways £780,000. In 1959 1,500 BR employees were convicted of theft[20].

Vandalism was and is almost always a crime committed against the railway from outside, and it too goes back to the earliest days of railways, as the records of the old companies attest. In the 1970s the Scottish Region had a Vandalism and Stone-Throwing Committee, which recorded instances of damage and injury. The cost of repairing wilful damage was put at over £100,000 a year in 1961 and £500,000 a year in 1975[21]. In 1974 a driver was killed when an overhead insulator was dislodged by stone-throwing boys near Garrowhill Station. Between 25 March and 11 April 1975 there were nine cases of injury, mostly by stones thrown at guards. Windscreens on multiple-units had to be replaced by toughened glass to protect drivers from large stones dropped from bridge parapets, and on lines classed as most vulnerable, the parapets were heightened. In April-May 1975, 675 instances of damage to upholstery on electric trains were recorded, along with 85 broken arm-rests, eleven route indicator glasses, and twelve destination indicator glasses. There were seventeen cases of body-side damage and 136 of lights breakage, and 36 fire extinguishers were removed or interfered with. This was a particularly bad period but the problem was endemic, shared with other public transport operators, and linked to wider and deep-rooted social and economic issues. The perpetrators were often children and railway police could not fail to note that lineside fencing was often pulled down close to schools. It was their elders who treated railway cuttings in some places as convenient dumping grounds for domestic debris of every kind. In the effort to stem the stream of incidents, staff were encouraged to be on the lookout. In April 1975 a second-man at Polmadie received £5 for apprehending a youth who was dropping light-bulbs from an overbridge at Crosshill, and £10 was given to a permanent-way man at Ayr who removed sleepers and lineside trough lids from the rails and alerted a signalman to halt trains until the line was checked. A paper from Leslie Soane to Sir Peter Parker in August 1980 called vandalism a (British) national disease. 'Black spots' in Scotland

Stirling Station in 1986, with a ScotRail-branded Class 101 dmu and a Class 47 locomotive. (Stenlake Collection)

Helensburgh Central Station in the 1980s. Recently the station has been refurbished. Through trains run between here and Edinburgh. (Stenlake Collection)

had been identified for regular patrolling, campaigns had been launched in schools, railway workers had been warned against leaving materials on lineside sites. The worst, though indirect, result of vandalism was the Polmont disaster of 30 July 1984, when a broken fence "subject to persistent vandalism"[22] allowed a cow to pass through on to the track. It was hit by the driving cab of the 17.30 push-pull express from Edinburgh to Glasgow, derailing the train, which was travelling at 85 mph. Thirteen people were killed, and 61 injured. In the 1980s the problem was tackled both by an education programme aimed at schools and by the introduction of a bright yellow vandalism prevention train which patrolled lines most at risk, but the problem was endemic. On 25 June 1994, two 17-year old youths placed concrete cable-trough covers on the line through Greenock, close to the later Drumfrochar Station site, which derailed the 22.45 Wemyss Bay-Glasgow train, killing the driver and a passenger. The perpetrators were traced and jailed for fifteen years for culpable homicide[23]. Nowadays a vandalism alert can bring a police helicopter on the scene in a very short time, but the problem remains. Linked to vandalism is the practice of graffiti, rarely an art form, which requires specialist scrubbing teams. Concern with vandalism and misuse of equipment is shared in 2016 by the British Transport Police and by the Rail Safety and Standards Board, which has produced a 'Trackoff' package for use by schools. Plans were going ahead in 2017 for the integration of the Scottish section of British Transport Police with the national force of Police Scotland, something enabled by the Scotland Act (2016).

Trespassing on the railway accounts for some 30 deaths a year in Scotland. Some of these may be suicides. Between 2010 and 2012 forty people committed suicide by jumping or lying in front of a train[24]. This too is not a new phenomenon, but a modern driver's windscreen view of such unstoppable events can cause deep and long-term shock, and treatment and care are given after such incidents.

PART THREE
THE PRIVATISATION ERA

11. Organising for Quality becomes Organising for Privatisation

Under Parker and Bob Reid British Rail had gradually risen from the low point reached in the 60s and 70s to a stage in which it was generally seen as efficient and providing a good public service. ScotRail had risen with it and indeed ahead of it, its new *esprit de corps* helping it achieve a higher level of punctuality and of customer approval than the majority of regions. Between 1984 and 1990 twenty-two stations had been opened or reopened (See Appendixes 6 and 7). In 1990 its fare income was £78.7 million, 8% over budget and a 13% improvement on 1989. By the early 1990s a 'Changing Face of ScotRail' promotional pamphlet could record that "The Scottish Region staff rallied under the ScotRail banner", and add with some pride that "All staff in contact with customers have had at least one charm school session." In 1990 Sir Bob Reid retired as BRB chairman, to be replaced by his namesake Sir Bob Reid (railway students refer to Bob Reid I and Bob Reid II). The new chairman was a Scot, born in Cupar, with a successful career in the oil industry. His prime task, though he did not know it for a few years, would be to preside over the break-up of British Railways, though he was not responsible for the chosen form of disposal.

Organising for Quality

Cyril Bleasdale was appointed director of the ScotRail sub-sector from February 1990, combining the business and production roles of his predecessors John Ellis and Chris Leah. He set up an integrated management team, which battled to cope with the many technical problems of the new 90 mph Class 158 "'InterCity' quality for Regional Railways passengers"[1] Express Sprinter diesel units, which though much heralded in anticipation, had been delivered eighteen months behind schedule – BREL Derby went through a management buyout in 1988-89 which appears to have wholly disrupted production. It was a "bitter disappointment" that the 1990 summer timetable could not be constructed, as intended, around the new trains[2]. When the 158s began to appear, first on the Edinburgh-Aberdeen route, a stream of train failures, as well as other operating problems, including delays on the single-track section from Usan to Montrose, prompted the management to set up a "problem-solving" team to resolve the issues, and 150 small improvements brought a gradual rise in customer satisfaction. Already-delivered units were sent back to BREL for modification under warranty as new sets came into service. With the problems eventually resolved, the 158s became popular with travellers. In May 1991, a pair of 158s made the Waverley-Queen Street run in 32 minutes 9 seconds, at an average 88 mph, with maxima of 107 mph, hailed by Regional Railways' head Gordon Pettitt as a world record for an underfloor diesel engine train[3]. For Pettitt, who was on the train, it was naturally a triumph for Regional Railways' choice of motive power; for the ScotRail staff, it was also a tribute to the skills of the Haymarket Maintenance Depot. In 1990-91 the North Berwick branch was electrified, the former G&SW line to Greenock via Kilmacolm was reopened as far as a new Paisley Canal Station on 27 July 1990, and the collapsed Ness Viaduct at Inverness rebuilt. These were real and welcome successes.

Scotland had its share of the accidents and near-accidents caused by trains passing signals at danger. Such SPAD incidents became highly controversial[4] when they occurred on 'single lead' junctions, where double track been reduced to single between the secondary and the primary line, meaning that trains entering and leaving the double line had to use the same track. At Bellgrove Junction on 3 March 1989 the 12.20 Milngavie-Springburn train left Bellgrove Station against a red light and collided on the single line with the oncoming 12.39 Springburn-Milngavie train killing the driver and a passenger. At Newton on 21 July 1991 the 21.55 Newton-Glasgow train hit the 20.55 Balloch-Motherwell, when "on the balance of probabilities" it passed a red signal[5], and both drivers and two passengers were killed. An innovation from the civil engineering side, single-lead junctions ostensibly reduced maintenance costs and allowed higher speeds. They were not welcomed by operating staff. Other accidents not in Scotland also showed the inherent susceptibility of such junctions to driver error, and the arrangements have been considerably modified, and 'double lead' restored at some of the busiest. TPWS (train protection warning system) since 2003 is designed to obviate such collisions and is itself being superseded by ETCS (European Train Control System) intended for high speed junctions.

In June 1990 the British Railways Board began a further stage of reorganisation, styled 'Organising for Quality' (OfQ), and building on sectorisation by creating nine business units as profit centres, or groups of profit centres. Suspected by some as a preparatory move to ease privatisation, OfQ was in fact a serious effort to maintain the action begun a decade before to make the railways more profit-conscious and to minimise their dependence on public subsidy, at a time when privatisation was a government option rather than a firm policy. The old regional system was abolished entirely, and the Scottish area board was finally dispensed with. 'Provincial' was renamed Regional Railways from 3 December 1990, and its HQ moved from London to Birmingham. In Scotland the former Region's functions were now split three ways, with ScotRail the largest element, employing some 10,000 people. The others, Freight and InterCity, respectively employing around 1,200 and 2,000 people in Scotland, were extensions of English-managed sectors. From 27 May 1991 ScotRail became the first Regional Railways sub-sector to implement the new OfQ management system, giving it increased power to take decisions and control its finances. In mileage terms, it was the largest of these sub-sectors, with 1,674 route miles, and the second-largest number of stations, at 311, and the only one to have its own distinctive identity. It was still very much an integrated railway, with responsibility for infrastructure, engineering and rolling stock, combined with a strong commercial focus centred on the concept of 'retail', with station and platform staff, ticket collectors and train cleaning teams all part of a single 2,500-strong retail section. A key point was that ScotRail, as owner of its assets, infrastructure, rolling stock and staff, was expected to trade among other rail businesses for the use of these assets: thus InterCity would buy use of ScotRail track and stations for its through trains between Inverness, Aberdeen and England. In a new reshuffle of area management, nine Service Managers were appointed, at Aberdeen, Ayr, Edinburgh, Fort William, Glasgow (North), Glasgow (South), Inverness, Perth and Stirling. At this time (1990-91) ScotRail was earning £78.7 million a year, 8% above its budget and 13% above 1989-90, and was providing 51 million passenger journeys a year[6].

The Freightliner terminal at Gushetfaulds, Glasgow, in the 1980s. Crane and trailers show signs of heavy use. (British Railways)

Echoing aims of a decade earlier, "customer needs" were to be at the forefront of concern, and "customer care training will be stepped up"[7]. One front-line customer business, trolley-based catering on trains, had been sublet since the early 1980s. From 1990 all train catering was leased to a private company, CCG services, whose 100 staff and 80 trolleys sold over 200,000 sandwiches a year, washed down by a million cups of tea and coffee, 300,000 soft drinks, 150,000 cans of export ale and 125,000 of lager, 12,000 miniature bottles of whisky, 10,000 of vodka, and 10,000 of water[8].

InterCity Scotland had a national manager based at Waverley Station, heading a sales team responsible for "half the passenger revenue in Scotland's Railways" including the sleeper trains. InterCity still owned the East Coast Main Line from Berwick to Edinburgh, the West Coast Main Line to the outskirts of Glasgow, and the newly-electrified Carstairs-Edinburgh line; and apart from freight-only lines like the Grangemouth branch, ScotRail owned the rest of the network[9]. Under OfQ the two divisions of Railfreight were made separate businesses from October 1991, with Trainload Freight specialising in bulks: metals, coal, petroleum and construction. Its Scottish Area Manager and Business Manager were in the metals division. Railfreight Distribution managed the container freight terminals at Gushetfaulds and Coatbridge and provided services for the automotive and chemicals industries as well as for general merchandise and export traffic. Freight traffic was slightly over 60 million tonnes, earning £60 million a year[10]. Alex Lynch, deputy director and financial controller of ScotRail, later its franchise development director, supervised the separation of InterCity and Railfreight accounts from those of the ScotRail passenger service.

Crossrail and the Airport Link

Glasgow's "missing link", the north-south Crossrail proposal, re-emerged in the early 1990s, energised by the Railway Development Society, and with a wide range of support, including the city's Chamber of Commerce, the Scottish Trade Union Congress and numerous local MPs – but not the railway professionals. In May 1991 ScotRail's general manager Cyril Bleasdale confirmed that "I understand that market research undertaken by SPTE demonstrated that the majority of customers currently using Glasgow

Central would be worse off if their trains were diverted via Crossrail… I can see little benefit in [further] discussing the matter"[11]. Another SPTE review in 1992 rejected it on grounds of social value. However, Crossrail's significance to the Glasgow Airport rail link got it included in a Strathclyde Regional Council document of 1992, 'Travelling in Strathclyde', backed by a powerful councillor, Malcolm Waugh, chairman of the Roads and Transportation Committee. Waugh remarked of Crossrail that "I didn't need that, but when I thought of the airport link, I needed it then to get people from all over Strathclyde to the airport"[12]. A light rail link to the airport from Paisley was the preference of the SPTE professionals, but not shared by their political masters who doubted whether people travelling to and from the airport would find a change of mode acceptable. For any direct rail link from the city centre and the incoming lines from the north and east to the airport, the existence of Crossrail was essential. Waugh's successor in 1996, Councillor Charles Gordon, an ex-NUR man[13], also backed it in similarly regal style, though noting "a lot of commuters who currently come in quite handily to Glasgow Central are going to be diverted away round Crossrail" and might not be pleased. He felt that social and environmental responsibilities should be considered: "there's got to be some vision and a bit of a leap of faith"[14], but a cost estimate of £80 million in 1996 helped to keep the project on the shelf. ScotRail's liaison manager with Strathclyde was quoted in 1996 as saying, "Certainly, we wouldn't put any of our own money into it"[15]. Gordon's leap of faith was required by the fact that successive cost-benefit analyses of the Crossrail project had shown negative results – but these took account only of specific effects and not of wider aspects or of potential changes in travel patterns. While traffic forecasts for 1980s projects, like the Cathcart Circle electrification, were often larger than the actuality, the Bathgate-Waverley, Stirling-Alloa and Borders lines have all greatly exceeded prediction – one of the issues that Transport Scotland must confront in future planning.

Privatisation is on the Agenda

ScotRail produced a positive marketing plan for 1992-93 with targeted revenue increases on its four designated route types, Express (up 13%), Long Urban (up 3.1%), Short Urban (up 5.1%) and Rural (up 6.3%) and was rewarded with a 9% increase in revenues[16]. Bleasdale maintained strong emphasis on customer care, and from the evidence of growing usage, ScotRail was generally doing what its users wanted. It was InterCity, not ScotRail, as operator of the sleeper services, which ended the provision of seated accommodation on the overnight trains from Inverness and Aberdeen to London on 10 May 1992. Seeing an opportunity, Stagecoach, the bus company, took its first step into railway operations with a contract to replace the service with own-branded carriages. This went live on 11 May, though only from Aberdeen as the full capacity of the Inverness train was now taken up by sleeping cars (Stagecoach ran a connecting road service from Inverness to Edinburgh). The contract was revised on 28 September 1992 to include the Glasgow-Euston overnight train, but Stagecoach ended the exercise, though not its interest in railways, on 3 October 1993.

By then a new Conservative government, under John Major, had been elected in April 1992. In Scotland Labour won 49 seats, the Conservatives eleven, the Liberal Democrats nine, and the SNP three. Railway privatisation was part of the new government's programme. With an irony that seemed to govern all three 20th century re-arrangements of the railways, just as a form of state ownership that worked well – cost-conscious, customer-oriented, seeking profits where they could be made – had been established, it was to be broken up to conform with a different political-economic philosophy. A majority of Scottish electors had supported parties that opposed privatisation, but two

Scots served as successive Ministers of Transport in the run-up to sell-off, Malcolm Rifkind (1990-92) and John MacGregor (1992-94). Rifkind had favoured privatisation of the existing set-up, but MacGregor's brief, formulated by the Treasury Privatisation Unit[17], was for a single corporation as permanent owner of track, stations and all installations, later named Railtrack. Simon Jenkins, a former BRB member, and co-founder of the Railway Heritage Trust (1985) that has done so much to refurbish historic railway structures, described Railtrack as "the Treasury's latest fad, the self-financing quango that it can control but need not finance"[18]. Twenty-seven route operators were to be granted fixed-term franchises by a semi-independent Franchise Director. After a lapse of 70 years, the concept of competition was once again invoked in official policy towards railway service, since some train operators would be sharing lines[19].

The Railways Act of 1993 cleared the way for British Railways to be disposed of. Two new bodies were set up to manage privatisation. The Office of Rail Regulation (ORR), independent of the Government, was to ensure that new train operating companies followed the franchise terms and also to look after the interests of passengers. The Office of Passenger Rail Franchising (OPRAF) was responsible to the government for overseeing the terms of franchises and subsidies – it was accepted that most franchises would be impossible to lease out, at least initially, without a system of subsidies in place to preserve services unprofitable in themselves but considered socially essential. Three new companies were formed to take over ownership of all passenger rolling stock and locomotives, which would be leased to franchise holders. Would-be franchise holders had to calculate the elements of revenue from services and subsidy, and balance these against the costs of providing the stipulated level of service, including the leasing charges, and payments to Railtrack for use of infrastructure, in order to make an offer which also assured their own required profit margin (See Appendix 1). Railtrack, rolling stock companies and franchise-holders were all supposed to make a profit for their shareholders.

A Class 86 locomotive enters Newton Station with a train from the south, all in post-1985 InterCity livery. (Stenlake Collection)

Preparation for Franchising:
the Return of Chris Green

With an annual turnover reckoned at £217 million, of which £87 million came from fares and £130 million fom subsidy, ScotRail was chosen as one of the first seven 'model franchises', which involved trimming its costs to make it a more attractive package to bidders. Pressure to shed staff was resisted, but routine maintenance work came virtually to a halt. In January 1993 Bleasdale had to impose a 'maintenance holiday' decreed by Regional Railways HQ as part of a 20% spending reduction. Painting of the Forth Bridge, famously a continuous task, was halted for a year, and the painters redeployed. Reopening of the Stirling-Alloa line had been planned for 1994 and Thornton-Leven had also been planned – in 1993 both "slipped off the radar" and a £26 million resignalling scheme for the Falkirk area was refused by Regional Railways HQ[20]. Newspapers caught the scent of infighting between ScotRail and Regional Railways, which had been pressing for further savings through service cuts: "ScotRail, however, has defended its services by producing savings in other areas, including cuts in staff at its Glasgow headquarters. Last month it announced it would save £600,000 by not painting the Forth Bridge this year. Managers have seen a summary of this year's changes, but do not believe any of them will adversely effect the quality of services. The only outright cut is believed to be the loss of one of the four trains a day on the Oban line. A ScotRail spokesman said: 'The policy is that there will be no detrimental effect on rail services before the Government releases more detail on what the effect of franchising will be'". *Modern Railways* reported that at one point the Department for Transport had wanted to make two franchises, Scotland East and Scotland West[21] – an echo of Sir Eric Geddes more than 70 years before.

Gourock Station, 1991. New canopies and a walkway to the ferry terminal were completed in 2011 (Stenlake Collection)

In 1993 there was some excitement around the potential of the Channel Tunnel to give Scotland better access to European markets and destinations. Indeed, trans-Tunnel sleeper trains from Glasgow to Paris and Brussels had been planned (and the cars built at a cost of £150 million) though the services never materialised. A consortium of BR, and the German, French and Belgian Railways had combined to form European Night Services, but this fell foul of a European Commission judgement on competition: that the same service must be offered to potential competitors. The venture was terminated in 1998[22]. When the Tunnel opened in May 1994, a link service from Edinburgh to London Waterloo was started, but little used, and was withdrawn in January 1997.

Uncertainty in the lives of railway users and workers was increased by government plans to effect a new reorganisation of local authorities, and in 1994 with its future unclear, the SPTA put an order for new Class 157 diesel units on hold, and suspended planned improvement work at Glasgow Central and Queen Street, Paisley Gilmour Street, and other stations. With pressure already growing for a second Forth road bridge, Bleasdale's work with Fife Regional Council resulted in consent from the Scottish Office for the council to invest £3.8 million in upgrading services to Edinburgh, including four new Class 157 units[23]. Speculation about a potential management buyout of ScotRail went on through 1993, with frequent mention of the names of Chris Green and John Cameron, farmer, railway enthusiast, and the only Scottish member at this time on the British Rail board (the number of Camerons involved in railway management is a curiosity). Bleasdale was also keen on a management buyout but was "understood to have lost an internal battle"[24] and retired at the end of March 1994.

As a preliminary to sale, ScotRail was made a separate entity as a division of the British Railways Board from 1 April 1994, a 'shadow franchise' working with the rolling stock companies and Railtrack[25]. The latter took control of track and signalling from the same date. Chris Green, by then head of InterCity, now wound up, returned to ScotRail as Director from 1 April, with the aim of mounting a management buy-out, and a stream of activity began, to reinvigorate the brand both by reaching the travelling public and by motivating the staff. ScotRail was one of Scotland's largest companies, with 4,100 employees and an annual turnover that had reached £300 million, though it now owned neither trains nor tracks nor stations. It was due to pay Railtrack £175 million a year for access to the rail network, plus leasing charges on stations, and to meet the cost of leasing and basic maintenance of the 280 trains providing 1,900 daily services. Maintenance depots were at Shields, Corkerhill, Haymarket and Inverness. Its name and livery were, however, the railway's public face. On a shadow franchise the BR logo was no longer considered appropriate, and a blue, red and yellow "swoosh" motif was substituted as part of the relaunch. Six area managers were appointed: for the North, based at Perth; for Queen Street; Glasgow Central; Yoker; Edinburgh (Steve Montgomery who would later head First ScotRail); and Ayr. Each area had a customer service manager, with North also having local managers at Aberdeen and Inverness.

New investment was badly needed: ScotRail's 29 routes were all in need of development. It was still operating some first-generation diesel units, and the Blue Trains were by now obsolescent. Green's plans included a 15-minute interval Edinburgh-Glasgow service, as part of a positive programme embracing most of the service developments which would happen over the next 20 years, as well as the Glasgow Crossrail and airport links. His draft budget for 1994-95 noted costs of £221 million, and passenger income of £96 million, supported by £110 million from SPTA and £115 million from the Franchise Director[26]. Investment and expansion of services was certainly not envisaged by the Franchise Director, however, whose brief was to form packages that would be attractive to bidders. As well as confronting a mountain of paperwork generated by the separation of ScotRail from the ownership of the BRB – a 100-page contract was required for the transfer of each station – and the new bureaucracy imposed by the relationships with Railtrack and the leasing companies, Green found himself under strong pressure to continue cost reductions.

Controversy arose in early 1995 when ScotRail, given responsibility for the Anglo-Scottish sleeper services following the dissolution of InterCity, proposed to abolish the London-Fort William train, at the behest of Roger Salmon, the Franchise Director. Not for the first time, war-cries from the Highlands disrupted plans made in London. As ever with proposed service cuts, contradictory figures on costs and earnings were quoted, though no-one denied that the sleeper required a substantial subsidy. ScotRail was accused of putting on a late-night 'ghost train', the 23.58 Maryhill-Bishopbriggs, using the 140-yard chord between Cowlairs North and East junctions, previously used only by the West Highland sleeper, in order to avoid a formal closure procedure. Campaigners against the sleeper closure took their case to the Court of Session, which ruled that the full procedure must be followed. The Fort William sleeper was eventually "reprieved"[27]. The now loss-making Motorail services were, however, cut at this time, including the Plymouth-Glasgow and Edinburgh trains.

This was not the kind of thing that Green, who had helped to save the overnight Fort William service ten years earlier, had come back for. Having hoped to build on ScotRail's "decade of growth" between 1984 and 1994 with continuing development, he resigned in February 1995. Though he made no public statement, it was hardly a secret that he thought the nature of the privatisation scheme was flawed, and the prospect of further enforced cuts to Scottish services in the interest of making a more attractive privatisation package directly conflicted with his plans for development and enhancement. A *Herald* article on 19 January 1996 referred to his "despairing insistence that Scottish services could not be maintained at anything near present level unless Government support increased." He was succeeded by John Ellis, who had been ScotRail general manager from 1987-90, a keen privatiser who also hoped to lead a management buyout. In December 1995 the ScotRail business and most of the old Scottish Region's assets and liabilities were vested in ScotRail Railways Ltd, a wholly-owned subsidiary of the BRB, set up as a vehicle for the privatisation process[28].

Until 31 March 1994 ScotRail, as part of Regional Railways, had no statutory requirement for separate audit and accounts. In its new incarnation, these formalities were required. Revenue for 1995 was shown as £71.9 million, with costs of £323.9 million including £170 million paid to Railtrack; for 1996 revenue was £89.2 million, with costs at £366.5 million. In the year to 31 March 1996, 49 million passenger journeys were made. The company employed 3,977 people. Since 1990 seventeen new stations had been added. During 1996 and into 1997, there was considerable disruption and loss of income from strikes mounted by the RMT Union in protest against productivity demands made on guards and conductors. In March 1996 the Health & Safety Executive required Railtrack to start emergency work on the Forth Bridge or face prosecution – painting had been in abeyance for three years rather than one[29]. New techniques of shot-blast and oxide paint were now to last for 25 years.

12. The ScotRail Franchise and the Formation of Transport Scotland

The First Franchise

Despite being selected as an early candidate for privatisation, ScotRail was almost the last franchise to be sold. The reason was external: Scottish local authorities had been reorganised from April 1996, replacing the region and district arrangement of 1975 with a mixture of regions and unitary authorities. The huge Strathclyde Region was now divided into twelve authorities and the Strathclyde Passenger Transport Authority had to be recast to take account of this. Most of these authorities were Labour-controlled and not happy about a profit-making company receiving public money to the tune of £105,568,000 to run railway services (See Appendix 1). Substantial concessions were extracted, including the provision of 38 three-car electric trains, and nine new 3-car diesel units to provide a 15-minute interval service between Edinburgh and Glasgow by March 2000; and special grant funding of £250 million over the franchise period to the SPTA, to reduce the demand on local authorities. In addition £1.2 million a year was to be paid annually to the SPTA to meet the costs of monitoring and working with the franchisee[1].

Also the PTA insisted on its full timetable of 520 routes to be protected by inclusion in the franchise terms, to the annoyance of OPRAF. It took until February 1997 to resolve all the issues, and National Express was named Preferred Bidder, beating the management buy-out bid led by Ellis – "frustrated by bus operators' readiness to gamble on cutting costs and an unstated reluctance in Whitehall to let railwaymen run trains"[2] – and three other bids including one from the Stagecoach bus company. The new franchise holder was also Scotland's largest bus operator, owner of Scottish CityLink coaches which since 1988 had been competing vigorously with the trains. This led to the franchise deal being referred to the Monopolies & Mergers Commission, which required National Express to divest itself of

ScotRail News shows how the new ScotRail logo was created, in April 1994. (British RAilways, Chris Green Collection)

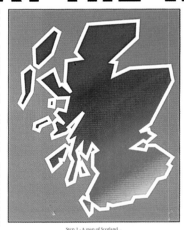

6 SCOTRAIL *News*

WHAT THE WHOOSH IS THAT?

WHAT IS THE WHOOSH? You should know it by now. Three bold sweeps of blue, red and yellow. The Whoosh is, quite simply, the symbol of the new ScotRail.

It is bright and colourful, it is cheerful and dynamic. And, although it is still early days, it will become totally, absolutely and unmistakably the identity of ScotRail.

You will see it on trains, in stations, on stationery, on uniforms, everywhere, in fact, that ScotRail has a presence.

More than 40 individual designs were looked at before ScotRail opted for the Whoosh. Its colours come from the Saltire and the Lion Rampant but it represents neither. ScotRail could have used a thistle, but then thistles are commonplace.

No, the Whoosh is unique. Created from a stylised map of Scotland it can go on to become a nationally known, instantly identifiable image that goes automatically with the new ScotRail. And if ScotRail can produce "the friendliest, most dependable way to travel in Scotland" then the Whoosh will become a symbol of all that's best in the railway industry.

Step 1 - A map of Scotland

Step 2 - in graphic form

Step 3 - the end result

Scottish CityLink within six months. The franchise was for seven years, with a built-in subsidy of £280.1 million in 1997-98, dropping to £202 million in 2003-04. This latter figure was 31% less than British Rail had claimed for ScotRail in 1996-97, a point emphasised by National Express, which also committed itself to running no less than the current number of train miles and to provide enhancements to stations and services[3].

Scotland's last publicly-owned trains were the 23.30 services between Edinburgh and Glasgow on 31 March 1997, with a staff champagne and whisky party on the eastbound train[4]. And so, after almost 50 years, the Scottish railway system entered a new phase of ownership and control. In half a century of nationalisation, there had been plenty of change. A Rip van Winkle from 1948 or before would have recognised much in the way of architecture, and semaphore signals still in many places, but little else would seem familiar. Some lines, like the Callander & Oban as far as Crianlarich, or the 'Port Road' from Dumfries to Stranraer, or those that once passed by such places as Muirkirk, Maud, Forfar, or Crieff, were already taking on the appearance of archaeological remains like the earthworks of the old North Britons. But shiny electric multiple units running under central Glasgow, local stations without staff but equipped with electronic screens and disembodied voices providing train information, power signal boxes controlling many miles, trains running from Glasgow to London in 4 hours 32 minutes, fast trainloads of containers with no brake van, would have seemed a vision of the far future come true. It was a reduced network, 1,894 miles (3,030 km) compared with the 3,730 miles (5,968 km) left by the LMS and LNER, but clearly still a live element in national life.

Now, the question was, what would happen under privatisation? Three other train companies (TOCs) ran passenger services into Scotland: Great North Eastern Railway to Edinburgh, with limited services to Glasgow, Aberdeen and Inverness; Cross-Country from south-west England to Edinburgh, Glasgow and Aberdeen (with a Penzance-Aberdeen service), and West Coast Trains between London and Glasgow via Lockerbie, the last two both owned by the Virgin Group. None required a Scottish subsidy, and competition with ScotRail was minimal (ScotRail did not run trains between Edinburgh and Berwick, and Dunbar was a GNER station). High hopes had been expressed for the economic benefits of franchising, sometimes with the same rhetorical bravado that the most enthusiastic advocates of nationalisation had shown 60 years earlier. One proponent of privatisation predicted that "…net contracted subsidies will decline rapidly… potentially, to nothing by 2012"[5].

The years between 1997 and 2000 were not good for the owners and users of privatised railways, even though passenger numbers continued on the rising trend that had begun in the late 1980s. Operational difficulties were caused by the three-year investment gap in routes, stations and rolling stock. In a book focused on the Scottish system it can only be noted in passing that the attempt to have as many as 27 train operating franchises was a failure, with punctuality declining and costs rising. In the next round the number of franchises would be fewer. Railtrack was a controversial creation from the start. In April 1996 John Welsby, chairman of the BRB, took the unusual step of publicly criticising the draft prospectus drawn up for its Stock Exchange flotation. The Minister of Transport, Sir George Young, made an aggressive reply accusing the old railway of being "a monolithic, monopolistic, slow-moving nationalised industry which never had the inclination or incentive to focus on the needs of its passengers or freight users"[6] – a curious response from a Minister busy creating a monolithic monopoly in the form of Railtrack. Owning ex-BR assets valued at £6.5 billion on which it was expected to achieve a 5.6% annual return, it was successfully floated as a

Entrance to Stirling Station, freshly branded with the ScotRail logo, 1997. Further modernisation and canopy renewed was completed in May 2016. (Stenlake Collection)

public limited company in May 1996, at £3.60 per share; the price peaked in November 1998 at £17.68 after a profit of £346 million was declared for 1997. Seen to be more focused on delivering shareholder results than infrastructure maintenance, which it outsourced to external contractors at costs up to three times the previous levels[7], Railtrack already had a reputation for ineffective management before the Hatfield crash of 17 October 2000 and the resultant sudden imposition of no less than 6,281 speed restrictions and temporary line closures, including the West Coast Main Line north of Carlisle for three days. By 28 October, though, Scottish services were mostly returning to normal. Compelled to pay huge amounts in compensation for the disruption, Railtrack posted losses of £534 million in 2000-01, and on 5 October 2001 it was placed in administration by the Labour government and the company was liquidated, with shareholders receiving £2.52 for each share. A new 'not-for-profit' state-owned company, Network Rail, was established to replace it from October 2002, owning and controlling all tracks and installations throughout the UK, with a Scottish office run by a local director. The rolling stock companies, set up in 1994, have been criticised from both sides of the political divide; having been sold by the Major government for £1 billion, subsequent sales have put their worth at three times that. In part their value increased because the increase in rail travel, coupled with the shortage of rolling stock caused by the pre-privatisation freeze on investment, heightened the demand for passenger accommodation. The companies made up to 44% return on turnover in their early years and were recovering the cost of new stock within a four to twelve year period, though it had a working life of up to 40 years[8]. Commentators pointed out that they were behaving exactly as commercial companies might be expected to do, and though there were accusations of market rigging, industry regulators were content to let the rolling stock companies follow their own code of practice.

The first franchise holders, mostly bus companies, were surprised to find that while bus deregulation had resulted in falling wages, rail privatisation was followed by pay rises, owing to the effectiveness or intransigence, depending on one's viewpoint, of the rail unions. They had also greatly overerestimated the amount of "efficiency" savings that could be sliced from railway operations. National Express, perhaps having relied too much on the rhetoric of the privatisers, found the ScotRail business much leaner than it had expected – its managing director admitted in 2002 that the BR men "knew how to squeeze a pound" – but it maintained a high ranking in performance standards. In the first two years of privatisation, its passenger journeys rose by 11%. In 1998, with 95.9% punctuality (arrival on time or within 10 minutes) and 99.4% 'reliability'. From 2000, after the establishment of the Scottish Parliament and Executive, the company subtitled itself 'Scotland's National Railway'. In 2002 it ran into financial trouble, forecasting a £115 million loss, primarily with its Central Trains franchise in England, but seeking also a renegotiation of its ScotRail contract. In a restructuring of the franchise agreement, subsidy payments due to fall instead took an upturn from 2002-03:

National Express subsidy (£ millions)						
1997-98	1998-99	1999-00	2000-01	2001-02	2002-03	2003-04
281	264	246	216	174	189	266

BBC News reported on 7 March that "a £34 million handout" of public money was going to National Express, to ensure that it maintained service levels[9].

ScotRail revenues were hit in 2002 and 2003 by pay disputes involving drivers and guards; when guards walked out on 28 March 2003 in protest against downgrading of their safety duties, some management staff were deployed as replacements. New official safety rules put the driver in charge of the train in the event of an accident or incident, with the guard's role to "assist passengers"[10]. The Anglo-Scottish services were now competing with low-cost airlines as well as coach companies, and "bargain berth" sleepers were introduced by ScotRail. In May 2002 an intending traveller from Glasgow to London and back again could choose from Virgin Trains at £29, ScotRail sleeper at £38, Go (air) at £55.25 and Easyjet at £61[11]. Under Peter Cotton as ScotRail managing director great efforts were made from 2002 and by 2004 (when it was named UK Rail Operator of the Year) the franchise had a list of achievements to chalk up, some of them only completed in the next incarnation of ScotRail. It provided the new train servicing facility at Eastfield in late 2004, introduced 74 new multiple-unit trains, 27 more than the franchise commitment, opened eight new stations, introduced the 15-minute interval Edinburgh-Glasgow service, and maintained above-average records of punctuality and customer satisfaction. Its essential failure was its inability to achieve the necessary level of profitability. To match the original proposed annual subsidy reductions, it needed to effect an improvement of 10% a year but only managed 0.4% in 1998-99 and 1999-2000, and a shortfall was incurred in the other years between 1997 and 2004.

National Express profit performance 1997-2004: 10% annual improvement targeted[12]:

1997-98	1998-99	1999-00	2000-01	2001-02	2002-03	2003-04
-0.7%	0.4%	0.4%	-3.2%	-12.8%	-2.5%	-3.2%

The 2000 Transport Act:
The Executive Gets a Look-In

There were other changes as successive Labour governments, in power from 1997 until 2010, grappled with the problems arising from the first privatisations[13]. The Transport Act of 2000 abolished the Office of Passenger Rail Franchise and set up a Strategic Rail Authority in its place, with a brief to exercise tighter control on franchise grants and closer monitoring of the train companies. This new body's relationship with the independent Rail Regulator was not wholly clear. The Regulator's brief was now to put passenger interests first while also promoting "high levels of cost-effective investment in the network". The Act also gave the devolved Scottish Executive (formed in 1999) a role in determining rail services provided by the ScotRail franchise: it was to define and give the SRA directions and guidance on its requirements, but the contract was to be let and managed by the SRA, which already, in August 2001, had identified ScotRail as "a heavy loss-maker"[14]. In January 2002 the SRA published a first strategic plan, which included the establishment of rail links to Glasgow and Edinburgh airports by 2010. In 2003 these proposals were noted merely as "being studied". In opposition, Labour had proposed to re-nationalise the railways, but the policy was repudiated by Alistair (later Lord) Darling, on the grounds that privatisation despite being "ill thought-out" had brought increases in investment and innovation. This was an odd statement since willingness of the private sector to invest had been notably lacking in rail privatisation[15]. A White Paper in July 2004 described the system as a public-private partnership, specified by the government and delivered by the private sector. As part of a "rail reform package", the Regulator was replaced on 5 July 2004 by a new Office of Rail Regulation, which would also assume responsibility for rail safety. The Strategic Rail Authority turned out to be short-lived, abolished by the next Transport Act which came along in 2005, and also provided for the transfer of its Scottish responsibilities to the Scottish Executive from July 2005.

The GNER London-Inverness service speeds down Glen Truim on a wintry April day in 1998. (Highland Railway Society)

The 2005 Transport Act
and the Formation of Transport Scotland

The 2005 Act gave distinct responsibilities and rights on passenger railway matters to the Scottish Executive, in liaison with the Office of Rail Regulation (Office of Rail and Road from 16 October 2015) and Network Rail. Establishing general future requirements, known as High Level Output Specifications (HLOS), is the responsibility of the Executive, now the Scottish Government. These specifications are passed to the ORR, along with a statement of funds available to achieve them. The ORR is not legally bound to implement all or indeed any of the specifications. As the independent economic regulator, it publishes a periodic review which determines the outputs that Network Rail has to deliver in contributing towards fulfilment of the HLOS (consistent with available funds), and the access charges that Network Rail will receive to fund the costs of these outputs. Network Rail has a right to reject ORR's final determination, if it believes that the outcome of the periodic review is unreasonable. ORR can then either revise its determination or refer the matter to the Competition and Markets Authority, something that has not yet been needed. ORR also has UK-wide responsibility for Health and Safety regulation on the railways (administered by the H&S Executive). Scottish Ministers have a formal role in a range of matters relating to Network Rail's finances and governance as they affect the Scottish route, including senior appointments and business planning. This is enabled by a Memorandum of Understanding between the Scottish Ministers and the UK Department for Transport, aligned to which is a separate debt limit of £3.3 billion to cover Network Rail's borrowing requirements for Scotland in Control Period 5 (CP5), which provides safeguards around Scotland's investment programme through to 2019[16]. It can be seen that important aspects of railway governance remain on a UK-wide basis. The ORR and Competition and Markets Authority are both non-ministerial government organisations, and since 2015 Network Rail has been reclassified as a government agency.

Transport Scotland was established by the Scottish Executive in 2005 as an external agency (quango in popular parlance) to plan and manage all aspects of government responsibility for all modes of transport. Its Rail Directorate was charged with supervision of the ScotRail franchise, though Transport

Class 47 No. 47712 restored in 2015 with the ScotRail livery of the 1980s push-pull expresses. Built in 1966, now owned by the Crewe Diesel Preservation Group, it carried the name *Lady Diana Spencer* between 1981 and 1991. Adjacent is 37401, Mary Queen of Scots, owned by Direct Rail Services. (Crewe Diesel Preservation Group)

Scotland has no control over the cross-border franchises (except for the Caledonian Sleeper service) other than to "provide input from a Scottish perspective". It was also to participate in a wider transport policy to serve the economy and the needs of travellers and shippers "in the most effective, productive and environmentally friendly ways", and manage the funding of Network Rail's delivery responsibility, monitor progress of new projects, advise Ministers on investment priorities, and liaise with the Office of Rail and Road. A separate Commercial Unit was set up to deal with commercial negotiations and procurements, including new rolling stock[17], and prepare for the next franchising round. Transport Scotland applied a new rigour to the franchise procedure and supervision, and rail users benefit from introduction of the station quality inspection report (SQUIRE) scheme, more stringent than that used in England. Based on a market research survey of passengers' priorities in 2006, it identifies five specific issues on trains and also in stations, and monitors these through inspections. Financial benefits or penalties are awarded to ScotRail, according to whether set targets are exceeded or missed[18]. At the same time, the SPTA was reformed into the Strathclyde Partnership for Transport (SPT), with responsibility for all regional transport co-ordination and planning, including freight traffic on road and rail, but no financial involvement with or operational control of railways[19]. Six similar bodies were set up in other regions, only one of which, ZetTrans in Shetland, has no concern with rail services. The others are for the Highlands and Islands, including Orkney (HITRANS), the North East (NESTRANS), Tayside & Central (TACTRAN), South East (SESTRAN), and South West (Swestrans). On the ashes of the SRA another organisation was set up as Passenger Focus Scotland, an independent "consumer watchdog" to speak for and protect the interest of rail travellers, though without specific powers.

West Coast and East Coast

The West and East Coast cross-border franchises both ran into trouble. The West Coast Main Line modernisation was completed in December 2005. Originally estimated to cost £2.5 billion, in the latter days of Railtrack it was alarmingly re-forecast at £14.5 billion. After the SRA and Network Rail got a firm, if belated, grip on the project, the final cost was £8.6 billion[20]. Twenty years after the APT experiments, the modernisation allowed Virgin Railways to use a development of APT tilting technology on its Italian-built Pendolino trains, which had been running on the West Coast Main Line since January 2004. Glasgow to London in 4½ hours was now a standard. Though more trains could now be provided, fears were already being expressed that the line would have insufficient capacity by 2015-20 if the levels of traffic growth seen in 2005-06 were maintained, and the prospect of an extension into Scotland of the HS2 project, giving 3-hour timings to London, was being aired[21]. Virgin Trains' franchise was extended to the end of 2012 while a bidding process went on for the next franchise, to run for fifteen years. This was awarded to First Group, but Virgin mounted a highly effective public, Parliamentary and legal campaign which forced the Department for Transport to admit that the evaluation process had been bungled, and the Virgin bid was accepted. Compensatory payments to First Group and other bidders cost the Department for Transport £44.6 million. The East Coast Main Line underwent its own saga. Great North Eastern Railway, a vehicle of Sea Containers plc, was the first franchisee, for seven years from 1996, extended to April 2005, and won a second franchise for seven years, with a possible 3-year extension. By late 2005 GNER was in financial straits, realised it had overbid, and defaulted on the franchise. The Government withdrew the franchise in December and put it up for new tenders, while GNER ran the line on a fixed-fee basis. National Express became the new franchise holder from December 2007 until 2015, but it in turn found the agreed terms too steep, and when the government refused further subsidy it defaulted on the agreement in July 2009. The franchise was again withdrawn and from November that year the trains were run by East Coast Trains, a subsidiary of the state-owned Directly Owned Railways. ECT ran the franchise very successfully until February 2015, when a new commercial franchise was agreed with Virgin Trains East Coast, a body owned 10% by Virgin Trains and 90% by Stagecoach. VTEC took over on 1 March 2015[22].

The Second Franchise

As noted above, as part of the devolution of powers, from 2000, the Scottish Executive was involved in placing the franchise of 2004, though the SRA controlled the process. The contract was won by another transport empire that had begun as a bus company, the Aberdeen-based First Group, which took over on 17 October. A celebratory 'breakfast party' was held at Paisley (Gilmour Street) Station[23]. Unlike National Express, it was not required by the Competition and Markets Authority to divest any of its road coach interests. The value of the 7-year contract was £1.98 billion, and First Group committed itself to investing £40 million. First ScotRail's managing director was Mary Dickson, the first woman to head a Scottish railway company. With passenger numbers continuing to rise, "Meet the Manager" sessions at stations voiced many complaints, and Dickson, who wore a name badge and talked to passengers on her daily commute between Edinburgh and Glasgow, reckoned that it would take "at least a year to change attitudes so that staff put passengers first"– this was ten years after the shadow franchise put "excellence in customer service" at the top of its agenda. Even so, customer satisfaction remained above the UK average. A Passenger Focus report in Autumn 2008 recorded that from Spring 2004 approval level never went below 83% and in one year reached 91% against a UK average ranging from

One of the wall panels in the refurbished station underpass at Kilmarnock, showing the town's railway history (Courtesy of WAVEparticle)

73% to 83% – though only 42% of respondents in that period thought that ScotRail dealt adequately with the specific problem of delays. While "overall satisfaction" for ScotRail was consistently high, another Passenger Focus issue, "Satisfaction with value for money for price of your ticket" ran at a lower level, 59% in Spring 2004, rising to 62% in Autumn 2008. But here too ScotRail's figures were still among the highest, bettered only by the small Merseyrail franchise. ScotRail's punctuality level also remained high, especially compared with trains coming up from England. The Commons Scottish Affairs Committee heard from Alec McTavish of the Association of Train Operating Companies on this on 24 April 2009:

McTavish: Let me explain the way in which we measure reliability. We measure on nought to ten minutes. A long-distance train is on time if it arrives within ten minutes of the scheduled time.

MP: It can be ten minutes late, and still be on time.

McTavish: Exactly[24].

In April 2008 First ScotRail's franchise was extended to 2015, with a revision of the terms which included the creation of a £73.1 million fund to be managed by Transport Scotland for general improvements. The money came from "converting future estimated revenue share payments… in return for a change in First ScotRail's revenue share and support arrangements". The three-year franchise extension was worth £900 million to First ScotRail and there was controversy over the fact that the deal had been done without external consultation process with interested parties and before the findings of a franchise review by Audit Scotland. Some observers felt that the Transport Minister and Transport Scotland had been outmatched by First Group's strong management team headed by Sir Moir Lockhead. However, the government, with its eye on the Glasgow Commonwealth Games in 2014, was also anxious to ensure continuity in the railway service during the run-up period. Transport Scotland's Finance Director resigned in November 2008 when it emerged that he had attended meetings about the franchise extension despite being a shareholder in First Group. Dr Malcolm Reed, Transport Scotland's chief executive, retired early by mutual agreement in February 2009. Audit Scotland's 2008-09 report on Transport Scotland gave unqualified approval to the accounts but made a number of recommendations both in terms of improving its management of the franchise, and improving stakeholder understanding, transparency and accountability. It also confirmed that the procedure for considering the franchise extension had been rigorous[25]. There was further embarrassment when it was announced that owing to a "methodology error" in the computer software used to produce overall passenger figures, First ScotRail's passenger totals for journeys originating in Scotland had been overstated by more than 7,000,000 in 2007 and 2008. This coincided with the franchise extension, but First ScotRail pointed out that the error, to do with the evaluation of SPT zone cards, originated during the previous franchise.

First Group appeared to have no trouble in maintaining both its road and rail interests: in 2009 it recorded a new coach leisure route from Glasgow to Largs, improved its overnight coach service from Glasgow to London, and completed "a major initiative to upgrade and rebrand the commuter coach service between Motherwell and Glasgow"[26]. Lockhead retired in March 2011 and Dickson (now Grant) left the company in the same year. Operations Director Steve Montgomery, whose career had begun in classic railway style as a signalman at Howwood in 1984, became managing director. By then, investment in new projects was beginning to show results. From December

2010 a cross-country service from Helensburgh to Edinburgh, via Glasgow, Airdrie and Bathgate, was running with Class 334 electric units, and new Class 380 units were on the Ayrshire and Inverclyde lines, with an enlarged maintenance base at Shields Road opened in February 2011[27]. In the snowy winter of 2010-11 Network Rail paid First ScotRail £1 million for weather-caused delays, and Transport Scotland revealed that since 2004 Network Rail had paid First ScotRail £2.8 million in compensation and the train company had paid Network Rail £2 million.

Well aware of of a train operating company's vulnerability to the vagaries of public opinion and the potential need for 'Crisis PR', First ScotRail employed a public relations consultancy to develop "extensive programmes of stakeholder engagement to build understanding of ScotRail's contribution to the life of the nation". Aimed at MSPs and members of other public bodies, the campaign was claimed to have improved favourability by double figures[28]. The company's operating profit in 2010-11 was £15.6 million, or £14.4 million after tax, and an interim dividend of £14 million was paid to the holding company, FirstRail Holdings Ltd (£18 million in the previous year). Turnover was £563.3 million (£524.6 million in the previous year). Its revenue grant from Transport Scotland was £270 million (£249.2 million in the previous year). Total net operating costs were £547,647,000 (£504,333,000), including staff costs of £164,708,000 for the 4,333 employees, making average pay around £38,000 a year. Directors received £1,032,000 including company contributions to pension funds. The company made charitable donations of £133,780 (£65,040 in the previous year). First ScotRail was judged Rail Operator of the Year in 2014, its third award of the title within six years. In the year to 31 March 2014 it received the largest subsidy of any TOC, £493.8 million; also the highest level of support per passenger-kilometre, 17.5 pence. Total turnover was £855 million, of which passenger fares accounted for £317 million, and a pre-tax profit of £25.7 million was recorded, with a dividend of £21 million going to the holding company[29].

Two Class 156 sets forming trains for Fort William and Mallaig cross at Glenfinnan Station. With the revitalisation of the station as a museum in 2009-13, the signal box, here definitely out of bounds, has been restored. (Stenlake Collection)

13. Infrastructure, Extension of the System and the Freight Problem

Edinburgh-Glasgow Improvement Programme (EGIP)

The first of a series of National Transport Strategy documents was published by Transport Scotland in 2006. A principal rail element in its 20-year perspective was the Edinburgh-Glasgow Improvement Programme (EGIP), an ambitious programme intended not only to increase the capacity of the Edinburgh-Falkirk-Glasgow main line but to incorporate electrification of the line from Cumbernauld through Stirling as far as Dunblane. Also included were electrification of the loop through Grahamston, and the busy freight-only Grangemouth branch, and the construction of an eastward-south chord at Dalmeny, enabling Glasgow-Edinburgh trains to stop at a new 'Edinburgh Gateway' station with a tram connection for Edinburgh Airport. It also incorporated the 'Garngad chord' to enable direct running between Queen Street Low Level, Cumbernauld, and stations beyond, which otherwise required reversal of direction at Springburn. The fastest timing between the city termini would be reduced to 35 minutes and there would be six trains an hour, with Class 380 electric units capable of acceleration from 0 to 60 mph in 50 seconds, compared to the 110 seconds taken by the Class 170 diesel units. The estimated cost was £1 billion, including the reconstruction of Queen Street, Haymarket and Cumbernauld stations.

Traditional building methods were retained in the heightening of this wall at Linlithgow in 2016, required as part of the EGIP scheme. Two class 170 Turbostar diesel units head for Edinburgh under the new catenary. (David Shirres)

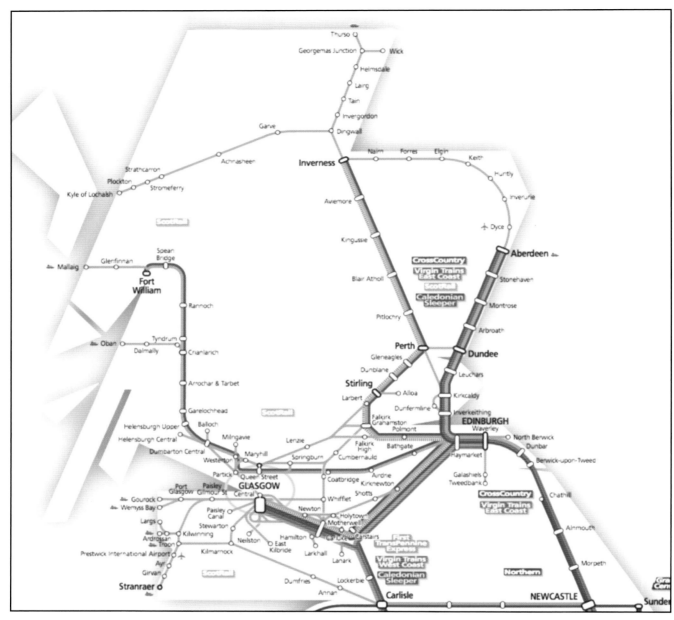

Diagrammatic map showing passenger routes in 2016. (ScotRail)

On the brink of the credit crunch and the switch to austerity policies that followed, Dr Malcolm Reed, former chief executive of the SPTE and now heading Transport Scotland, told an interviewer that planning assumptions were for 23% passenger growth by 2014[1]. In the event, growth in passenger journeys in the period was around 14%. In August 2008 Transport Scotland and Network Rail anticipated completion of Edinburgh Gateway by 2011, with the Dalmeny chord, the Garngad chord and an improved interchange station between Edinburgh and North Clyde line trains at Bellgrove by 2016. The worldwide financial crash beginning in September 2008 put many projects in jeopardy. In the aftermath of the crisis spending reviews were inevitable, and perhaps it it is more remarkable that two thirds of the EGIP programme survived than that a third was dropped, amended, or deferred, bringing its forecast cost down from £1 billion to £650 million. Following a six-month public consultation period, a Network Rail strategy review in July 2012 held the Waverley-Queen Street service to its present four per hour, though with longer, eight-car trains to increase capacity. Minimum journey time was now to be 42 minutes. Extension of the electrified line from Cumbernauld to Dunblane was at first deferred to a later spending period, but realisation that failure to provide this extension would make the regular 42-minute Edinburgh-Glasgow schedule (EGIP Key Output 3) impossible led to its inclusion in Network Rail's "rolling programme of electrification" for completion in December 2018, at a cost of £159.6 million, compared to an estimated £104.7 million in 2012[2], along with the loop through Grahamston to Polmont. The chord at Dalmeny, which would have enabled the new Edinburgh Gateway Station to serve Glasgow-Edinburgh trains, was abandoned, reducing the connections of the airport interchange to north-south services only, and the Garngad chord was also dropped[3].

From August 2012 electrification between Springburn and Cumbernauld went ahead, completed in May 2014. A final business case for EGIP was published on 27 January 2014, setting the cost at £742 million and introducing the prospect of an EGIP Phase 2 from 2025, "subject to affordability and other considerations including High Speed Rail and and wider capacity issues". Edinburgh Gateway Station opened on 11 December 2016. Full electrification between Waverley and Queen Street was deferred until end of 2017 and completion of the entire project is expected to be in 2019[4].

Two thousand cctv cameras were installed on 230 ScotRail trains in 2005-06, at a cost exceeding £2 million. More than half of stations also had surveillance cameras: the highest proportion in Britain[5]. Also in 2005 the Adopt a Station scheme was launched, to foster the value and appearance of local stations for their communities: 160 stations had been adopted by 2013. Transport Scotland decreed in 2008 that the ScotRail name and "saltire" livery was to be maintained irrespective of who held the franchise, thus assuring a continuing national identity across the system, including the former Strathclyde trains, which had had a distinctive livery of their own, initially orange and black, replaced from February 1997 by "carmine and cream"[6].

An SPT-liveried Class 318 electric multiple unit (introduced 1986-87) stands at Ayr Station. The Station Hotel, built by the G&SWR in 1866, rises above. It closed suddenly in 2013 and is now unused. (Stenlake Collection)

The privatisation era's first reinstatement of a closed line was the extension of Argyle Line services to Larkhall on 12 December 2005. Passenger trains between Stirling and Alloa returned on 19 May 2008, with coal trains running on to Kincardine to supply Longannet Power Station. This line's construction cost of £85 million greatly exceeded the original estimate of £37 million, but passenger numbers, forecast at 155,000 a year, were 402,000 in 2014-15. Also in 2008 double track was restored on the former G&SW line between Gretna and Annan. The prime scheme was the 30.5 mile Borders Railway (see below). Network Rail embarked on a new phase of improvements to Waverley Station from 2006, with four new platforms, remodelled tracks and user-friendly entrances – glass-enclosed escalators replaced the notorious wind-trap of the Waverley Steps to Princes Street. The Paisley Canal line was electrified from November 2012. Network Rail's original estimate for the 8.8 km route was £20-28 million, but when cost-benefit analysis established that the scheme justified a maximum spend of no more than £12.2 million, First ScotRail and Network Rail worked out a way of achieving this, and the scheme was completed to budget. Lower wires were permitted on the basis that electric trains would be multiple units only. If freight services resumed to the Hawkhead oil terminal, they would have to operate at night with the wire de-energised. ScotRail also waived compensation payments for engineers' line occupancy[7] between June and December 2012.

Glasgow Airport Access

Austerity policies had an impact on other projects as well as EGIP. Network Rail produced its first Scotland Route Utilisation Strategy, after thorough discussions with Transport Scotland, ScotRail and other interest-groups, in November 2006. The National Transport Strategy in 2006 and a Strategic Transport Projects Review in 2008 were both overtaken by events. For the Scottish government there were challenging issues, including the future of the Glasgow Airport rail link and the related question of the north-south Crossrail link in Glasgow itself. Following a fresh examination of the Crossrail plan, involving the new curve between High Street and Bell Street, and the 'Strathbungo link' from Muirhouse Junction to the former City Union line, which rated the project's benefit-cost ratio at a low 0.75-1.25, Transport Scotland rejected the scheme in 2008[8], but it still has many proponents who dispute the decision, pointing out that the link would be a game-changer that cannot be judged on the basis of existing traffic patterns. The Glasgow Airport rail link, involving a new branch from the Inverclyde line, between Paisley Gilmour Street and St. James Stations, to the terminal, was approved by the Parliament in 2009 and preliminary work had already begun when it was axed under austerity measures. Glasgow Airport had 8.7 million passengers in 2015 apart from staff and visitor movements, and confirmation of the project's renewal came in 2016 as the flagship element in the £1.13 billion Glasgow and Clyde Valley city deal – a funding agreement between the UK Government, the Scottish Government and eight local authorities across Glasgow and the Clyde Valley[9]. In November 2016 after a further consultants' appraisal, agreement was reached on the train-tram option, a £144 million scheme involving tram-trains capable of running both on heavy rail between Glasgow Central and Paisley, and on light rail to the airport. Hopes were expressed for completion by 2025[10].

The Borders Railway

The final version of Transport Scotland's 2009 Strategic Transport Projects Review indicated in a single brief mention that "the Waverley rail link is under development"; admittedly it was a document on future plans rather than a progress report, but it rather played down a remarkable project. If

Madge Elliot, campaigner for the Borders Railway, had a Freightliner locomotive named in her honour at Waverley Station on 4 June 2015. (Freightliners Ltd)

Strathclyde's Councillor Gordon had thought that vision and faith were required for an £80 million rail scheme catering for the huge numbers using Glasgow Airport, what combination of these qualities might be needed to procure a £294 million railway from Edinburgh over the hills to Galashiels and Tweedbank? Yet one was shelved and the other is triumphantly running. Campaigning for renewal of the Waverley Route was muted in the 1970s and 80s but gained strong momentum in the 1990s. The need for regional regeneration, with continuing depopulation, the shrinkage of the woollen industry, the huge expansion of forestry, and heavy road congestion in the vicinity of Edinburgh all helped to give the campaign a strong regional base of support. A venture to set up a timber-transporting railway using part of the old Border Counties line from Kielder to Riccarton, thence south to Longtown on the former main line (then terminus of a freight branch from Carlisle) did not succeed in 1998 but gave added momentum to a grass-roots movement which became the Campaign for Borders Rail in 1999. A feasibility study by the Scott Wilson Group that year did not result in a positive cost-benefit analysis but local pressure compelled public transport bodies and local authorities to form a Waverley Railway Joint Committee. The decision to create Edinburgh's Crossrail scheme, vigorously promoted by the Capital Rail Action Group (CRAG) and other organisations reflecting a growing interest in sustainable and environmentally-friendly transport, extended trans-city passenger services south-east to Newcraighall, on the still-extant end section of the Waverley Route in 2002, providing a helpful doorstep for continuance southwards, and the beyond-forecast success of the Bathgate lines was a further fillip[11]. Despite a "business case" survey in 2004 which found the project to be economically unviable, but was strongly contested, the Scottish Parliament passed the Waverley Railway (Scotland) Act on 14 June 2006. Even then hurdles remained. The new Transport Scotland organisation had shown scant enthusiasm for the project, and the tendering procedures collapsed in 2010-11 when two potential contractors pulled out. Management of the scheme was assumed by Network Rail, who undertook to complete the line by mid-2015 for £294 million, and, with contractor BAM Nuttall, succeeded within both time and budget. A train first travelled the line – at 30 miles the longest railway constructed in Britain since the West Highland, 111 years before – on 13 May 2015; public services began on 6 September and the railway was formally opened by the Queen three days later[12]. In its first year the line carried a million passengers, against a top forecast of 647,000, and the Campaign for Borders Rail found it necessary to cut through the official self-congratulations to remind everyone of the role of the local activists, in the face of (at best) official indifference, to get the line restored[13].

Looking into the Future:
The McNulty Report

"Every so often a bald-headed businessman writes a report on the efficiency of the railways, and everyone panics," wrote the journalist Julian Glover[14], commenting on a study entitled 'Realising the Potential of GB Rail' which appeared in May 2011. Led by Sir Roy McNulty, the Northern Irish businessman and former head of the Civil Aviation Authority, subtitled 'The Rail Value for Money Study', it was commissioned by the ORR and the Department for Transport to give a progress report on fifteen years of privatisation, and a set of recommendations for the future. From the Scottish viewpoint, there were some odd aspects. Despite the 'GB' title neither the Scottish Government nor its TS agency had any acknowledged part in its formation or brief. Its only mentions of Scotland were a reference to the Airdrie-Bathgate line as costing along with the (vastly more expensive) Thameslink scheme £1 billion, and a note with a faintly colonialist tinge that the study had "important linkages" for Scotland and Wales and that "the Department for Transport should work closely with devolved administrations to secure as consistent [an] approach as necessary"[15]. However, the study had some cogent things to say, not least about

A Class 170 train crosses the 14-arch Ferryden Viaduct over the South Esk, near Montrose, in 2016. (big55012)

privatisation, whose primary object "is understood to have been to reduce the level of public subsidy for an industry that was seen as being in long-term and possibly terminal decline", something which was certainly not spelled out in the Railways Act of 1993. McNulty pointed out that in fact rail passenger traffic was currently forecast to double in the next twenty years. Listing seven other aims of the privatisation project, including reduction of government investment, he made the masterly understatement that there was "still some distance to to go before these objectives are fully achieved"[16]. The basis of his case was that though railway passenger traffic had gone up by 57% since privatisation, operating cost per passenger had remained virtually unchanged, and the thrust of his proposals was that at least 30% could be cut from operating costs by 2018-19. He identified eight specific barriers to efficiency which had to be overcome, as well as a general "lack of leadership within the industry", and set out his solutions to overcoming these problems, with a timetable for implementation. Some were specific, like the formation of a Rail Delivery Group of industry leaders to drive the broad cost-saving strategy forward, subsequently established as the RDG; the decentralisation of Network Rail, now in hand; the creation of alliances between Network Rail and train operating companies in order to achieve cost-effective solutions to future requirements (set up in Scotland); and differentiated approaches for infrastructure and operations on "lower-cost regional railways". In other cases a problem was merely identified and left to the companies to sort out – noting that railway wages and salaries had risen above inflation, McNulty remarked that this could not continue, and that the industry would have to introduce pay restraint at all levels. At the same time, though, improved employee relations were "a key enabler" to bring about significant change. On a still-vexed issue, the study stated firmly that driver-only operation should be the default position, with a second traincrew member only "where there is a commercial, technical or other imperative". Even from the measured Whitehallese prose of the study, it was clear that stations were considered to be overstaffed and that TOCs should review this "as a matter of priority"; also that the rolling stock leasing companies needed to be more closely regulated, with the suggestion that the Department for Transport should "in the longer term establish new vehicles to procure and hold rolling stock in the public interest"[17].

McNulty's report was certainly closely read in Scotland, where the railway system was already well-suited to achieving his key aims, with a single TOC, its own Network Rail route plan, and devolved political and financial control. Indeed, when the House of Commons Transport Committee interviewed interested parties after publication of the report, Network Rail's chief executive, Sir David Higgins, cited the collaboration on the Paisley Canal electrification as evidence that alignment of Network Rail and Train Operating Company could and did result in substantial cost reductions[18].

Privatised Freight
and Parcels Services, 1991-2016

British Rail's parcel and postal traffic was renamed Rail Express Systems in October 1991, by which time its main function was carrying letter mail for the Post Office. The Red Star station-to-station parcels service, introduced in 1963 and incorporated in the Parcels sector in October 1987, was extracted for separate sale and disposed of to a management buyout on 5 September 1995. A scheme known as Railnet was devised in 1996, based on dedicated postal trains between a London hub, six points in England and one in Scotland, at Shieldmuir, by Mossend. In the same year Rail Express Systems was sold to North & South Railways (later English, Welsh & Scottish). In June 2003 the Post Office, dissatisfied with the service, made a premature end to its rail

contract, and the Shieldmuir distribution centre was served only by road. From 2004 a limited rail service into Shieldmuir was restored, first with GB Railfreight, then with DB Cargo UK, on a current contract that runs until 2018.

A container train pulls out of the Coatbridge Freightliner depot behind a US-built General Electric Class 70 locomotive in 2016. (Freightliners Ltd)

How to divide and prepare the rail freight business for privatisation was a vexed question: subsidies were not available, and the BRB's policy appeared to be one of "rationalisation", as ever a euphemism for reduced services. By the 1990s Freightliner had become primarily an import-export service to the principal container ports, none of which were in Scotland, and its internal operations shrank to the point where the Gushetfaulds depot closed in 1993, with its residual traffic transferred to Coatbridge. Sir Bob Reid told the House of Commons Scottish Affairs Committee in November 1992 that rail freight was uncompetitive with road haulage under 400-500 kilometres except for full trainloads[19]. Soon afterwards rail freight charges were more then doubled.

As part of preparation for privatisation, the Trainload Freight business sectors were reformed in 1994 as shadow franchises: Transrail, Loadhaul and Mainline Freight, on a geographical rather than the previous commodity basis, with services in Scotland allocated to Transrail, whose base was in Cornwall. Railfreight Distribution continued to run Freightliner, including Scottish terminals, until 1996. Transrail was a proactive shadow outfit, concerned chiefly with coal traffic, but it also started a regular wagonload freight system, branded 'Enterprise', which restored freight operations at selected points, including Lairg and Georgemas on the Far North line. New hopes for international freight potential were briefly stimulated in January 1996 when blocks of Ledmore marble were sent from Lairg via the Channel Tunnel to Carrara in Italy[20].

Privatisation of rail freight was organised on a quite different basis to the passenger service. There were no franchises and the companies which acquired the various parts of British Rail's freight business owned their own rolling stock. The new freight companies, all English-based, obtained access to Scottish routes from Railtrack and set up their own depots as traffic or contracts required. The largest operator, English, Welsh & Scottish Railways, which took over Railfreight Distribution and Transrail, including the latter's 'Enterprise' wagonload service, in February 1996, was a subsidiary of the Wisconsin Central Railroad company, itself owned by Canadian National (after subsequent ownership changes it is now DB Cargo). Freightliner was sold to a management buyout on 25 May 1996, helped by a 4-year track access grant. Other operators, Colas Rail, GB Railfreight and Direct Rail Services (state-owned and originally set up to transport nuclear waste) also ran services based on container operations and bulk loads.

The challenge to freight by rail was evident: in 1994 road transport accounted for 71% of goods lifted in Scotland, and if only road and rail were considered, road's share went up to 96%. The trend was an established one: in 1981 rail's share had been 7.8%, in 1990 it was 5.8%. Most of the goods lifted were for delivery within Scotland, with 10% going elsewhere in the UK, and 1% for export. A Conservative Government Green Paper asserted in 1997 that the introduction of private sector investment and initiative "have revitalised rail freight services in, to and from Scotland", though the tonnage of freight lifted was later seen as an "all time low"[21]. Through freight trains from Scotland to Europe via the Channel Tunnel had been forecast in 1993, though they did not come about, and the forecast for freight traffic through the Tunnel was far greater than the reality. At Mossend, near Motherwell, a European freight terminal was laid out in 1993, now Mossend International Freight Park.

By 1996 locomotives were in very limited use for passenger trains and the freight companies either owned their own or leased them. Coal remained a substantial element in the freight market, and the Hunterston port, no longer handling iron ore after the closure of the Ravenscraig steel works in 1992, found a new role in importing coal, carried forward by rail to the huge power station at Longannet. A short-lived attempt to restore a Motorail service, with cars by overnight rail and passengers by air, came and went in 1999[22]. Alloa marshalling yard, from the 1950s, already much reduced, was finally closed in 1998. Ayrshire coal, now obtained by opencast methods, was loaded by conveyor onto trains at four railheads: Killoch, Chalmerston, and the new terminals opened in 2005 at Crowbandsgate (New Cumnock), and Greenburn on the reinstated (2004) mineral branch from Bank Junction on the Dumfries-Kilmarnock line. On the West Highland, the paper mill at Corpach switched to road transport in 2001 and closed down in September 2005, and in June 2001 Freightliner ceased to carry aluminium ingot traffic from Fort William, though some other aluminium-related traffic remained[23]. Initiatives in carrying timber traffic from Kinbrace went on between 2001 and 2005; timber traffic from Arrochar, and from Crianlarich and Taynuilt, did not last beyond 2009. In 1999 the Department for Transport and the Scottish Executive awarded the logistics company TDG Nexus a £10 million freight facilities grant to build a new intermodal rail terminal south of the dock area. The following year a similar level of grant was awarded to BP Oil to upgrade rail handling facilities at their Grangemouth refinery and four distribution railheads across Scotland. Since 1995, TDG European Chemicals has provided the necessary platform to enable TDG to tailor a specific road/rail service for BP's polyethylene output, at first with Freightliner, then with EWS[24].

Railtrack's difficulties and the delays in modernising the West Coast Main Line discouraged diversifying of freight traffic and it was not until the

Scottish Executive was enabled to set up Transport Scotland in 2005 that the issue of rail freight was given some attention. The Executive's Local Government & Transport Committee issued a report on freight transport in 2006, but suggested no rail-related initiatives other than maintaining freight facilities grants. At that time the virtual elimination of railborne coal traffic in Scotland within ten years was not suspected, and concentration on passenger franchising left the freight operators to make what they could of Scottish opportunities. The total tonnage of rail freight lifted in Scotland fell from a high of 14.31 million tonnes in 2005-06 (75% of it being coal and minerals) to 8.43 million tonnes in 2012-13, by which time 48% was coal and minerals, and container traffic exceeded coal traffic[25]. Closure of Longannet Power Station in March 2016 and the conversion of English stations to biomass burning ended Hunterston's coal traffic, making a further massive reduction in Scottish freight carriage.

Even before that, by 2013 positive action on railborne freight was clearly needed. Organisations like Scottish Enterprise were realising that without a viable railfreight system, new industrial and commercial projects might be hampered or lost. Network Rail's plan for its 'Scotland Route', published in 2013, identified railfreight markets as including intermodal, Royal Mail, construction, coal, and other bulks. Intermodal and biomass traffic were particularly seen as growth areas. Encouragingly, general merchandise had risen by 25%[26]. Though primarily concerned with Control Period 5 (2015-19), Network Rail reported "industry-supported" forecasts as indicating a growth in total freight traffic to 22 million tonnes in 2030, which would require infrastructure investment to be achievable. An important issue was that of loading gauge. Freight vehicles were now larger. The largest rail-borne containers were 9ft 6in high and 2.6 metres wide (Gauge W12), too big to fit on many lines built for 19th century clearances. Apart from the West Coast Main Line, able to take Gauge W10, 9ft 6in high by 2.5 metres wide[27], most Scottish lines, including Glasgow-Grangemouth, were restricted to the 9ft high W9 gauge, and some, Inverness to Elgin, for example, have a clearance rated at W7. Use of new "lowliner" wagons, first introduced in 1991 though in limited numbers, have widened the range of container routes to include Glasgow-Aberdeen, Perth-Inverness and Glasgow-Fort William, though infrastructure improvements are also needed to enable fully effective use of railfreight, including longer passing loops to hold trains up to 775 metres long.

In 2015 the Scottish Government had £12 million-worth of funds in grants available for freight facilities, compared with £7.5 million in England and Wales. The UK-wide Freight Transport Association's Scottish Freight Council identified priority routes for upgrading as Mossend-Aberdeen-Elgin, Gretna-Mossend (WCML), Hunterston-Mossend and Coatbridge, with extended or dynamic loops on the Gretna-Dumfries-Kilmarnock, Ayr-Mossend and Perth-Inverness lines[28]. Logistics companies such as the Malcolm Group, since 2004 based at Elderslie's West of Scotland Rail Terminal, J.G. Russell (Leith, Hillington, Coatbridge, Inverness and Aberdeen), P.D. Stirling (Mossend) and Stobart (Grangemouth) have made operating agreements for container trainloads. Regular intermodal services now include Mossend-Inverness, Mossend-Daventry (England), Grangemouth-Aberdeen, Grangemouth-Elderslie, Grangemouth-Daventry, and Coatbridge-Daventry. Supermarket supplies, mineral water and whisky are among the prime items carried. New Spanish-built Class 88 dual-mode locomotives, capable of 100 mph and able to switch from electric to diesel traction and so requiring no change of motive power, are due to appear on DRS services in 2016-17. DRS has also diversified into special passenger services, for cruise trains like Belmond's 'Royal Scotsman', and in conjunction with the seaborne cruise

Intermodal working in 2012 at the Russell Group's Coatbridge Containerbase, with containers hauled by rail from Daventry, England. (John G. Russell (Transport) Ltd)

liner industry. Transport Scotland recorded 119 freight stations in 2014[29], Traffic Scotland, a road information system, identified 44 freight railheads in 2015, and Network Rail listed eleven intermodal terminals: Aberdeen (Dyce and Craiginches), Coatbridge, Elderslie, Glasgow (Hillington), Grangemouth (DB Cargo, Malcolm, Forth Ports), Inverness, Mossend (International Rail Park and Euroterminal). No intermodal facilities were recorded at the ports of Dundee, Leith or Stranraer.

The chicken-egg issue forms a subtext to all discussions on freight between infrastructure providers and service promoters. Network Rail was evidently wary of providing facilities which might be underused or abandoned early[30]. It is hard to sell a railfreight service on a route which has no provision for such a service. Despite disappointing results for Scottish freight via the Channel Tunnel, a 2015 Scottish Parliament committee report on freight transport highlighted the role of railfreight in connecting Scotland to European markets via the Tunnel[31] in what was both a sober assessment of inadequacies and a call for action. Transport Scotland embarked on a "refresh" of the national freight strategy, and in March 2016 it issued a new document, 'Delivering the Goods: Scotland's Rail Freight Strategy', drawing on submissions from companies and bodies engaged in railfreight, and declaring that railfreight was a "key component" of the rail sector's economic contribution. Acknowledging the steep decline in coal and steel traffic, the document stressed the need to develop smaller markets, with a £30 million Scottish Rail Freight Investment Fund available in Control Period 5 (2014-19) for such purposes as day-to-day operation of the rail network, new lines, new electrified routes and additional gauge clearance. Certain problems were identified: the limited train paths available on some lines, a lack of 'resilience' (deviation possibilities in the event of engineering works or floods, back-up staff availability, etc.), and Network Rail's inflexible approach on site investment and leasing. The paper's tone was largely aspirational, with much emphasis on the desirability of joint initiatives and on action beyond 2019. It did not address the finding that the freight grant applicability was in some ways too restrictive (for example, not extending to provide a 'pool' of low-bed container wagons). The Joint Freight Board, a forum combining all transport systems, was to find ways of overcoming barriers to innovation which the Freight Working Group could implement, while joint action was to be taken to counter the reported views of potential users that rail freight was hard to access, inflexible, expensive and unreliable. It also acknowledged that freight had been playing a very much second-fiddle role to passenger development and promised a greater emphasis, with a Strategic Freight Network to be identified, the freight funding system to be revised, and a specific freight section incorporated in the Ministerial High Level Output Specifications for 2019-24 (though this will cover only cross-border freight). Comments and proposals from bodies like the Rail Freight Group, while keen to urge on Transport Scotland and its political masters at Holyrood in moves to develop rail freight traffic, often reveal a degree of criticism or frustration; an echo of 1938 crops up in the RFG's complaint about "lack of a level playing field": "… investment appraisal in recent times has failed to adopt a neutral, cross-modal approach to road and rail upgrades on key corridors such as Perth-Inverness"[32].

Per tonne of cargo, rail generates 76% less carbon dioxide than road transport, and the government's commitment to rail freight development is closely linked to European Union targets for modal shift from road to rail/water by 30% in 2030 and 50% in 2050, for distances over 300km/188 miles (while the future of Scotland in a United Kingdom which has voted to leave the European Union has made many issues uncertain, trading with Europe is likely to require adherence to specific European guidelines or rules). To achieve that in Scotland will not be easy. The influence of environmental statistics on the commercial decisions of freight consignors is not clear. While financial responsibility for passenger services is vested with the Scottish Government, it neither buys nor specifies freight services, and there is no domestic rail freight company. It is obviously desirable for Transport Scotland to maximise use of the state-subsidised railway tracks, with freight trains paying access charges to the rail network (though such charges are one of the problems cited by the industry). Among the numerous public agencies, private companies, and independent bodies involved in rail freight, it is the only one in a position to take ownership of the issue. In November 2016 the Arup consultancy was hired by the Scottish Government and the Scottish Freight Joint Board to review the potential for rail freight.

A panoramic view of the modernised station at Stirling with its new canopies, completed in May 2016. (Derek MacLeod Contruction Ltd)

14. The Third Franchise, and Pointers to the Future

Not One Franchise, but Two

From 1975 to 2014, the number of road vehicles licensed in Scotland rose from 1,300,000 to 2,821,000, including 2,370,000 private cars, more than one for every two people in the country[1]. In the 1960s, expert forecasters would have assumed from these figures that railway passengers (commuters apart) would be rarer than ptarmigans in 2014, but in fact over 96 million rail passenger journeys were made in 2014-15, more than ever before. During a Parliamentary debate on 11 December 2008 on the First ScotRail franchise extension, the then Transport Minister said that the SNP government hoped that the next franchise would be a "not for profit" one, but this aspiration was not pursued. By the time its franchise was up for renegotiation, First ScotRail could point to a strong record. There had been a low point in May 2012 when Steve Montgomery, joined with his Network Rail counterpart, David Simpson, to apologise for poor service in the Glasgow-Inverclyde-Ayrshire area, caused by bad weather, vandalism and engineering works, and promised a return to standard. First ScotRail was fined £576,000 under Transport Scotland's SQUIRE quality control regime for failure to meet standards of cleanliness and effacement of graffiti between March 2014 and March 2015. In June 2014 it won the Award for Business Excellence from Quality Scotland, and in Spring 2015 it enjoyed a customer satisfaction rating of 87%, seven points above the UK average, and had been UK Rail Operator of the Year three times in the previous six years. New franchises, however, are granted on the case made for future value rather than past achievement. National Express mounted a powerful case, led by Mary Grant, who had been First ScotRail's managing director from 2004 to 2011 and would have the

A Class 158 Super Sprinter at Keith Junction in 2016, before the Aberdeen to Inverness upgrading. (big55012)

Ex-British Railways Class 73 73966, re-engined and owned by GB Railfreight, in Caledonian Sleepers livery at Fort William, 2016. (Caledonian Sleepers)

same role with her new employer if the contract were won. Other contenders included Arriva, MTR (Hong Kong) and the incumbent First Group. Abellio (the international arm of the state-owned Netherlands Railways) and National Express emerged as front runners. Abellio's subsidy requirement was £776 million while National Express's was £747 million, but Abellio's bid was rated 7.9% ahead of National Express on the Quality aspect. The final outcome on 18 October 2014 was a lead of 0.24%, a win by a whisker. National Express was said to be "baffled" by the quality ratings[2] and there was talk of seeking a judicial review, but this was not pursued, and Abellio assumed management of ScotRail on 1 April 2015.

The Caledonian Sleeper service was made a separate franchise by Transport Scotland. By 2015 it was formed of two trains each way, with London Euston as the southern terminus. One train had Aberdeen, Inverness and Fort William portions combining and separating at Edinburgh; and on the other Glasgow/Edinburgh portions combined and divided at Carstairs. Some MSPs and commentators commented adversely on the additional franchise as an unnecessary and undesirable fragmentation of the passenger service, but the government insisted that it was desirable for the development of the sleeper operation. Serco plc acquired the franchise in May 2015 for a fifteen-year period, supported by a £100 million investment from the Scottish and UK governments, including £60 million for building of 75 new sleeping cars at CAF in Spain, to be delivered in 2018 – the existing rolling stock was 30 years old or more and required high maintenance to be acceptable to users. In 2011-12 the sleeper service had a directly attributable cost of £25.8 million, excluding fixed track access cost which was assumed to be £5 million for the purpose of the new franchise, and attributable revenue of £19.5 million. Sleeper traffic had been declining, but a "full business case" published on 20 June 2014 by Transport Scotland anticipated that the fall would be reversed by new trains and an "improved product offer", though it hedged this with a note of the difficulty of accurately forecasting demand and usage levels. Arriva, First Group and Serco formed the short list of bidders, with 50/50 value being placed on subsidy level and quality offer. Serco's subsidy requirement was £187 million, and its experience in "migration and mobilisation" of businesses and services during phases of transition was considered an important plus in evaluating its bid. A 50/50 profit share was built in between limits of 7% and 15% above a preset level; after five years of the franchise, any losses would also be equally shared[3]. Serco took over the Caledonian Sleepers on the night of 31 March-1 April 2015 and established its HQ at Inverness Station. Brand-liveried locomotives are used on the service, with refurbished former Southern Region Class 73/9 electro-diesels north of Edinburgh and Glasgow and Class 92 electric locomotives on electrified lines, all leased from GB Railfreight.

At the inception of Abellio's franchise in 2015, the DOO issue was still very much a live one, with ScotRail seeking to extend the 'Strathclyde Manning Agreement' beyond the SPT area to the new Bathgate line, whose Class 334 trains were designed for driver-only operation, and the RMT Union doing its best to make the issue one of safety for the travelling public rather than one of jobs or pay levels. This was an argument now 30 years old. Passenger surveys have consistently expressed a preference for a conductor to be on board[4]. With many stations unmanned, this is a critical issue for disabled passengers in particular (possibly passengers would prefer to have an automated, driverless train rather than no-one to provide 'customer care'). In September 2016, after a summer of strikes and dispute, a draft agreement was reached between the RMT and ASLEF unions and Abellio, allowing for the continuance of conductors on current and new electric trains. Hitachi Class

Track works in 2016 – a Babcock road-rail vehicle (RRV) on the line at Crianlarich, November 2016. (big55012)

385 trains under construction were now to be fitted with conductor-operated door controls. While ScotRail described the settlement as a win-win for both sides, it appeared that the union campaign had been the real victor[5]. There can be no doubt that since privatisation the rail unions have been of great benefit to their members: paradoxically, if their wish for a state-owned railway were fulfilled, they might find negotiation more difficult.

The Shaw Report

Almost five years after McNulty came the report into the future of Network Rail by Nicola Shaw, then chief executive of the HS1 Channel Tunnel rail link; and as with McNulty's, the government paid it the compliment of acting on at least some of its recommendations (unlike celebrated previous reports, both of these treated railways as a positive force rather than a basket case). As far as Scotland was concerned, much of what Shaw recommended was already in place, including a Network Rail Scottish office and director, and a "deep alliance" with Abellio-ScotRail since May 2015. However, she recommended deeper "route revolution" with freedom for routes to build up their plans based on passenger and freight requirements (under independent regulation), with an onus on route management to find new private sector sources of funding development. Structurally, Network Rail "could be, and should be, more agile in how it responds to the changing wants and needs of its customers"[6]. The formation of a Britain-wide "virtual freight route" with powers and responsibilities identical to other routes was recommended. The report made no comment on the Scottish government's wish for fully devolved responsibility for rail infrastructure[7], but its exclusion of Scotland from certain recommendations because of devolved "funding route enhancement" proposals showed the increasingly uncomfortable divide between Holyrood funding and Westminster regulation. The new (2016) UK government responded quickly to Shaw's recommendation for a decentralised Network Rail and went considerably further by announcing the intention to involve train operating companies in infrastructure investment and maintenance. The Transport Minister, Chris Grayling, was reported as saying that "We think, with hindsight, that the complete separation of track and train into separate businesses at the time of privatisation was not right for our railways"[8]. It will not escape the reader that the trend of proposals and policies in 2015-16 bears a distinct resemblance to the sectorisation established by British Rail in the 1980s and dismantled in the 1990s.

High Speed, ScotRail, ORR, Network Rail and Transport Scotland

Since 2006 proposals have existed for a High Speed rail link between Glasgow and Edinburgh, enabling a journey time of 30 minutes. A Transport Scotland paper entitled 'Fast Track Scotland' was published in 2011, endorsed by Transport Minister Derek Mackay, expressing the view that it was essential for Scotland to be incorporated into a High Speed Rail programme extending north of Birmingham[9]. In its five-year National Planning Framework No. 3, published in June 2014, the Scottish government set down firmly that "Connectivity is key… with High Speed Rail between Edinburgh and Glasgow, and in time, on to London".

A subsequent business plan for the project, never published, may have dampened this enthusiasm[10]. Mackay informed the Scottish Parliament in January 2016 that "it was not possible to progress planning" on the HS Edinburgh-Glasgow line until there was confirmation of the route of a High Speed line coming up from England – a project to which the Westminster

Customer service: ScotRail station guide Michelle assists a passenger at Glasgow Central in 2016. (ScotRail)

government had made no commitment of any kind. In March 2016 the HS2 company produced a set of five possible options for HS routes into Scotland, measured against enhancement of the existing routes[11], at estimated costs ranging from £29 billion to £43 billion, exclusive of the Glasgow-Edinburgh line, itself estimated at around £6 billion. At the end of 2016 all these proposals remained in the realm of the potential. One of the principal arguments in favour of High Speed Rail is that only a 3-hour journey from Glagow or Edinburgh to London could effect a significant shift in usage from air to rail. In 2015 3,120,700 air journeys were made between Scotland's three busiest airports, Aberdeen, Edinburgh and Glasgow, and London Heathrow. This compares with 2,107,000 journeys between all Scottish stations and London in 2013-14[12]. The implications of a large-scale shift to rail are clear, both for train and station capacity and for airport development, but have not been addressed (they are also highly relevant to the Scottish government's target of reducing "greenhouse gas" emissions to 66% less than 1990 levels by 2032). Network Rail's provisional long-term forecast for rail passenger capability in 2043 is 6,700 a day on the Glasgow-London route, and 12,400 on Edinburgh-London[13].

In 2015, ScotRail had 4,966 employees, 743 more than in 1994 (Network Rail had a further 2,320 railway workers). It managed 358 stations, including the Network Rail-owned Waverley and Glasgow Central. Both of these were rated as Grade A historic buildings, as were twelve others, while 59 were classed as Grade B and 14 as Grade C; such classification of working stations could not impede modifications and alterations but moderated its impact on historic structures. Network Rail looked after 1,916 route miles on which 92.7 million passenger journeys had been made in 2014-15, compared with 78.3 million in 2010-11. Passenger revenue had doubled within the previous ten

Aberdeen Station was refurbished and modernised in 2009. (Wikimedia Commons/ Waldemar Zboralski)

years, or by 59% in real terms, allowing for inflation. In March 2016 the Oxera consultancy produced a paper for TS and the Rail Delivery Group, 'What is the Economic Contribution of Rail in Scotland?' Its quantification of gross value added (the value of outputs less the value of inputs purchased) came to a direct contribution of £462 million plus an indirect contribution of £206 million[14]. The 'ScotRail Alliance' between the new train operator and Network Rail was announced in May 2015, to provide an integrated approach in managing the £2.7 billion provision for infrastructure in Control Period 5, 2014-19. Hailed by the participants as a "deep alliance" and "Track and train together in one business", it was more cautiously described by Derek Mackay as "a more integrated approach"[15]. Network Rail's 'Scotland Route' programme covered six "markets": the Glasgow and Edinburgh conurbations, Interurban, Rural, Anglo-Scottish, and Freight. It looked forward to providing 125 million customer journeys a year by 2020 and to replacing all signal boxes (71 in 2015) with two Rail Operating Centres, plus the RETB centres at Inverness and Banavie, by 2029, opening the way to the "digital railway", with real time traffic management enabling more frequent services and minimising delays on the network[16]. As of December 2016 no Strategic Outline Business Case for digital railway development was being undertaken in Scotland.

With the 2015 franchise, the stage was set for seven years, though the inception of Control Period 6 from 2019 might change the scenery or even remove some of it. Abellio-ScotRail's term would come to an end just a century on on from the Big Five companies' final year. A hundred years before that, in 1822 there had only been the horse-drawn Kilmarnock & Troon line to point to the future of railways. Who then would have predicted the position in 1923? And what would be the position in 2022? That Scotland would still need and want its railways hardly seemed in doubt. But what the new arrangements would be, and indeed what the status of the government in Edinburgh would be and what the relationship of Scotland to the UK and the EU would be – at the end of 2016 these things were far from certain.

The ORR, with a branch office in Glasgow, in addition to control of 'Health & Safety' issues, supervises the work of Network Rail, publishing an annual assessment. On inspecting work on Scottish projects in 2015, the ORR concluded that Network Rail was in breach of its licence, through failures of cost and project control, delays and lack of information to Transport Scotland as funding agent. Network Rail, with its Scottish office and its plans for the "Scotland Route", though a far more effective organisation than Railtrack, was a UK-wide company dependent on government agencies for two-thirds of its income (and hence providing a huge hidden subsidy to train operating companies) and with an enormous cumulative debt of £41 billion that was transferred to the public sector balance sheet from the beginning of 2014. In 2011-12 more of Network Rail's funds (£1.32 billion) were used to service its debt than in track maintenance (£968 million)[17]. Costings of Network Rail's Britain-wide plans for Control Period 5, at £38.5 billion, were already admitted in 2015 to be underestimated.

The Scottish Ministers' High Level Output Requirements, published in June 2012, had set out the key tasks for 2014-19 as; 1. Improvement of journey times (and hence greater line capacity); 2. Safety improvements as laid down by the Department for Transport; 3. Carbon reduction per train and freight-tonne kilometre in line with the key performance indicators set by the ORR for Control Period 5. Network Rail published 'Delivering a Better Railway for a Better Scotland: Our Plans for 2014-19' in 2013. Five items were listed: route enhancement between Aberdeen and Inverness, the creation of a Forth Bridge visitor centre (the bridge was named as a UNESCO world heritage site in 2014), the Borders Railway, the Edinburgh-Glasgow Improvement Project, and time/capacity enhancement on the Highland Main Line. The document recorded 30% growth in passenger traffic since 2004, and predicted 15% further growth by 2019, with a longer-range forecast of 115% growth in the Edinburgh area, 38% in the Glasgow area, 48% on rural lines, and a more modest 11% in freight traffic[18]. During those years total passenger journeys were climbing towards the 100 million mark. Network Rail's 'Scotland Route' plan, also published in 2013, noted some of the problems and difficulties facing railway enhancement: there were 934 known mining hazards, 4,400 bridges to be maintained or adapted, and Scotland has 44% of the rock cuttings on British railways. Flooding was another concern, with many stretches of track vulnerable to exceptional rainfall: in 2007 Network Rail had reported that each year flooding was responsible for the loss of around 100,000 train minutes, or 1,666 hours, requiring compensation costs of some £3 million[19].

Transport Scotland acquired a new chief executive, Roy Brannen, formerly Director of Trunk Roads and Bus Operations, in November 2015, and Scotland's alert rail lobby will no doubt closely watch his organisation's policies and performance, as well as its responses to criticism, which often sound testy and defensive, reminiscent of the early years of BR's Scottish Region[20]. As one of six directorates within Transport Scotland, the railway needs strong management and vision to ensure that the agency takes full advantage of its potential in reducing road congestion. The plan for dualling the A9 trunk road between Perth and Inverness while making only limited improvement to the Highland Main Line's capacity, has been criticised, recalling a comment made almost 50 years before, in 1969, by Robert MacLennan MP to the Select Committee on Scottish affairs, on exactly the same topic: "If the Scottish Office invests in roads which compete with Ministry of Transport subsidy to a rail service, does this make any sense?" Now of course a single Scottish-based agency manages investment in both road and rail, with the associated issues of air pollution, congestion, and supporting national economic growth. The Scottish Government's draft budget for 2017-18 shows a 17.8% increase from the actual 2016-17 expenditure on motorways and trunk roads, from £820.6 million to £967 million; and a 3.2% increase on total rail expenditure, from £751.8 million to £775.8[21].

Even in an industry inured to constant organisational change, 2015 and 2016 were years of exceptional flux. Network Rail, whilst awaiting the findings of the Shaw Report into its constitution and structure, was reported in 2016 to be considering selling much of its property, including major stations – a portfolio that includes Edinburgh Waverley and Glasgow Central – and even one of its eight "routes", to the private sector. Its options will be defined by government policy at Westminster. In 2016 the Scottish Government announced that it was seeking full devolution of Network Rail in Scotland: "… there remains a clear misalignment between the Scottish Government's primary responsibility for the funding and specification of Network Rail activities in Scotland, and the level of direct control and influence around how its responsibilities are discharged"[22]. In July 2016 the ORR gave a generally positive report on Network Rail's project management, but warned against time and cost overruns in some cases, including the Edinburgh-Glasgow Improvement Project (EGIP). Transport Scotland supplemented the ORR's report by commissioning the international EY Consultancy to carry out its own inspection, which echoed the ORR assessment but added a few criticisms of its own, the most basic being that under the present system, Transport Scotland lacks the "commercial leverage" a funds provider should have over the contractor[23]: an important element in the Scottish Government's case for infrastructure control. In November 2016, the ORR expected Network Rail to exceed its budgeted spending in Scotland by £43 million "largely because of £52 million higher costs on the EGIP and rolling programme of electrification enhancement projects"[24].

Merging of the Association of Train Operating Companies into the Rail Delivery Group was announced on 24 October 2016, creating a powerful body though also one that internalises some conflicts of interest in tackling the role of "agent for change" in supporting the growth of "UK plc"[25]: train operating companies are, or were, intended to be competing organisations. This was followed by a UK government announcement that some of Network Rail's powers would be transferred to train operating companies[26]. The scope of intention appeared to go well beyond the Network Rail-ScotRail alliance. In an industry that requires long-term planning, while potential infrastructure needs up to 2043 have been clearly set out in the NR Scotland Route Study of July 2016, the sources and nature of funding the system's development beyond 2020 remained studiously vague at the end of 2016. Before its merger the Rail Delivery Group issued a paper on 23 September 2016, committing itself to supporting the government's national transport strategy and promising advice for Scottish Ministers in forming their high-level output specifications for railways 2019-24, which were due to be published as part of the Office of Rail & Roads' 2018 Periodic Review. It noted "investment opportunities" such as Edinburgh Suburban Line enhancement (for freight), gauge improvement to Grangemouth and on the former G&SWR main line, quadruple tracking on the East Coast Main Line from Edinburgh to Drem, with dynamic loops between Drem and Berwick, and increased capacity on the Greenhill-Dunblane-Perth line. Three years before, Network Rail had already included a significant caveat in its 'Delivering a Better Railway for a Better Scotland': "… choices will have to be made about striking the right balance between running more trains and reducing costs or further improving performance. Growth in demand makes it inevitable that we will find it harder in the future to deliver continuous improvement on a railway that, due to geography or costs, can only expand to a limited extent"[27].

These comments hint at future intimations that railway development is

One of ScotRail's new Hitachi Class 385 electric units, due for introduction in 2017, inside the maintenance depot. (ScotRail)

approaching either the blank wall of full capacity or a financial hurdle which will dwarf previous records. Line occupancy at certain locations is said to be almost at capacity. Even as further reinstatement of closed lines, including St. Andrews and Leven, is canvassed, the vital, intensively-used east-west and north-south lines in central Scotland, particularly into Glasgow, will reach load limits and have to be supplemented. The Network Rail/ScotRail Scotland Route Study of July 2016, a long-term outlook document, is intriguing, with its four alternate levels of forecast for each of Scotland's rail markets: Prospering in Global Stability, Prospering in Isolation, Struggling in Global Turmoil, and Struggling in Isolation. In November 2016 Humza Yousaf, Minister for Transport and the Islands, launched a 'Consultation on Scotland's Rail Infrastructure Strategy from 2019', as a preliminary to setting out the Government's High Level Output Specifications for 2019-2024. While asserting that "investment in rail will remain a priority", this document notes that "the effects of further fiscal consolidation", along with changes in the way Network Rail has been funded since 2015, mean that rail projects will have to compete for capital funding with areas such as health and education. What is clear from the 2016 consultation paper is that the agenda is being managed by the experts and professionals. Comment is invited on their plans, which focus on improvements to existing infrastructure and rolling stock. Alternative or additional schemes are not allowed for. Regional transport authorities nursing new rail projects, and national and local rail action groups, will need to be on their mettle. No extension to the railway system has been approved by the Scottish government since the Waverley Railway Act of 2006.

By the late months of 2016 the shine on Abellio's franchise was wearing thin. Punctuality was slipping and overcrowding was normal on some commuter services. Performance on the new Borders line, the Milngavie line and the Far North line, among numerous others, was said to be unacceptable. Public protests led the government to demand an improvement plan from the franchisee, which produced a document listing 249 actions to be undertaken, mostly of a routine nature and over an unspecified period. In part at least, the storm was created by a combination of political tactics and media jumping on an easy target, and Abellio moved into large-company damage-limitation mode, hiring lobbyists and publicists[28]. Sharp exchanges were made between it and Transport Minister Yousaf, who suggested it might lose its franchise at the half-term break-point. Abellio responded by suggesting that ministers shared the blame by "fixing the number of seats", and also criticised its alliance partner Network Rail for delays and cost overruns[29]. 54% of "delay minutes" were caused by Network Rail's over-running on maintenance work, or other failures within NR's province. The public performance measure (PPM) of train service, for April-October 2016 was 89.5%, against a target of 92%, reduced by the ORR in November to 91%[30]. Presumably this adjustment of the goal posts was related to many of the attendant circumstances being beyond ScotRail's control. Performance slipped again to 86% in October-November, but improved to 89% in December-January. In December the Scottish Government announced a £3 million package for season ticket holders, giving them a week's free travel as a "thank you" for their patience[31]. It remains to be seen whether this is a temporary situation until Abellio's new trains are delivered in 2017 and the current major construction projects are completed, or whether it reflects inadequate commitment to the task from the franchise holder.

How tranquil the days before the war, and in the 1950s, seemed in rosy retrospect, with trains puffing briskly through the Buchan countryside, racing along Strathmore, hauling sleeping cars from Stranraer over the Port Road's viaducts… Looking back through almost nine decades, it seems that the essential features of the story are the three great upheavals, each followed by attempts to put things together again. The first was the Grouping of 1923, of which a joint LMS-LNER statement observed in 1946, "It is a matter of record that the amalgamations under the Railways Act 1921 involved an administrative upheaval which was much more prolonged and disrupting, and far less productive of economies, than was anticipated". The second was Nationalisation in 1947-48, an attempt to put together an over-centralised monolith with scant consideration for a radically changed operating environment. The third was Privatisation in 1994-97, a hurriedly-confected programme which narrowly avoided disintegration and whose worst excesses Scotland has largely avoided. All three upheavals were government-led, with the last two driven by economic-political doctrines deployed for their own sake – and all on the basis that the system must be reformed. Each time, professional railway people (and many civil servants and local authority workers since the 1960s) have striven to make working sense out of the grand schemes. In 2017, the Scottish railway system had more attention and focus, more bodies both official and unofficial concerned with its performance and future operations (actual or potential), more planning, more monitoring, more controls of all types, than ever in its history. The extent to which it is enmeshed by separate organisations with regulatory or inspectorial powers already noted in this chapter, their various programmes and functions indicated by a host of acronyms, would astonish its previous owners and operators. This is a curious consequence of "liberalisation", perhaps surprising to the advocates of a free market in railway operation, just as is the continuing requirement for huge levels of subsidy. No British government, except in wartime, has ever been able to see the railways as other than a problem, whether as a monopoly, or a lame-duck relic of one, or an expensive necessity. Can the Scottish government see things differently, understanding that there are bigger and wider problems, to which railways can actually be part of the solution?

TIMELINE 1923-2016

(For station openings and closures see Appendices 6 and 7)

1920s

1923 LMS and LNER take over all Scottish railway assets and services from 1 January. H.P. Burgess is general manager of the LMS, Ralph Wedgwood of the LNER. Donald Matheson appointed deputy general manager (Scotland) of LMS; James Calder is general manager (Scotland) of the LNER. Closure of Burntisland Works.

1924 Strike by ASLEF members in January against companies' proposals on pay and conditions. Gleneagles Hotel opened, 2 June.

1925 Sir Henry Fowler becomes chief mechanical engineer of the LMS. Closure of St. Margaret's Works.

1926 General Strike, 4-14 May. Accident at St. Margaret's, three killed. Burgess retires; Sir Josiah Stamp joins the LMS.

1927 LMS instals water troughs at Floriston and Strawfrank. Stamp becomes LMS Chairman as well as President of the Executive. Matheson retires; T.H. Moffat is LMS chief officer for Scotland.

1928 Rail Unions accept 2½% wage cut. Third class sleeping cars introduced. 'Queen of Scots Pullman', Glasgow-Harrogate-London, introduced. 'Flying Scotsman' runs non-stop between Edinburgh and London. Dinwoodie collision, four killed. Pinwherry goods runaway, 2 July, two enginemen killed. Railways (Road Traffic) Act. New freight classifications introduced. David MacBrayne (1928) Ltd formed, owned by LMS and Coast Lines.

1929 Last vestige of passenger tax removed. Scottish Motor Traction Co. reconstituted: LMS and LNER each own 25%. Waterloo St. Bus Station opened in Glasgow.

1930s

1930 The 2½% pay cut restored (May), new cuts in September.

1931 Fowler retires; Ernest Lemon appointed LMS chief mechanical engineer.

1932 Buchanan Street Station rebuilt. Lemon appointed an LMS vice-president; W.A. Stanier appointed chief mechanical engineer. New LMS-LNER traffic pooling agreement. John Ballantyne appointed LMS chief officer for Scotland. Passenger services end on Lauder, Dolphinton and Gullane branches. Closure of Campbeltown & Machrihanish Light Railway.

1933 Road & Rail Traffic Act modifies charging arrangements. Railways begin experimental air services.

1934 James Calder retires as LNER General Manager (Scotland), succeeded by George Mills as divisional General Manager. Port Eglinton Junction crash, 6 September: nine killed. Highland Airways begin Inverness-Kirkwall flights.

1935 Glasgow Subway converted to electric traction.

1936 Pay increases restore most of 1931 cuts.

1937 Castlecary smash, 10 December: 39 killed. Ministry of Transport takes responsibility for trunk roads.

1938 Railway companies launch 'Square Deal' campaign. Closure of Edzell and Leadhills branches. William Whitelaw retires as LNER chairman but remains on Scottish Area board until he dies in 1946. Sir Ronald Matthews succeeds as LNER chairman.

1939 Railways pass under State control for war period from 1 September. Sir Ralph Wedgwood retires as GM of LNER, succeeded by (Sir) Charles Newton. LMS establishes Gourock-Dunoon car ferry. Saltcoats derailment, 5 August: four killed.

1940s

1940   Railway Air Services, requisitioned 1939, handed back for service on specified routes. Wagons break away on Highland line: two enginemen killed, 5 March.

1941 Lord Stamp killed by bomb, 16 April; Sir Charles Royden appointed LMS chairman. Malcolm Speir appointed LMS Chief Officer, Scotland. R.J. Inglis replaces Mills as LNER Divisional GM. Sir Nigel Gresley dies; Edward Thompson becomes chief mechanical engineer of LNER. Palace Hotel, Aberdeen, burns down: six staff die. Gretna Green crash: three deaths, 24 January. Clyde Blitz, March.

1942 Cowlairs crash, 30 January: fourteen die. Falkirk Tunnel accident, three workmen killed, 18 June. Scottish Wagon Co. in liquidation.

1943   LNER sets up Control Districts.

1944   Derailment at Mossband, 15 May: three passengers killed. T.F. Cameron replaces Inglis as LNER Divisional GM.

1945 Railway workers' week reduced from 48 to 44 hours, June.

1946   A.H. Peppercorn succeeds Thompson as chief mechanical engineer of LNER.

1947   Transport Act: Railways in Great Britain to be state-owned. Former G&SWR-CR lines linked at Stevenston, 16 June.

1948   State ownership of railways begins, 1 January. Scottish Region established under T.F. Cameron as Chief Regional Officer. Huge floods disrupt train services in South East, August: effects last for two years.

1949   Enginemen stage unofficial strike, May-June. Closure of Moniaive branch, 2 July. Scottish TUCC set up, July.

1950s

1950   Closure of North Fife and Whithorn lines. Post-flood bridge repairs completed, 5 May. Lauder branch reopens after floods (freight only), 20 November. Train fire near Beattock, 8 June: five killed. Townhill wagon repair works opened.

1951   Polmadie locomotive depot modernised. Alloa Jct accident, 10 January: two passengers killed. New Burntisland control centre opened, September.

1952   'Clan' class locomotives introduced.

1953   Transport Act: Railway Executive abolished. Sir Brian Robertson appointed chairman of BTC. Regional structure amended: Sir Ian Bolton appointed chairman of Scottish Area Board. Scottish Transport Group (STG) formed to operate MacBrayne's and Caledonian Steam Packet Company (CSP), then amalgamated as Caledonian MacBrayne Ltd (CalMac). 'Starlight Specials' inaugurated, 11 April. *Princess Victoria* sinks in North Channel, 31 January: 133 people die. Collision at Gollanfield, 15 June, three killed.

1954   Two-mile diversion line built around Loch Luichart hydro-electric scheme, Dingwall-Kyle line. Last railway horse parade: all to go by end of year. Construction of Ravenscraig steel works begins.

1955   BTC unveils Railway Modernisation Plan. T. F. Cameron retires; first A. E. H. Brown (dies) then James Ness appointed General Manager of Scottish Region (from 1 January 1956). First car-sleeper service introduced. New 'Hielan' Piper' goods service. Derailment at Wormit, 28 May, three killed.

1956   Thornton marshalling yard opens. Trials of diesel railcars on Galashiels, Crieff, North Berwick branches. Observation car introduced between Fort William and Mallaig. Third class redesignated second.

1957   Restrictions on BR rates and charging system partially relaxed. Scottish Region runs "TV train".

1958   Transport Act. Collision at Paisley Gilmour Street, 20 May: one passenger killed.

1959   Ernest Marples becomes Minister of Transport. Bolton retires; Frank Donachy replaces him as a part-time member of BTC board. Donald Cameron appointed Scottish Board chairman. Reappraisal of Modernisation Plan. Closure of Kilmarnock Works, and Lochgorm Works, Inverness. Ravenscraig Steelworks completed.

1960s

1960 Three traffic divisions set up. Stedeford Report on BR. Guillebaud Inquiry into Railway pay. Glasgow Electrification Phase 1 opens 7 November, trains withdrawn 30 December. Caledonian Steam Packet (Irish Services) Co. formed. Castlecary collision, 9 September: 70 injured.

1961 Glasgow electric service restored, 1 October. 'Deltic' diesel-electric locomotives speed up Edinburgh-London service. Robertson retires from BTC, Dr Richard Beeching is chairman, 1 June.

1962 Transport Act: BTC dissolved and British Railways Board established. South Clyde electric services begin, 27 May. Perth marshalling yard opened 12 March. Traffic survey undertaken in Scotland, closures begin. "Starlight Special" service ends this year. Scottish Railway Development Association (later SAPT) formed. *Caledonian Princess* enters Stranraer-Larne service, December. Scottish Region loses responsibility for workshops. Railway workers' week reduced from 44 to 42 hours.

1963 'Reshaping of Britain's Railways' published, 27 March. BTC is replaced by British Railways Board. W.G. Thorpe succeeds Ness as General Manager of Scottish Region. Highland Transport Board set up. Millerhill Marshalling Yard in full operation, 9 August. Blue Circle Cement Works open at Dunbar. Red Star parcels service introduced, 1 April. Large-scale closures begin.

1964 Line and station closures continue despite widespread protest. Stanley Raymond succeeds Beeching as BRB chairman. Cameron retires as Scottish Board chairman but remains on board until 1972. W.G. Thorpe is chairman as well as general manager. Craiglockhart Spur reinstated in Edinburgh. Forth Road Bridge opened.

1965 Beeching's Second Stage report published. BRB adopts trading name of British Rail. Gushetfaulds Freightliner terminal opened. Closure of Dundee West Station, 1 May, of the Dumfries-Challoch Junction line, 14 June, and Princes Street Station, 6 September. 'Highland Lines' management set up.

1966 Barbara Castle becomes Minister of Transport. Closure of St. Enoch and Buchanan Street Stations, 27 June, 7 November. 'Motorail' name introduced. Tay Road Bridge opened.

1967 Last steam locomotives in Scotland are withdrawn. Raymond removed as BTC chairman, November, replaced by Henry Johnson. Gordon Stewart succeeds Thorpe as chairman/general manager of Scottish Region. Highland Lines organisation disbanded. Passenger service between Perth and Kinnaber Jct withdrawn, 4 September. Electrification of Gourock and Wemyss Bay lines.

1968
Richard Marsh replaces Castle as Minister of Transport. Transport Act creates PTAs and allows for public subsidy of railways. Two-tier management established. Buchanan House, new Scottish Region HQ, fully open, 1 January. Aberdeen and Edinburgh Freightliner terminals opened; Freightliner put under control of National Freight Corporation. Old Course Hotel at St. Andrews opened, June. Observation cars withdrawn. Cowlairs Works close, engineering operations centre on St. Rollox, now known as Glasgow Works. *Antrim Princess* enters Stranraer-Larne service, December.

1969
Clydeport Container Terminal opened at Greenock, rail link to be laid (opened 1971, closed 30 September 1991). Railway workshops become British Rail Engineering Ltd (BREL), October. National Freight Carriers (NFC) set up, with a controlling interest in Freightliners. NCL and Scottish Transport Group set up. Closure of Waverley Route, 6 January, of Thornton Junction-Leven passenger service, and Inverurie Works. Landslide blocks Dingwall-Kyle railway for two weeks, November. Montrose Field, first large North Sea oil discovery.

1970s

1970 Closure of Kinross-Bridge of Earn line to facilitate motorway construction. West Coast electrification, Weaver Junction-Glasgow, approved. Railway shipping division named Sealink. Longannet Power Station begins generation

1971 Decimal coinage introduced. Richard Marsh succeeds Johnson as Chairman of BRB. Stewart retires, Alex Philip is general manager, Lord Taylor of Gryfe chairman, of Scottish Region. M8 motorway opened. Camping coaches withdrawn.

1972 Coal strikes: '3-day week' temporarily introduced, January-February. Closure of Barassie Works. Transport 2000 (later Railfuture) founded.

1973 United Kingdom joins the EEC. OPEC create energy crisis through cut in oil production. Longannet Power Station in full production. Greater Glasgow Passenger Transport Authority (GGPTA) set up. Dingwall-Kyle line 'reprieved'. Collision at Shields Junction, 30 August: five killed.

1974 Coal strikes, February-March: 3-day week reintroduced. Transport Act replaces subsidies for individual unremunerative lines with Public Service Obligation block grant. David Cobbett succeeds Philip as general manager, Scottish Region. West Coast electrification completed to Glasgow, 6 May. Scottish Region and GGPTA produce Clyderail proposals.

1975 Inflation reaches 24.6%. Local authorities reorganised into Regions and Districts GGPTA reformed as Strathclyde PTA. TOPS system introduced in Scottish Region. Derailment at Lunan Bay, 26 October, one fatality.

1976 InterCity 125 trains introduced. Peter Parker takes over as chairman of BRB from Marsh. John Palette succeeds Cobbett as general manager, Scottish Region. Freightliners returned to BR control.

1977 Leslie Soane succeeds Palette as general manager, Scottish Region. Speedlink wagonload service launched, September. First part of St. Fergus gas terminal opens.

1978 'Winter of discontent' 1978-79. Transport Act returns Freightliner to BR.

1979 First independence referendum, 1 March. Margaret Thatcher forms a Tory Government, 3 May. Scottish Region and Scottish Bus Group agree on marketing co-operation. Argyle Line opened, 5 November. Collapse of Penmanshiel Tunnel 17 March: two killed, line closed until August. Paisley collision, 16 April: seven killed. Invergowrie collision, October: five killed. Craigentinny Maintenance Depot rebuilt. Hunterston Ore Terminal opened. Fraserburgh line completely closed.

1980s

1980 Transport Act deregulates road coach services. Glasgow Subway modernisation complete. Falkirk Tunnel closed between 9 March and 8 December for repairs. Chris Green appointed Chief Operating Manager.

1981 Open Station programme begins, to 1984. Rationalisation of areas within Scottish Region, 27 down to sixteen. Transport Act 1981 establishes British Rail Investments Ltd, Sealink, British Transport Hotels and hovercraft interests transferred to it. Disposal of BT hotels begins: complete by 1984. Completion of electrification Coatbridge-Mossend. Closure of Cadder and Sighthill yards.

1982 Reorganisation of railways into Business Sectors begins. Closure of Townhill wagon works and of freight service to Forfar.

1983 Bob Reid replaces Parker as BRB chairman; he is also chief executive, September. George Mackie succeeds Soane as general manager Scottish Region, Chris Green is deputy general manager. Ian Campbell, vice-chairman of BRB takes over chair of Scottish Regional board from Roderick MacLeod, who joins BRB. The Serpell Committee report published: options for the future. Scottish Bus Group initiates Citylink services, October. Nightrider passenger service introduced. Closure of Townhill Wagon Works. ScotRail identity established 22 September. British Transport Hotels sold, March. Closure of Kilmacolm line, 10 January.

1984 Miners' strike halts coal traffic. Chris Green succeeds Mackie as GM, Scottish Region. Stranraer Harbour modernised. Seasonal steam service introduced, Fort William-Mallaig. Radio Electronic Token Block (RETB) system introduced on Kyle line, October. Red Star-plus Parcel service test-launched, October. Derailment at Polmont, 30 July: thirteen killed.

1985 Stations opened: Porthleven, Livingston, Bridge of Allan. RETB introduced on Wick & Thurso line, November. BR five-year plan for sector management introduced. ScotRail is designated a sub-sector of 'Provincial'. Glasgow Central, Queen Street, Dundee and Aberdeen stations refurbished. Glengarnock Steelworks close. 'Strathclyde Manning Agreement', October. Transport Act provides for bus deregulation from 16 October 1986. APT project terminated.

1986 Jim Cornell succeeds Green as general manager. Edinburgh-Bathgate electrified line opened, March. Paisley-Ayr electrification, 1 September. Closure of Gartcosh steel strip mill. Loch Lomond steamer withdrawn, 28 September. Glasgow Works become part of the BR Maintenance Group, April.

1987 John Ellis succeeds Cornell as general manager, ScotRail. Yoker operations centre opened.

Electrification of Kilwinning-Ardrossan Harbour and Ardrossan-Largs completed, January. Coatbridge-Motherwell reopens for passengers. Freightliners, Speedlink and Railfreight International grouped as Railfreight Distribution. Second class renamed Standard, 11 May.

1988 New ScotRail management structure from 22 May. Number of area managers cut from ten to four. RETB complete on West Highland and Oban lines. Haymarket becomes a specialised "Sprinter" maintenance depot. John Cameron joins BRB (to 1993).

1989 Airdrie line extended to Drumgelloch. Yoker Integrated Electronic Control Centre fully active, December. BREL sold off, April. Ness Viaduct collapses, 7 February. Bellgrove collision 6 March, two killed. Scottish Bus Group restructured for sell-off. Irvine signalling and telecommunications works close, March.

1990s

1990 Economic downturn to mid-1993. Provincial is renamed Regional Railways. Paisley Canal line reopened, 27 July. Sir Bob Reid (I) steps down as BRB chairman, replaced by namesake Sir Bob Reid (II). Cyril Bleasdale succeeds Ellis as general manager of Scotrail, is also Provincial Manager, ScotRail. NUR and NUS merge to form Rail, Maritime & Transport Workers' Union (RMT). Ness Viaduct rebuilt, 9 May.

1991 Electrification of East Coast Main Line completed. North Berwick electrification, 8 July. Speedlink (wagon load) business terminated. Newton crash, 21 July: 4 killed. Scottish Bus Group sell-off completed.

1992 National financial crisis follows two years of recession. Ravenscraig Steelworks close. BR's 'Organising for Quality' initiative begins: Sectors take over all operations and infrastructure from Regions, April. Government introduces "Passengers' Charter". Eastfield depot closed.

1993 Railways Act 5 November: privatisation authorised. Rutherglen-Whifflet line, Northern Suburban Phase 1 (Maryhill) and Cowlairs chord to enable Cumbernauld services opened. Rail Users Consultative Council (RUCC) replaces TUCC. Gushetfaulds Freightliner terminal closes.

1994 Railtrack established. Shettleston Fabrication Works closed 23 December. Bleasdale retires, April. ScotRail Railways Company formed as a subsidiary of BRB in preparation for privatisation; Chris Green takes

over as director, 1 January. Channel Tunnel opened, 4 May. Mossend Eurocentral Freight Terminal opens. Signal workers' strike. Vandals derail train near Drumfrochar, 25 June: two persons killed.

1995 Rolling Stock Maintenance (Glasgow) sold to Railcare, 6 June; BRIS Infrastructure Design Unit (Glasgow) sold 18 August. Rail Express Systems sold to EW&SR, 9 December. Largs Station wrecked when a train overruns the buffers, 11 July. Flooding closes Argyle Line from 11 December to 24 September 1995. Sir Bob Reid (II) retires; John Welsby is BR chairman. Chris Green resigns; John Ellis is ScotRail Director. Fort William sleeper controversy.

1996 Unitary local authorities introduced. ScotRail takes over Anglo-Scottish sleeper service, March. Motherwell-Cumbernauld electrification completed. BRIS Track Renewal and Infrastructure Maintenance companies (Scotland) sold, 8 and 14 February. Freightliner transferred to management buy-out, 25 May.

1997 ScotRail franchise acquired by National Express Group, 10 February. Alastair McPherson is managing director. Railfreight Distribution sold to EW&SR, 22 November.

1998 Monopolies & Mergers Commission reports on National Express Group's acquisition of ScotRail franchise.

1999 Scottish Parliament convened, 12 May. Intermodal terminal set up at Grangemouth.

2000s

2000 Post-Hatfield crash precautions cause widespread rail slowdown. Nick Brown succeeds McPherson as ScotRail managing director. Transport Act renames RUCC as Rail Passengers' Committees.

2001 Strategic Rail Authority (SRA) formally starts work, 1 February. Railtrack goes into administration, October. Scottish Executive takes over responsibility for funding the ScotRail franchise. ScotRail negotiates a revised subsidy deal.

2002 National Express aided in financial restructuring after forecasting huge loss. Peter Cotton succeeds Brown as ScotRail managing director. "Edinburgh Crossrail" services begin, 4 June. Network Rail set up to replace Railtrack.

2003 Strikes over new safety rules.

2004 ScotRail (National Express) named Rail Operator of the Year. ScotRail franchise awarded to First Group from 1 October. First ScotRail managing director is Mary Dickson (Grant). Portobello-Newcraighall line opened. Elderslie intermodal terminal set up (Malcolm Rail). Community Rail Development Strategy launched.

2005 Railways Act: responsibility for ScotRail devolved to Scottish Government; Transport Scotland is set up under Dr Malcolm Reed (until 2009). Strathclyde PTA becomes Strathclyde Partnership for Transport; six other regional Transport Partnerships established. Rail Passengers' Council (later Passenger Focus) replaces Passengers' Committees, 27 July. Hamilton-Larkhall line opened, 9 December. WCML upgrade allows speeds up to 125 mph with tilting trains. Adopt a Station scheme launched.

2006 Waverley Railway (Scotland) Act, June, authorises Borders Railway. Transport Scotland assumes responsibility for railways. SRA wound up, 30 November.

2007 Edinburgh-Glasgow Improvement Programme (EGIP) is announced, 27 September. First TransPennine take over Glasgow/Edinburgh-Manchester Airport services.

2008 International financial crash: austerity period begins. Stirling-Alloa line reopened, 19 May. First ScotRail is UK Train Operator of the Year. Network Rail opens Larbert training centre.

2009 Scottish Government publishes its Strategic Transport Programme Review. Glasgow Airport rail link cancelled. New Partick interchange station opened, 31 March.

2010s

2010 Electrification completed between Airdrie and Bathgate, making a fourth Edinburgh-Glasgow route. ScotRail starts Edinburgh-Dunbar service.

2011 Grant resigns from First Group, Steve Montgomery appointed managing director of First ScotRail. McNulty Report, 'Realising the Potential of GB Rail'. Shields Road electric service depot opened. Last Glasgow-Stranraer boat train.

2012 First Group's ScotRail franchise extended to 2015. EGIP project plans curtailed. 'Alliance' between NR and ScotRail speeds up and reduces cost of Paisley (Canal) electrification.

2013 Modernisation of Haymarket Station completed, December.

2014 Glasgow-Cumbernauld and Rutherglen-Whifflet electrification works completed, May and December. Community Rail Partnership three-year programme starts.

2015 Borders Railway opened to Tweedbank, 6 September. Carmuirs Aqueduct replaces tunnels, 28 March. ScotRail franchise acquired by Abellio, to start from 1 April. 'ScotRail Alliance' between Network Rail and Abellio, May. Work begins on Phase 1 of Aberdeen-Inverness improvement. Rail Regulator functions pass to Office of Rail and Roads (ORR).

2016 Longannet Power Station closes, 24 March. Shaw Report on Network Rail. Decentralisation of NR and involvement of TOCs in infrastructure projects are announced. Edinburgh Gateway Station opens, 11 December.

APPENDIX 1

State Subsidy and Commercial Profit

As many people are dubious or unclear about the combination of public subsidy and private profit-taking that is a current feature of railway operation in Scotland, it may be helpful to give a neutral explanation of how it is intended to work. The system rests on the idea that a well-ordered market can maintain a socially-beneficial stability in the trading of any commodity from treacle pies to transport. The working of the market establishes *social efficiency*, meaning the optimal distribution of resources in society. For a railway service this involves taking into account all costs and benefits external to provision of the service (e.g. infrastructure: everything from station toilets to signalling) as well as the internal costs and benefits associated with the provision of one (train, train crew, profit margin). In a pure market, when you buy a ticket its price will cover your proportion of the provider's external and internal costs in carrying you. This is known as the *marginal cost*, marginal in this context referring to a single act of consumption by an individual. In the case of rail travel this would put the ticket price beyond most people's ability to pay, so instead the concept of *marginal social cost* is used. The supplier's cost of providing the service, and the ticket buyer's cost of using it, are both subsidised by contribution from a third party, normally the taxpayers. The ideal of social efficiency is achieved when marginal social cost equals marginal social benefit. Marginal social benefit, in the train ticket, might include helping to reduce road congestion and environmental pollution, with their associated costs to society as a whole, and the benefit of getting to work in less time. A price that is over or under its marginal social cost is *inefficient*, because the benefit to the 'winner' is less than the loss to the rest of society, and so the total of general welfare is reduced. Competition between service providers is the vital necessity to keep any such inefficiency within tolerable limits. Various financial formulae exist to fix the right level of marginal social cost.

A service provider needs to raise capital in order to finance its operations, and therefore must pay interest or dividends to the capital providers. Its internal costs will include the profit element necessary to maintain and develop the business at the requisite level of capital resources. This profit element must be included in the calculation of marginal social cost. Franchise agreements normally incorporate some form of profit-capping or sharing to prevent the provider from making excessive profits.

From 1998 the application of marginal social cost pricing was required across all inland transport modes in European Union states, the intention being to secure not only a maximisation of *allocative efficiency* in the level and mix of the rail industry's output – and that of the wider transport sector – but also to limit government intervention and free the industry to define its own role in response to market signals. (Allocative efficiency is achieved when service production precisely meets consumer needs in terms of volume and cost).

There is no consensus among advocates of a market-based economy about the way to manage the railway market. For one, "Meticulous planning of privatisation acts against market-based reforms, as the optimal structure of a railway system is unknown. Therefore a special effort has to be made to allow the privatised railway system the freedom to adjust according to entrepreneurial potential, market demand, the costs of contractors and the availability of finance without government straitjacket"; while for another, "it seems clear that organisation (command and control) is superior to markets and contracts as a mode of railway operation. This is far from a novel observation… It is no accident that railways were and always have been vertically integrated entities, for that is the market-preferred solution to the provision of railways." (Oliver Knipping, in Hibbs et al., *The Railways, the Market & the Government*, 169f; David Tyrall, *Ibid.*, 122).

Competition, so fundamental to market theory, is virtually non-existent within the Scottish railway system. It can only be simulated by 'benchmarking' against other railway systems, an artificial procedure that requires external, non-market intervention and supervision.

APPENDIX 2

Location of Area Managers under Two Tier as first set up (1968)

Glasgow Division
Ardrossan, Ayr, Beattock, Bellgrove, Bellshill, Carstairs, Coatbridge, Dumbarton, Dumfries, Falkirk, Fort William, General Terminus (Glasgow), Grangemouth, Greenock, Irvine, Johnstone, Kilmarnock, Lenzie, Motherwell, Oban, Paisley, Partickhill, Rutherglen, Sighthill, South Glasgow, Stirling, Stobcross, Stranraer.

Edinburgh Division
Aberdeen, Bathgate, Dunbar, Dundee, Dunfermline, Edinburgh Goods, Fraserburgh, Hawick, Kirkcaldy, Millerhill, Montrose, Perth.

Highlands
Aviemore, Dingwall, Dufftown, Elgin, Keith, Invergordon, Inverness, Kyle of Lochalsh, Pitlochry, Thurso.

Stationmasters
Glasgow Central, Glasgow Queen Street, Edinburgh Main.

Depot Managers
Glasgow Parcels, Glasgow High Street.

Depot Engineers
Aberdeeen, Corkerhill, Dundee, Eastfield, Haymarket, Inverness, Leith Central, Polmadie, Thornton.

(Freightliner depot managers at Gushetfaulds and Portobello not included)

Oban Station and harbour on 10 June 1961. A return excursion train to Cardiff and Bristol is about to depart. Shipping includes a fishery cruiser, TS *Queen Mary*, and the Inner Isles mailship *Claymore*. (Robert Darlaston)

APPENDIX 3

Freight Train Connections at Mossend Yard in November 1988.

At this time there was still substantial coal, mineral and steel traffic. English and Welsh locations italicised. Asterisk indicates Speedlink service, (F) Freightliner.

*Arrochar
*Bescot (West Midlands)
Blyth
Cardiff
Carlisle
Clitheroe
(F)Coatbridge
*Coedbach (Swansea)
*Corpach
*Craiginches (Aberdeen)
Dalston (London)
*Deanside (Glasgow)
Dee Marsh
*Dover
Ellesmere Port
*Falkland Junction (Ayr)
(F)Felixstowe
Fort William
Gartcosh
*Gloucester
*Grangemouth
Grimethorpe
Gunnie (Coatbridge)
Hardendale

Healey Mills
Hunterston
*Inverness
Larbert
Llandarcy
*Mallaig Junction
Margam Yard
*Millerhill
(F)Motherwell
Oakleigh
*Oban
(F)Pengam
Ravenscraig
*Ripple Lane (London)
Sheerness
(F)Southampton
*Stirling
(F)Stratford (London)
*Stoke Gifford (Bristol)
*Tavistock Junction
(F)Tilbury
*Tyne Yard
*Warrington
*Whitemoor (March, Cambridgeshire)
*(F)Willesden (London)
*Wisbech
Wishaw

The 17.15 Oban-Glasgow train pulled by Class 5 No. 44786 of St Rollox depot, near Balquhidder on 3 September 1959. (Robert Darlaston)

APPENDIX 4

Abellio's Train Fleet, 2016

2	class 68 diesel locomotives
100	Mark II carriages
48	Class 156 2-car Super Sprinters
48	Class 158 2-car Express Sprinters
55	Class 70 3-car Turbostars
16	Class 314 electric 3-car units
21	Class 318 electric 3-car units
29	Class 320 3-car electric units
40	Class 334 Juniper 3-car electric units
38	Class 380 Desiro 3/4 car electric units

Due for delivery from 2017
46   Class 385 Hitachi 3-car and 24 4-car units

For possible delivery in 2018
27   refurbished and shortened (5-car) Class 43 HST sets

Serco Caledonian Sleepers
53   Mk III sleeping cars
22   Mk II seated cars
On order: 75 Mark V sleeping cars (2018)

Ex-NBR 0-4-0 saddle tank No. 50 (1897) as BR 68116 with a coal-cart tender, at its home depot, Kipps, in the heart of the Monklands coal and iron country. It was withdrawn in 1958. (North British Railway Study Group)

APPENDIX 5

Travel Trends

Unless otherwise noted these figures are from Transport Scotland statistics, some of which are based on samples or estimates.

Car remains by far the dominant, and still rising, form of personal transport, with 64% of total journeys in 2014-15. While rail journey numbers rose slightly, rail's share of total journeys fell back from 2.1% in 2013-14 to 1.7% in 2014-15

Index figures: taking 2005 as a base year (100), rail passenger numbers had risen to 134 by 2015, car travel kilometres to 104, air passenger numbers to 107, while bus passenger numbers had fallen to 87. In 2010 buses carried 5.5 times more passengers than trains; in 2015 the figure was 4.36.

A. Average annual miles of surface personal travel in Scotland

	1995-99	2008-10	2011-12
Rail	346	405	483
Local Bus	557	571	405
Car	3,427	3,525	5,315

RAC Federation. On the Move: Car, Rail and Bus Travel Trends in Scotland, 2013; Transport Scotland Statistics. Transport & Travel 2015, 4. Personal Travel

B. Bus, Rail and Air Journeys, 2006-2014 (millions/percentage of journeys to work)

	2006		2014	
Bus journeys	476	11.8%	414	10.2%
Rail journeys	69.8	3.6%	86.7	4.2%
Passengers at all airports	24.4	--	25.5	--

Transport Scotland. National Transport Strategy, Refresh, 2015.

220

C. Rail Passenger Journeys Originating In Scotland, 1960-2013 (millions per year)

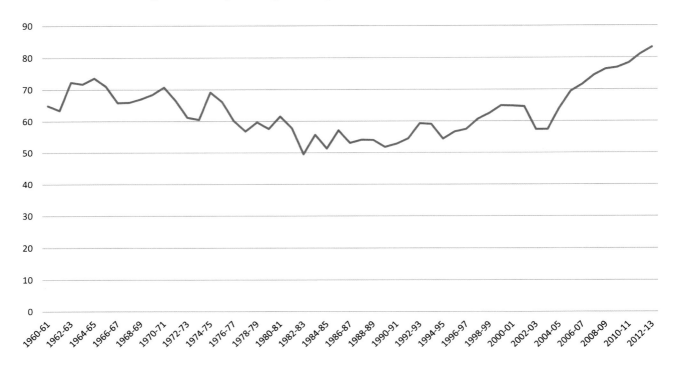

D. Freight tonnage lifted in Scotland, 1993-2013 (millions of tonnes per year)

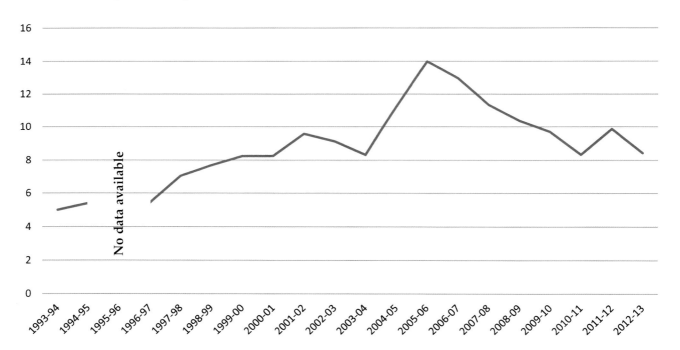

APPENDIX 6

Stations opened or reopened

Stations within cities are shown under the city name.
(G) indicates freight only (selected locations).

A. Stations opened or reopened between 1923 and 1947

Carfin Halt 1 October 1927
Croftfoot 1 January 1931
Edinburgh, Balgreen Halt 29 January 1934
Edinburgh, East Pilton Halt 1 December 1934
Glasgow, Corkerhill December 1923
Glasgow, Garrowhill 16 March 1936
Glasgow, Hillington East 19 March 1934 (as Hillington to 1 April 1940)

Glasgow, Hillington West 1 April 1940 (as Hillington to 3 March 1952)
Glasgow, Kings Park 6 October 1928
Glasgow, Mosspark 1 March 1934 (as Mosspark West to 3 May 1976)
Heads of Ayr (Butlin's Holiday Camp) 17 May 1947
Williamwood 4 September 1928
Woodhall 1 October 1945

B. Stations opened or reopened between 1948 and 1981

Alness 7 May 1973
Balmossie (Balmossie Halt until 1983) 18 June 1962
Duncraig 3 May 1976
Dunlop 5 June 1967
Edinburgh, Kingsknowe 1 February 1971
Glasgow, Anderston 5 November 1979
Glasgow, Argyle Street 5 November 1979
Glasgow, Bridgeton (was Bridgeton Cross) 5 November 1979
Glasgow Central (LL) 5 November 1979
Glasgow, Dalmarnock 5 November 1979
Glasgow, Drumry 6 April 1953

Glasgow, Exhibition Centre (Finnieston to 1987) 5 November 1979
Glasgow, Garscadden 5 November 1960
Glasgow, Hyndland (new) 5 November 1960
Glasgow, Maryhill Park (formerly Maryhill) 19 December 1960
Glasgow, Partick 17 December 1979
Greenock, Branchton 5 June 1967
IBM 9 September 1978
Lochwinnoch (Lochside to 1985) 27 June 1966
Muir of Ord 4 October 1976
Rogart 12 June 1961

C. Stations opened or re-opened between 1982 and 2016

Airbles 15 May 1989
Alloa 19 May 2008
Ardrossan Town 19 January 1987
Armadale 4 March 2011
Auchinleck 12 May 1984
Baillieston 4 October 1993
Bargeddie 4 October 1993
Bathgate 24 March 1986
Beauly 15 April 2002
Blackridge (formerly Westcraigs) 1 January 2010
Bridge of Allan 13 May 1985
Edinburgh, Brunstane 3 June 2002
Caldercruix 3 February 2011
Camelon 27 September 1994
Carmyle 4 October 1993
Chatelherault 12 December 2005
Conon Bridge 8 February 2013
Curriehill 5 October 1987

Dalgety Bay 28 March 1998
Drumfrochar 24 May 1998
Drumgelloch 15 May 1989
Dumbreck 30 July 1990
Dunfermline, Queen Margaret 26 January 2000
Dunrobin Castle 13 June 1985
Dyce 15 September 1984
Edinburgh Gateway 11 December 2016
Edinburgh, Newcraighall 3 June 2002
Edinburgh Park 4 December 2003
Edinburgh, South Gyle 1 May 1985
Edinburgh, Wester Hailes 11 May 1987
Eskbank 6 September 2015
Falls of Cruachan 20 June 1988
Galashiels 6 September 2015
Gartcosh 9 May 2005
Glasgow, Ashfield 3 December 1993
Glasgow, Corkerhill 30 July 1990

Glasgow, Crookston 30 July 1990
Glasgow, Gilshochill (originally Lambhill)
	3 December 1993
Glasgow, Kelvindale 29 September 2005
Glasgow, Maryhill (formerly Maryhill Park)
	3 December 1993
Glasgow, Mosspark 30 July 1990
Glasgow, Mount Vernon 4 October 1993
Glasgow, Possilpark 3 December 1993
Glasgow, Priesthill & Darnley 23 April 1990
Glasgow, Summerston 3 December 1993
Glenrothes with Thornton 11 May 1992
Gorebridge 6 September 2015
Greenfaulds 15 May 1989
Greenock Whinhill 14 May 1990
Gretna Green 20 September 1993
Howwood 12 March 2001
Kilmaurs 12 May 1984
Kirkwood 4 October 1993
Larkhall 12 December 2005
Laurencekirk 18 May 2009
Livingston North (exLNER) 24 March 1986

Livingston South 6 October 1984
Loch Awe 1 May 1985
Loch Eil Outward Bound 1 May 1985
Merryton 12 December 2005
Milliken Park 15 May 1989
Musselburgh 3 October 1988
New Cumnock 27 May 1991
Newtongrange 6 September 2015
Paisley Canal 30 July 1990
Paisley Hawkhead 12 April 1991
Portlethen 17 May 1985
Prestwick International 5 September 1994
Sanquhar 27 June 1994
Shawfair 6 September 2015
Shieldmuir 14 May 1990
Stepps 15 May 1989
Stow 6 September 2015
Tweedbank 6 September 2015
Uphall 24 March 1986
Wallyford 30 June 1994
Whifflet 21 December 1992

St Enoch Station, Glasgow, and its hotel. An aerial view from the 1950s. (Author's Collection)

APPENDIX 7

Stations closed

Where there are two dates, the first indicates passenger closure and the second freight closure (selected stations), which sometimes preceded passenger closure. Goods-only stations (select listing) are noted as (G). An asterisk indicates subsequent reopening, on or near the same site.

A. 1923-1929

Arbirlot 2 February 1929, 24 May 1965
Bargeddie* 24 September 1927
Braeside Halt August 1926
Carmyllie 2 December 1929
Charlestown 1 November 1926, 24 February 1964
Cuthlie 2 December 1929
Denhead 2 December 1929
Edinburgh, Granton East 2 November 1925,
    1 June 1966
Edinburgh, Trinity 2 November 1925

Glasgow, Broomhouse 24 September 1927
Glasgow, Gorbals 1 June 1928
Glasgow, Shields 1 November 1924
Hillside February 1927
Lyneside 1 November 1929
Macmerry 1 July 1925, 2 May 1966
Renfrew, King's Inch 19 July 1926
Renfrew Porterfield 19 July 1926
South Queensferry Halt 14 January 1929
Winton 1 July 1925

B. 1930-1939

Abbotsford Ferry 5 January 1931
Aberchalder 1 December 1933
Aberdeen, Don Street 5 April 1937
Aberdeen, Holburn Street 5 April 1937
Aberdeen, Hutcheon Street 5 April 1937
Aberdeen, Persley 5 April 1937
Aberdeen, Pitfodels 5 April 1937
Aberdeen, Ruthrieston 5 April 1937
Aberdeen, Schoolhill 5 April 1937
Aberdeen, Woodside 5 April 1937
Aberlady 12 September 1932
Alloway 1 December 1930, 7 December 1959
Annan Shawhill 27 April 1931
Ardrossan North 4 July 1932
Auchenmade 4 July 1932
Auchmacoy 31 December 1932
Avonbridge 1 May 1930
Balnacoul 14 September 1931
Banavie Pier 4 September 1939, 6 August 1951
Bankfoot 13 April 1931, 7 September 1964
Banknock 1 February 1935
Bardowie 2 July 1931
Bathgate Lower 1 May 1930, 28 October 1963
Bents 1 May 1930
Bieldside 5 April 1937
Blackstone 1 May 1930
Blairadam 22 September 1930
Boarhills 22 September 1930
Boddam 31 October 1932
Bonnybridge 28 July 1930, 7 December 1964

Bonnybridge Central 1 February 1935
Bowhouse 1 May 1930
Brackenhills 1 December 1930
Braeside Halt August/November 1926
Broomlee 1 April 1933
Bullers o' Buchan 31 October 1932
Burghead 14 September 1931, 7 November 1966
Cairneyhill 7 July 1930
Caldarvan 1 October 1934
Calderbank 1 December 1930
Cauldcots 22 September 1930
Causewayend 1 May 1930
Chapelhall 1 December 1930, 4 April 1961
Clackmannan 7 July 1930
Cleland (Old) 1 December 1930
Coltfield Platform 14 September 1931
Colzium (G) 2 May 1955
Commonhead (Airdrie North) 1 May 1930
Crossgatehall Halt 22 September 1930
Cruden Bay 31 October 1932
Culross 7 July 1930
Denny 28 July 1930
Dennyloanhead 1 February 1935
Dolphinton (LNER) 1 April 1933
Drumclog 11 September 1939
Drymen 1 October 1934, 5 October 1959
Dundee Esplanade 2 October 1939
Dunure 1 December 1930
Edinburgh, Leith Walk 31 March 1930
Edzell 27 September 1938, 7 September 1964

Eskbridge 22 September 1930
Fauldhouse & Crofthead 1 May 1930
Fingask Halt 2 November 1931
Fochabers Town 14 September 1931, 28 March 1966
Forest Mill 22 September 1930, 1 December 1953
Fort Augustus 1 December 1933
Gairlochy 1 December 1933
Gargunnock 1 October 1934
Gartness 1 October 1934
Giffen 4 July 1932
Gifford 3 April 1933
Gilmerton 1 May 1933
Glasgow, Bellahouston Park Halt 1 January 1939
Glasgow, Botanic Gardens 6 February 1939
Glasgow, Kirklee 1 May 1939
Glencorse 1 May 1933, 1 July 1959
Glengarnock High 1 December 1930
Glenside 1 December 1930
Gogar 22 September 1930
Gullane 12 September 1932
Halbeath 22 September 1930, 28 December 1964
Hatton 1 November 1932
Heads of Ayr (original) 1 December 1930
Hopeman 14 September 1931, 30 December 1957
Humbie 3 April 1933
Invergarry 1 December 1933
Invergloy 1 December 1933
Inverkeilor 22 September 1930
Irvine Bank Street 28 July 1930
Jamestown 1 October 1934
Kelty 22 September 1930, 25 January 1965
Kilbagie 7 July 1930
Kilbirnie South 1 December 1930
Kilsyth (New) 1 February 1935
Kilwinning East 4 July 1932
Kincardine 7 July 1930, 30 March 1968
Kingsbarns 22 September 1930
Kinneil 22 September 1930
Kippen 1 October 1934, 5 October 1959
Kirkliston 22 September 1930, 7 February 1966
Knoweside 1 December 1930
Lamancha 1 April 1933
Lauder 12 September 1932, 1 October 1958
Leadhills 2 January 1939
Leslie 4 January 1932, 9 October 1967
Letham Grange 22 September 1930
Lethenty 2 November 1931
Loanhead 1 May 1933, 22 July 1968
Loch Tay 11 September 1939

Lochanhead 25 February 1939
Longhaven 31 October 1932
Longriggend 1 May 1930
Loudounhill 11 September 1939
Luffness Platform 12 September 1932
Lugton High 4 July 1932
Lunan Bay 22 September 1930
Macbiehill 1 April 1933
Maidens 1 December 1930, 28 February 1955
Manuel Low Level 1 May 1933
Maxwelltown 1 March 1939
Methven 27 September 1937, 25 January 1965
Milltimber 5 April 1937
Montrose (LMS) 30 April 1934
Morningside (LNER) 1 May 1930
Morningside (LMS) 1 December 1930
Mount Melville 22 September 1930
Murtle 5 April 1937
Newhouse 1 December 1930
Newmains 1 December 1930
Oldmeldrum 2 November 1931
Ormiston 3 April 1933, 24 May 1965
Oxton 12 September 1932
Pencaitland 3 April 1933
Pitlurg 31 October 1932
Port of Menteith 1 October 1934
Ratho Low Level 22 September 1930
Rawyards 1 May 1930
Roslin 1 May 1933
Ryeland 11 September 1939
Saltcoats North 4 July 1932
Saltoun 3 April 1933
Sauchie 22 September 1930
Seton Mains Halt 22 September 1930
Slamannan 1 May 1930, 20 October 1958
Smeaton 22 September 1930
Stracathro 27 September 1938
Strathord 13 April 1931
Stravithie 22 September 1930
Thornbridge Halt 1 August 1938
Torryburn 7 July 1930
Turnhouse 22 November 1930
Wanlockhead 2 January 1939
West Cults 5 May 1937
Westfield 1 May 1930
Whifflet (LNER) 22 September 1930
Whitburn 1 May 1930, 10 August 1964
Whiterigg 1 May 1930
Winchburgh 22 September 1930

C. 1940-1949

Airdrie (LMS) 3 May 1943, 6 July 1964
Balerno 1 November 1943, 4 December 1967
Bankhead 2 June 1945
Bridge of Dee 26 September 1949
Calder 3 May 1943
Catrine 3 May 1943

Crossford 3 May 1943
Crossgates 26 September 1949
Currie 1 November 1943
Dalkeith 5 January 1942, 10 August 1964
Dolphinton (LMS) 2 June 1945
Dumfries House 13 June 1949

Dunscore 3 May 1943
Dunsyre 2 June 1945
Earlston 13 August 1948, 19 July 1965
Edinburgh, Bonnington 16 June 1947
Edinburgh, Colinton 1 November 1943
Edinburgh, Easter Road 16 June 1947
Edinburgh, Junction Bridge 16 June 1947
Edinburgh, Juniper Green 1 November 1943
Fort George 5 April 1943, 11 August 1958
Fushiebridge 54 October 1943
Gartsherrie 28 October 1940
Glasgow, Kelvinside 1 July 1942
Glasgow, Mount Vernon* (LMS) 16 August 1943
Glassford 30 September 1948
Gordon 13 August 1948
Greenlaw 13 August 1948
Haddington 5 December 1949, 30 March 1968
High Blantyre 30 September 1945, 1 June 1968
Holywood 26 September 1949
Irongray 3 May 1943
Jedburgh 13 August 1948, 10 August 1964
Jedfoot 13 August 1948
Kirkbank 13 August 1948
Kirkland 3 May 1943

Livingston* 1 November 1948
Lybster 1 April 1944
Marchmont 12 August 1948
Meikle Earnock Halt 12 February 1943
Mid Clyth 1 April 1944
Moniaive 3 May 1943, 4 July 1949
Newbigging 2 June 1945
Newtonairds 3 May 1943
Nisbet 12 August 1948
North Leith (LNER) 16 June 1947, 5 February 1968
Occumster 1 April 1944
Overtown 5 October 1942
Plaidy 22 May 1944
Quarter 30 September 1945
Ravelrig January 1945
Rigg 1 November 1942
Stepford 3 May 1943
Strathaven North 30 September 1945
Strathpeffer 23 February 1946, 26 March 1951
Tarbolton 4 January 1943, 6 January 1964
Thrumster 1 April 1944
Turnberry 2 March 1942, 28 February 1955
Ulbster 1 April 1944
West Wemyss 7 November 1949

D. 1950-1959

Abercairney 1 October 1951
Aberfoyle 1 October 1951
Abernethy 19 September 1955
Airth 20 September 1954
Alford 2 January 1950
Allangrange 1 October 1951
Almondbank 1 October 1951
Alva 1 November 1954, 24 February 1964
Alyth 2 July 1951, 25 January 1965
Amisfield 19 May 1952
Annbank 10 November 1951, 6 July 1964
Ardler 11 June 1956
Armadale* 9 January 1956, 19 July 1965
Auchencruive 10 September 1951
Auchendinny 5 March 1951
Auchenheath 1 October 1951
Auchterarder 11 June 1956
Auchterhouse 10 January 1955
Auchterless 1 October 1951
Auchtermuchty 5 June 1950, 5 October 1964
Auldbar Road 11 June 1956
Auldgirth 3 November 1952
Avoch 1 October 1951, 13 June 1960
Baldovan 10 January 1955, 25 January 1965
Baldragon 10 January 1955
Balfron 1 October 1951
Balgowan 1 October 1951
Balmore 2 April 1951
Banff Bridge 1 October 1951
Bannockburn 2 January 1950, 4 May 1964
Barrasford 15 October 1956

Bathgate Upper 9 January 1956
Beith North 4 June 1951
Bellshill (exLNER) 10 October 1951
Biggar 5 June 1950
Birchfield Halt 7 May 1956
Birnie Road 1 October 1951
Blackford 11 June 1956
Blairgowrie 10 January 1955
Blanefield 1 October 1951
Bogside (Fife) 15 September 1958
Bo'ness 7 May 1956, 7 May 1965
Bothwell (exLMS) 5 June 1950
Bothwell (exLNER) 4 July 1955, 6 June 1961
Bowland 7 December 1953, 23 March 1964
Bowling 5 February 1951
Brechin 4 August 1952, 2 May 1981
Brocketsbrae 1 October 1951
Broomieknowe 10 September 1951
Broughton 5 June 1950
Buchlyvie 1 October 1951
Buckhaven 10 January 1955
Bucksburn 5 March 1956
Burnbank 15 September 1952
Cairntable Halt 3 April 1950
Caldercruix* 9 January 1956
Campsie Glen, 1 October 1951
Careston 4 August 1952
Cargill 11 June 1956
Carham 4 July 1955
Carmont 11 June 1956
Carronbridge 7 December 1953

Cassillis 6 December 1954, 31 October 1961
Causewayhead 4 July 1955
Chirnside 10 September 1951, 7 November 1966
Clocksbriggs 5 December 1955
Clydebank East 14 September 1959
Coatbridge (exLNER) 10 September 1951
Cockburnspath 18 June 1951
Colfin 6 February 1950
Collessie 19 September 1955
Colliston 5 December 1955
Colzium (G) 2 May 1955
Commondyke 3 July 1950
Coulter 5 June 1950
Cove Bay 11 June 1956, 28 October 1963
Craigo 11 June 1956
Cronberry 10 September 1951
Cummertrees 19 September 1955
Cumnock (2nd) 10 September 1951, 1 July 1959
Cunninghamhead 1 January 1951
Curriehill 2 April 1951
Dairsie 20 September 1954
Dalchonzie Halt 1 October 1951
Dalrymple 6 December 1954
Dalserf 1 October 1951
Dirleton 1 February 1954
Donibristle Halt 2 November 1959
Drongan 10 September 1951
Dronley 10 January 1955
Drum 10 September 1951
Drumlithie 11 June 1956
Drumshoreland 18 June 1951
Dubton 4 August 1952
Dumgoyne 1 October 1951
Dundee East 5 January 1959
Dundee, Magdalen Green 11 June 1956
Dunning 11 June 1956
Duns 10 September 1951
Eassie 11 June 1956
East Grange 15 September 1958
Edinburgh, Barnton 7 May 1951
Edinburgh, Davidson's Mains 7 May 1951, 1 June 1966
Edinburgh, Easter Road Park Halt 7 April 1952
Edinburgh, House o' Hill Halt 7 May 1951
Edinburgh, Millerhill 7 November 1955
Edinburgh, Newhailes 6 February 1950
Edrom 10 September 1951
Esslemont 15 September 1952
Falkland Road 15 September 1958, 10 August 1964
Fallside 3 August 1953
Farnell Road 11 June 1956
Fordoun 11 June 1956
Forgandenny 11 June 1956
Forteviot 11 June 1956
Fortrose 1 October 1951, 13 June 1964
Friockheim 5 December 1955
Fyvie 1 October 1951, 3 January 1966
Gartmore 2 January 1950
Gateside 5 June 1950

Glamis 11 June 1956
Glasgow, Anderston Cross 3 August 1959
Glasgow, Bellahouston 20 September 1954
Glasgow, Calderpark Halt 4 July 1955
Glasgow Green 2 November 1953
Glasgow, Kelvin Bridge 4 August 1952
Glasgow, Mount Vernon (exLNER) 4 July 1944
Glasgow, Parkhead North 19 September 1958
Glasgow, Robroyston 11 June 1956
Glasgow, Stobcross 3 August 1959
Glasgow, Summerston* 2 April 1951
Glasgow, Victoria Park 2 April 1951
Glassaugh 21 September 1953
Glasterlaw 2 April 1951
Glenboig 11 June 1956
Glenbuck 4 August 1952
Glencarse 11 June 1956
Gourdon 1 October 1951
Greenloaning 11 June 1956
Greenock, Lynedoch 2 February 1959, 7 March 1966
Greenock Princes Pier 2 February 1956
Gretna 10 September 1951
Guay 3 August 1959
Guthrie 5 December 1955
Hamilton (exLNER) 15 September 1952
Haywood 10 September 1951
Holehouse 3 April 1950
Howwood* 7 March 1955
Humshaugh 15 October 1956
Hurlford 7 March 1955, 6 July 1964
Inchture 11 June 1956
Innerpeffray 1 October 1951
Innerwick 18 June 1951
Inveramsay 1 October 1951, 2 November 1964
Inverbervie 1 October 1951, 23 May 1966
Johnshaven 1 October 1951
Johnstone North 7 March 1955, 4 May 1964
Jordanstone 2 July 1951
Justinhaugh 4 August 1952, 4 September 1967
Kemnay 2 January 1950
Killearn 1 October 1951
Killochan 1 January 1951
Killywhan 3 August 1959
Kilmany 12 February 1951, 5 October 1964
Kilsyth 6 August 1951, 4 May 1964
Kinbuck 11 June 1956
Kinfauns 2 January 1950
King Edward 1 October 1951, 1 August 1961
Kingennie 10 January 1955, 9 October 1967
Kingsmuir 10 January 1955, 9 October 1967
Kirkbuddo 10 January 1955, 9 October 1967
Kirkgunzeon 2 January 1950
Kirkinner 25 September 1950
Kirriemuir 4 August 1952, 21 June 1965
Larkhall East 10 September 1951
Lasswade 10 September 1951
Lauriston 1 October 1951
Leadburn 7 March 1955, 5 February 1962

Leith Central 7 April 1952
Lennoxtown 1 October 1951
Leysmill 5 December 1955
Liff 10 January 1955
Lindean 10 September 1951
Lindores 12 February 1951
Locharbriggs 19 May 1952, 4 May 1964
Lochearnhead 1 October 1951
Lochee 10 January 1955
Lochee West 10 January 1955
Lochmaben 19 May 1952
Lochside 4 July 1955
Longforgan 11 June 1956, 25 January 1965
Lugar 3 July 1950
Luncarty 18 June 1951
Luthrie 12 February 1951, 5 October 1964
Lyne 5 June 1950
Macduff 1 October 1951, 1 August 1961
Madderty 1 October 1951
Marykirk 11 June 1956
Meigle 2 July 1951 25 January 1965
Menstrie 1 November 1954, 28 January 1965
Methil 10 January 1955, 30 December 1978
Methven Junction 1 October 1951
Millisle 25 September 1950
Milton of Campsie 1 October 1951
Moffat 6 December 1954
Monikie 10 January 1955
Montgreenan 7 March 1955
Monymusk 2 January 1950, 3 January 1966
Muchalls 4 December 1950
Munlochy 1 October 1951
Netherburn 1 October 1951
Newburgh 19 September 1955
Newpark 14 September 1959
Newtonhill 11 June 1956
Newtyle 10 January 1955, 7 September 1964
North Water Bridge 1 October 1951
Ochiltree 10 September 1951, 6 January 1964
Palnure 7 May 1951
Parkhill 3 April 1950
Peebles (exLMS) 5 June 1950, 1 August 1959
Penicuik 10 September 1951, 27 March 1967
Philpstoun 18 June 1951, 23 March 1964

Plains 18 June 1951
Plean 11 June 1956
Polton 10 Septermber 1951, 18 May 1964
Portlethen* 11 June 1958
Portpatrick 6 February 1950
Rankinston 3 April 1950, 2 November 1959
Ratho 18 June 1951
Redcastle 1 October 1951
Rosemount Halt 10 January 1955
Rosslyn Castle 10 September 1951
Rothienorman 1 October 1951, 3 January 1966
Ruthven Road 1 October 1951
St. Cyrus 1 October 1951
St. Fillans 1 October 1951
Saughtree 15 October 1956
Selkirk 10 September 1951, 2 November 1964
Shieldhill 19 May 1952
Skares 10 September 1951
Sorbie 25 September 1956
Sprouston 4 July 1955
Stanley 11 June 1956, 6 December 1965
Stobo 5 June 1950
Strathblane 1 October 1951
Strathmiglo 5 June 1950
Tannadice 4 August 1952
Tibbermuir 1 October 1951, 27 January 1964
Tillietudlem 1 October 1951, 4 January 1966
Tillyfourie 2 January 1950
Tochieneal 1 October 1951
Torrance 2 April 1951
Trabboch 10 September 1951
Turriff 1 October 1951, 3 January 1966
Twechar 6 August 1951
Uphall* 9 January 1956
Wartle 1 October 1951
Wemyss Castle 10 January 1955, 28 December 1964
Westcraigs 9 January 1956
Whauphill 25 September 1950
Whitehouse 2 January 1950
Whithorn 25 September 1950, 5 October 1964
Wigtown 25 September 1950, 5 October 1964
Wilsontown 10 September 1951, 4 May 1964
Wishaw South 15 September 1958, 5 April 1965
Woodburn 15 September 1952

E. 1960-1970

Aberdeen, Kittybrewster 6 May 1968
Aberdour 18 May 1964
Aberfeldy 3 May 1965, 25 January 1965
Abington 4 January 1965
Aboyne 28 February 1966, 18 July 1966
Ach-na-Cloich 1 November 1965
Achterneed 7 December 1964
Advie 18 October 1965
Airdrie, Hallcraig (G) 6 July 1964
Airdrie South (G) 4 January 1965
Allanfearn 3 May 1965

Alloa* 7 October 1968, 13 July 1974
Alness* 13 June 1966
Alves 3 May 1965
Anstruther 6 September 1965
Appin 28 March 1966
Ardrossan Montgomerie Pier 6 May 1968
Ardrossan Town* 1 January 1968, 3 April 1972
Arnage 4 October 1965
Auchengray 18 April 1966
Auchindachy 6 May 1968
Auchinleck* 6 December 1965

Auchnagatt 4 October 1965, 28 March 1966
Auldearn 6 June 1960
Aultmore (G) 3 October 1966
Ayr Cattle Market (G) 1 March 1965
Ayr Newtonhead (G) 4 October 1965
Ayton 5 February 1962
Back o' Loch Halt 7 September 1964
Baillieston* 5 October 1964
Balado 15 June 1964
Ballachulish 28 March 1966
Ballachulish Ferry 28 March 1966
Ballater 26 March 1966
Ballifurth Farm Halt 18 October 1965
Ballinluig 3 May 1965
Balnaguard 3 May 1965
Balquhidder 28 September 1965
Banchory 28 February 1966
Banff 6 July 1964
Barcaldine Platform 28 March 1966
Barleith 6 April 1964
Barrhead South (G) 28 October 1963
Barrmill 5 November 1962
Beauly* 13 June 1960
Beith Town 5 November 1962
Belses 6 January 1969
Benderloch 28 March 1966
Bilbster 13 June 1960
Blacksboat 18 October 1965
Blackwood 4 October 1965
Boat of Garten 18 October 1965
Bogside (Ayrshire) 2 January 1967
Bonnybridge High 6 March 1967
Bonnyrigg 10 September 1962
Borrobol Platform 29 November 1965
Bower 13 June 1960
Braidwood 2 July 1962
Bridge of Allan* 1 November 1965, 4 May 1964
Bridge of Dun 4 September 1967
Bridge of Earn 15 June 1964
Bridgefoot Halt 6 July 1964
Brodie 3 May 1965
Broxburn Junction (G) 19 July 1965
Brucklay 4 October 1965
Buckie 6 March 1968
Buckpool 7 March 1960
Bunchrew 13 June 1960
Burnmouth 5 February 1962
Cairnbulg 3 May 1965
Cairnie Junction 6 May 1968
Calcots 6 May 1968
Callander 1 November 1965, 7 June 1965
Cambus 7 October 1968
Cambus o' May 28 February 1966
Cambusavie 13 June 1960
Camelon* 4 September 1967
Cameron Bridge 6 October 1969
Canonbie 15 June 1964
Cardrona 5 June 1962

Carmyle* 5 October 1964
Carnwath 18 April 1966
Carron 18 October 1965
Castle Douglas 14 June 1965
Castle Kennedy 14 June 1965
Castlecary 6 March 1967
Castlemilk (G) 6 April 1964
Cleghorn 4 January 1965
Closeburn 11 September 1961
Clovenfords 5 February 1962
Clunes 13 June 1960
Clydebank Riverside 5 October 1964
Coalburn 4 October 1965
Coatdyke (G) 15 July 1968
Cobbinshaw 18 April 1966
Comrie 6 July 1964
Conon Bridge* 13 June 1960
Cornhill 6 May 1968
Coupar Angus 4 September 1967
Craigellachie 6 May 1968
Crail 6 September 1965, 18 December 1966
Crathes 28 February 1966
Crawford 4 January 1965
Creagan 2 March 1966
Creetown 14 June 1965
Crianlarich Lower 28 September 1965, 4 February 1971
Crieff 6 July 1964, 11 September 1967
Cromdale 18 October 1965, 4 November 1968
Crook of Devon 16 June 1964, 20 April 1964
Crosshouse 18 April 1966, 6 July 1964
Crossmichael 14 June 1965
Cullen 6 May 1968
Culloden Moor 3 May 1965
Culter 28 February 1966
Cults 28 February 1966
Cumnock (Old) 6 December 1965, 7 September 1964
Dailly 6 September 1965
Dailuaine 6 October 1965
Dalbeattie 14 October 1965, 3 May 1965
Dalcross 3 May 1965
Dalguise 3 May 1965
Dalmellington 6 April 1964
Dalmuir Riverside 5 October 1964
Dalnaspidal 3 May 1965
Dalvey Farm Halt 18 October 1965
Darvel 6 April 1964
Dava 18 October 1965
Daviot 3 May 1965, 7 September 1964
Delny 13 June 1966
Dess 28 February 1966
Dinnet 28 February 1966
Dinwoodie 13 June 1960
Dollar 15 June 1964
Dornoch 13 June 1960
Douglas West 5 October 1964
Doune 1 November 1965
Dreghorn 6 April 1964
Drummuir 6 May 1968

Drumpark 5 October 1964
Drybridge 3 March 1969, 2 November 1959
Dufftown 6 May 1968, 7 November 1966
Dullatur 5 June 1967
Dundee West 3 May 1965
Dunfermline Upper 7 October 1968
Dunlop* 7 November 1966
Dunphail 18 October 1965
Dunragit 14 June 1965
Dunrobin* 14 November 1965
Duror 28 March 1966
Dyce* 6 May 1968, 10 August 1964
Dysart 6 October 1969, 26 April 1965
East Fortune 4 May 1964
East Linton 4 May 1964
Easthaven 4 September 1967
Eastriggs 6 December 1965
Ecclefechan 13 June 1960, 28 October 1963
Edderton 13 June 1966
Eddleston 5 February 1962
Edinburgh, Abbeyhill 7 September 1964
Edinburgh, Balgreen Halt, 1 January 1968
Edinburgh, Blackford Hill 10 September 1962
Edinburgh, Corstorphine 1 January 1968
Edinburgh, Craigleith 30 April 1962
Edinburgh, Craiglockhart 10 September 1962
Edinburgh, Dalry Road 30 April 1962
Edinburgh, Duddingston 10 September 1962
Edinburgh, East Pilton 30 April 1962
Edinburgh, Gorgie East 10 September 1962
Edinburgh, Granton High (G) 5 February 1968
Edinburgh, Granton Road 30 April 1962
Edinburgh, Joppa 7 September 1964
Edinburgh, Kingsknowe* 6 July 1964
Edinburgh, Leith Walk East (G)
Edinburgh, Leith Walk West (G)
Edinburgh, Lothian Road (G) 3 August 1964
Edinburgh, Merchiston 6 September 1965
Edinburgh, Morningside Road 10 September 1962
Edinburgh, Murrayfield 30 April 1962
Edinburgh, Newhaven 30 April 1962
Edinburgh, Newington 10 September 1962
Edinburgh, Piershill 7 September 1964
Edinburgh, Pinkhill 1 January 1968
Edinburgh, Portobello 7 September 1964
Edinburgh Princes Street 6 September 1965
Edinburgh, St. Leonards (G) 22 July 1968
Edinburgh, Saughton (G) 24 February 1964
Edinburgh, Scotland Street (G) 6 November 1967
Elderslie 14 February 1966
Elie 6 September 1965
Elliot Junction 4 September 1967
Ellon 4 October 1965, 11 September 1967
Elvanfoot 4 January 1965
Embo 13 June 1960
Eskbank* & Dalkeith 6 January 1969
Evanton 13 June 1966
Eyemouth 5 February 1962

Falls of Cruachan Halt* 1 November 1965
Findochty 6 May 1968
Flemington 4 January 1965
Forfar 4 September 1967
Foulis 13 June 1960
Fountainhall 6 January 1969
Fraserburgh 4 October 1965, 6 November 1979
Gailes 2 January 1967
Galashiels* 6 January 1969, 28 April 1969
Galston 6 April 1964
Garmouth 6 May 1968
Garnkirk 7 March 1960
Gartcosh* 5 November 1962
Gartly 6 May 1968
Gatehouse of Fleet 14 June 1965
Gilbey's Cottages 18 October 1965
Gilnockie 15 June 1964
Glasgow, Bridgeton Cross* (exLMS) 5 October 1964
Glasgow Buchanan Street 7 November 1964
Glasgow Central LL* 5 October 1964
Glasgow, College (G) 1 January 1968
Glasgow, Cowlairs 7 September 1964
Glasgow Cross 5 October 1964
Glasgow, Crow Road 6 November 1960
Glasgow, Cumberland Street 14 February 1966
Glasgow, Dalmarnock* 5 October 1964
Glasgow, Eglinton Street 1 February 1965
Glasgow, High Street (G)
Glasgow, Hyndland (old) 5 November 1966
Glasgow, Ibrox 6 February 1967
Glasgow, Kelvin Hall (Partick Central to 1959)
     5 October 1964
Glasgow, Maryhill Central 5 October 1964
Glasgow, Maryhill Park* 29 February 1964
Glasgow, Parkhead Stadium 5 October 1964
Glasgow, Partick West 5 October 1964
Glasgow, Possil 5 October 1964
Glasgow St. Enoch 27 June 1966
Glasgow, St. Rollox 5 November 1962
Glasgow, Scotstoun East 5 October 1964
Glasgow, Scotstoun West 5 October 1964
Glasgow, Shields Road 14 February 1966
Glasgow, Strathbungo 28 May 1962
Glasgow, Tollcross 5 October 1964
Glasgow, Whiteinch Riverside 5 October 1964
Glasgow, Yoker Ferry 5 October 1964
Glassel 28 February 1966
Glenbarry 6 May 1968
Glencarron 7 November 1964
Glen Douglas 15 June 1964
Glenfarg 15 June 1964
Glenluce 14 June 1965
Glenwhilly 6 September 1965
Golf Club House Halt 6 July 1964
Gollanfield 3 May 1965
Gorebridge* 6 January 1969
Grandtully 3 May 1965
Grange 6 May 1968

Grangemouth 29 January 1968
Grantown on Spey East 18 October 1965
Grantown on Spey West 18 October 1965
Grantshouse 4 May 1964
Greenhill 18 April 1966
Greenock Upper 5 June 1967
Gretna Green* 6 December 1965
Guard Bridge 6 September 1965
Halkirk 13 June 1966
Happendon 5 December 1964
Harburn 18 April 1966
Hassendean 6 January 1969
Hawick 6 January 1969, 28 April 1969
Heads of Ayr (2nd) 9 September 1968
Heriot 6 January 1969
Highlandman 6 January 1964
Hollybush 6 April 1964
Hoy 29 November 1965
Imperial Cottages Halt 18 October 1965
Inches 5 October 1964
Innerleithen 5 February 1962
Inveresk 4 May 1964, 25 January 1965
Inverugie 3 May 1965
Keith Town 6 May 1968
Kelso 16 June 1964, 30 March 1968
Kennethmont 6 May 1968
Kentallen 28 March 1966
Kilbarchan 27 June 1966
Kilbirnie 27 June 1966
Kilbowie 5 October 1964
Kilconquhar 6 September 1965
Kildary 13 June 1960
Kilkerran 6 September 1965
Killiecrankie 3 May 1965
Killin 29 June 1965
Killin Junction 28 September 1965
Kilmaurs* 7 November 1966
Kinaldie 7 December 1964
Kincraig 18 October 1965
Kingshouse Platform 28 September 1965
Kingskettle 4 September 1967
Kinloss 3 May 1965
Kintore 7 December 1964, 7 November 1966
Kirkandrews 7 September 1964
Kirkbride 7 November 1964
Kirkcowan 14 May 1965
Kirkcudbright 3 May 1965
Kirkintilloch 7 September 1964, 4 April 1966
Kirkpatrick 13 June 1960
Kirkton Bridge Halt 3 May 1965
Kirtlebridge 13 June 1960
Knock 6 May 1968
Knockando 18 October 1965
Ladysbridge 6 July 1964
Lamington 4 January 1965
Langholm 15 June 1964, 18 September 1967
Langloan 5 October 1964, 3 April 1967
Largo 6 September 1965

Larkhall* 4 October 1965
Laurencekirk* 4 September 1967
Law Junction 4 January 1965
Leith George Street (G) 22 July 1968
Leith North 30 April 1962
Lentran 13 June 1966
Lesmahagow 4 October 1965, 6 April 1964
Leven 6 October 1969
Lhanbryde 7 December 1964
Loch Awe* 28 September 1965
Loch Skerrow 9 September 1963
Lochty (G) 8 August 1964
Lochwinnoch 27 June 1966
Logierieve 4 October 1965
Longmorn 6 May 1968
Longside 3 May 1965
Lonmay 4 October 1965
Lossiemouth 6 April 1964, 28 March 1966
Loth 13 June 1966
Lugton 7 November 1966
Luib 28 September 1965
Lumphannan 28 February 1966, 15 June 1964
Lundin Links 6 September 1965
Manuel 6 March 1967, 5 April 1965
Mauchline 6 December 1965, 1 November 1965
Maud 4 October 1965
Mawcarse 15 June 1964, 25 January 1965
Maxton 15 June 1964
Melrose 6 January 1969, 18 May 1964
Milliken Park* 18 April 1966
Milnathort 15 June 1964, 4 May 1970
Mintlaw 3 May 1965
Mossend 5 November 1962
Moy 3 May 1965
Muirkirk 5 October 1964, 7 September 1964
Muir of Ord* 15 June 1960
Mulben 7 December 1964
Murthly 3 May 1965
Musselburgh 7 September 1964, 7 December 1970
Muthill 6 July 1964
Neilston Low Level 7 November 1966, 5 October 1964
Nethercleugh 13 June 1966
Nethy Bridge 18 October 1965
New Cumnock* 6 December 1965, 7 September 1964
New Galloway 14 June 1965
New Luce 6 September 1965
Newcastleton 6 January 1969
Newmachar 4 October 1965
Newmilns 6 April 1964, 6 July 1964
Newport on Tay East 5 May 1969, 2 January 1967
Newport on Tay West 5 May 1969
Newseat Halt 3 May 1965
Newtongrange* 6 January 1969
Nigg 13 June 1960
North Connel 28 March 1966
Oakley 7 October 1968, 28 December 1964
Orbliston 7 December 1964
Ordens Halt 6 July 1964

Orton 7 December 1964
Oyne 6 May 1968
Paisley Abercorn 5 June 1967
Paisley Hawkhead* 14 February 1966
Paisley West 14 February 1966
Park 28 February 1966
Parton 14 June 1965
Patna 6 April 1964
Peebles East 5 February 1962
Perth, Princes Street 28 February 1966
Peterhead 3 May 1965, 7 September 1970
Philorth Bridge Halt 3 May 1965
Pinmore 6 September 1965
Pinwherry 6 September 1965
Pitcaple 6 May 1968
Pitmedden 7 December 1964
Pittenweem 6 September 1965, 18 July 1966
Pittenzie Halt 6 July 1964
Pomathorn 5 February 1962
Ponfeigh 5 October 1964, 4 April 1966
Portessie 6 May 1968
Portgordon 6 May 1968
Portknockie 6 May 1968
Portsoy 6 May 1968
Racks 6 December 1965
Rathen 4 October 1965
Renfrew Fulbar Street 5 June 1967
Renfrew South 5 June 1967
Renfrew Wharf 5 June 1967
Reston 4 May 1964
Rhu 15 June 1964
Riccarton Junction 6 January 1969
Rogart* 13 June 1960
Rosewell & Hawthornden 10 September 1962
Rosslynlee Hospital Halt 5 February 1962
Rothes 6 May 1968, 4 November 1968
Rothiemay 6 May 1968
Roxburgh 15 June 1964, 10 August 1964
Rumbling Bridge 15 June 1964
Rutherford 15 June 1964
Ruthwell 6 December 1965
St. Andrews 6 January 1969
St. Boswells 6 January 1969
St. Combs 3 May 1965
St. Fort 6 September 1965
St. Monance 6 September 1965
Salzcraggie Platform 29 November 1965

Sandilands 5 October 1964
Sanquhar* 6 December 1965
Shankend 6 January 1969
Sinclairtown 6 October 1969
Skelbo 13 June 1960
Southwick 3 May 1965
Spey Bay 6 May 1968
Springside 6 April 1964
Steele Road 6 January 1969
Stepps* 5 November 1962
Stobs 6 January 1969
Stonehouse 4 October 1965, 7 December 1964
Stow* 6 January 1969
Stranraer Town 7 March 1966
Strathaven Central 4 October 1965
Strathyre 28 September 1965
Strichen 4 October 1965
Struan 3 May 1965
Symington 4 January 1965
Tarff 3 May 1965
Tauchers 7 December 1964
Tayport 22 May 1966
Thankerton 4 January 1965
The Mound 13 June 1960
Thornhill 6 December 1965
Thornielee 6 November 1960
Thornton Junction 6 October 1969
Throsk 18 April 1966
Tillicoultry 15 June 1964, 23 May 1966
Tillynaught 6 May 1968
Tomatin 3 May 1965
Torphins 28 February 1966
Towiemore 6 May 1968
Tullibardine 6 July 1964
Tynehead 6 January 1969
Uplawmoor 2 April 1962
Urquhart 6 May 1968
Walkerburn 5 February 1962
Wamphray 13 June 1966
Waterside 6 April 1964
Watten 13 June 1960
West Ferry 4 September 1967
Whifflet Lower 5 November 1962
Whifflet Upper 5 October 1964
Whistlefield Halt 15 June 1964
Wormit 5 May 1969, 14 August 1967

F. 1970 onwards

Balloch Pier 28 September 1986
Beattock 3 January 1972
Bridge of Weir 10 January 1983
Errol 30 September 1985
Fairlie Pier 1 July 1971
Glasgow, Bridgeton (Bridgeton Central 1954-65)
        5 November 1979
Glasgow, Corkerhill* 10 January 1983

Glasgow, Crookston* 10 January 1983
Glasgow, Mosspark* 10 January 1983
Glasgow, Partickhill* (resited as Partick) 17 December 1979
Houston 10 January 1983
Kilmacolm 10 January 1983
Kinross 5 January 1970
Leith East (G) 31 December 1973
Paisley Canal* 10 January 1983

Number of Station Closures per Year in Scotland (closures to passengers only)

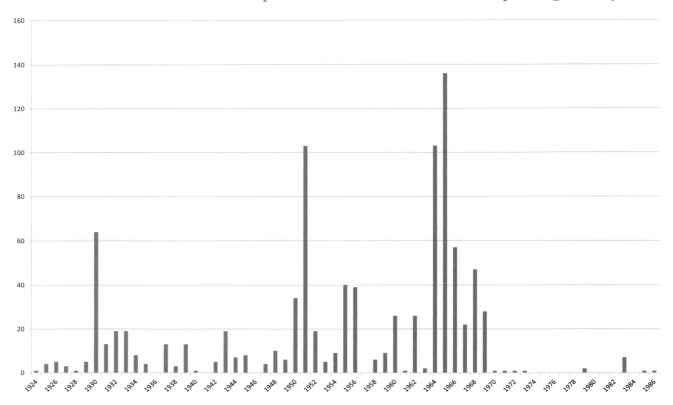

Exterior view of Fort William Station, 1954. (David Kelso)

London and North Eastern Railway Company

QUEENSFERRY FERRY

TABLE of TOLLS and CHARGES

Leviable by the London and North Eastern Railway Company on the Ferry between North and South Queensferry, in terms of the Schedule to the London and North Eastern Railway Order, 1925.

SCHEDULE

PART I.

	Tolls and Charges.
For every—	
Motor Car seated for not more than three persons	7/6
Motor Car seated for more than three but for not more than ten persons	10/-
Motor Car or Motor Char-a-banc seated for more than ten persons	25/-
Motor Cycle Car (three wheels) seated for two persons	5/-
Motor Bicycle	2/6
Motor Bicycle with side-car	5/-
Motor Tricycle seated for one person	3/-
Motor Tricycle seated for two persons	4/-
Motor Van or Lorry (inclusive of load, if any)	7/6 Per ton
Motor Hearse	Minimum charge 10/-, Fractions of 10 cwt. to be charged as 10 cwt.
Motor Ambulance Van	10/-
Ordinary Bicycle	8d.
Tandem Bicycle	1/-
Ordinary Tricycle	1/6
Perambulator or Child's Mail Cart (non-folding)	9d.
Child's Mail Cart (folding)	4d.

The toll or charge for passengers shall in each case be charged in addition to the toll or charge for the vehicle.

PART II.

	Tolls and Charges.
For every—	
Four-wheeled passenger vehicle drawn by one horse, mule or ass, and for every two-wheeled passenger vehicle	6/-
Four-wheeled passenger vehicle drawn by two or more horses, mules or asses:—	
Seated for not more than six persons	10/-
Seated for more than six but not more than twelve persons	15/-
Seated for more than twelve persons	20/-
Wagon or Vehicle for carrying goods, wares or merchandise:—	
When drawn by one horse, mule or ass	4/-
When drawn by two or more horses, mules or asses	6/-

with an addition of 1/- for every two cwt. beyond the first sixteen cwt., inclusive of load, if any.

Part II.—(continued)

	Tolls and Charges.
For every—	
Hearse (horse drawn)	15/-
Ambulance Van (horse drawn)	7/6
Caravan	7/6 per ton or fraction of a ton.

A Vehicle under this Part of this Schedule shall be charged as a passenger vehicle or as a vehicle for carrying goods, wares or merchandise according to the principal purpose for which such vehicle is constructed or ordinarily used; and the toll or charge for passengers, horses, mules and asses shall in each case be charged in addition to the toll or charge for the vehicle.

PART III.

	Tolls and Charges.
For every—	
Saddle Horse, Carriage Horse or led Horse	2/6
Cart Horse or Wagon Horse	1/6
Stallion	7/6
Mule, Ass, Cow, Ox or Heifer	1/6
Bull	2/6
Calf, Sow or Hog	9d.
Sheep or Goat	4d.
Lamb or Kid	3d.
Dog	6d.

The toll or charge for passengers shall be charged in addition to the toll or charge for a horse or other animal.

PART IV.

	Tolls and Charges.
For every—	
Passenger	7d.
Corpse	10/- in addition to the toll or charge for Hearse or other conveyance.
Organ (Street) on wheels	2/6
Barrow (loaded)	1/6
Barrow (empty)	9d.
For Goods, Wares or Merchandise when not carried in a Van, Lorry, Wagon or other vehicle for which a charge is made either for the load or by weight	10d. per cwt.
For Parcels:—	
Up to 28 lbs.	6d. each
Over 28 lbs. but not exceeding 100 lbs.	9d. each
For Luggage	The toll or charge for goods, wares or merchandise, with a free allowance of 100 lbs. for each passenger.
For a Special Sailing	£7 7s.

Edinburgh, August 1925.

J. CALDER, General Manager, Scotland.

Hugh Paton & Sons, Ltd., Printers, Edinburgh

SOURCES

ARCHIVES

National Archives, Kew (NA), National Records of Scotland (NRS), National Railway Museum, York (NRM), Parliamentary Papers (PP), Railways Archive on-line (RA)

THESES, PAPERS & PAMPHLETS

Arnott, Robert, *TOPS: Story of a British Railways Project.* DATE. (Railways Archive)

British Railway Companies, *The Railways' Plan for Air Transport.* 1944.

British Railway Companies, *British Railways and the Future.* 1946

British Railways, *The Modernisation and Re-Equipment of British Railways.* 1954

British Railways, *The Reshaping of British Railways.* 1963

Blake, George, *Glasgow Electric.* BR (Sc) 1960.

Buttle, G.W., *A Signal Failure: The Origin and Management of British Railways*, 1948-64. Durham University, 2008

Davies, R.A.M., *Public Passenger Transport in Inter-War Britain: the Southern Railway's Response to Bus Competition, 1923-39.* University of York Railway Studies, September 2014

Divall, Colin, *What Happens if we Think about Railways as a Kind of Consumption?* Institute of Railway Studies & Transport History, York, 2007

Docherty, Iain, *Making Tracks: the politics of local rail transport in Merseyside and Strathclyde, 1986-96.* University of Glasgow, 1998

Edwards, Roy A., *Management Information and Management Practices: Freight Train Operation in Inter-War Britain.* London School of Economics, DATE

Elgar, J. and Simpson, R., *The Impact of the Law on Industrial Disputes in the 1980s.* Centre for Economic Performance, November 1994.

Gardiner, R., *Railway Transportation in Scotland.* LNER, 1937.

Gilchrist, A.O., *A History of British Railways' Electrical Research.* Institute of Railway Studies & Transport History Working Paper No. 11 (2008)

Glaister, S., *Competition Destroyed by Politics: British Rail Privatisation.* Centre for the Study of Regulated Industries Occasional Paper No. 23. University of Bath School of Management, 2004

Lawrenson, D.M., *Engineering and Accountancy as Determinants of Change in Manufacturing Industry: A Case Study of Railway Mechanical Engineering.* Leicester University, 1971

Merkert, Rico, *The Restructuring and Future of the British Railways System.* Working Paper 586, Institute of Transport Studies, Leeds University, 2005

LNER, First Report of the LNER Post-War Development Committee, September 1943

Nash, C.A., and Smith, A.S.J., *Passenger Rail Franchising: The British Experience.* ECMT Workshop on Competitive Tendering for Passenger Rail Services, ITS, University of Leeds 12 January 2006.

Pringle, Gordon. *RETB Next Generation:* Network Rail Project Review for IRSE Scotland, 16 February 2016

Schabas, M., 'Regulatory Policy', 8, in Research Centre Seminar on Privatisation & Deregulation of Transport, August 1997.

SMT, *The Scottish Motor Traction Company Ltd: A Short History* (1945)

Sjöblom, G., The Shift from Railways to Roads. Economic History Yearbook, Vol. 48, Issue 1.

NEWSPAPERS AND JOURNALS

Accounting Forum
Backtrack
British Railways Magazine (BR (Sc) Mag.)
Commercial Motor
Dundee Courier
Glasgow Herald/Herald (Glas. Her./Her.)
Financial Times
Guardian
Highland Railway Journal (HRJ)
Independent
International Railway Journal
Journal of Transport Economics & Policy
Journal of Transport History (JTH)
LMS Magazine
LNER Magazine
Modern Railways (Mod. Rlys.)

New Scientist
Provincial Express (ScotRail)
Public Money Management
Rail Engineer
Rail News
Railway Gazette (Rly. Gaz.)
Railway Gazette International (Rly. Gaz. Int.)
ScotRail Staff Bulletin (*Newsline* from 1987)
Scotsman (Scmn.)
Scottish Transport Review
Socialist Standard
Sunday Times
Surveyor
Times
Trans-Pennine Magazine

ONLINE DOCUMENTS

Bowman, A., and others, *The Great Train Robbery: Rail Privatisation and After*. Centre for Research on Socio-Cultural Change (CRESC), June 2013

Francis, P., Bellamy, P., and Crisp, G., *Twentieth-Century Air Raid Precaution Control Centres*

Horne, M.A. (comp.), *A Century of Change: Britain's Railways and the Railway Studies Association* (Nebulous Books)

archive.org. *Transport in the Highlands* (1962 report with statistical appendices)

Tyrrall, D. and Parker, D., *The Fragmentation of a Railway: A Study of Organisational Change on British Railways*. Open University Accounting & Finance Research Unit, November 2001

BOOKS

Aldcroft, D., *Britain's Railways in Transition*. London, 1968

Bagwell, P.S., *The Railwaymen*. 2 vols., London, 1963, 1982

Bagwell, P.S., *The Transport Revolution, 1770-1985*. London, 1988

Barker, Theo, and Savage, C.I., *An Economic History of Transport in Britain*. London, 2006

Baxter, David (ed.), *British Locomotive Catalogue, 1825-1923, Vol. 4*. Ashbourne, 1984

Baxter, David, and Mitchell, Peter (eds.), *British Locomotive Catalogue 1825-1923, Vol. 6*. Southampton, 2012

Bergqvist, R., Wilmsmeier, G., and Cullinane, K., *Dry Ports: A Global Perspective*. London, 2013

Bonavia, M., *History of the LNER*, 3 vols. London, 1982-83

Bonavia, M., *Railway Policy Between the Wars*. Manchester, 1981

Bonavia, M., *British Railways: the First 25 Years*. London, 1981

Bonavia, M., *The Nationalisation of British Transport*. London, 1986

Boocock, Colin, *British Rail at Work: ScotRail*. London, 1986

Bradley, S., *The Railways: Nation, Network and People*. London, 2015

Cairncross, A.K., *The Scottish Economy: A Statistical Account of Scottish Life*. Cambridge, 1954

Chick, Martin, *Industrial Policy in Britain, 1945-51*. Cambridge, 1958

Clark, Andrew, *Pleasures of the Firth*. Catrine, 2012

Clay, John F. (ed.), *Essays in Steam*. Shepperton, 1970

Clinker, C.R., *Register of Closed Passenger Stations and Goods Depots in England, Scotland & Wales, 1830-1977*. Bristol, 1978

Crump, N., *By Rail to Victory*. London, 1947

Docherty, Iain, *Making Tracks*. Aldershot, 1999

Dyos, H.J. and Aldcroft, D., *British Transport: An Economic Survey from the 17th Century to the 20th*. Leicester, 1969

Ellis, C. Hamilton, *British Railway History, vol 2*. London, 1959

Ellis, C. Hamilton, *LMS: A Railway in Retrospect*. London, 1970

Faulkner, R. and Austin, C., *Holding the Line*. Addlestone, 2012

Fenelon, K.G., *Railway Economics*. London, 1932

Fenelon, K.G., *British Railways Since the War*. London, 1933

Fenelon, K.G., *British Railways Today*. London, 1940

Ferguson, N., and Stirling, D., *The Caledonian in LMS Days*. Easingwold, 2007

Fiennes, Gerard, *I Tried to Run a Railway*. 2nd ed., London, 2016

Gourvish, T.R., *British Railways, 1947-74*. Cambridge, 1986

Gourvish, T.R., *British Rail, 1974-97*. Oxford, 2002

Gourvish, T.R., *Britain's Railways 1997-2005*. Oxford, 2008

Greville, M.D. and Spencer, J., *A Handbook to Closed Passenger Lines of Scotland up to 1939*. Caterham, 1963

Harris, Nigel, *Competition and the Corporate Society: British Conservatives, the State, and Industry, 1945-64*. London, 1974

Haywood, Russell, *Railways, Urban Development and Town Planning in Britain, 1945-2008*. Aldershot, 2009

Henshaw, David, *The Great Railway Conspiracy*. Hawes, 1991

Hibbs, J., Knipping, O., Merket, R., Nash, C., Roy, R., Tyrall, D.E. and Wellings, R., *The Railways, the Market and the Government*. London, 2006

Holland, Julian, *Dr Beeching's Axe: 50 Years On*. Newton Abbot, 2013

Hughes, Geoffrey, *LNER*. London, 1986

Jackson, Tanya, *British Rail: The Nation's Railway*. Stroud, 2013

Joy, Stewart, *The Train That Ran Away*. London, 1973

Kellas, James G., *The Scottish Political System*. Cambridge, 1989

King, Benjamin, Biggs, Richard, and Criner Eric, *Spearhead of Logistics: A History of the US Army Transportation Corps*. Washington DC, 2001

Larouche, Pierre, *Competition Law and Regulation in European Telecommunications*. London, 2000

Loft, Charles, *Government, the Railways, and the Modernisation of Britain*. London, 2006

Loft, Charles, *Last Trains*. London, 2013

McGregor, John, *The West Highland Railway, 120 Years*. Stroud, 2014

McKillop, Norman, *The Lighted Flame*. London, 1950

McKillop, Norman, *Enginemen Elite*. London, new ed. 1972

MacKinnon, D., Shaw, J., and Docherty, Iain, *Diverging Mobilities? Devolution, Transport, and Policy Innovation*. Oxford/Amsterdam, 2008

Middlemass, Thomas. *Mainly Scottish Steam*. Newton Abbot, 1973

Morris, Lord, *Fifty Years in Politics and the Law*. Cardiff, 2011

Mullay, A., *Scottish Region: A History, 1948-73*. Stroud, 2006

O'Brien, P., *A New Economic History of the Railways*. London, 1977

Peel, Dave, *Starlight Specials*. Stroud, 2014

Pettitt, Gordon and Comfort, Nicholas, *The Regional Railways Story*. Addlestone, 2015

Pollins, H., *Britain's Railways: An Industrial History*. Newton Abbot, 1971

Pryke, R.W.S. and Dodgson, J.S., *The Rail Problem*. London, 1975

Quick, M., *A Chronology of Railway Passenger Stations in Great Britain*. Oxford, 2009

Rhodes, Michael, *British Marshalling Yards*. Sparkford, 1988

Ross, David. *The Highland Railway*. New ed., Catrine 2010

Ross, David, *The Caledonian: Scotland's Imperial Railway*. Catrine, 2013

Ross, David, *The North British Railway: A History*. Catrine, 2014

Roth, R. and Divall, C., *From Rail to Road and Back Again?* Farnham, 2015

Savage, C.I., *Inland Transport*. London, 1957

Simnett, W.E., *Railway Amalgamation in Great Britain*. London, 1923

Sinclair, Neil T., *Highland Railway: People and Places*. Derby, 2005

Spaven, David, *Waverley Route*. Edinburgh, 2012

Spaven, David, *Highland Survivor*. Inverness, 2016

Stewart, V. and Chadwick, V., *Changing Trains: Messages for Management from the ScotRail Challenge*. Newton Abbot, 1987

Summers, L.A., *British Railways Steam, 1948-70*. Stroud, 2014

Webster, Gordon, *The West Highland Lines: Post-Beeching*. Stroud, 2014

Wolmar, Christian, *Fire and Steam*. London, 2007

NOTES AND REFERENCES

These books are referred to in abbreviated form:
Gourvish, T.R., *British Railways, 1947-74:* Gourvish I
Gourvish, T.R., *British Rail, 1974-97:* Gourvish II
Gourvish, T.R., *Britain's Railways 1997-2005:* Gourvish III

Chapter 1

1. Its growth is traced in Ross, *Getting the Train.*
2. Ross, *Great North of Scotland*, 196.
3. Simnett, *Railway Amalgamation*, chapters 2-6. For Scottish companies see Ross, *Highland, Caledonian, Glasgow & South Western, North British*, and *Great North*.
4. Dyos and Aldcroft, *British Transport*, 292f.
5. *Times*, 5 and 19 May 1921; NA. CAB24/123/7. Memo to Cabinet, 4 May 1921.
6. RA. Railways Act 1921.
7. Norman McKillop recalled that "the first lot of dungarees that came to Haymarket were not exactly 'made to measure'… the skinny ones could amost turn round inside the new uniforms" (*Enginemen Elite*, 63).
8. See *JTH*, Vol. 7, No. 2, September 1986. Butterfield, P., 'Grouping, Pooling & Competition'.
9. *Scmn.*, 18 May 1928: Report on Railway Roads Bill.
10. In view of Matheson's acceptance of high office in the LMS it is of interest to note a correspondence in the *Scotsman* during July 1947, in which two writers claiming friendship with Matheson state that he had battled against the amalgamation of the Caledonian Railway into the LMS and fought tooth and nail for a purely Scottish grouping. While respect should be accorded to personal memories, the present writer has found no other evidence for these claims. He certainly commended the Grouping arrangement to his staff. See Ross, *Caledonian*, 189.
11. Hughes, *LNER*, 12.
12. Hughes, *op. cit.*, 16; Bonavia, *The Nationalisation of British Transport*, 47.
13. Ellis, *British Railway History II*, 329.
14. Bonavia, *Railway Policy Between the Wars*, 16.
15. *Ibid.*, 19.
16. *Times*, 11 November 1926. This was probably a Class B12, of which several appeared on the ex-GNSR lines.
17. Middlemass, *Mainly Scottish Steam*, 28.
18. *Ibid.*, 55.
19. *Scmn.*, 19 April 1923.
20. *Scmn.*, 14 April 1923.
21. *Scmn.*, 21 December 1926.
22. Quoted in *Scmn.*, 1 January 1923.
23. NRM. *LMS Mag.*, February 1926, 55.
24. Bonavia, *Railway Policy Between the Wars*, 33.
25. *Scmn.*, 20 May 1928.

26. *Scmn.*, 22 January, 12 June 1924.
27. *Scmn.*, 24 February 1925; Ross, Highland, 68f. The rails from Aultmore to Buckie were removed in 1937.
28. *Scmn.*, 16 January 1926.
29. *JTH*, vol. 9 No. 2, September 1988. Crompton, G.W., 'The Role of Railway Volunteers in the General Strike'.
30. NRS. BR/LNE8/779/22.
31. *JTH*, *op. cit.*
32. *Scmn.*, 24 July 1926.
33. *JTH*, *op. cit.*, see also *Wishaw Herald*, 14 May, *Hamilton Advertiser*, 22 May 1926. The damaged line was said to have been blown up.
34. McKillop, *op. cit.*, 178.
35. Middlemass, *op. cit.*, 147.
36. Fenelon, *Railway Economics*, 135.
37. NA. RAIL 421/146, Freight Transport in Container Trucks. See also Keith Harcourt in Roth & Divall, *From Rail to Road and Back Again?* 'Railway Containers in the United Kingdom and Europe', 109ff.
38. Ross, *NBR*, 206f. See also Theses, Edwards, 83.
39. *Scmn.*, 2 June 1928. The heaviest item moved by rail in Scotland was a 143-ton stator taken forward from Reston Junction to Dalmarnock in August-September 1956. With a height of 12 ft $5^7/_8$ ins and 12ft 10 in wide, it was moved only on Sundays. The load could be shifted one foot to either side to help in clearing immovable obstructions (*BR (Sc) Mag.*, September 1956).
40. See *Scmn.*, 18 November 1927.
41. In 1923 LMS directors received £47,504 in total, and LNER directors £25,000.
42. *Times*, 12 August 1931.
43. NA. RAIL 390/238. Joint Committee Minutes, 16 June, 7 July 1931.
44. *Scmn.*, 2 May, 23 May 1928.
45. *Scmn.*, 24 March 1949.
46. PP. Report of Select Committee on the Western Highlands and Islands of Scotland, 24 July 1928, 104. Letter to GPO, 9 February 1928.
47. *Ibid.*, 18f, 28.
48. *Scmn.*, 21 November, 19 October 1928.
49. *Scmn.*, 21 November 1928; PP. vol 3, 607. HoC Sessional Papers, 1928-29.
50. The issues are well explained in Davies, R.A.M., 'Public Passenger Transport in Inter-War Britain: the Southern Railway's Response to Bus Competition, 1923-39'. See Theses.
51. *Scmn.*, 30 July, 16 August 1929.
52. *Scmn.*, 30 June 1930; SMT: *History*, 12.
53. In 1937 the toll was halved when a ferry opened at Bonawe (*Commercial Motor*, 7 May 1937)

Chapter 2

1. *Scmn.*, 23 March 1928, 25 August 1924. Inverurie Works enjoyed a reputation for efficiency and tranquil industrial relations.
2. *Scmn.*, 2 January 1931.
3. McKillop, *The Lighted Flame*, 188ff.
4. PP. 1931. Cmd 3751.
5. *Ibid.*, 231, 232.
6. *Scmn.*, 17 April, 20 July 1931.
7. *Scmn.*, 3 June 1931.
8. NRS. BR/LIB/S/6/211. Report of Railway Pool Committee, LMS/LNER, 1932.
9. *Scmn.*, 17 February 1931.
10. *Scmn.*, 20 June 1931.
11. Pollins, *Britain's Railways*, 195f.
12. *Scmn.*, 17 February 1934, 21 January 1935.
13. *Rly. Gaz.*, 27 June 1924.
14. It worked until 31 December 1940, by which time the hotel was a military training centre.
15. *Scmn.*, 10 March 1932.
16. *Scmn.*, 23 March 1933
17. NRS. BR/LIB/S/6/211. Report of Railway Pool Committee. See further details in Stirling & Ferguson, *The Caledonian in LMS Days*; also *JTH*, Vol. 7, No. 2, September 1986. Butterfield, P., 'Grouping, Pooling and Competition'.
18. *Scmn.*, 10 October 1933.
19. Gardiner, *Railway Transportation Progress in Scotland*, 28. He records that the ticket "induced a native of these parts to see how far he could reduce the average receipt per mile by travelling 2339 miles during one week in the Edinburgh No. 1 area, for a ten-shilling note."
20. *Scmn.*, 26 December 1933.
21. *Scmn.*, 7 June 1930, 27 July 1932, 24 January, 28 June 1933.
22. *Scmn.*, 28 June 1933; 17 September, 3 August 1936.
23. PP. Ministry of Transport, Report of the Committee on Main-Line Electrification (1931); LNER. First Report of the Post-War Development Committee, September 1943; *Scmn.*, 30 January 1935
24. *Scmn.*, 5 April 1937.
25. Bonavia, *Railway Policy Between the Wars*, 54. Roth & Divall, *From Rail to Road and Back Again?* 120.
26. It was not the last in service: No. 112 ran until February 1940.
27. *Scmn.*, 31 December, 19 August 1935.
28. *Scmn.*, 14 January 1936.
29. *Scmn.*, 28 January 1935.
30. *Scmn.*, 28 July 1936; Gardiner, *op. cit.*, 39.
31. *Scmn.*, 18 August 1933.
32. *Scmn.*, 12 July 1932.
33. See *HRJ*, Vol. 5, No. 78, 15ff. David Stirling, 'Finding Fodderty'.
34. Ministry of Transport Statistics, 1930-31, 1935-36.
35. Bagwell, *Transport Revolution*, 241, notes this and also that the 3-day return ticket at a single fare was introduced in 1935.
36. *Scmn.*, 19 July 1934.
37. Gardiner, *op. cit.*, 30.
38. PP. Cmd. 4110, 1931-32. 43.
39. *Scmn.*, 26 May 1933.
40. *Scmn.*, 18 March 1937.
41. *Scmn.*, 9 April 1938, 29 September 1937.
42. *Times*, 22 May 1933; Gardiner, *op. cit.*, 21.
43. Ministry of Transport Railway Returns 1931, 1936]
44. *Scmn.*, 21 July 1933.
45. Gardiner, op.cit., 25.
46. Stirling & Ferguson, *op. cit.*, 43.
47. *Scmn.*, 20 December 1934.
48. *Scmn.*, 2 November 1934.
49. *Scmn.*, 25 April 1935; 12 February 1936.
50. *Scmn.*, 19 August 1935.
51. *Scmn.*, 1 July 1938.
52. Gardiner, *op. cit.*, 19.
53. These 'super-power' engines were deemed necessary since the trains were beyond the haulage capacity of a single 'Pacific' and 'Pacifics' were not allowed to run double-headed. See Coster, P.J., 'From Cock o' the North to Saint Johnstoun', in Clay, *Essays on Steam*, 109ff. But Gresley also wanted to design an engine that might bear comparison with André Chapelon's designs on the SNCF.
54. *Scmn.*, report of talk in Glasgow by N. Ridley, LNER advertising representative, 9 March 1935.
55. RA. Accident Reports.
56. Quoted in Gardiner, *op. cit.*, 2.
57. Cairncross, *The Scottish Economy*, 71.
58. *Scmn.*, 28 May 1936.
59. *Scmn.*, 17 July 1936.
60. *Scmn.*, 6 March 1937.
61. NA. RAIL/418/209. Review of the LMS Commercial Organisation, 1940. 35.
62. NA. CAB 24/286/6. Report on the railway "square deal" proposals.
63. *Scmn.*, 28 July, 13 August 1937.
64. See Theses etc., Sjöblom, 1, 3.
65. *Scmn.*, 3 July 1939.
66. *Scmn.*, 16 February 1939.
67. Noted in 'British Railways & The Future', 1946.
68. NA. CAB 24/286/6.
69. *Scmn.*, 31 January 1936.
70. *Scmn.*, 22 July 1932.
71. *Rly. Gaz.*, 21 July 1939.
72. See the valeofleven.org website for their history.
73. Theses, Lawrenson, 293.
74. *Scmn.*, 1 February, 1 March 1929.
75. Stirling & Ferguson, *op. cit.*, 43f.
76. *Times*, 8 March 1934.
77. Theses, Lawrenson, 292
78. NRS. LMS/4. Circulars, etc.

Chapter 3

1. *Backtrack*, 19, No. 4, 2005. Forsythe, R.N., 'The Railways of R.O. Bishopton'.
2. Quick, Passenger Stations. These halts were not in the public timetable.
3. NRS. BR/BRB/S/2/20.
4. See Ross, NBR, 207f for details of the earlier arrangement.
5. Savage, *Inland Transport*, 295.
6. Savage, *op. cit.*, 284.
7. *Rly. Gaz.*, 25 May 1945.
8. NRS. BRB/RB/S/2/20.
9. Crump, *By Rail to Victory*, 43, 66.
10. Online documents. Francis et al, '20th Century Air Raid Precautions', 27.
11. NA. RAIL 412/206, LMS War Journal I, 5.
12. Savage, *op. cit.*, 515f.
13. NA. Rail 421/206. LMS War Journal I, 297.
14. *Times*, 25 February 1946.
15. *Rly. Gaz.*, 5 January 1940.
16. NAS. LMS/4. Circulars.
17. NA. RAIL 421/206. LMS War Journal I, 323, 108, 310.
18. *Times*, 27 September 1940.
19. McKillop, *Enginemen Elite*, 139. NA. RAIL 421/206. LMS War Journal I,., 144, 266.
20. PP. Cmd 5926, 1939. Schedule of Reserved Occupations (Provisional).
21. *Scmn.*, 16 March 1940.
22. *Scmn.*, 18 February, 12 March, 1942.
23. *Scmn.*, 18 August 1942.
24. NRS. BR/LMLN/1/13. LMS/LNER Joint Committee, 20 April 1943.
25. *Scmn.*, 22 February 1944.
26. Crump, *op. cit.*, 128.
27. Savage, *op. cit.*, 113; Crump, *op. cit.*, 22.
28. *Scmn.*, 2 February 1942; Railways Archive: Report on the Accident at Cowlairs East Junction on 30th January 1942.
29. *Scmn.*, 8 November 1939. Gerard Fiennes, then an assistant superintendent in Edinburgh, gave a picturesque account of the event. The guard assumed his colleagues were on the engine, and passing through Waverley he acknowledged the gesticulations of platform staff with a wave. It was his birthday and he thought they were wishing him many happy returns. Fiennes, *I Tried to Run a Railway*, 30f.
30. Three "old and worn-out" washbasins in the station's hairdressing salon were replaced by three from the hotel, and £7 10s duly paid by the joint station committee to the LNER (NRS. BR/LMLN/1/13. LMS & LNER Joint Committee).
31. Quoted in Savage, *op. cit.*, 191.
32. *Rly. Gaz.*, 7 July 1944. This traffic lasted well into the 1960s: in 1960 Scottish Region despatched 204,000 tons of seed potatoes.
33. Savage, *op. cit.*, 576.
34. Savage, *op. cit.*, 630.
35. Savage, *op. cit.*, 491f.
36. *Scmn.*, 2 September 1940.
37. NA. RAIL 421/206. LMS War Journal I, 255.
38. NA. RAIL 421/207. LMS War Journal, II, 185.
39. See for example *Scmn.* 4 March 1944, report of LNER o.g.m.
40. In *HRJ* No. 20, early 1992, J.L. Stevenson recorded that this train acquired the 'Jellicoe' name given to the First World War coal trains to Grangemouth. It normally included a sleeping car to Perth and a 'canteen coach' staffed by Salvation Army volunteers between Perth and Thurso (Ed Nicoll, *HRJ* No. 35.
41. *Scmn.*, 7 April 1941, 4 February 1942; *BR (Sc) Magazine*, April 1952. Contrary to suggestion in the latter, parachutes were not employed.
42. NA. 421/206. LMS War Journal I, 87.
43. NRS. LMS Railway: Chief Civil Engineer's Dept. History of the Department During the War of 1939-45.
44. Noted in Stirling & Ferguson, *The Caledonian in LMS Days*, 83.
45. Several people were injured when a re-routed passenger train hit a light engine at the point where the LMS and LNER lines met (*Scmn.*, 25 March 1940).
46. *HRJ*, Vol 5, No. 78, 15ff. Stirling, David, Finding Fodderty. He also notes that Macnaughton tube mines were laid to destroy access in the case of invasion.
47. *Rly. Mag.*, 29 May 1942.
48. *Rly. Gaz.*, 8 September 1944.
49. Crump, *op. cit.*, 143, 46.
50. *Rly. Gaz.*, 18 May 1945.
51. King, Biggs, & Crine, *Spearhead of Logistics*, 218f.
52. NA. RAIL 421/206. LMS War Journal I, 222.
53. NRM. First Report of the LNER Post-War Development Committee.
54. NRM. *Ibid.*
55. *Scmn.*, 6 March 1943.
56. *Times*, 3 March 1945.
57. Estimated figures, quoted in Savage, *op. cit.*, 634.
58. *Rly. Gaz.*, 29 March 1940.
59. NRM. The Railways' Plan for Air Transport, 1944.
60. *Times*, 25 February 1946.
61. *Accounting, Business & Finance History*, Vol. 12 No. 3, November 2002, Crompton, G. and Jupe, R., 'An Awkward Fence to Cross: Railway Capitalisation in the Inter-War Years'.
62. Online Documents. Horne, *A Century of Change*, 57.
63. See for example Wolmar, *Fire & Steam*, 264: "The railways were on their knees and ripe for nationalisation."

Chapter 4

1. NRS. GD 344/2/29.
2. NRM. Report on Visit to USA by LNER Mechanical Engineers, October-December 1945, p. L/16.
3. *Scmn.,* 24 April 1946. The Forth Bridge Railway, owner of the bridge, was still a separate body, jointly owned by the LNER and LMS until 1947.
4. *Scmn.,* 12 October 1946.
5. NRM. 'British Railways and the Future.'
6. January 1947. Bagwell, *Railwaymen,* II, points out that Government stocks at the time were returning only 2.5%.
7. Theses. Buttle 'A Signal Failure?' 62.
8. *Rly. Mag.,* 28 March 1947.
9. PP. Cmd 7459. Scottish Office, 'Industry and Development in Scotland, 1947.'
10. *Times,* 24 December 1946.
11. In 1949, see Theses etc. Glaister S., 'British Rail Privatisation', 5.
12. PP. *Hansard* 9 July 1947. HL vol 150, cc261-394.
13. Although the regional border coincided with the national border, Carlisle's Kingmoor locomotive depot was treated until 1958 as a Scottish Region enclave, with sub-depots at Dumfries, Stranraer, Newton Stewart and Beattock.
14. *Scmn.,* 27 November 1947.
15. PP. Cmd 7459, 1948. Industry & Employment in Scotland, 1947; BTC Annual Report 1948.
16. *Scmn.,* 11 December 1947.
17. Gourvish, I, 54,63. Pollins, *Britain's Railways,* 168.
18. Bonavia, *The Nationalisation of British Transport,* 51.
19. According to Michael Bonavia they held 'informal' lunches instead. See Theses, Buttle, 'A Signal Failure?' 82.
20. NA. AN 6/1. Memorandum from CRO's to RE, 16 June 1948.
21. LNER online Encyclopedia, 'The Gresley A4 Pacifics'. Norman McKillop ascribes the first run to Driver Jim Swan and 60029 *Woodcock,* but *Woodcock's* first non-stop run via St. Boswells was not until 27 August. Their feats bear out his claim that "the bunch of us who became 'possessors' of Gresleys went slightly haywire on the care, maintenance and sheer devotion we lavished on these 'horses' of ours" (McKillop, *Enginemen Elite,* 86, 76).
22. *Scmn.,* 18 May 1949; 8 September 1948.
23. *Scmn.,* 16 November 1948.
24. *Scmn.,* 13 June, 20 September 1949.
25. NRM. *BR (Sc) Mag.,* 23 April 1950.
26. NRM. *BR (Sc) Mag., Ibid.*
27. NA. MT74/1. Hurcomb on Post-War Policy for Inland Transport.
28. NA. CAB 134/139. Cabinet Investment Programme Committee: Railway Investment in 1949.
29. NA. MT 74/1. Railway Executive: British Railways & the Future.
30. *Rly. Gaz.,* 11 May 1951; *BR (Sc) Mag.,* April 1952.
31. RA. Accident Reports; *Rly. Gaz.,* 23 February 1951.
32. *Scmn.,* 10 May, 19 June 1950. The public relations department was primarily concerned with producing publicity material.
33. *Scmn.,* 19 September 1950.
34. *Scmn.,* 20 May 1947, 6 March 1950.
35. NA. AN 97 19/19. Branch Lines Committee.
36. *Scmn.,* 25 November 1949.
37. *Scmn.,* 1 July 1950; *Dundee Courier,* 26 January 1951. The curious earlier history of this line is given in Ross, *NBR.*
38. *Scmn.,* 31 March 1950.
39. *Scmn.,* 2 December 1950; *Glas. Her.* 5 March 1951. NA. AN6/5. Circular of 27 April 1951.
40. *Rly. Gaz.,* 7 July 1950, 16 March, 22, 29 June, 4 August and 28 September 1951.
41. Gourvish, I, 110. *Ibid.,* 675, from BTC Minutes of 26 March 1953.
42. NA. BTC Statistics, 12/26, quoted in Gourvish, I, 675, note to p. 71.
43. *Rly. Gaz.,* 22 June 1951.
44. *Rly. Gaz.* feature, 28 September 1951; *Scmn.,* 7 March 1950.
45. In *Backtrack,* 2014, issue 28, 134, R.A.S. Hennessey noted that Frederick Bisacre, then an electrical engineer with Merz & McLellan, had recommended electrification of Glasgow's suburban railways at 1.5kV in the 1920s.
46. See Haywood, *Railways, Urban Development and Town Planning,* ch 4.

Chapter 5

1. NA. PREM1 1/559. Hurcomb to Minister of Transport & Civil Aviation, 1 August 1952.
2. NA. CAB129/69/11. Reorganisation of the Railways. PP. Transport Act 1953. 16 (9).
3. *Ibid.,* 16 (7). 20 (2) (c).
4. Gourvish I, 144. *Independent,* 14 June 2004.
5. NRS. DD17/1182. Highlands & Islands Transport Charges 1951-54. Railway officials held up announcement of the members of the new Scottish Area Board to coincide with publication of the new charges, in the hope that it would deflect attention from the increases.
6. See Gourvish I, 149ff
7. Bonavia, *British Railways: the First 25 Years,* 29, notes that Cameron lived in an apartment in Edinburgh's North British Hotel and commuted by car to Glasgow.
8. Peel, *Starlight Specials,* gives a detailed account of the service.
9. NRM. *BR (Sc) Mag.,* May 1956.
10. *Rly. Gaz.,* 25 October 1957.
11. NRS. BR/RSR/1/106. Scottish Region Quarterly Reports.]*BR (Sc) Mag.,* September 1958.
12. NRM. *BR (Sc) Mag.,* September 1952.
13. NA. CAB/129/83. BTC Review of Financial Situation, 21 September 1956.

14. NRM. *BR (Sc) Mag.*, September, October, November 1952.
15. See Bonavia, *History of the LNER*, III, 81.
16. NA. AN85/17.
17. RA. Electrification of Railways: Report of a Committee Appointed by the Railway Executive and the London Transport Executive.
18. NA. AN 88/77. Riddles memo to BTC, January 1952.
19. *Scmn.*, 26 September 1950.
20. Scmn, 10 April 1948.
21. *Scmn.*, 11 and 12 January 1950.
22. *Scmn.*, 8 September 1950.
23. NRM. *BR (Sc) Mag.*, October 1954. *Rly. Gaz.*, 12 April 1957.
24. *Rly. Gaz.*, 15 July 1960.
25. NRS.BR/RSR/1/106. *Rly. Gaz.*, 14 April 1961.
26. RA. Modernisation of British Railways: The System of Electrification for British Railways'.
27. Braking systems were an unfortunate aspect of modernisation. The Modernisation Plan anticipated all rolling stock to be air-braked, as recommended by a specialist panel. In February 1956 the BTC decided to retain vacuum brakes, as the most common system in use. This was finally countermanded in 1964, but by 1975 only 5% of the wagon stock was air-braked and 47% had no power brakes at all (BRB Operations Planning Team Report August 1975, noted in Gourvish, I, 435).
28. NRM. *BR (Sc) Mag.*, December 1956.
29. NRM. *BR (Sc) Mag.*, September 1956.
30. *Ibid.*, January 1959; March 1958.
31. PP. Cmd 813. 1958-59, Reappraisal of the 1956 Plan; Pollins, *Britain's Railways*, 171.
32. Quoted in Gourvish, I, 200.
33. *Rly. Gaz.*, 5 October 1959.
34. NRM. *BR (Sc) Mag.*, July 1959.
35. *Ibid.*
36. NRM. *BR (Sc) Mag.*, January 1958.
37. NRM. *BR (Sc) Mag.*, August 1958.
38. NRM. *BR (Sc) Mag.*, July 1958.
39. Sinclair, *Highland Railway: People and Places*, 123.
40. *Rly. Gaz.*, 2 August, 13 December 1957.
41. *Times* 12 February; *Rly. Gaz.*, 15 February, 24 May 1957.
42. *Ibid.*, 24 May 1957. In the end, of course, the opposite happened.
43. NRS. BR/RSR/18. Report on Progress of Diesel Schemes in Scottish Region. *Rly. Mag.*, 29 December 1961.
44. NRM. *BR (Sc) Mag.*, March 1958.
45. *Times*, 2 March 1955; Gourvish, I, 206.
46. *Glas. Her.*, 8 January, *Rly. Gaz.*, 12 February 1960.
47. Noted in *Commercial Motor*, 12 February 1960: the road haulage industry always kept a close eye on railway initiatives.
48. *Rly. Gaz.*, 13 March 1959.
49. See Gourvish, I, 212.
50. BTC. Reappraisal of the Modernisation Plan, introduction. Robertson was perhaps referring to the economic recession of 1958 "when a relatively small fall in heavy industrial production produced financial crisis on the railways" – see Harris, *Competition & the Corporate Society*, 192.
51. Aldcroft, *British Railways in Transition* 9, 175; Gourvish, I, 293.
52. MoT Highway Statistics 1965.
53. PP. Cmd 813. Reappraisal of the 1956 Plan, 9, 17, 20, 26. 1958-59.
54. NRM. *BR (Sc) Mag.*, September 1958.
55. Theses, Buttle, 238f, from NA. MT115/248. Letter to Watkinson from Robertson, 15 July 1959.
56. NA. AN174/910. The lengthy exchange of memoranda between Region and BR headquarters on the creation of this moderately senior post, salary bracket £2400-£3205, shows the strength of the central bureaucracy.
57. NA. MT132/32. MOT Railways B Division, 23 January 1960.
58. PP. *Hansard*, vol 619, 1960. Statement on British Railways, 10 March 1960.
59. Online Documents. Francis et al, *Air Raid Precautions*, 66f.
60. PP. HoC Papers 1959-60. No. 254-1.
61. PP. HoC Papers 1959-60. No. 254-1. Appendix 47, Annex 6, Tables 1 and 4.
62. BTC Report & Accounts for 1959.

Chapter 6

1. *Mod. Rlys.*, January 1962.
2. *Rly. Gaz.*, 29 September 1961, *Mod. Rlys.*, Ibid.
3. PP. 1959-60, vii, 233. Select Committee Report on BR, 11 July 1960.
4. NA. CAB134/1433. SAG Preliminary Report, 17 June 1960. See also Faulkner & Austin, *Holding the Line*, 27.
5. Gourvish I, 111.
6 PP. Central TUCC for Great Britain, Annual Report 1962.
7. NA. AN174/827.
8. NA. *Ibid.*
9. NA. MT96/174.
10. Gourvish, I, 38.
11. PP. Cmnd 2045. Scottish Home Dept., 1959-60; Cd 1727. Scottish Development Dept., 1961-62.
12. *Mod. Rlys.*, March 1962.
13. PP. *Hansard*, HoC 27 June 1962.
14. *Times*, 23 July, 27 August 1962. Bagwell, II, 135f.
15. The MP for Berwick, J.P. Mackintosh, in a parliamentary debate on Scottish transport, registered his disappointment with the leadership of British Railways in Scotland, which "has too often has taken its remit to be a quick attempt to close a line which alternative methods of manning and running could make economic" (PP. *Hansard*, vol. 743, cc1135-78. HC debate 10 March 1967).

16. NA. AN/13/2713. SAG report September 1960, para 77.
17. RA. Transport Act 1962, 2,2.
18. RA. *Ibid.*, 36,1.
19. RA. *Ibid.*, 1962, 22 (i).
20. Reshaping of BR, 3f.
21. *Mod. Rlys.*, February 1962.
22. Reshaping of BR., 24f, 40.
23. *Ibid.*, 13, 16.
24. Faulkner & Austin, *Holding the Line*, 33.
25. Reshaping of BR, 97.
26. *Ibid.*, 100f.
27. NRS. BR/RSR/4/1668.
28. *Times*, 29 March 1963. In fact Loch Lomond steamer services went on until 1981, and Balloch Pier station survived until 1986. *Maid of the Loch* was being restored to working order in 2016.
29. *Geography*, Vol. 48, No. 3, July 1963, 335.
30. NAS. DC1/646. *Mod. Rlys.*, January 1962.
31. *Glas. Her.*, 19 April 1963.
32. Holland, *Dr Beeching's Axe*, 8. Loft, *Government, the Railways and the Modernisation of Britain*, 53ff, gives a balanced account of Marples' role in policy making and execution.
33. Henshaw, *The Great Railway Conspiracy*, Faulkner and Austin, *Holding the Line*, passim.
34. Road Haulage Association, *The World's Carriers*, April 1960, quoted in Faulkner & Austin, *Holding the Line*, 25.
35. NA. MT124/1243.
36. NA. CAB129/116/16.
37. Reshaping of BR, Table No. 1, pp 100-101.
38. Loft, *Last Trains*, 179.
39. Father of the railway campaigner and writer David Spaven, see Bibliography.
40. Gourvish I, 442.
41. Quoted in Loft, *op. cit.*, 187. A detailed breakdown of the Highland lines' traffic, though not including earnings or costs, was published in 'Transport in the Highlands', a 1962 study of all transport forms in the region, commissioned by the Minister of Transport and the Secretary of State for Scotland. Acknowledging the certainty that the lines ran at a loss, it pointed out that "the value of the peripheral services such as the Highland lines cannot of course be assessed properly by taking them on their own, apart from the main network. An operating loss on the fringes…may be offset to some extent by the value of traffic which they bring to the rest of the undertaking…" and "no line should be closed until adequate substitute services by road are provided" (archive.org, 'Transport in the Highlands', paras 96, 100, 101).
42. Figures from Gourvish I, quoting BRB (Sc) RT/TS2/24/79/Pt 1. Ironically, the very length of the Far North and Kyle lines may have helped in the effort to preserve them. The total emptiness north and west of Inverness shown on Beeching's map was striking, in quite the wrong kind of way. As Sir David Serpell would discover in 1982, to publish a map showing a heavily cut-back railway system was to invite a wave of hostile reaction.
43. *Rly. Gaz.*, 1 May 1964.
44. Spaven, *Waverley Route*, 69, 76. Closure of the line was later said to have contributed to the failure of the Borders Economic Plan (Kellas, *The Scottish Political System*, 55).
45. NRS. BR/RSR/4/1525. Closure of Unremunerative Lines. Bob Symes, one of the leaders of the project, expected to base the operation on carrying timber from Kielder Forest (report on BBC News, 18 June 2002).
46. Spaven, *op. cit.*, 137f.
47. The new Minister of Technology, Frank Cousins, formerly general secretary of the Transport & General Workers' Union, claimed to have "sacked Beeching", while the Minister of Transport, Tom Fraser, had wanted Beeching to conduct a survey across the whole spectrum of inland transport.
48. *Mod. Rlys.*, February 1965.
49. See *Hansard*, HC Deb 20 December 1963 vol 686 cc1634-63.
50. Gourvish notes that this document was largely the work of James Ness as BRB planning director.
51. *Mod. Rlys.*, November 1965.
52. NA. AN 174/825.
53. NRS. BR/RSR/4/157. Meetings between BR (Sc), Scottish Office and MoT, 1969-1972.
54. Gourvish I, 459.
55. Joy, *The Train That Ran Away*, 13.
56. Joy, *Ibid.*, 29; Pryke, R.W.S. and Dodgson, J.S., *The Rail Problem*, 275; Hibbs, John, 'Seeking a Market Solution' in Hibbs et al., *The Railways, the Market and the Government*, 57.

Chapter 7

1. NRS. BR/RSR/1/148. Gourvish, I, 169, 191. NA. AN174/910. BR (Sc) circular, 27 April 1960.
2. *Times*, 28 November 1960.
3. *Mod. Rlys.*, February 1962.
4. BR (Scottish Region). Blake, *Glasgow Electric*.
5. *Rly. Gaz.*, 29 September, 20 October, 1 December 1961.
6. *Mod. Rlys.*, July 1962. Incidentally, Glasgow's last tram route ended on 4 September 1962.
7. *Rly. Gaz.*, 16 October 1964, 5 February 1965.
8. See doublearrow.co website. Much the same had been done in 1923 and 1948 but this was a more thorough exercise.
9. *Times*, 10 August 1968.
10. NRM. *BR (Sc) Mag.*, April 1960.
11. *Rly. Gaz.* 24 June, 9 September 1960, 21 April 1961.
12. *Ibid.*, 27 January 1961.
13. Peel, *Starlight Specials*, 113.
14. A4 running officially ended on 3 September 1966, but the route's last steam-hauled scheduled services

were worked by A4 'Pacific' 60024 *Kingfisher*, already technically withdrawn. On 13 September it hauled the 17.15 Aberdeen-Glasgow and returned next day with the 08.25 Glasgow-Aberdeen (RCTS 'Green Books' Pt2A, 132), courtesy of Allan Rodgers.

15. *Mod. Rlys.*, July 1962.

16. NRS. BR/RSR/4/1492. *Rly. Gaz.*, 2 June 1961.

17. NA. AN 183/30.

18. *Rly. Gaz.*, 23 March 1962. BTC Annual Report 1963, 47.

19. The train was hauled by ex-LMS 2-6-4T No. 42274. Eight of the former companies' engines are preserved, though not all in working order: Highland Railway No. 103, GNSR No. 49 *Gordon Highlander*, NBR Nos. 673 *Maude* and 256 *Glen Douglas*, Caledonian Nos. 123, 419 and 828, and G&SWR No. 322. Also preserved are the 'Scottish' LNER engines No. 246 *Morayshire* and No. 3442 *The Great Marquess*.

20. *Rly. Gaz.*, 29 November 1963.

21. ORR.gov.uk. Letter to Network Rail, 15 April 2016.

22. See Rhodes, *British Marshalling Yards*, for details on Millerhill, Mossend, Perth and Thornton.

23. *Rly. Gaz.*, 8 June 1962, 9 August, 20 and 27 September 1963.

24. See Gourvish, I, 490. The episode is described in slightly different terms in Fiennes, *I Tried to Run a Railway*, 80.

25. *Times*, 10 June 1965.

26. NRS. BR/RSR/4/1525. See Appendix 7.

27. RA. BR 'Freightliner' brochure.

28. Commercial Motor, 28 October 1966, 21 April 1967.

29. *Mod. Rlys.*, February, April; *Times*, 27 May, 1968. *Mod. Rlys.*, April, reported that the Aberdeen terminal had been installed in a hurry to keep a meat container contract. An anecdote in the memoirs of Lord Morris of Aberavon, Barbara Castle's deputy, records that "When the chairman of the nationalised road company was summoned off a golf course and ordered to buy the company, which he did, the union saw we meant business" – a complacent conflation of a prolonged and intensive set of negotiations which ended with substantial concessions on job security extracted by the NUR (*Fifty Years in Politics and the Law*, 72). See also *Mod. Rlys.*, June 1965; NA. MT157/34. PP. *Hansard*, HoL, 7 March 1967; Gourvish, I, 546.

30. *Mod. Rlys.*, February 1965.

31. Gourvish I, 425.

32. NRS. BR/RSR/4/1525. 24 November 1969.

33. Gourvish I, 38, also 'The Sea Container Revolution', in Roth & Divall, *From Rail to Road and Back Again?* 139.

34. Gourvish, II, 500ff.

35. Note to a B.R. Magazine article, 'Shotgun Wedding: the Difficult Business of Ordering a Scottish Region', by Neil McLellan, date unestablished. Jim Summers collection. Gourvish I, 344, 346.

36. See Gourvish I, 165.

37. NA. AN174/825. See also NRS. BR/RSR/1/48, 'Report on Future Organisation of Scottish Region', May 1968.

38. *Mod. Rlys.*, February 1965.

39. NA. AN/174/827. 'Report on Re-Organisation of Management Structure (Two-Tier) in the Scottish Region', December 1969.

40. NA. AN174/825. Memo from GM (Sc) to Head of BR Management Staff Committee, 18 August 1967. It is also true that the completed or impending axing of lines and stations would reduce activity to a point that scarcely justified a separate divisional structure at Inverness, but that was an ancillary reason.

41. *Mod. Rlys.*, April 1968.

42. NA. AN174/825.

43. NRS. BR/RSR/18/1.

44. NA. AN 174/827.

45. NRS. BR/RSR/1/148. 'Report on Future Organisation of Scottish Region, May 1968'.

46. NA. AN174/826.

47. A *New Scientist* article on 14 February 1963 reported that following research begun in 1957, a first computer-created timetable would appear in June, for the East Coast Main Line.

48. PP. HoC Select Committee on Scottish Affairs, 1968-69. Although the Scottish total grant was the third largest, after North West and South East England, it was the largest per head, representing £1 17s 9d a year for each person compared with £1 0s 8d per head in England.

49. PP. HoC Select Committee on Scottish Affairs, 1968-69. Appendix 23.

50. PP. *Hansard*, HoC, 18 December 1968. Adjournment debate of the closure of Inverurie Works.

51. It is one of the numerous lines with a vigorous local campaign for reinstatement.

52. NRS. BR/RSR/4/1525. Gourvish, I, 524. Incidentally, the 1962 Transport Act (para 6) empowered the BRB to provide hotels "in places where those using railway services provided by the Board may require them."

Chapter 8

1. The concept of rigid fixed costs was increasingly challenged by economists. See Joy, *The Train That Ran Away*; and also in 'Railway Costs & Planning', *Journal of Transport Economics & Policy*, Vol. 23, No. 1, January 1989.

2. Joy, *op. cit.*, 128, reported that Scottish Region proposed every passenger service for a grant, except the East and West Coast main lines.

3. Pryke & Dodgson, *The Rail Problem*, 251.

4. Pryke & Dodgson, *op. cit.*, 195.

5. PP. *Hansard*, HoL 22 April 1970. Debate on Scottish railway services. See also See Loft, Last Trains, 258.

6. Quoted in Faulkner & Austin, Holding the Line, 61.

7. Loft, Last Trains, 263.

8. PP. HoC Papers No. 84, 1972-73.

9. NRS. BR/RSR/1/49. 'The Central Belt of Scotland', September 1970.

10. Pryke & Dodgson, *op. cit.*, 27.

11. Pryke & Dodgson, *op. cit.*, 153, 155, 157.

12. PP. *Hansard*, HoL. 22 April 1970, Debate on Scottish rail services.

13. *Times*, 6 May 1974.

14. NA. AN 192/933.

15. NRM. Mackie, G., 'Scottish Transport into the 80s', 9f, 12. An obituary of Leslie Soane, general manager 1977-83, pays tribute to his "consummate skills" in making alliances with councils and the Scottish Office to ward off closures in 1977 (*Times*, 17 November 1999).

16. Gourvish, I, 384.

17. See *Hansard* Vol. 875 cc1004-116, HC Deb 24 June 1974.

18. Pettitt & Comfort, *The Regional Railways Story*, Appendix F7, 209.

19. Joy, *op. cit.*, 132.

20. Pettitt & Comfort, *op. cit.*, 10.

21. Boocock, B*ritish Rail at Work: ScotRail*, 25f. See also Nick Lawford, 'One at Each End', on 6lda28.com.

22. Chris Green to the author, 2016.

23. See *Surveyor*, vol. 173 issue 5097, 31 May 1990, 10-13, Hubbard, G., Glasgow's Missing Link'.

24. Findings of TRL Glasgow Rail Impact Study, quoted in Theses: Docherty, 152.

25. Quoted in Gourvish II, 30.

25. An account of this is in Faulkner & Austin, *Holding the Line*, 65ff. Incidentally, Gourvish in II, 29 notes that Parker established "something of a MacMafia" in appointing "shrewd", "resilient" and "determined" Scots to the British Rail Board: Robert Reid, Ian Campbell and James Urquhart, joining the already-serving David Bowick, though in some cases their Scottishness was of a fairly Anglo kind.

27. Gourvish, I, 62f; NRS. BR/RSR/4/1/63.

28. A first-hand account, with photographs, of this incident can be found on the derbysulzers.com website at 'Snowy Days in 1970's'.

29. See RA for inspectors' reports into these accidents. Perusal of accident reports, and of operating rule books, give a salutary reminder of the responsibility and complexity of trainmen's and signalmen's tasks, especially at junctions.

30. NRM. Mackie, *op. cit.*, 25.

31. RA. TOPS: Story of a BR Project by Robert Arnott: a first-hand account by the project leader which also gives useful insights into how a nationwide scheme was introduced across regional and departmental frontiers.

32. Quoted in *Trans-Pennine Magazine*, issue 18, December 1977.

33. Roth & Divall, *From Rail to Road and Back Again?* 143ff.

34. NA. AN 192/933.

Chapter 9

1. NA. AN/192/933.

2. Quoted in *New Scientist*, 13 January 1983. Travers Morgan was a road rather than a rail consultancy.

3. Online Documents: Tyrrall, D. and Parker, D., 'The Fragmentation of a Railway: A Study of Organisational Change in British Railways'.

4. PP. HoC Transport Committe evidence. 9 April 1986. One committee member said, "What puzzles me is that an InterCity train arrives in Edinburgh and is then a non-InterCity train to Aberdeen." Reid replied that it did not matter to the passenger, but managerially, it was a good way to run things.

5. This paragraph draws on Tyrrall and Parker, *op. cit.*

6. NRS. BR/RSR/4/1/63. Management Committee, 21 February 1983.

7. Gourvish, II, 112f.

8. Gourvish, II, 125.

9. Joy, 'Railway Construction & Planning' in *Journal of Transport Economics & Policy*, Vol. 23, No. 1, January 1989. Gourvish, I, 395.

10. Scottish Transport Statistics.

11. NRS. BR/RSR/4/1182. Open Stations Policy. Scotland Operating Plans 1983, 15, and 1984, 21.

12. Quoted in Pettitt & Comfort, *The Regional Railways Story*, 18.

13. Conversation with the author, 2016.

14. BR (Sc). Scotland Operating Plan 1982, 48.

15. Jim Summers, in conversation with the author.

16. BR (Sc). Scotland Operating Plan 1982, 19.

17. A full account of the BIT is given in Scottish Region Document COM MPT/557, January 1982. It did not survive into privatisation. In November 2006 the SAPT, in its comments on the Network Rail draft Route Utilisation Schedule, asked for a "regular interval" timetable. ScotRail's timetable, with those of other TOCs, is prepared at Network Rail's offices in Milton Keynes.

18. *Mod. Rlys.*, February 1995.

19. Boocock, *British Rail at Work: ScotRail*, 75. Jim Summers describes much of the rolling stock as "rubbish" which ScotRail somehow managed to keep running (conversation with the author, 2016). See also Pettitt & Comfort, *op. cit.*, 27.

20. Chris Green would have liked 60 (conversation with the author, 2016).

21. Boocock, *op. cit.*, 72.

22. MacKinnon, Shaw & Docherty, *Diverging Mobilities*, 74.

23. SPTA, 'The Way Ahead', December 1983.

24. SPTA. Electric News No. 2, February 1985.

25. ScotRail. Strathclyde Rail Review, 1985: A Turning Point.

26. Noted in Gourvish, II, 157.

27. NA. CAB128/74/5. 24 June 1982.

28. Theses, etc. Elgar, J. and Simpson, R., 'The Impact of the Law on Industrial Disputes in the 1980s.'

29. *Guardian*, obituary by Geoffrey Goodman, 14 August 2001.

30. Strathclyde University, 'The Scottish Economy' document FEC, 11 February 1985. See also Gourvish II, 185; *Mod. Rlys.*, October 1985; and a somewhat biased account of the episode in Stewart & Chadwick, *Changing Trains*, 98f.

31. Theses, Docherty, 169. This thesis and subsequent book give valuable insights into the value and limitations of the railways to Strathclyde Regional Council's broad social strategy.

32. *Ibid.*, 218.

33. Jim Summers, deviser of the service, recalls that the aim was to send fully-loaded trains south, with no advertised stops in England, an aim ultimately subverted by the Eastern Region, which took the opportunity of removing one of its own trains and making the 'Nightrider' halt at intermediate points, so losing its lustre as an 'exclusive' express service (conversation with the author, 2016).

34. *Mod. Rlys.*, February 1985.

35. *Ibid.*, April 1984, February 1985.

36. Boocock, *op. cit.*, 27.

37. *Mod. Rlys.*, August 1984; March 1984: now the 'Jacobite' run by West Coast Railways.

38. PP. HoC Transport Committee, evidence from Sir Bob Reid, 9 April 1986.

39. Moir Lockhead, chief engineer of Glasgow Corporation Transport in the early 1980s, later founder of First Group, recalled meeting Chris Green at that time: "Green made quite an impression, and, shrewdly, Moir incorporated aspects of Green-think into his own portfolio…" (Interview with Andy Milne on *Railway People* website, 11 April 2006).

40. *Mod. Rlys.*, April 1985.

41. Pettitt & Comfort, *op. cit.*, 22.

42. Theses, etc. 'Gilchrist, History of British Railways' Electrical Research', 17ff.

43. Scottish Region: 'Operation Phoenix', July 1983, 6.

44. Network Rail. Pringle, Gordon, 'RETB Next Generation: Project Review for Institution of Railway Signal Engineers (IRSE) Scotland', 16 February 2016.

45. Chris Green to author; Pettitt & Comfort, *op. cit.*, 28.

46. Boocock, *op. cit.*, 61f, records the saga of the operations and engineering staffs' work to keep the West Highland sleepers running.

47. Stewart & Chadwick, Changing Trains.

48. *Mod. Rlys.*, September 1985.

49. Scotland Operating Plans, 1980-85; ScotRail Review, 1984-85.

50. ScotRail Operating Plan 1982, 9. One is tempted to ask how it could have taken until 1982 to learn this particular lesson. In fact BR had produced a document after the severe winter of 1962-63, 'Lessons of the Winter' (NA. AN183/30) but perhaps it was regarded as a historical rather than a practical document.

Chapter10

1. Conversation with the author, 2016.

2. Pettitt & Comfort, *op. cit.*, 31.

3. Gourvish, I, Appx J, 502.

4. PP. HoC Transport Committee, Minutes of Evidence 3 July 1991.

5. 'ScotRail Provincial Express', July 1987.

6. ScotRail, 'Newsline Special', June 1988.

7. Strathclyde Transport pamphlet, 1988. Jim Summers Collection.

8. PP. *Hansard*, vol. 124 HoC, cc 378-96, 8 December 1987.

9. Scottish Region, 'Newsline', No. 4, March 1988.

10. See PP. *Hansard*, 6th Series, Vol. 100. HoC, 24 June 1986. ScotRail Staff Bulletin, March & September 1985, July 1986; Spaven, *Highland Survivor*, 212ff.

11. *Glas. Her.*, 11 February 1987; see also Spaven, *op. cit.*, 219.

12. *Her.*, 24 March 1999. It was not a Railtrack commitment. Campaigning for a direct line continues, though the fate of the inland loop via Lairg complicates the issue.

13. Spaven, *op. cit.*, 238ff, 239; Jim Summers, in conversation with the author, 2016. Full details of the bridge replacement are in *Journal of the Permanent Way Institution*, Summer 1990, 134-155. C. R. Ford records diplomatically that a lightweight bridge was "decided to be a false economy and the design was therefore full BS5400RU loading" (*Ibid.*, 149).

14. Gourvish, T., 'The Sea Container Revolution' in Roth & Divall, From *Rail to Road and Back Again?*133ff.

15. ScotRail. Staff Bulletin No. 1, Autumn 1984.

16. *Commercial Motor*, 7 April 1984.

17. ScotRail, Staff Bulletin, January 1987.

18. Roth & Divall, *op. cit.*, 147

19. NA. CAB 134/690. NA. MT132/88, 8 July 1959.

20. *Rly. Gaz.*, 23 June 1961, *Glas. Her.*, 11 March 1975.

21. RA. Accident Reports. Polmont Derailment.

22. *Her.*, 23 December 1994.

23. *Her.*, 23 December 1994.

24. *Her.*, Report by Caroline Wilson, 22 July 2012.

Chapter 11

1. Pettitt & Comfort, *The Regional Railways Story*, 50.

2. ScotRail. 'Express Spotlight, January 1990.

3. Letter to Bleasdale, 7 May 1992, with copies to Sir Robert Reid and some other senior figures (Private collection).

4. *Glas. Her.*, 16 May 1990.

5. RA. Report of an Inquiry into the Collison on 21 July 1991 at Newton Junction.

6. ScotRail. 'Scotland's Railways', 24 June 1991.

7. Scotrail. *Ibid.* The fact that in 2006, First ScotRail managing director Mary Dickson could still say "We're getting better at customer service, but there's still room for more intelligent thinking" (*Scmn.* interview, 26

January 2006) indicates either that a sense of "customer service" does not come naturally to many Scots, or that some staff preferred to decline the role of company ambassador.

8. ScotRail factfile 1994.

9. ScotRail. 'Scotland's Railways', 24 June 1991. Regional Railways. 'Focus', June 1991.

10. ScotRail. 'Scotland's Railways', *Ibid.*

11. Theses. Docherty, 220.

12. Docherty, *Making Tracks*, 155

13. Later MP for Glasgow Cathcart, 2005-11

14. Docherty, *Ibid.*

15. Theses. Docherty, 220f.

16. *Mod. Rlys.*, April 1994.

17. Few civil service teams have earned such opprobrium as has been heaped upon this body, particularly in relation to its handling of rail privatisation.

18. *Times*, 6 March 1993.

19. A Parliamentary select committee observed in 1872 that "Committees and commissions carefully chosen have for the last thirty years clung to one form of competition after another; it has nevertheless become more and more evident that competition must fail to do for the railways what it has done for ordinary trade and that no means have yet been devised by which competition can be permanently maintained" (quoted in Dyos & Aldcroft, *British Transport*, 157: not a book on the Treasury's reading list, it would seem).

20. Pettitt & Comfort, *op. cit.*, 55; *Mod. Rlys.*, April 1994.

21. *Her.*, 8 March 1993. *Mod. Rlys.*, April 1994.

22. Larouche, *Competition Law and Regulation in European Telecommunications*, 184f. The cars were eventually sold to VIA Rail, Canada, for C$125 million (*Rly. Gaz. Int.*, 1 January 2001).

23. *Mod. Rlys.*, March 1994.

24. *Her.*, 10 August 1993.

25. Railtrack came into existence in March 1993, first as a division of BR; Pettitt & Comfort, *op. cit.*, 61, note that one of the projects identified by its first chairman, Sir Robert Horton, as beneficial to Regional Railways was Glasgow Crossrail.

26. *Mod. Rlys.*, June 1994.

27. *Times*, 30 January 1995. PP. *Hansard*, HoC 23 March, HoL 27 March 1995; *Her.*, 4 May 1995. The case against closure was led for the Highland Regional Council by Andrew Hajducki QC, author of several books on Scottish railway history. Interestingly, Simon Jenkins suggested that the sleeper services should be a separate sub-franchise (*Spectator*, 1 April 1995): an idea taken up 20 years later).

28. PP. Cmd 3773. Monopolies & Mergers Commission. National Express Group and ScotRail Railways Ltd: report on the merger situation, 1997-98.

29. *Times*, 29 March 1996.

Chapter 12

1. *Mod. Rlys.*, April 1997.

2. Pettitt and Comfort, *The Regional Railways Story*, 66.

3. PP. Cmd 3773. Monopolies & Mergers Commission, 'National Express Group and ScotRail Railways Ltd: Report on the Merger Situation, 1997-98'.

4. Pettitt and Comfort, *op. cit.*, 67.

5. Research Centre Seminar on Privatisation & Deregulation of Transport, August 1997. Schabas, M., 'Regulatory Policy', 8.

6. Gourvish, III, 439.

7. *Accounting Forum*, 51ff, quoting National Audit Office, 2000.

8. David Tyrrall in Hibbs, et al, *The Railways, the Market & the Government*, 113, 117.

9. Theses. Nash & Smith, Passenger Rail Franchising. BBC (Scotland) 7 March 2002.

10. *Times*, 29 March 2003.

11. *Times*, 23 May 2002.

12. Theses. Nash and Smith, *Ibid.*

13. Several Westminster-based Scottish politicians were involved with Transport administration. In 1997-2001, with Transport part of the Department for the Environment, Transport and the Regions, the ministers of state responsible for Transport were successively Gavin Strang, John Reid, Helen Liddell and Lord 'Gus' Macdonald. From 2002 until 2006 Alistair Darling was Secretary of State for Transport, combining the role with that of Secretary of State for Scotland.

14. Gourvish, III, 96.

15. It is tempting to suppose that as a former Transport Minister, Darling was happy to see private enterprise having a go at "sorting" the railways.

16. Network Rail Monitor Scotland, Qtrs 1 and 2 of CP5. 1 December 2015.

17. In the case of Abellio/ScotRail, responsibility for train procurement has been passed to the franchisee.

18. Transport Scotland. SQUIRE results, general overview, 2016-17, ist quarter. The "fines" are applied for the improvement of passenger facilities. A National Audit Office report noted that TOCs normally factor in a sum for such penalties when making franchise bids. See PP. HC 132, 20 July 2005. NAO: 'Maintaining and Improving Britain's Railway Stations', 22.

19. The combination of financial ease without responsibility led the SPTA's top management into laxities that were labelled as making the organisation "a byword for scandal" in the Glasgow *Evening Times* (31 January 2016).

20. PP. HC 22. Comptroller and Auditor-General's report on modernisation of WCML, 2006-07.

21. *Ibid.*

22. Theses, etc. McCartney, S. and Stittle, J., 'Carry on up the East Coast: A Case Study in Railway Franchising'. *Public Money Management*, No. 31 (2), 2011, 123-30.

23. *Sunday Times*, 17 October 2004.
24. PP. HoC. Scottish transport links and the credit crunch. 2008-09.
25. Audit Scotland. Report on Transport Scotland, December 2009, 85.
26. First Group report and accounts 2009. Chief executive's operating review, 13.
27. First ScotRail. Annual report for year ending 31 March 2011.
28. Pagoda Porter Novelli website: case studies.
29. ORR. Statistical Release, 2013-14. *Her.*, 6 December 2014.

Chapter 13

1. *Rly. Gaz. Int.*, 5 March 2008.
2. See TS. Commercial Assurance Review of the Rail Major Projects Portfolio, 26 Oct 2016.
3. *International Railway Journal*, 11 April; Railfuture Scotland, 3 October 2015.
4. TS, EGIP site; Audit-Scotland, Scotland's Key Infrastructure Project, 2013.
5. *Scmn.*, 20 September 2005.
6. *Scmn.*, 28 July 2008.
7. See *Rail Engineer*, 3 December 2012.
8. TS. Strategic Transport Projects Review, Report 3, Annex 3. Glasgow Crossrail.
9. The 'city deal' was an inducement from Westminster in the course of the 2014 referendum campaign, dependent on a 'No' result. It did not appear that the airport owner was expected to contribute to this enhancement of its future prospects.
10. Glasgow Airport Media Centre, 24 November 2016.
11. Crossrail trains originally ran from Bathgate and Dunblane but since 2009 come from Fife.
12. The Queen came in a train pulled by the ex-LNER A4 'Pacific' 4488 *Union of South Africa*, belonging to the former BRB board member John Cameron. The full story of the line is told in Spaven, *Waverley Route: The Life, Death and Rebirth of the Borders Railway*.
13. CBR press release, 17 August 2016.
14. *Guardian*, 16 May 2011.
15. 'Realising the Potential of GB Rail, 43.
16. *Ibid.*, 41.
17. *Ibid.*, 60, 62.
18. PP. HoC 329-i. Transport Committee, 19 June 2012. Disparaging references were made to engineers', or engineering companies', tendency towards "gold-plating": designing a project to specifications higher than its actual operations required, costing more and taking longer.
19. PP. HoC Scottish Affairs Committee, 25 November 1992. See also Gourvish, II, 412ff.
20. Friends of the Far North Line, news release, January 1996.
21. PP. Cmd 3565. Keeping Scotland Moving. A Scottish Transport Green Paper, 1996-97; Scottish Transport Statistics No. 12, 1990-91, and Statistical Trends, Freight Transport 1974-2009.
22. *Scottish Transport Review*, 5, Spring 1999.
23. Webster, *The West Highland Lines: Post-Beeching; Freight* magazine, 23 December 2015.
24. *Freight, Ibid.*
25. TS. Scotland Transport Statistics, 2015.
26. Network Rail. 'Delivering a Better Railway for a Better Scotland'. Oxera report: Scottish Transport Statistics.
27. The Rail Freight Group in its submission to Transport Scotland's consultation on rail freight strategy, 19 January 2016, observed that when damage to the Lamington viaduct closed the WCML in December 2015-February 2016, it suddenly became possible to transport 9ft 6in containers on the previously lower-rated Dumfries-Kilmarnock line.
28. Freight Transport Association. Response to TS Railfreight Consultation, 2016.
29. TS. Scotland Transport Statistics 2015.
30. NR's 2007 Plan for Route 25 (Highlands) made reference to a proposed deep water port in the inner Moray Firth area, which remains in the realm of potential; and though its National Freight Utilisation Strategy gave a robust forecast for future growth, especially Glasgow-Fort William and Inverness-Invergordon, it was not tempted into providing for increased freight traffic.
31. Infrastructure & Capital Investment Committee 29 June 2015.
32. RFG submission to Transport Scotland's consultation on railfreight strategy, 19 January 2016.

Chapter 14

1. Transport Statistics Scotland 2015.
2. *Passenger Transport,* 24 December 2014.
3. Transport Scotland: Caledonian Sleeper Franchise, full business case. 20 June 1015.
4. The McNulty 2011 'Rail Value for Money' study totally ignores this aspect, with a focus wholly on system 'efficiency'.
5. *Railnews* online, 21 September 2016.
6. Shaw Report. Section R2.3.
7. Shaw chose the example of Scottish Water and its regulator, the Water Industry Commission for Scotland, as an example of benchmarking in the public sector (in this case with privatised English water suppliers) to indicate how comparison of routes could be achieved within a decentralised NR and partially decentralised ORR framework. See Shaw Report, R2, Box 5.
8. *Independent*, 3 December 2016.
9. TS. Fast Track Scotland – Making the Case for High Speed Rail Connections in Scotland.
10. Scottish Government. NPF3. 2, 23. *Scmn.*, 15 January 2016.

248

11. HS2 Ltd. Broad Options for Upgraded and High Speed Railways to the North of England and Scotland; see also Greengauge 21. Linking North to South: A Review of the HS2 Ltd Report, June 2016.
12. Transport Scotland, Statistics 2015 .
13. See NR. Scotland Route Study, July 2016.
14. Oxera Ltd. 'What is the Economic Contribution of Rail in Scotland?' 2015, 28.
15. *Mod. Rlys.*, 15 May 2015; Network Rail, Operating Review, Scotland: Strategic Report 2016, from NR Annual Report & Accounts, 2016, 22.
16. Network Rail. Network Specification: Scotland, April 2015. See also the digitalrailway.co website.
17. *Accounting Forum*, 39, 1. March 2015, 51-63. Bowman, A., 'An Illusion of Success: the Consequences of British Railways Privatisation'.
18. Network Rail. 'Delivering a Better Railway for a Better Scotland', 12.
19. Network Rail, to Scottish Parliament's Rural Affairs and Environment Committee, 19 December 2007.
20. TS responses can have an "auntie knows best" flavour. When cyclists were campaigning in 2015 for more folding seats on trains to provide bicycle space, currently 2 spaces per three or four-coach train, and the Government was encouraging people to get out and take exercise, TS insisted on maximising the number of fixed seats.
21. gov.scot/Publications/2016/12/6610/14.
22. TS. Consultation on Scotland's Rail Infrastructure Strategy from 2019.
23. ORR. Enhancements improvement programme. Review of implementation in Scotland, September 2016; TS. Commercial Assurance Review of the Rail Major Projects Portfolio, 26 October 2016.
24. ORR. NR Monitor Scotland, 1 April-15 October 2016 (24 November 2016).
25. As stated in the RDG's 2015 document 'Britain's Future, Britain's Railway'.
26. Written statement to House of Commons, 6 December 2016.
27. Network Rail. Delivering a Better Railway, 2013.
28. At an unfortunate moment a Scottish newspaper discovered that Abellio's parent company was extolling the value of the ScotRail franchise in its annual report: "the capital invested is relatively limited while a return on investment is achieved of 18 per cent" (*Daily Record*, 2 October 2016). It is noticeable that in its public documents and signage, Abellio's logo has become more prominent than 'ScotRail', but public sympathy may move in the contrary direction.
29. Scottish media, October-December 2016, *passim*.
30. ORR. NR Monitor Scotland, 1 April-15October 2016 (24 November 2016).
31. *Guardian*, 16 December 2016.

Two Class 26 diesels fitted with token exchange apparatus, on the Inverness train at Kyle of Lochalsh, July 1961. The Portree mail shp MV *Loch Nevis* is at the pier. (Stenlake Collection)

Index

Note: Timeline entries are indexed
when not referred to in the text.
Appendix entries are not indexed

1. EVENTS, ORGANISATIONS, TOPICS AND ROUTES

2. PERSONS AND PLACES

Wemyss Bay Station in 1964. In subsequent refurbishments, the clock and the stag's head have gone. (Stenlake Collection)